PARENTAL ENGAGEMENT AND EARLY CHILDHOOD EDUCATION AROUND THE WORLD

Exploring the importance of parental engagement in early childhood education, this book delves into research and practices in 25 countries to bring students, researchers, teachers and policy-makers insights into working families around the world. The incorporation and consideration of parental engagement and involvement in early childhood education are a new phenomenon to many countries. Yet, increasing research recognises the importance of parental engagement and involvement in early childhood education services, and the role both parents and teachers play to support children's learning and development. Using a range of materials from curriculum to policy documents, Garvis et al. demonstrate differences in practices and terminologies pertaining to the topic and provide an international perspective on the importance of parental involvement and engagement in early childhood education services.

The content covers a range of countries as well as countries beyond an 'Anglo-Saxon' perspective. The different policy settings across these countries highlight how countries work with, and involve, parents differently, which is useful for jurisdictions where early childhood education is a developing aspect of a country's education system. Looking at cultural influences, partnership approaches, parental collaboration, institutional dominance and child involvement in parent meetings, the content offers readers real understanding of parental engagement and involvement in different settings.

The readership includes students in early childhood education, and researchers, teachers, policy makers, and general members of the public interested in parental engagement or involvement in early childhood education across the globe.

Susanne Garvis is Professor of Education (early childhood) and Chair of the Department of Education at Swinburne University of Technology. She has extensive experience in early childhood research and has worked at both Australian and Swedish universities on national and international projects. Her particular focus is quality improvement and policy development.

Sivanes Phillipson is Professor of Education at Swinburne University of Technology. She is the Routledge Editor for the Evolving Families Series, which focuses on issues, challenges and empirical best practices surrounding evolving families that impact upon their survival, development and outcomes. Sivanes has over 100 publications to her name including books, peer-reviewed papers and book chapters. She has authored and co-authored/edited eight published books focusing on teacher education and parent engagement, with the latest four books published with Routledge.

Heidi Harju-Luukkainen is Professor of Education and Vice Director of Kokkola University Consortium Chydenius at the University of Jyväskylä, Finland. She also works as a professor of Education at Nord University, Norway. She holds a Ph.D. degree in education, special education teacher qualification and a qualification in leadership and management from Finland. She has published more than 200 international books, journal articles and reports as well as worked in multiple projects globally. Harju-Luukkainen has worked at top ranked universities in the USA like UCLA, USC as well as in many Nordic research universities. She has developed education programs for universities, been a PI of PISA sub-assessments in Finland and functioned as a board professional.

Alicja Renata Sadownik, Ph.D., is an associate professor at the Western Norway University of Applied Sciences (Bergen, Norway). She received her Ph.D. in Social Sciences from the University of Gdansk (Poland). Since the last six years her research focuses on childhood(s), early childhood education settings and parental cooperation in the context of migration and socio-cultural diversity. Her works have been published in journals such as *European Early Childhood Education Research Journal*, and *Contemporary Issues in Early Childhood SAGE Journal*, among others. She is also one of the editors of "Young children in the world and their rights 30 years with the UNCRC" (Springer 2021).

"A new and broad collection of policy and practice insights into home–early childhood partnerships that benefit children, families and education systems around the world."

Associate Professor Alexandra C. Gunn,
University of Otago, New Zealand

Evolving Families
Series Editor: Sivanes Phillipson

This series focuses on issues, challenges and empirical best practices surrounding evolving families that impact upon their survival, development and outcomes. The aim of this series is twofold: (1) to showcase the diversity of evolving families and the multiple factors that make up the function of families and their evolution across time, systems and cultures; (2) to build on preventative, interventionist, engagement and recovery methods for the promotion of healthy and successful evolving families across generations, social and political contexts and cultures.

Teachers' and Families' Perspectives in Early Childhood Education and Care
Early Childhood Education in the 21st Century Vol II
Sivanes Phillipson and Susanne Garvis

Policification of Early Childhood Education and Care
Early Childhood Education in the 21st Century Volume III
Edited by Sivanes Phillipson and Susanne Garvis

Growing Children's Social and Emotional Skills
Using the TOGETHER Programme
Joanna Grace Phillips, Sivanes Phillipson and Gaye Tyler-Merrick

Parental Engagement and Early Childhood Education Around the World
Edited by Susanne Garvis, Sivanes Phillipson, Heidi Harju-Luukkainen and Alicja Renata Sadownik

For more information about this series, please visit: www.routledge.com/Evolving-Families/book-series/EF

PARENTAL ENGAGEMENT AND EARLY CHILDHOOD EDUCATION AROUND THE WORLD

Edited by Susanne Garvis, Sivanes Phillipson, Heidi Harju-Luukkainen and Alicja Renata Sadownik

LONDON AND NEW YORK

First published 2022
by Routledge
2 Park Square, Milton Park, Abingdon, Oxon OX14 4RN

and by Routledge
605 Third Avenue, New York, NY 10158

Routledge is an imprint of the Taylor & Francis Group, an informa business

© 2022 selection and editorial matter, Susanne Garvis, Sivanes Phillipson, Heidi Harju-Luukkainen and Alicja Renata Sadownik; individual chapters, the contributors

The right of Susanne Garvis, Sivanes Phillipson, Heidi Harju-Luukkainen and Alicja Renata Sadownik to be identified as the authors of the editorial material, and of the authors for their individual chapters, has been asserted in accordance with sections 77 and 78 of the Copyright, Designs and Patents Act 1988.

All rights reserved. No part of this book may be reprinted or reproduced or utilised in any form or by any electronic, mechanical, or other means, now known or hereafter invented, including photocopying and recording, or in any information storage or retrieval system, without permission in writing from the publishers.

Trademark notice: Product or corporate names may be trademarks or registered trademarks, and are used only for identification and explanation without intent to infringe.

British Library Cataloguing-in-Publication Data
A catalogue record for this book is available from the British Library

Library of Congress Cataloging-in-Publication Data
A catalog record for this book has been requested

ISBN: 978-0-367-42389-6 (hbk)
ISBN: 978-0-367-42390-2 (pbk)
ISBN: 978-0-367-82391-7 (ebk)

DOI: 10.4324/9780367823917

Typeset in Bembo
by Apex CoVantage, LLC

CONTENTS

List of contributors   xi
List of figures   xix
List of tables   xx

1. An introduction to parental involvement in early childhood education and care: a global perspective   1
   Susanne Garvis, Heidi Harju-Luukkainen, Alicja Renata Sadownik and Sivanes Phillipson

2. The cultural interface of parental involvement in the Australian context   9
   Wendy Goff and Sivanes Phillipson

3. Parental involvement in early childhood education in Azerbaijan   24
   Ali Kemal Tekin, Ulviyya Mikayilova and Nigar Muradova

4. Parental involvement in early childhood education in Belarus   40
   Natallia Bahdanovich Hanssen and Volha Mamonka

5. Parental involvement in Croatian early childhood education: challenges and opportunities   50
   Adrijana Višnjić Jevtić

6 Parental involvement in Czech Republic: towards a
   partnership approach?   63
   Martina Kampichler

7 Parental involvement in early childhood education
   in Denmark   74
   Katharina Jacobsson

8 Parental perspective in the Finnish early childhood
   education context   90
   *Karoliina Purola, Heidi Harju-Luukkainen
   and Jonna Kangas*

9 Educational partnership: parental collaboration
   in German ECEC settings   99
   Emely Knör

10 Parental involvement in early childhood education
   in Ghana   109
   Francis R. Ackah-Jnr

11 Parental involvement in early childhood education in
   Hong Kong: critical analysis of related policies   122
   Aihua Hu

12 From institutional dominance to parental involvement:
   models of working with families in Hungarian
   Kindergartens   136
   Anikó Varga Nagy, Sándor Pálfi and Eleonora Teszenyi

13 Children's participation in parent meetings in
   light of the history of preschool policy documents
   in Iceland   151
   Kristín Dýrfjörð and Guðrún Alda Harðardóttir

14 Parental involvement in early childhood education
   in Jordan: policy and practice   162
   Fathi Ihmeideh and Ali Kemal Tekin

15 Parental involvement in ECE in Norway   174
   Alicja Renata Sadownik and Ruth Ingrid Skoglund

16 The state of parent involvement in early childhood
education: case of Oman 185
Ali Kemal Tekin, Laila Al-Salmi and Maryam Al-Mamari

17 Parental involvement in ECEC in Poland 199
Alicja Renata Sadownik and Ewa Lewandowska

18 Collaborating with parents for South Sámi language
learning: a study in an indigenous preschool in Norway 211
Heidi Harju-Luukkainen, Karianne Berg and Asbjørn Kolberg

19 Parent participation in preschool education in Serbia:
challenges and perspectives 221
Dragana Pavlović Breneselović, Lidija Miškeljin and Tijana Bogovac

20 Taming the Tiger: exploring parental involvement
in early childhood education in Singapore 232
*Eugenia Koh-Chua, Sarah Somarajan, Lucas Ku-Wang and
Sivanes Phillipson*

21 Parental involvement in early childhood education in
Catalunya, Spain 246
*Sílvia Blanch Gelabert, Ana María Forestello and Gabriel
Lemkow-Tovias*

22 Parental involvement in Swedish preschools:
a reflection of current steering documents 256
Tina Yngvesson and Susanne Garvis

23 Parental involvement in early childhood education
discourse in Uganda 269
Godfrey Ejuu

24 United Kingdom – four nations in one country:
diversity in policy, research, and practice 280
Catherine Carroll-Meehan

25 Family engagement in early childhood:
policy and practice in the United States 292
*Carola Oliva-Olson, Mari Estrada, Soodie Ansari,
Annie White and Jaime Matera*

26 International trends in parent involvement of *sayings*,
   doings, and *relatings* 306
   Alicja Renata Sadownik, Sivanes Phillipson,
   Heidi Harju-Luukkainen and Susanne Garvis

Index *317*

CONTRIBUTORS

Francis R. Ackah-Jnr is a lecturer at Griffith University College and researcher at the Griffith Institute for Educational Research, Griffith University. He has cutting-edge teaching and research expertise in inclusive education, early childhood and leadership. His research interests include parent-school-community partnerships, professional development, education policy and law, social justice, human rights, and methodological expertise in qualitative and quantitative research.

Guðrún Alda Harðardóttir is a former associate professor of Early Childhood Education at the University of Akureyri. She currently operates a preschool in Iceland and works there as pedagogista. She is a former head of the Preschool Teacher's union in Iceland. Her research interests are children's; learning opportunities, empowerment, democracy and pedagogical documentation.

Maryam Al-Mamari graduated with a bachelor's degree from Sultan Qaboos University (SQU) in Oman and earned her master's degree in Early Childhood Education from the University of Texas at Austin. Currently, she is a lecturer at SQU and her research interests include curriculum in ECE, agency producing learning/teaching, ECE policy and teacher preparation.

Laila Al-Salmi earned her MAT and Ph.D. degree from the University of Texas at El Paso, USA. Her research interests focus on bilingual development at childhood, parental involvement, and early education teacher preparation. She is currently an Assistant Professor in Early Education Department at Sultan Qaboos University in Oman.

Soodie Ansari is the Early Learning Dual Language Support Coordinator at San Mateo County Office of Education. She has dedicated her career to designing professional development and peer learning opportunities to expand and challenge educators' approach to authentic family engagement and culturally and linguistically responsive practices. She holds a master's degree in Child Development from University of California, Davis.

Natallia Bahdanovich Hanssen is a leader of the Research Group on Special Needs Education, and an associate professor at the Faculty of Education and Arts at Nord University in Bodø, Norway. Natallia's research is currently linked to early childhood education, special needs education, inclusive education, comparative studies, language difficulties, aesthetic and special needs education, bullying, psychosocial learning challenges and behavioral and relational impairments.

Karianne Berg is an associate professor, Faculty of Education and Arts, Nord University, speech language therapist and engaged in master in speech language therapy and master in special education. Her research interests include speech language therapy and user involvement, language and culture.

Sílvia Blanch Gelabert holds a Ph.D. in Educational Psychology and Degree in Clinical Psychology. She is a professor of the Basic, Developmental and Educational Psychology Department in the School of Education of the Universitat Autònoma de Barcelona (2004 at present). Her work includes teacher training for ECE Teachers, family support and family groups.

Tijana Bogovac is a preschool pedagogue from Serbia. She works in preschool institution Cukarica, in Belgrade, as an expert associate. She studied International Master programme in Early childhood education and care. Tijana is interested in the issues of teachers' professionalism, preschool education in international perspective and innovative practices.

Catherine Carroll-Meehan has worked as an early childhood teacher, leader/manager and academic for the past 30 years. Catherine worked as a lecturer at Queensland University of Technology prior to moving to the UK in 2006 at Canterbury Christ Church University. Catherine is currently at the University of Portsmouth as Head of School of Education and Sociology.

Kristín Dýrfjörð is an associate professor of Early Childhood Education at the University of Akureyri. She has experience as a preschool principal, has taken part in the development of the National Curriculum at the Ministry of Education. She is current president of OMEP Iceland. Her research interests are policy studies, neoliberalism in early childhood education and the connection between science and creativity in early childhood.

Mari Estrada is a lecturer in Early Childhood Studies and pre-credential programs at California State University Channel Islands. She led statewide efforts for family engagement and workforce development. She holds a doctorate in Education from the University of California, Santa Barbara. Her research includes dual language learners and effective work teams.

Ana María Forestello holds a Ph.D. degree in Pedagogy and is a professor of the Childhood Education Degree at Universitat de Vic-Universitat Central de Catalunya and at Universitat Autònoma de Barcelona. Ana is involved in two research teams: Childhood, Family and Education (ERIFE) and Education, Neuroscience, Experimentation and Learning (GRENEA).

Susanne Garvis is a professor of education (early childhood) and Chair of Department of Education at Swinburne University of Technology, Australia. Her research focuses on enhancing quality and learning within early childhood education and care. She has worked on numerous national and international projects in both Australia and Europe.

Wendy Goff is a lecturer at Swinburne University of Technology, Australia. Wendy's research focuses on adult relationships. She is particularly interested in how adults might come together to support the learning and development of children. Throughout her career, Wendy has worked as a pre-school teacher, a primary school teacher, and a social welfare worker. She joined the tertiary setting in 2010 and teaches in the undergraduate and postgraduate secondary, primary and early childhood teacher education programs.

Godfrey Ejuu is an education psychologist with specialized training in Early Childhood Education and Development. He has been involved in research in the area of Early Childhood and is an expert in Early Childhood curriculum designing, early childhood indigenous knowledge, early learning and development standards, Instructional materials for Early Childhood Care and Development (ECCD), Monitoring and Evaluation of ECD programmes, ECD policies and ECD community mobilization and advocacy. Currently, he heads the early childhood education department at Kyambogo University, a public university in Uganda.

Heidi Harju-Luukkainen is a professor (Nord university, Norway) and holds a Ph.D. degree in education, special education teacher qualification and a qualification in leadership and management from Finland. She has published more than 150 international books, journal articles and reports as well as worked in more than 25 projects globally. Her research areas are early childhood education, justice in education and international student assessment.

Aihua Hu is an associate professor in the Department of Pedagogy, Religion and Social Studies at Western Norway University of Applied Sciences (HVL). She is also affiliated to KINDKnow center. Her research interests include teacher education &

teacher development, early childhood education, transition, sustainability, education policy, and comparative and international education.

Fathi Ihmeideh is an associate professor of Early Childhood Education (ECE) at the Hashemite University in Jordan. He received his Ph.D. from University of Huddersfield, UK. He has over a decade of experience in university teaching, developing ECE curricula, preparing and evaluating ECE programs, and creating parental involvement programs. He is involved in leading research projects in the field of ECE.

Katharina Jacobsson is an associate professor at Nord University, Faculty of Education and Arts, Norway. She educates at the SEN teachers' program, the school headmasters' program and on teacher's education. Research interest mainly focuses on school improvement, leadership in schools, professional development and children with special needs.

Martina Kampichler is a sociologist and works as a researcher at the Institute for Research in Inclusive Education at Masaryk University Brno. Her research interests include sociology of childhood, Czech family and work-care policies as well as the provision of early childhood education.

Jonna Kangas works as a university lecturer in the Playful Learning Centre, Faculty of Education Science, The University of Helsinki. Her research focus is on play-based learning and pedagogy in early childhood education. She aims to understanding learning processes through joy and participation, and she uses findings for designing innovative teacher training programs.

Emely Knör, M.A., is a qualified childhood educator in Germany. Her previous work focuses on further education of pedagogical professionals in language education and the perspective of children in the quality discourse. Currently, she is involved in an international research project of the University of Education in Weingarten, Germany, on family centres.

Eugenia Koh-Chua is pursuing her Ph.D. research in education at Swinburne University of Technology. She has a master's degree in Inclusive and Special Education from Monash University and worked extensively with parents, teachers and students from diverse cultural and socio-economic backgrounds in Singapore. Her research interests include parental involvement in children's education, risky play and inclusive education.

Asbjørn Kolberg is an associate professor, Faculty of Education and Arts, Nord University and coordinator of the university's South and Lule Saami Teacher Education Programme. Research interests include children's literature in a contemporary and historical perspective, critical text analysis, representations of indigenous people in literature and media and South Saami history, language and culture.

Lucas Ku-Wang is a Ph.D. candidate in Education at Swinburne University of Technology. He is also a qualified early childhood teacher who has worked in preschool settings across Melbourne. His current research focuses on highlighting and explaining children's mathematical endeavours and creativity in Australian early years' settings through investigating teachers' perceptions and practices.

Gabriel Lemkow-Tovias holds a Ph.D. in Philosophy and is a lecturer in the BA in Early Childhood Education Degree, Faculty of Social Sciences of Manresa (UVic-UCC). Gabriel is a member of the Lab 0_6: Discovery, Research and Documentation Centre for Science Education in Early Childhood and research coordinator of the GRENEA group (Research Group in Education, Neuroscience, Experimentation and Learning).

Ewa Lewandowska is an assistant professor at The Maria Grzegorzewska University in Warsaw. She researches on early childhood education and parental collaboration in relation to sustainability and children's rights. She focuses on children's perspectives on sustainability, parental collaboration and ECE quality.

Volha Mamonka is an associate professor at Belarusian State Pedagogical University BSPU, Institute for Inclusive Education. Volha's research is currently linked to early childhood education, special needs education, inclusive education, and parental involvement. Mamonka has published more than 70 works, including scientific articles in national and international journals.

Jaime Matera is assistant professor of Anthropology at California State University Channel Islands, where he teaches and conducts research on human-ecological interactions. His work emphasizes the importance of identifying sources of vulnerability and resilience in building family and community resilience.

Ulviyya Mikayilova is an assistant professor at ADA University, Azerbaijan, and an adjunct lecturer at Moscow School of Social and Economic Studies. She studied in Manchester University and was a recipient of Fulbright scholarship in 2006. She is the executive director of the Center for Innovations in Education (CIE). Her research interests are teachers' professional development and social inclusion of children with disabilities.

Lidija Miškeljin is an assistant professor at the University of Belgrade – Faculty of Philosophy, Department of Pedagogy and Andragogy and Chair for Early Childhood Education. She has participated in international projects on ECEC in Serbia and lectured at College for Preschool Teacher Education. Her research interests are childhood studies; action research; early childhood education policies and systems; professional development.

Nigar Muradova received her B.Sc. degree in Social Sciences and Psychology and master's degree in Clinical Psychology from The Baku State University. She is currently a faculty member at Azerbaijan State Pedagogical University. She has scientific publications in pedagogical psychology and her research interests include family-school relations, psychological factors of parenting, and intra-family relations.

Anikó Varga Nagy, Ph.D., is an associate professor of Early Childhood Education at the University of Debrecen, Hungary. Her research interests are in comparative education, history of education and Roma children's education. She is the Placement & Practice Assessment Co-ordinator for Early Childhood Students. She was the Co-Chair of EECERA 2018.

Carola Oliva-Olson is an associate professor at California State University Channel Islands. Her work includes preparing early care and education teachers to effectively work with children and their families from birth to age eight. She leads national and State workforce development professional development, research and advocacy. Dr Oliva-Olson has been appointed to the California Governor's Early Childhood Policy Council. She is a bilingual former toddler, preschool, kindergarten, first- and second-grade teacher and coach.

Sándor Pálfi is a professor of Early Childhood Education at the University of Debrecen, Hungary. His research interests include the principles of Project Pedagogy, children's free play and a child-centred pedagogical approach. Before entering Higher Education he ad worked in the early years sector for 25 years as a Kindergarten Pedagogue. He was the Chair of EECERA 2018.

Dragana Pavlović Breneselović is a full professor at the University of Belgrade – Faculty of Philosophy, Department of Pedagogy and Andragogy, senior researcher at the Institute of Pedagogy and Andragogy and Head of the Chair for Early Childhood Education. Research interests include systemic changes; professional development; family–preschool partnership; research with children; child well-being.

Sivanes Phillipson is a professor of education at Swinburne University of Technology. She is also the Routledge Editor for Evolving Families Series, a series that focuses on issues, challenges and empirical best practices surrounding evolving families that impact upon their survival, development and outcomes. Sivanes' research interest and experience centre around family studies in particular parental engagement in early learning and care as the basis for children's formal learning and whole wellbeing. Her most recent work from an Australian Research Council Linkage is a resource website, www.numeracyathome.

com, that facilitates and enables parents and educators to engage in early mathematical learning.

Karoliina Purola is completing her Ph.D. at the University of Helsinki. Throughout her career, she has worked as a service leader in the Finnish municipal early childhood education and care (ECEC) provision. Her research focuses on parental participation in ECEC, with several published articles on this topic.

Alicja Renata Sadownik, Ph.D., is an associate professor at Western Norway University of Applied Sciences and Kindergarten Knowledge Center for Systemic Research on Diversity and Sustainable Futures. She researches on childhood(s), ECE settings and parental cooperation in the context of migration and sociocultural diversity. She approaches the complexity of differences from intersectional perspectives.

Ruth Ingrid Skoglund, Ph.D., is an associate professor at Western Norway University of Applied Sciences and Kindergarten Knowledge Center for Systemic Research on Diversity and Sustainable Futures. Her research has focus on parental cooperation and supervision, the phenomenon of recognition as well as inclusion and exclusion processes in children groups and social perspectives on bullying.

Sarah Somarajan is an adjunct university lecturer in Singapore with more than 10 years of classroom experience with young adults. She has a master's degree in education from Monash University, Australia. Sarah is keenly interested in educational research, specifically education policy, teacher training and early childhood education.

Ali Kemal Tekin is an associate professor and an international expert in Early Childhood Education (ECE). He holds master's and Ph.D. degrees from The Pennsylvania State University. He has numerous publications and conference appearances including keynote speeches at international level over 20 countries. His research interests are parent involvement, early bilingual education, motivation and efficacy of ECE teachers. He also serves for international organizations such as UNESCO, NAEYC, and AECE.

Eleonora Teszenyi is a lecturer in early childhood at the Open University, UK with experience in leading master's programmes and teaching on undergraduate and postgraduate courses. She has worked in the early years' sector for 22 years and her doctoral research focuses on early childhoodpedagogy. Her other research interests include parent partnerships and work-based learners in Higher Education.

Adrijana Višnjić Jevtić is an assistant professor at the University of Zagreb, Faculty of Teacher Education. She is involved in professional development programs for early childhood teachers in Croatia and Europe. Her research interests are ECE, family-school cooperation and early childhood teachers' competences and professionalism. She is a member of OMEP, EECERA and TACTYC.

Annie White is an assistant professor with the Early Childhood Studies program at California State University Channel Islands and worked extensively with Head Start. Dr White is a life-long learner and scholar practitioner, and holds a doctorate in Leadership in Education. Her research interests include learning stories and family engagement.

Tina Yngvesson holds M.Sc. degrees in educational research and international business and is currently a Ph.D. research fellow at Nord University in Norway as well as working full-time as a preschool class teacher. Alongside various international and national research projects in child- and youth sciences, she also works as a preschool teacher in a Swedish primary school.

FIGURES

2.1	Leximancer concept map – the four key concepts and their associated sub-concepts and connections when parents and educators explain parental involvement	14
2.2	Leximancer concept map – the four key concepts and their associated sub-concepts and connections of a parent's role	16
2.3	Leximancer concept map – the four key concepts and their associated sub-concepts and connections of the educator's role	19
2.4	Visual Representation of Parental Involvement	22
19.1	Systemic operationalization of partnerships through dimensions of roles (Pavlović Breneselović, 2011)	227
20.1	Leximancer concept map displaying the intersection of the key concepts within the main themes of Child and Play	239
20.2	Leximancer concept map displaying the connectivity of the key concepts within the main theme of Play in relation to Child outcomes	241
24.1	Child poverty rates in England, Wales, Scotland, and Northern Ireland: Households Below Average Income	282
26.1	Leximancer concept map showing themes of parental involvement – Parent Involvement Sayings, Parent Involvement Doings and Parent Involvement Relatings	309

TABLES

2.1	Demographic information of the educator participants	12
2.2	Demographic information of the parent participants	13
3.1	Structure of General Education System in Azerbaijan	25
3.2	Reliability Analysis of the Scale	31
3.3	Demographic Characteristics of the Participants (N = 360)	32
3.4	Descriptive and Frequency Results for the Likert Items of the Scale (N = 360)	33
3.5	Main Effect Results of the Factorial ANOVA (N = 360)	34
3.6	Interaction Effect Results of the Factorial ANOVA (N = 360)	35
3.7	Focused ANOVA Results for Each Group of Interaction Effect (N = 360)	35
5.1	Codes and frequencies of data	56
7.1	Six types of involvement	81
7.2	Goals from the national curriculum in which parental cooperation is mentioned (Ministry of Higher Education and Science, App. 2, 2017)	83
7.3	Examples from the six universities' knowledge and proficiency goals	84
8.1	Parental collaboration as objectives and concept of studies in teacher education programmes	95
11.1	Guiding questions for data analysis adapted from Edmondson (2000)	125
11.2	Overview of the analyzed policies	125
12.1	Outline of the five parent involvement models	142
15.1	Parental participation	182

16.1	Frequency distribution of the participants	191
16.2	Challenges of parental involvement	193
21.1	Successful examples of family-school initiatives	252
24.1	Themes emerging in research about family involvement from systemic literature review in the UK (2015–2020)	286

1
AN INTRODUCTION TO PARENTAL INVOLVEMENT IN EARLY CHILDHOOD EDUCATION AND CARE

A global perspective

Susanne Garvis, Heidi Harju-Luukkainen, Alicja Renata Sadownik and Sivanes Phillipson

Introduction

A broad range of research has shown that parental involvement is an important factor within early childhood education to support a child's learning and development (Epstein, 1995; Janssen & Vandenbroeck, 2018). Many governments have created a place for parental involvement in early childhood education curricula. Furthermore, a more limited number of studies have compared early childhood parental involvement in curricula across countries and in one such recent comparative study, Janssen and Vandenbroeck (2018) compared parental involvement in 13 early childhood education and care curricula and identified three curricula approaches that demonstrated a lack of "unanimity in top-down constructions of parental roles and responsibilities" (p. 813). These approaches were (1) school-like, (2) rights based and (3) ambivalent perspectives on parental involvement. The authors concluded that the lack of consensus in the curricula further challenged the notions of how partnerships should proceed and advocated for a stronger focus on democratic partnerships. Thus, there is a clear lack of research especially from a comparative and international cross-cultural perspective especially within parental involvement (Janssen & Vandenbroeck, 2018).

Building on previous work in the field, this international volume expands current research to include a collection of 24 countries on parental involvement in early childhood education and care settings. Early childhood education services are organised from each country's own cultural, social and political contexts, which are reflected in the policy documents and further in the work of teachers. How these different policy documents recognise and view parents are varying and they position parents differently in connection to early childhood education services. The intention of this book is to make visible the complexity around parent's possibilities to collaborate and to get involved in their child's early childhood educational environment across the globe. We help fill current gaps in knowledge and contribute significantly to the early childhood education profession and policy development. Epstein (1995) has constructed a model for parental involvement in school, pointing at various aspects, dimensions and levels that the parental involvement may actually take place on. By analysing parental involvement country by country, we can reconstruct, following dimensions of Epstein-inspired parental involvement that are either implied in polices or reported by research quoted by the chapters' authors.

Across the globe, we notice that various terms such as parental involvement, parental engagement, home-school partnership and parental partnership are used. In this book, we encompass all these different terms under the same umbrella of 'parents' to provide a collective understanding of how early childhood services and parents co-exist. We do not specifically focus on specific terms or their philosophical foundations, but rather interested in how early childhood services and parents work together. We have also chosen to use the term 'parental involvement' based on ideologies of positioning parents as equals in involvement. Similarly with terminology, we engage with the term early childhood education and care as an umbrella term to encompass the vast terms used, such as but not limited to, preschool, day care, kindergarten and childcare across different countries. Our general definition covers early childhood education and care for children aged birth to starting school age (which again varies by country).

Traditions in parental involvement

Different policy, social and cultural contexts of each country seem to establish various approaches for parental collaboration. The pedagogical literature (Bennet, 2005) distinguishes at least two main traditions within this topic. The first is preschool oriented, where children's future school performance is at stake. The approach focuses on a home-based involvement of parents, continuing the child's education at home, and thus continuing the preschool's work. This tradition contributes to fostering cognitive and behavioural dispositions (Bourdieu, 2004) high level of which will help the child to succeed in the institution of school. This approach requires parents to understand the ECEC as preparatory for school. The parents should be adequately informed by the ECEC about the child's developmental progress towards school readiness, and how it could be supported by the family activities.

The social pedagogy tradition focuses on the community being the setting of a child's development. Here, the parents are a link between the local community and the ECEC, communicating with the ECEC to co-created and benefit of community's resources and initiatives. This perspective on parental collaboration is more focused on ECEC-based involvement, transforming it into a local community centre where various initiatives can create arenas for children's activities, both completing for the home (Epstein, 1995).

The social focus of the social pedagogy approach is in line with the traditional approach's goals regarding positive school performance. Creating arenas where children can access other competences, sets of meanings, activities and ways of being beyond the home strengthens not only the children's cultural and social capital but also the ECEC (community of parents and professionals) in its interaction with local community and local government.

Policies and pedagogies described in this book assume, strengthen or facilitate particular approaches to parental involvement. Most of the chapters, however, combine these approaches at the level of either description of practice or future recommendations. For example, the UK policy focuses on parental home-based involvement in the child's learning, supporting the family from the level of community and local government. Poland in the steering documents focuses on information flow regarding the child's development progress and school readiness, shedding formal and economic responsibility for preschools to the local governments and making community engagement through parents easier. The Scandinavian curricula (Sweden and Norway) point at the necessity of collaboration between the home and ECEC to strengthen conditions for the child's overall development. These documents, however, operate in the highest social trust (ESS, 2018) and at a high level of voluntary, collective initiatives, which shows that the social pedagogy tradition may be taken for granted by the steering documents (which then intend to strengthen the preschool approach). Singapore for example demonstrates how policy's documents try to loosen parental academic admissions and introduce a more holistic approach towards development, while the parents and professionals aware of primary schools' academic rigour focus on the child's school readiness. What is clear is that contextual and cultural understanding is also needed when understanding parental involvement across different countries.

Overview of the book

Across the chapters of this book, it is clear that parental involvement is viewed from different perspectives. Therefore, for the reader of this book, it is important to note that different learning spaces in different cultures define partnership with the parents from different perspectives.

The context of Australia is shared in Chapter 2. The chapter focuses on how parents perceive, define and enact parental involvement within the early childhood education and care context. A specific aim of the chapter is to explore ways that different perceptions and definitions of parental involvement can come together to guide future research practice. A framework is shared at the end of the chapter to help shape parental involvement in Australian early childhood education and care.

Chapter 3 introduces parental involvement in Azerbaijan and presents survey results that are first of its kind. There are no previous scholarly works that have presented the status of parental involvement in early childhood education in Azerbaijan. The chapter explores the degree to which Azerbaijani parents become involved with and interact with their child's schooling. The chapter also highlights the influence of parent and child demographic characteristics such as the parent's age and gender, child's gender, educational level, the number of children and marital and employment status have on parental involvement. The chapter provides in-depth information about the background, current practice and suggestions for the improvement of parent involvement in ECE.

Chapter 4 presents the complexity of policy, practice, theoretical approaches and teacher education addressing the issue of parental involvement in Belarus. The policies developed after the Soviet era underline the importance of parental involvement by creating opportunities for both formal and less formal forms of involvement. Parents are, however, mostly involved with extracurricular arrangements and excluded from major decision making. This outcome is quite surprising as the existing theoretical approaches focus on partnerships that support children's school readings and attitudes towards learning. The authors argue for wider improvements following the outlook on current actual parental roles together with a weaker support for teacher education within this area of knowledge and practice.

Parental involvement in Croatia is discussed in Chapter 5 with the help of a literature review and a research that included a total of 180 interviews of early childhood education teachers. The chapter highlights that although there is a public interest for a teacher-parent relationship, there is a lack of research in the area conducted within the Croatian context. Further, the chapter discusses the importance of parental involvement and teachers' responsibilities in raising the question of whether the teachers in Croatia have the required competencies to support parental involvement.

Chapter 6 presents the parental involvement in ECEC within the Czech Republic. Parental involvement is understood through a review of the developing system of 30 years in relation to the aftermath of the state-socialist educational system. Thus, the chapter begins with a more general introduction to the Czech ECE system, featuring a short historical contextualisation and a concise overview of the relevant transformations in the last three decades. Parental involvement is then explored and critiqued with issues associated with power and the reproduction of inequalities.

The context of parental involvement in Denmark is shared in Chapter 7. Intentions from the Danish steering documents for early childhood education and care and parental involvement are discussed, with gaps highlighted on what is needed for future development around parental involvement. The chapter shows that all of Epstein's six types of parental involvement were found in Danish steering documents. A new theme also emerged on the concept of 'improving' which seemed to articulate the importance of collaboration between parents and community to enhance the educational environment.

Chapter 8 demonstrates the current situation in parental involvement in the Finnish ECEC context. In reviewing the Finnish ECEC steering documents, cooperation with parents is seen as central. Parents' attitudes towards their own participation in ECEC as well as teachers' attitudes towards parents and cooperation are important factors for successful outcomes. Universities in Finland train teachers for cooperation with parents by teaching them not only how to conduct a plan for a child's development and learning with the parents but also how to meet the diversity of families. The authors suggest developing new structures for parental participation in Finland.

From Chapter 9, we learn that parental role is one of the three central standards of early childhood education and care (ECEC) in Germany. The decentralised system of ECEC in Germany leads to a heterogeneous implementation of the required 'Erziehungs- und Bildungspartnerschaft' (education partnership). The chapter specifically focuses on exploring current debates around parental engagement in Germany and provides insights into the theoretically conveyed ideal of parental collaboration.

In Chapter 10, the country of Ghana is introduced. The chapter shows the important roles parents play in regard to children's early learning, education and socialisation. The chapter reviews policy and legal frameworks with current research within Ghana. The key ideas are highlighted around attention to parent involvement and the use of practical enactment. Key ideas to develop and strengthen parents' engagement and collaboration with early childhood education are discussed.

Chapter 11 shares the context of Hong Kong by analysing how policies stipulate parental involvement within early childhood education. Critical questions adapted from a policy analysis are used to guide the overarching analysis process, showing the differentiations within parental involvement in Hong Kong. The chapter aims to provide a policy-level picture around parental involvement and provide suggestions for improved policies and practices.

In Chapter 12, the legislative requirements and theoretical background that frame the work between kindergartens and families in Hungary are reviewed. In this chapter, the authors discuss the shift in practice from the socialist regime to the present day, with a focus on five distinct models of family engagement. The chapter concludes by identifying key points in strengthening the relationships between families and early childhood education, and explores ways of working together that benefit children, families and kindergartens.

Chapter 13 explores the context of Iceland through an exploration of children's participation in the light of history of preschool policy documents. In the chapter, the authors describe an innovative project that showcased a parent meeting in cooperation with five-year-old children. Drawing on Habermas' (2007) theories of democracy and empowerment, the chapter shows the importance of including children. The backdrop of policy development in Iceland's preschools is also shared, showing the importance of parental involvement.

Chapter 14 presents the parental involvement in Jordan. As the institutional ECE in Jordan starts at the age of four or five, the authors begin with the country's policies and strategies in motivating parents to provide stimulating, loving and protective environments. Next in the chapter, parental involvement initiatives are presented along with related established theoretical models (such as Epstein's model). The research overview presented in this chapter points at the professionals' negative attitudes towards parents, contrasted by teachers' appreciation of parental involvement generally. The chapter concludes with a complex overview of aspects and conditions for parental involvement that require improvement, where more professionalisation of teacher education, more precise description of PI in steering documents followed by national initiates helping spreading them in the field, stay central.

In Chapter 15, Norway is explored through an exploration of Norwegian steering documents for the ECE sector and teacher education. Concepts of 'understanding' and 'collaboration' are discussed, showing changes over time. The findings are important for showing how parental collaboration is featured in different documents, including teacher education. The authors try and reconstruct an un-average perspective about services. The findings suggest that the full publication of parental surveys beyond average score reporting.

The context of Oman is presented in Chapter 16. This chapter discusses the paradoxical landscape of parental involvement, starting with the global awareness of the importance for the child's holistic development as well as an important social investment. No matter the importance of ECEC for society's futures, Oman seems to put the onus of responsibility of ECEC on private sector's investment. This approach is shadowed by parental involvement not being mentioned in steering documents, making parental involvement random in nature, depending on knowledge and beliefs of individuals. Even though parental involvement is relevant for teacher education, high-quality teachers are not a priority as the private sector seeks for lower qualified teachers in order to capitalise on greater profits. The chapter highlights the lack of recognition of the parents' role in ECEC, and the limiting of parental involvement mostly to one-way communication and home-based activities. A complex array of improvements is suggested by the authors of the chapter.

The context of parental involvement in Poland is presented in Chapter 17. In this chapter, the authors discuss how parental involvement is conceptualised in the steering documents for early childhood education and ECEC teacher education. Further, they point out that there is a lack of research conducted on the field, which is a challenge in raising the profile for parental involvement in the country. In their concluding thoughts, the authors argue that the perspective held about parents in policy documents and the challenges that follow these policy assumptions are problematic. This perspective might be seen as a reason for growing parental engagement in creating ECEC alternatives for their children.

Within Chapter 18, teachers working with parents in the South Sami language are explored. Indigenous Sámi languages are from the Nordic countries and North-West Russia. The chapter takes a closer look at parental collaborations in a South Sami indigenous preschool. Through structured interviews, perspectives of practice and language support structures became known. The study also highlights a clear lack of research within Norway and the importance of teachers to receive training.

Chapter 19 focuses on the phenomenon of civic rights in relation to parental involvement in early childhood education that are of importance in a young democracy like Serbia. Parental involvement is considered as a marker of quality indicator for ECEC in Serbia. The chapter touches upon the supportive policies for involvement of diverse families in different ways including the difficulties and challenges in implementing those policies. Through a description of best practices in a pilot programme and discussion of associated strengths and weaknesses of teacher education in Serbia, the authors provide suggestions of systemic improvements necessary to empower professionals to have dialogues and build a trusting relationship with parents.

Chapter 20 presents parental involvement in early childhood education in Singapore, a country that in 2018 advocated a policy for more play-based and holistic approach in preschool education. The policy however is counter-intuitive to the existing societal practice that carries the concept of 'tiger parenting'. 'Tiger parents' lean heavily on children's school readiness and high academic achievement, and they do so by providing children home-coaching and extra enrichment programmes. This chapter reveals that parents and educators embrace the play-based government reforms yet experience some dissonance because of the academic rigour and expectations in primary schools in Singapore.

In Chapter 21, we learn about increasing interest around parental involvement in Catalonia, Spain, that has led to changes in the ECEC setting's practices and the promotion of research in this field. This chapter focuses on the laws, the main family support services to promote parental engagement with the community and the parental involvement in the schools. Details from a successful project on parent-school meetings are also shared to propose suitable strategies for engagement.

Chapter 22 presents parental involvement in Sweden, which has a broad and an important objective. It maps the current state of parent involvement in the Swedish preschool. This mapping is explored against the background of steering documents that investigated how parental involvement is reflected in practice as well as in teacher education. The chapter presents a literature review along with steering analysis in problematising current teacher education programs' lack of content regarding parental involvement. The chapter puts forth the issues around cultural sensitivities that may dominate many families and/or individual children during the assimilation process into Swedish preschool (and society).

The context of Uganda is shared in Chapter 23. The chapter author reflects on current practices and documents that are used to guide implementation of practices. Some practices appear to be treasured by parents, while others are done by parents to please government agencies. This varied approach creates a tension between policy and practice providing disjuncture within early childhood education and care in Uganda.

In Chapter 24, the complexity of a four-nation education paradigm of the United Kingdom is discussed in relation to parental involvement in the early childhood context. Though the intention is to build a common value of parental importance for the child's learning and well-being, each of the nations has developed different policies and strategies. The chapter discusses the challenges in sustaining appropriately qualified teachers working with children from birth to five years as an important quality standard in facilitating parental involvement, and thereby engagement, in early childhood education.

Chapter 25 presents parental involvement perspectives from the United States of America. As the United States becomes increasingly diverse, it has become imperative for educators and policymakers to integrate, and not replace, cultural norms and home language into educational practices and policies. In addition, collaborating with parents is seen as important in order to create and promote a home environment where learning at an early age is not only supported but also valued and validated. This approach increases the likelihood that children will succeed in school and in life. At the end of the chapter, the authors provide us with a local snapshot of family engagement efforts from San Mateo County in California, USA.

We would like to thank all of the peer reviewers who were involved in the chapters, providing useful feedback and suggestions. Their contribution has been amazing given the new Covid-19 environment we move in.

Finally, we hope that new insights and perspectives can be gained by readers of the book. The intention is to develop new reflections, questions and ways of working within the early childhood sector. Countries can learn from other countries, while also being able to 'stop in time' and review and evaluate their own ways of working with parents. We dedicate the book to the parents and early childhood teachers in the field and hope new possibilities can flourish.

References

Bennett, J. (2005). Curriculum issues in national policy-making. *European Early Childhood Education Research Journal*, *13*(2), 5–23. doi:10.1080/13502930585209641

Bourdieu, P. (2004). The forms of capital. In S. Ball (Ed.), *The Routledge Falmer reader in sociology of education* (pp. 46–58). London: Routledge Falmer.

Epstein, J. (1995). School/family/community partnerships: Caring for the children we share. *Phi Delta Kappan*, *76*(9), 701–712.

ESS. (2018). *European social survey: Round 9*. Retrieved from www.europeansocialsurvey.org/data/download.html?r=9

Habermas, J. (2007). *Mellan naturalism och religion: Filosofiska uppsatser*. Gothenburg, Sweden: Daidalos.

Janssen, J., & Vandenbroeck, M. (2018). (De)constructing parental involvement in early childhood curricular frameworks. *European Early Childhood Education Research Journal*, *26*(6), 813–832. doi:10.1080/1350293X.2018.1533703

2
THE CULTURAL INTERFACE OF PARENTAL INVOLVEMENT IN THE AUSTRALIAN CONTEXT

Wendy Goff and Sivanes Phillipson

Introduction

Early Childhood Education and Care (ECEC) in Australia (defined from birth to eight years of age) is steered by three key documents: (1) *The National Quality Framework (NQF);* (2) *The National Quality Standard (NQS);* and (3) *The Early Years Learning Framework (EYLF)*. The National Quality Framework for ECEC is a federal document that is used to align the regulatory requirements of Australia's six states and two territories (Organisation for Economic Co-operation and Development [OECD], 2016). The National Quality Standard (NQS) is an essential component of the NQF and provides a national benchmark for the high quality of ECEC services across the country. The third key document steering ECEC in Australia is the Early Years Learning Framework (EYLF). The EYLF is Australia's first National Curriculum Framework for children from birth to eight years and is embedded in the National Quality Standard.

All three steering documents highlight the direction of ECEC in Australia and also the importance of educators coming together with families to support the learning and development of children. The NQF emphasises building and maintaining 'collaborative partnerships with families and communities' and standard 6 of the NQS defines the minimum requirements for ECEC settings to achieve this collaboration as:

> providing families with information, sharing key documentation about children with families, maintaining enrolment records that reflect children and family health needs, displaying and providing information about children to families, enabling families to access and have input into governance and providing an administrative space that facilitates family consultation.
>
> *(NQS Standard 6)*

DOI: 10.4324/9780367823917-2

Principle 2 of the EYLF also highlights parental collaboration and suggests that the learning outcomes embedded in the curriculum framework 'are most likely to be achieved when early childhood educators work in partnership with families' (Australian Government Department of Education, Employment and Workplace Relations, 2009, p. 13).

What is interesting about the three key documents that are steering the work of ECEC in the Australian context is that there is no explicit discussion about the level of involvement of parents in such partnerships and as a result there is little guidance offered in relation to the role that parents might play in their children's education. In this chapter, we examine how educators and parents perceive, define and enact parental involvement within the context of early childhood education in Australia, and explore ways that these perceptions and definitions might come together to guide future research and practice. ECEC is defined across different settings in the Australian context; this includes prior-to-school and school-based settings.

Parental involvement in Australia

In the Australian context, the term parental involvement is often juxtaposed with the term 'parental engagement' to demonstrate the differences between parents' interactions with their child's learning at home, at school, and within the wider community, with a parent's active involvement in the life and work of children, educators, and schools (see Jennings & Bosch, 2011; Emerson, Fear, Fox, & Sanders, 2012). The two terms *parental engagement* and *parental involvement* are also often used interchangeably by researchers and policy-makers in the Australian context despite some advocacy for the use of the term 'parental engagement' in the Australian research literature (Emerson et al., 2012; Bond, 2019). In their work exploring parent and educator roles in educational settings, Emerson and colleagues suggest that the term parental engagement better reflects the complexity of parenting in relation to children's education and care, and affords a more authentic lens for researchers to examine the parental role (Emerson et al., 2012). They propose that the term parental involvement is limited in its ability to describe the various activities and supports that parents afford to their children outside of the formal schooling system because there is an underlying assumption that involvement means involvement with school (Emerson et al., 2012). Other Australian researchers have addressed this issue by examining parental involvement through an analytical lens of family-school partnership (Daniel, 2015; McDonald, O'Byrne, & Prichard, 2015). This has facilitated a way to understand the complex nature of a parent's involvement in their child's education and care across the different contexts in which children live and learn.

Parental involvement has been positively associated with improved academic performance and enhanced educational outcomes (Duan, Guan, & Bu, 2018) and in the Australian context, education policy has traditionally targeted parental involvement for the notion of 'greater student success' (see *the National Partnership Agreement on Low Socio-Economic Status School Communities and the Parent Engagement Project*). However, more recent advancements in educational policy have seen a shift away from the educational outcomes of children and towards those involved in parental involvement (see *the Learning Potential App*). There has also been some research done in Australia that has begun to examine parent and educator perspectives of parental involvement.

In an exploratory study that was focused on parent and teacher understandings about parental involvement in an Islamic school in Australia, Gurr (2010) found that whilst all participants in the study believed in the importance of parental involvement that there was little consensus on what parental involvement might look like in practice. Stacey (2016) also examined the nature of parent-school relationships at a selective public high school in NSW, Australia. Comparable to the findings of Gurr (2010), a key finding in the study was the conflicting understandings of parents and educators when defining parental involvement.

Interestingly, Bond found a distinct disconnect between how schools think parents engage and how parents describe, define, and enact their engagement (Bond, 2019). Bond's findings are reflected earlier by Chenhall and colleagues who explored parental involvement through in-depth interviews with Indigenous parents, policy-officers, and educators (Chenhall, Holmes, Lea, Senior, & Wegner, 2011). A key outcome from this study was an inconsistency between how parents described parental engagement and what the policy and school community assumed about parental engagement. Perceptions of engagement held by policy officers and educators were primarily centred around notions of a parent's visibility within the school community, whereas parents explained engagement through the representation of a lack of visibility. According to parents, a high level of engagement would result in a parent stepping back from the school community and entrusting educators and schools to do their job (Chenhall et. al., 2011).

The differences in educator and parent perceptions are important considerations. Not only do they provide insight into how parents and educators perceive their roles and the roles of other stakeholders, but they also provide a starting point for remedying or improving the supports afforded to young children. However, identifying and problematising difference can also act as a barrier for seeking out new ideas for convergence. In the study presented in this chapter, we attempt to move beyond notions of difference and seek out ways for difference to exist harmoniously in the context of parental involvement.

Method

The aim of this research is to establish how a small representation of Australian educators and parents perceive, define and enact their roles in early childhood education in Australia, and to examine how these perceptions and definitions might come together to support young children's learning and development. The research questions are:

(i) How do Australian educators and parents explain parental involvement in ECEC?
(ii) How do Australian educators and parents perceive their role and the role of others in the context of parental involvement in ECEC?

After permission to conduct research was granted, by University and Department of Education Ethics committees, educator participants were recruited via an existing network that was established in a previous research project (Wu & Goff, 2021). This network was chosen for ease of accessibility and for the different EC settings/contexts that were represented within the network. The network was situated in a high socio-economic status area in an inner eastern suburb of Melbourne, Australia. Parent participants were recruited from the same network and were also drawn from different EC settings/contexts. It should be noted that not all participants lived in the same geographical location as the network. The EC settings/contexts within the network cater to a wide demographic of educators and parents, who do not necessarily live in the same suburb. In fact, some of the families in the network are students who live in outer suburbs but have chosen the ECEC context because of their proximity to the local university.

Data were collected through a qualitative open-ended survey. The instrument was structured around short open-ended questions and was designed to elicit rich, detailed, and first-person explanations about the roles that parents and educators play when coming together to support children's education and care. Questions were organised around three key ideas: (1) Defining parental involvement; (2) the roles of parents; and (3) the roles of educators. There were 12 questions in total. A total of seven educators and six parents participated in this study. Table 2.1 presents the demographic information of the educator participants. Table 2.2 presents the demographic information of the parent participants. There were 13 participants in total.

TABLE 2.1 Demographic information of the educator participants

Participant	Teaching Experience	Context	Local to the Area
One	6.4 years	Long Day Care	Yes
Two	3.1 years	Long Day Care	No
Three	3 years	Long Day Care	No
Four	8 years	Sessional Kinder	Yes
Five	11 years	Primary School	Yes
Six	4 years	Long Day Care	No
Seven	2 years	Primary School	No

TABLE 2.2 Demographic information of the parent participants

Participant	Age	Context	Local to the Area
One	28 years	Long Day Care	No
Two	28 years	Playgroup/Sessional Kinder	No
Three	41 years	Primary School	No
Four	28 years	Primary School	No
Five	30 years	Long Day Care	No
Six	22 years	Long Day Care	No

Analysis

The survey data were collated and analysed using the Leximancer software, which uses verbatim logarithm as the basis of its sorting and categorisation of themes. The logarithmic analysis within Leximancer provides confidence for an open correlation and interpretation of data in relation to repeated hits of verbatim taking into account different accounts of responses (Smith & Humphries, 2016). Leximancer allows both an individual view and comparative view of groups of participants – a collated and a comparative view of how both parents and educators explained parental involvement. Only the four main key concepts and sub-concepts are reported as the main themes of parental involvement explained within the context of this study.

Results

The following results initially highlight how this small sample of Australian educators and parents explains parental involvement in ECEC, followed by how the participants explain their role and the role of others in the context of parental involvement.

How did the Australian educators and parents explain parental involvement in ECEC?

Figure 2.1 shows the Leximancer key concepts in relation to the first research of this study. The concept of the ***child*** had the largest number of verbatim counts in the data set (111), with the sub-concepts of ***parents*** and ***learning*** drawn upon to explain parental involvement. There was a strong focus on the outcomes of parental involvement relative to the child, and these outcomes were closely linked to ***parents*** and ***learning***. This was reflected in comments such as "It [parental involvement] is important for children to thrive, and involves parents being interested in their children's education" and "If you want the best for your child you should care about your child's education and care so yes, it [parental involvement] is important". The

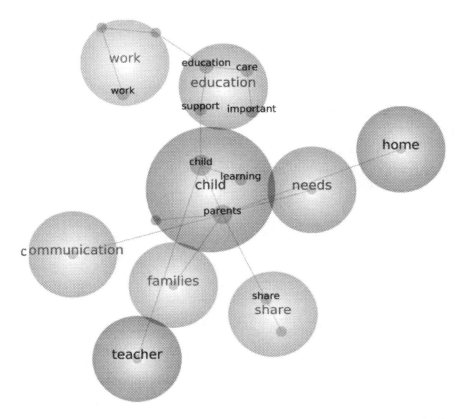

FIGURE 2.1 Leximancer concept map – the four key concepts and their associated sub-concepts and connections when parents and educators explain parental involvement

sub-theme of *parents* was often drawn on to highlight the positive impact of parental involvement on the *child*: "Parents are the most important people in children's lives so we want them to be involved in their children's education and care" but it was also used to explain some of the challenges: "There are some parents who demand all your time. This can be a challenge when you are trying to make sure that all parents are involved in their children's learning". The sub-theme *parents* was also closely linked to the sharing of information about children, and in relation to parental involvement, was drawn on to explain how information is shared in specific contexts: "All parents sign and acknowledge our requirements when they enrol their child". The sub-concepts teacher, communication, home, families, and needs were also evident and discussed in relation to the child.

The concept with the second largest verbatim count (48) was *education* with the sub-concepts of *support*, *care,* and *important* also visible. Similar to the concept of the *child*, the concept of *education* was explained relative to the child but was drawn on more specifically to explain what parental involvement encompasses. The sub-concepts of *support, care,* and *important* were embedded in the concept of *education* and used as a way for participants to explain parental involvement in practice. This was reflected in comments such as "It is important for me to be involved in my child's education and care and to forge a partnership with the centre/school in order to best support my child".

Work was the concept with the third highest verbatim count (27) and was identified as impacting on the concepts of education and the child, and the different sub-concepts within each of these concepts. *Work* was also used to define parental involvement in relation to other ways of working together: "*partnerships may be a more professional working relationship*". And to highlight the pressures of work in relation to parental involvement: "I'm always rushing to get to work and that's hard".

The concept identified with the fourth highest verbatim count was *share* (23) with the sub-concept of *information* also visible. *Share* was primarily centred on the actions of parental involvement and included detailed descriptions about how *information* was accessed by parents: "There are many parent Apps and portals where the teachers share on your child's attributes as well as informing us on upcoming events to attend". As well as how information was communicated by educators: "We share information in many ways: face-to-face; discussion; email; telephone; and the school's compass system". Individuals also offered specific information about their role in relation to parental involvement: "I have adopted an open-door policy and encourage parents to visit my classroom whenever they want to".

In summary, the child was identified as the central focus of the educators and parents in the study when explaining parental involvement. There was a consistent focus on outcomes and benefits to the child, and these outcomes were closely aligned with learning and the role of the parent. Education is described as the core business of parental involvement with the concepts of support and care, and having a sense of importance, used to explain parental involvement in action. Work was identified not only as a barrier to parental involvement but also as a way to describe the working relationship between educator and parent. Share was another concept drawn upon to describe the actions of parental involvement and was primarily used to explain how the educators shared information with parents or how parents come to access information.

How do the Australian parents in the study explain their role and the role of others in the context of parental involvement?

The key concept of *the child* was again identified with the highest verbatim count (48) in parent data and was central to the way parents defined and explained their role in parental involvement (refer to Figure 2.2). The sub-concepts of *education, care, involvement, important,* and *school* were also visible but were explained relative to, or through, the key concept of *the child*. In fact, notions of *the child* were explicitly connected to parental responsibility and obligation, and closely aligned to

16 Wendy Goff and Sivanes Phillipson

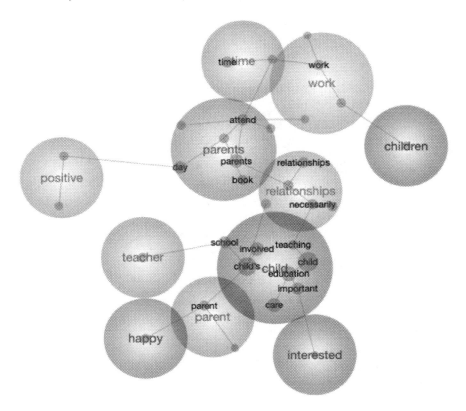

FIGURE 2.2 Leximancer concept map – the four key concepts and their associated sub-concepts and connections of a parent's role

beliefs about 'good' parenting. Parents demonstrated this in comments such as "My involvement is really important because I am his mother. I have a responsibility to him to be involved and interested in everything that he does" and "As a parent my role is to be as involved as possible to give my child the best possible outcomes and opportunities in life". The sub-concepts of **education, care,** and **important** were used to justify and explain parental involvement and provided further insight into why parents should be involved: "If you want the best for your child you should care about your child's education and care". The key concept of **the child** was also drawn on to explain the parent role in 'action' and was evident in comments such as "Parental involvement means being present in my child's learning and life. It means being interested in what he's doing with his carers and helping them when they need it" and "If I am happy and kind to [the educators] they are happy and kind to my child, and they know that I am happy with the care they provide". Other connected concepts such as *teacher, work,* and *parent* were highlighted in the data set and primarily explained through the key concept of the **child.**

The concept with the second highest verbatim count (29) was **parents** with the sub-concepts of ***day, attend,*** and ***book*** also visible. The concept of **parents** was directly related to role and provided a detailed description of the action of parental involvement. The sub-concepts of ***day, attend,*** and ***book*** were drawn on to describe the different ways in which parents enacted this role, including how they communicated with educators and the wider school on a day-to-day basis. This was captured in comments such as "[T]he centre involved me in his day by having a book that came home for me to read that outlined what his day entailed" and "[We are] communicating either through notes in his book or face-to-face". It was also captured in comments that reflected school expectations: "We are asked to help fundraise for the school, they send notes home for special days . . . and we are asked to attend".

The third visible concept in the data set was the concept of ***relationships*** with a verbatim count of (15). The sub-concepts of ***involvement, necessarily,*** and ***partnership*** were also evident. ***Relationships*** were described as central to the parent's role in parental involvement with the sub-concept of ***involvement*** used as a way to explain this centralisation. ***Relationships*** were also described specific to the individual and relative to personal circumstances. This central and personal nature of ***relationships*** was reflected in comments such as

> I work fulltime and only get to attend the service fortnightly while my partner attends the other week. I think this makes it difficult to have involvement to a full capacity because it takes longer to build **relationships** with educators and other parents

Relationships were also linked to the perceived role of the teacher "I value an educator who genuinely likes my child. When you know that an educator doesn't like your child it is hard to work with them". There was also an acknowledgement that relative to parental involvement, ***relationships*** can be diverse in nature "Relationships can be negative or positive in nature". The sub-concept of ***partnership*** was not only described as being crucial to ***relationship***, "I believe [that] without a partnership you can't forge a relationship" but also drawn on to highlight the unique nature of ***relationship*** relative to parental involvement: "Partnership and relationship are not **necessarily** the same. Most **relationships** in an education setting are built on respect and having the same goals to meet outcomes for children".

The concept with the fourth highest verbatim count (10) was ***time***. Time was used by parents to describe the perceived role of the teacher: "The time and extra efforts of our teachers are valued by me" and also to add to the description of the parental role: "Talk to the teacher, ask questions, offer your time (if you can)" and "I make myself available on school drop off and to acquaint myself with the teacher and see how my child is going". ***Time*** was also identified as a barrier to parental involvement: "You want to talk but you have to be at work on time".

In summary, the child is again a central focus of the parents in the study when explaining their role in parental involvement, with notions of parental responsibility, obligation, and beliefs about 'good' parenting the primary motivations for being involved. The actions of parental involvement were explained through daily interactions, shared information, communications with educators, being interested in a child's learning and development, and the building and maintenance of relationships. Parents described relationships and relationship building as distinct from 'partnership' but have indicated that both concepts are important for parental involvement. The offering of time was highlighted as being valued by parents when discussing the educator's role in parental involvement. It was also described as both an action and a barrier when defining the parent role and was linked to wider parental responsibilities such as work and other children. The educator's role and what educator actions are valued by parents were explained relative to the child with adjectives such as being happy, positive, and interested drawn on to highlight both the actions and the relationship. Information sharing from educator to parent was also highlighted as a key component of the educator's role and a building block for relationship.

How do the Australian educators in the study explain their role and the role of others in the context of parental involvement?

Figure 2.3 shows how the key concept of **parents** was identified with the highest verbatim count (54) in educator data and was central to the way educators defined and explained their role in the context of parental involvement. The sub-concepts of **children, care, important,** and *family* were also visible and embedded in the key concept of **parents**. Educators identified **parents** as their primary focus when supporting the learning of children, and as critical people in a child's education and care. This focus was evident in comments such as "There is an ethical obligation to support parental involvement" and "Parents are the most important people in children's lives, so we want them to be involved in their children's education and care". **Parents** were also identified as an important component of the educator's role in the wider context of ECEC "The curriculum sends a strong message that children do best when parents are involved in their children's learning" and "We are required to involve the family through the EYLF". When explaining their role in parental involvement, educators suggested that it involves "Working closely with parents so they are involved in their child's education" and that educators should "respect a parent's right to be involved in their child's learning in their own way". It was also explained relative to the individual: "Our centre has various practices that we put in place but personally I just try to make a personal connection with the parents that I work with".

The concept with the second highest verbatim count (25) was the concept **sure**. The sub-concepts of **information, share,** and **year** were also identified. **Sure** was closely aligned with the actions of the educators' role and was tied into what was perceived as the most important elements of that role *(making sure)*. This concept was evident in comments such as "I make **sure** that I am relentless in sending

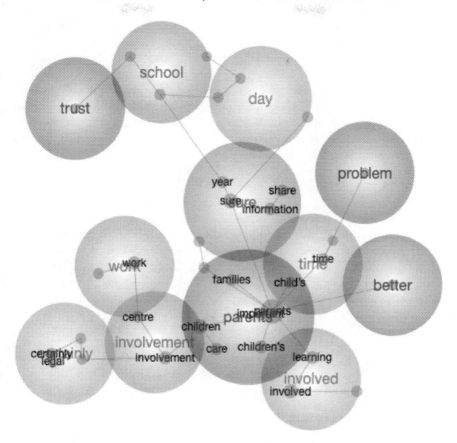

FIGURE 2.3 Leximancer concept map – the four key concepts and their associated sub-concepts and connections of the educator's role.

information home and I make **sure** that all parents know what my expectations are at the start of the **year**" and also in comments such as "We make **sure** that everyone in the room knows about the family" and "I make **sure** that I acknowledge every parent who comes into the room". Being **sure** to **share information** was also highlighted as a key component of an educator's role: "We **share information** in many ways: face-to-face; discussion; email; telephone and the school's compass system". As was an educator's ability to receive information **shared**: "Be open to learning from parents".

The key concept of *involved* had the third highest verbatim count (18) with the sub-concept of *learning* also highlighted. The concept *involved* was used primarily to define parental involvement. It was also used interchangeably with the concept of *involvement*: "[Parental involvement] means that parents become a part of the centre and work alongside educators to support their children" and "It means being

involved in your child's learning". It was also drawn on to highlight educator and parent roles: "[Parental involvement] requires educators to be encouraging and supporting parents to be involved in the learning, care and development of their children".

Time was the key concept with the fourth highest verbatim count (14) with the sub-concept of *the child* also identified. The concept of *time* did not emerge in the traditional sense of the passing of time but instead it was a concept drawn upon to explain how educators used their time working to engage in parental involvement: "[Parents] are already important parts of their child's lives. In a service it is up to us to make the **time** to find out how they want to be involved and what best suits them". *Time* was also referred to as a measurement of involvement: "Parental involvement refers to a parent's degree of involvement in their child's education" and in the more traditional sense: "You know what you should be doing but you just don't have the time to do it".

In summary, the educators in the study identified parents as their primary focus when supporting the learning of children, and as critical people in a child's education and care. The educator's role was explicitly explained through the provision of information and also the provision of support to parents to be or become involved. The role of parents was explained relative to parenting and supporting children's learning, with the key concept of being involved used to define and explain the parent role. The use of time was closely linked to role and drawn on to explain how educators engaged in parental involvement.

Discussion and conclusion

Most research that has examined educator and parent perceptions of parental involvement in the Australian context has stressed and problematised the differences found between parent and educator perspectives (Gurr, 2010; Chenhall, Holmes, Lea, Senior, & Wegner, 2011; Bond, 2019). With our study, we sought to initially identify a combined perspective of parental involvement in order to understand how the parents and educators in the study explained their different roles. The purpose of our investigations was not to problematise difference but to seek out a way for educators and parents to come together. The cultural interface provides a different schema to work from in that it affords a way to move beyond difference and examine parental involvement through a lens of convergence (Nakata, 2007). We now draw on the cultural interface to discuss the findings of this study.

The results showed that the parents and educators in this study positioned the child at the centre of parental involvement with the perceived core business or purpose of parental involvement to improve educational outcomes. This positioning of children and identified shared purpose of parental involvement was the space in which educator and parent found 'mutual ground'. Nakata describes this space as the cultural interface, a reconfiguration of the lived space of individuals as they merge together as one to navigate new terrain (Nakata, 2007).

Concepts of support and care describe the action of parental involvement with the 'working relationship' described as the primary driver. The sharing of information emerged as a key action of parental involvement and was primarily explained through the educator sharing information with parents. This finding aligned with how educators positioned parents as their primary focus, and the provision of information and support to parents a core component of their role. It also aligned with parents who, although positioning children as their primary focus, explained their role through daily interactions and communications with educators. Nakata explains the interface as "a space of many shifting and complex intersections between different people with different histories, experience, language, agendas, aspirations and responses" (Nakata, 2007, p. 199). The central focus of educators and parents in relation to role is indicative of this notion but the alignment of perspective in relation to the sharing of information represents what Nakata explains as intersection, where two worlds meet and become entangled through and because of the interface (Nakata, 2007). This intersection was evident in different ways. For example, parents explained their role through notions of parental responsibility, obligation, and beliefs about 'good' parenting. And although this was not as explicit in the combined analysis, there was an emphasis placed on outcomes and benefits to the child that were also closely aligned with the role of the parent evident in the data. Educators explained the role of the parent through the notions of parenting and supporting the learning of children, and whilst this explanation was not tethered to notions of 'good' parenting, it was still an explicit focus. These synergies highlight what Nakata explains as the knowledge that is operationalised in the realities of a converged social world (Nakata, 2007). What is interesting about this finding is that not only does it provide a window into the social world of parental involvement but it also opens up another avenue for investigating parental involvement theoretically. This finding is important particularly in the Australian context where there is an emphasis on partnership, collaboration, and the relationship between educator and parent in research and policy, rather than an explicit focus on parenting or the parent role (Woodrow, Somerville, Naidoo, & Power, 2016).

In conclusion, the findings of this study provide good insight into what parental involvement might look like in action (see Figure 4). When considering the roles of the educators and parents in the study, parental involvement emerges as a linear process that is centred on the child but is dependent on the educator to determine and share information. There was an expectation from parents that educators will share expert knowledge with them, and that the information shared will enable them to better support their children's education. There was also an expectation from the educators that parents will both receive and apply the information shared and will use this information to enhance the learning of children. This is a vital conclusion because the reciprocity in the study does not appear to lie within the relational aspects of parental involvement, but in the information that is shared, suggesting that a new process for investigating parental involvement in Australia.

The study hence provides insight into educator and parent perspectives of parental involvement in the Australian context. While the study is a small representation

22 Wendy Goff and Sivanes Phillipson

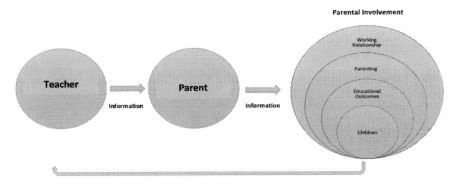

FIGURE 2.4 Visual Representation of Parental Involvement

of Australian parents and educators, in an attempt not to problematise the differences found within educator and parent perspectives, we have proposed a new consideration for Australian research and policy, and a suggested framework for future research and policy directions.

References

Australian Government Department of Education, Employment and Workplace Relations. (2009). *Belonging, being and becoming: The early years learning framework for Australia.* Retrieved from https://www.acecqa.gov.au/sites/default/files/2018-02/belonging_being_and_becoming_the_early_years_learning_framework_for_australia.pdf

Bond, M. (2019). Flipped learning and parent engagement in secondary schools: A South Australian case study. *British Journal of Educational Technology, 50*(3), 1294–1319.

Chenhall, R., Holmes, C., Lea, T., Senior, K., & Wegner, A. (2011). *Parent-school engagement: Exploring the concept of "invisible" indigenous parents in three North Australian school communities.* Darwin, Australia: The Northern Institute.

Daniel, G. (2015). Patterns of parent involvement: A longitudinal analysis of family-school partnerships in the early years of school in Australia. *Australasian Journal of Early Childhood, 40*(1), 119–128.

Duan, W., Guan, Y., & Bu, H. (2018). The effect of parental involvement and socioeconomic status on junior school students' academic achievement and school behaviour in China. *Frontiers in Psychology, 9*, 1–8.

Emerson, L., Fear, J., Fox, S., & Sanders, E. (2012). *Parental engagement in learning and schooling: Lessons from research.* A report by the Australian Research Alliance for Children and Youth (ARACY) for the Family-School and Community Partnerships Bureau. Canberra: ARACY.

Gurr, D. (2010). Parental involvement in an Islamic school in Australia: An exploratory study. *Leading and Managing, 16*(2), 62–76.

Jennings, K., & Bosch, C. (2011). *Parent engagement in children's education.* Canberra: Prepared for the Family, School & Community Partnerships Bureau.

McDonald, M., O'Byrne, M., & Prichard, P. (2015). *Using the family partnership model to engage communities: Lessons from Tasmanian child and family centres.* Parkville: Centre for

Community Child Health at the Murdoch Children's Research Centre and the Royal Children's Hospital.

Nakata, M. (2007). The cultural interface. *The Australian Journal of Indigenous Education, 36,* 7–14.

Organisation for Economic Cooperation and Development. (2016). *OECD factbook 2015–2016: Economic, environmental and social statistics.* Paris: OECD Publishing. doi:10.1787/factbook-2015-en

Smith, A. E., & Humphreys, M. S. (2006). Evaluation of unsupervised semantic mapping of natural language with Leximancer concept mapping. *Behavior Research Methods, 38*(2), 262–279.

Stacey M. (2016). Middle-class parents' educational work in an academically selective public high school. *Critical Studies in Education, 57,* 209–223. http://dx.doi.org/10.1080/17508487.2015.1043312

Woodrow, C., Somerville, M., Naidoo, L., & Power, K. (2016). *Researching parent engagement: A qualitative field study.* Penrith: Western Sydney University. doi:10.4225/35/5715bcdd2df24

Wu, B., & Goff, W. (2021). Learning intentions: A missing link to intentional teaching? Towards an integrated pedagogical framework. *Early Childhood Education Journal.*

3
PARENTAL INVOLVEMENT IN EARLY CHILDHOOD EDUCATION IN AZERBAIJAN

Ali Kemal Tekin, Ulviyya Mikayilova and Nigar Muradova

Introduction

Azerbaijan is a sovereign nation and former Soviet republic located in the South Caucasus region of Eurasia. It is neighboring to the Caspian Sea on the east, Russia and Georgia on the north, Armenia on the west, and Iran on the south. The population of this Caucasus State is estimated to be 10,392,109 according to the United Nations (UN) Population Division (2020) with a median age of 31.7, of whom 2,236,000 reside in the capital, Baku. The official and predominant language is Azerbaijani and the main revenues of this developing nation are coming from oil and natural gas. The nation has taken important steps to improve its educational system to advance its society and in 2017, expenditure on education was 6.94% of the total government expenditure according to the UNESCO Institute for Statistics. The Ministry of Education (MoE) is the central body overseeing the education system. As illustrated in Table 3.1, there are five main stages in Azerbaijan's general education system.

Structure and organization of the ECE system in Azerbaijan

Early childhood education (ECE) in Azerbaijan is split between two education levels – preschool and primary education. Preschool education is for children from 1 to 5/6 years of age. It is provided in nurseries (to children of less than 3 years of age), kindergartens– to 3–5/6-year-olds. Preschool education in Azerbaijan is not compulsory. School readiness programs for 5–6-year-old children are provided either at kindergartens (as a part of preschool education) or at primary schools. Primary education is the first level of the compulsory general education system. The admission age is 6 (see also Table 3.1).

DOI: 10.4324/9780367823917-3

TABLE 3.1 *Structure of General Education System in Azerbaijan*

Voluntary General Education	Full Secondary Education	14–17	3 years (9–11 grades)
Compulsory General Education	Basic Secondary Education	10–14	4 years (5–8 grades)
	Primary Education	6–10	4 years (1–4 grades)
Necessary	School Readiness	5–6	1 year
Voluntary	Preschool Education	3–5	3 years
Voluntary	Infant and Toddler Education	1–3	3 years

Supervised by the MoE, primary education as well as school readiness programs are embedded in general education schools. Under the MoE are 4,418 public general schools (MoE, 2019) with 642,832 (SSC, 2019) children being educated in 1–4 primary education grades. A total of 98,061 children are enrolled in school readiness programs provided at primary/general education school levels (SSC, 2019). Urban/rural disparity with regard to enrollment to these school readiness programs is not large (54,253 children in urban area versus 43,808 in the rural area) (SSC, 2019).

On the other hand, kindergartens are supervised by local authorities. But the MoE participates in the development and implementation of the state policy for preschool education. Under local authorities are 1,803 state kindergartens and nurseries providing services to 126,866 young children from between the ages of 1 and 5 (including those enrolled to school readiness programs), which is 28.5% of the total population of children at that age group (SSC, 2019). There is a disparity in enrollment rates to preschool education between urban and rural child population: 39.8% in urban area versus 17.9% rural area.

Key steering documents about role of parents in education

Parental involvement in ECE is regulated by several strategic documents and legislative acts. The development concept paper "Azerbaijan 2020: Vision for Future" was adopted in 2012. It emphasizes the importance of introducing a state-public governance model for educational institutions (EIs) through the involvement of parents into governance.

The State Strategy on Development of Education was adopted in 2013. It also strategizes the need for involvement of parents in the governance of EIs through participation in parent–teacher associations and other self-governing bodies (3.2.3.). One of the strategic goals is the development of the Competent Parent program aimed to promote the pedagogical–psychological enlightenment of parents (1.1.2).

The General Education Law and *The Preschool Education Law*, both adopted in 2019, also support the idea of democratic and participatory governance and its transparency (articles 20.6 and 15.6 correspondingly) to be ensured through creating parent councils at EIs. Both laws recognize parents as participants of educational process (articles 21.0.5 and 16.0.6 correspondingly), their right for choosing an EI for children (articles 24 and 19 correspondingly), a right to be informed about organization and quality of teaching process, child behavior and learning motivation, as well as a right to participate in a governance of EI; partner with an IE and propose recommendations for improvement of teaching process and school facilities. *The General Education Law* (article 24) recognizes the rights of parents to provide donations, while the Preschool Education Law also recognizes the rights of parents (article 19) to be informed about child nutrition, health care, and other services provided by preschool EI; to defend rights of their child to get education, as well as participate in organization of various events in the EI. *The General Education Law* obliges schools to collaborate with parents and keep them informed about the achievements of the child (article 23.3.11), and his/her school attendance (article 24).

Both laws have similar provisions regarding the responsibilities of parents such as the responsibility for creating conditions for the holistic development of a child, to follow internal guidelines and procedures of EIs, and to partner with them. *The General Education Law* states a responsibility of parents to attract their child to education in a school while *The Preschool Education Law* states that preschool education can be conducted in a family environment; and in areas where preschool EIs are not available, family-based or community-based or short-term playgroups could be organized, following the parents' wish (article 8.7). Both laws make leadership and teachers of preschool EIs responsible for collaboration with parents for the education and development of a child.

The Law on the Rights of a Child was adopted in 1998. It recognizes parents as responsible for defense of rights and dignity of a child (article 7), to ensure a child' healthy growth and development, per universal and national values; to prepare a child for independent living, develop a full potential of a child, meet a child's both material and moral needs, and defend child interests (article 19). The government can intervene in parents' rights only in case of emergency.

National mechanisms are established to provide participation of parents in the governance of ECE EIs. Intending to promote effective parent engagement in ECE programs, the Education Law mandates a parental board at EIs (SABER Country Report, 2018). *The Exemplary Charter of Preschool Educational Institutions* informs that leaders of parent councils could be invited to meetings of the highest governing body – Pedagogical Council, MoE (2009). A similar provision is made in the *Exemplary Charter of General School*, MoE (2010).

Parental involvement in ECE teacher education curricula

Parental involvement is included in the curricula of pre-service teacher training colleges and universities. However, considering that faculty are given the autonomy in designing the courses, scope, and extent of teaching parental involvement, much depends on individual faculty decisions.

In Baku State Pedagogical University, for example, the third-year preschool teacher bachelor students are taught a specific course "Parenting Issues in a National Family Environment." Besides, topics related to parental involvement are taught to special education students as a part of a preschool Pedagogy course, for example, "A Role of Families in a Child Care and Development" and "Forms of Collaboration between Kindergarten and Family" (two academic hours per each topic). In regional Pedagogical Universities such as Ganja State Pedagogical University or Lankaran State University, "Unity of Families and Preschool Institutions" topic is taught as a part of Preschool Pedagogy course (two or four academic hours per course). Parent involvement is included in the textbooks of Preschool Pedagogy for Higher Education approved by the Ministry of Education (MoE). However, the universities have a commitment to teach parent involvement as a separate course upon demand from the field.

Parental involvement is not covered by the curricula of primary school teacher students at the same university. However, that topic is covered by some individual faculty. In a primary school teacher college in Baku, parental involvement is taught to primary school teacher students as a part of specific subject teaching skills. For instance, the topic "A Role of Family in Teaching Elementary Math Concepts" (six academic hours) is delivered to primary school teachers within an elementary math teaching subject.

Parental engagement in a teaching practice

The Handbook for Principals of Preschool Educational Institutions (MoE, 2015) was developed by the State Institute of Education and has a specific chapter on Forms and Methods of Work with Parents. The Handbook states the importance of building collaborative relations with parents and promoting parent engagement referring. Emphasizing the need for individualization of work with parents, the Handbook informs about five levels of parental involvement, which could be differentiated to some extent by the Epstein's types of family involvement (Epstein et al., 2002):

- One Time Parental support to the preschool institution (*volunteering*);
- Sometimes employing parenting skills in a teaching process (*volunteering*);
- Constant parent volunteering in a preschool institution (*volunteering*);
- Collaboration with a teacher at a classroom level in defining teaching strategies (*communicating and volunteering*);
- Participation of parents in a discussion of any priority issues (*communicating and involvement in decision-making*).

A role of preschool institutions/teachers is to know parents and their characteristics/strengths very well, to build positive and trustful relations with parents (*communicating*), to benefit from parental competencies empowering them to be involved in a teaching process, to motivate them to be engaged in a teaching process. Preschool teachers are recommended to collaborate with parents for a more smooth transition of a child to schooling in two ways: 1) strengthening parenting competencies through social discussions, workshops, individual conversations, group advising, round table discussions, and setting up parental corners in preschool EI (*parenting and learning at home*); 2) involving parents in the organization of entertainment and other events in a preschool institution (*volunteering*). The handbook lists collective, individual, and information sharing work forms with parents and describe each work form as, for example, forms and methods for parent education and enlightenment, which include home visits, parent conferences, information exchange, surveys, open-door days (*collaborating with the community*), Q&A sessions, advising parents, etc. (*parenting, communicating and learning at home*). There is no such a Handbook for Primary school leaders/teachers.

Parental Involvement practices are also recommended to teachers working in community-based preschool education groups covering 3–5-years-old children. Teachers are obliged to conduct regular parent conferences to discuss various issues related to child development and learning, and do joint planning of activities and shared decision-making. Minutes of each meeting are prepared, countersigned by parents and kept. Manuals on parenting skills were distributed to communities where the community-based preschool education model is piloted, and community leaders were trained as trainers on parental involvement and engagement (ASIPDE, 2017). Recently it was decided to create a parent association uniting community leaders and active parents. It is planned that the parent association will be implementing joint projects with community-based preschool education centers (AzEdu Education Portal, 2019).

While in a preschool education, parental involvement is institutionalized, in a primary education context, parental involvement is still mainly elaborated through innovative project experience such as, for example, "Child Safety on Internet" (*making parents aware about rules of safe usage of internet to protect children from harmful information impact*) (Ombudsman Office, 2010), Effective School project (Yagublu, 2012) (*strengthening school-family-community links and promoting development of a school community*), Healthy School-Healthy Nation project (since 2014) (improving parenting skills and strengthening parental engagement through on-going trainings) (Azerbaijan Muellimi, 2019).

Parent involvement is one of the key components of the listed project. The importance of this is built on a firm recognition that schools cannot fulfill their mission without the support of competent and committed parents and that schools are losing a traditional role of a center of a community without parents' and community support and are under the growing risk of isolation and ineffective functioning.

Innovative experience is challenging. It would be relevant to share reflections of the "Effective School" project coordinator on the experience of strengthening parent engagement which is similar to other aforementioned projects' experience:

> It is not sufficient anymore to organize social and cultural events such as meetings with well-known people, competitions, interest clubs. Schools to

develop effectively and to form a school community, need to develop open communication with parents. . . . We decided to start a process of building a school community through supporting families to be active and responsible parents will be probably the most productive way. In 12 project schools a two-day long "Communication skills" training was conducted with the joint participation of primary school teachers, school psychologists, and parents. The training was about parenting skills to care about a child, create a positive climate at a family, strengthening family relations, and other both pedagogical and psychological issues. The topics such as "Communication culture and skills", "How to help a child to regulate emotions", "Ways of developing partnership with a child", "Alternatives to punishment", "How to strengthen a child independence", "How to praise a child", "Shy child", "Whimsy child" were explored together. Parents often do not have the competencies and knowledge necessary to effectively manage various problems being faced daily. We were glad to read that training participants while evaluating training effectiveness, asked to invite fathers as well. School psychologists and teachers refused to provide such training further admitting that do not feel well prepared for doing this. Another challenge is a lack of reader-friendly practical materials on parenting and for parents in Azerbaijani language.

Recommendations produced by the Effective School project's experience on parental involvement are summarized as below:

- Parent involvement requires new approaches and tools. Training, psychological counseling, and advising could be one of the possible ways;
- Schools should search for ways for involving fathers and grand-fathers;
- School psychologists' work should be diversified and become more practice-oriented/practical;
- A life-learning concept should be explored with teachers, parents, and pupils to achieve a shared understanding (Yagublu, 2012).

"Healthy School-Healthy Nation" project experience does not seem as challenging. Project documents share the description of activities aimed to strengthen parent involvement in 38 pilot primary schools:

> Our project goal is to involve parents and strengthen partnership with them. This should be done systematically. We have always been relying on parent support. Monthly meetings with parents are organized in a format of workshops. Topics are proposed based on our observations and recommendations of parents. We usually start with the education of parents of 1st graders. The topics are about "Influence of a child health with her/his school performance", "How to ensure hygiene at home and how it is connected with her/his learning", "How to build partnership between parents and teachers", "Joint practice-joint competence ", "Mutual support", "Division of responsibilities", "Developing learning and teaching resources ", "Trust in

relations". We also organize joint games and competitions between parents and children.

(Azerbaijan Muellimi, 2019)

Study

Investigation of family engagement in ECE among Azerbaijani parents

Although parents' roles are considered as critical universally (Tekin, 2011), there is no research on parental involvement in Azerbaijani education available publicly. Therefore, it is critical to conduct empirical research on parent involvement issues in Azerbaijan. To initiate a series of such investigations, the authors started with researching the degree to which Azerbaijani parents become involved with and interact with their child's school. Second, the influence of their demographic characteristics including their age, gender, child's gender, educational level, the number of children, and marital and employment status on their engagement is another emphasis to be investigated as claimed by Tekin (2016) because it will provide information for the differences of involvement levels among the parents with different backgrounds and characteristics, and accordingly lead to ideas to improve the parent involvement in ECE. Addressing the potential influence of demographic variables on parent involvement will also present an opportunity to compare the results with other studies in the existing literature. For example, some research studies found parents who are older (Katzev, 1994), female (Hung, 2005; Fleischmann & Haas, 2016), married (Tartori, 2018), and unemployed (Fuller, 2017), and with female child (Baker & Milligan, 2016), higher educational level (McQuiggan, Megra, & Grady, 2017), and fewer children in the household (Zedan, 2011) showed greater level of engagement in their children's education. Thus, this study is of great importance. The research questions of this study are: (1) What is the level of family engagement of Azerbaijani parents in their young children's education? and (2) What are the influences of age, gender, child's gender, educational level, the number of children, and marital and employment status on their engagement?

Method

Instrument. A modified version of the Family Engagement Scale (FES) was used for this study. The original instrument was developed by Gehlbach (2015) and included six items targeting the degree to which families become involved with and interact with their child's school. All items were rated on a 5-point Likert scale. The scale ranged from 1 (almost never) to 5 (weekly or more) or 1 (not at all involved) to 5 (extremely involved) to measure the level of participants' engagement in their young children's education. The authors went through the adaptation procedures to use the FES scale in Azerbaijani context and employed a panel of experts to review and revise the original scale. Based on the panels' review and agreement, two more items were added to the scale to strengthen the scale in the given context. Back translation procedures were also completed. Along with the FES scale, a demographic survey consisted of seven items and was used to gather information on participants' demographic characteristics. Consequently, the Azerbaijani version of the scale consisting of eight items was used in the study. As shown in Table 3.2, Cronbach's alpha value for the scale was calculated as 0.77. Thus, the reliability analysis for each scale showed that each scale's summated value had an acceptable level of reliability (Muijs, 2011).

Participants and Data Collection. Since Azerbaijani parents who have children enrolled in second and third grades were of interest, a convenient sampling method was used in this study. According to the National Association for the Education of Young Children (NAEYC), children aged between 0 and 8 are called "Young Children" (2020). Therefore, the participants recruited for this study were representative of ECE studies. The eligible parents were the ones who had their child in the same school at least for one year. The others were excluded from the study since their answers would not be valid for addressing the research questions. The authors contacted the administrators of six public primary schools in Baku and explained the scope of the study and received permission to collect the parents through those schools. 500 FES and demographic surveys along with the informed consent forms including information about the contact details of the researchers, purpose, procedures, duration, confidentiality, and eligibility of the study were distributed to the potential participant parents through the schools. They were given two weeks to complete and return the survey. Although participation was voluntary, a high number of parents – 401 – agreed to join the study, and subsequently completed and returned the surveys. After eliminating the spoiled ones, 340 participants' data were analyzed. Initially, demographic characteristics retrieved from the data are indicated in Table 3.3.

The average age of the participants was found to be 33.50. Therefore, the cutoff point for age was determined to be used in further analysis. Similarly, the average number of children was found to be 2.3 and thus the cutoff point for the number of children in participants' families was determined to be 2.

Data Analysis and Results. The researchers used SPSS 23.0 (Statistical Package for the Social Sciences) for Windows to conduct and complete the data analysis procedure. Both descriptive and inferential statistical techniques do analyze the data and answer the research questions. At the outset, descriptive statistics provided information about the level of Azerbaijani parents' family engagement as depicted in Table 3.4.

TABLE 3.2 *Reliability Analysis of the Scale*

Scale	Number of Participants	Number of Items	Cronbach's Alpha
Family Engagement	360	8	.77

TABLE 3.3 Demographic Characteristics of the Participants (N = 360)

Variable		N	Valid %
Age	≤33	210	58.3
	>33	150	41.7
Gender	Male	48	13.3
	Female	312	86.7
Child's Gender	Male	197	54.7
	Female	163	45.3
Educational Level	Less than High School	26	7.2
	High School	203	56.4
	University and above	131	36.4
Number of Children in the Family	≤ 2	242	67.2
	> 2	118	32.8
Marital Status	Married	335	93.1
	Single	25	6.9
Employment Status	Employed	122	33.9
	Unemployed	238	66.1

As it is shown in Table 4, the median Likert point was three; therefore, cutoff point to analyze the means was determined to be three. The results indicated that the participants' level of engagement in their young children education showed variety across the items, ranging from $M = 2.28$, $SD = 1.34$, which was calculated for Item 7 (their involvement in parent training programs or workshops at the child's school to improve their skills to help their child's learning) to $M = 4.55$, $SD = 0.94$ for Item 1 (how often they meet in person with teachers in their child's school). For the overall scale, the results $M = 25.88$ with $SD = 6.30$ showed central tendency in terms of the averages and it infers that participants' level of family engagement in their children's education is very marginally above the average possible ($3 \times 8 = 24$). The frequency results also showed variety across the FES items. For example, only 4.7% of the participants reported that they were extremely involved in decision-making processes at school, whereas 55.8% claimed to be involved in school activities weekly or more. Hence, for the first research question, the results showed that the Azerbaijani parents' level of engagement in their young children's education was average.

The second research question was about to see if there is any influence of demographic characteristics of the parents such as their age, gender, child's gender, educational level, the number of children in their family, marital status, and employment status (IVs) on the degree to which they become engaged and interact with their child's school (DV). This is supposed to be investigated by conducting inferential statistical analysis. Therefore, Factorial ANOVA was employed to compare the means for the participants' family engagement across the demographic variables. The results are illustrated in Table 3.5.

TABLE 3.4 Descriptive and Frequency Results for the Likert Items of the Scale (N = 360)

Question					M	SD
1. How often do you meet in person with teachers at your child's school?					4.55	.94
Almost never	Once or twice per year	Every few months	Monthly	Weekly or more		
10 (2.8%)	12 (3.3%)	18 (5%)	47 (13.1%)	273 (75.8%)		
2. How involved have you been with a parent group(s) at your child's school? (For example, doing activities together for the benefit of your children and school)					3.43	1.03
Not at all involved	Slightly involved	Somewhat involved	Quite involved	Extremely involved		
19 (5.3%)	44 (12.2%)	106 (29.4%)	144 (40%)	47 (13.1%)		
3. In the past year, how often have you visited your child's school to be involved in activities?					4.14	1.20
Almost never	Once or twice per year	Every few months	Monthly	Weekly or more		
20 (5.6%)	27 (7.5%)	35 (9.7%)	77 (21.4%)	201 (55.8%)		
4. In the past year, how often have you discussed your child's school with other parents from the school?					3.38	1.56
Almost never	Once or twice per year	Every few months	Monthly	Weekly or more		
73 (20.3%)	47 (13.1%)	36 (10%)	77 (21.4%)	127 (35.3%)		
5. How involved have you been in decision-making processes at your child's school such as deciding together on teaching approach and learning environment?					2.63	1.27
Not at all involved	Slightly involved	Somewhat involved	Quite involved	Extremely involved		
103 (28.6%)	58 (16.1%)	87 (24.2%)	95 (26.4%)	17 (4.7%)		
6. In the past year, how often have you done something voluntarily to help and improve your child's school?					2.58	1.31
Almost never	Once or twice per year	Every few months	Monthly	Weekly or more		
93 (25.8%)	103 (28.6%)	60 (16.7%)	71 (19.7%)	33 (9.2%)		
7. In the past year, how often were you involved in parent training programs or workshops at your child's school to improve your skills to help your child's learning?					2.28	1.34
Almost never	Once or twice per year	Every few months	Monthly	Weekly or more		
149 (41.4%)	71 (19.7%)	61 (16.9%)	50 (13.9%)	29 (8.1%)		
8. In the past year, how often did you receive school communication such as by parent information packets, telephone calls, newsletters, email, parent–teacher conferences, home visits, and school websites?					2.88	1.48
Almost never	Once or twice per year	Every few months	Monthly	Weekly or more		
96 (26.7%)	58 (16.1%)	70 (19.4%)	64 (17.8%)	72 (20%)		

TABLE 3.5 Main Effect Results of the Factorial ANOVA (N = 360)

Variable	df	Mean Square	F	Sig.
Age	1	128.74	3.38	.067
Gender	1	33.57	.88	.348
Child's Gender	1	23.06	.61	.437
Educational Level	2	29.01	.76	.467
Number of Children in the Family	1	1.97	.05	.820
Marital Status	1	23.99	.63	.427
Employment Status	1	37.39	.98	.322

Factorial ANOVA helps to see the main effects (IVs) and interaction effect on DV, where the interaction effect is the degree of the influence sourced from the interaction between different levels across the IVs on the DV at a significant level. In this study, however, the Factorial ANOVA results revealed that there was no statistically significant difference between the group means across the IVs as seen in Table 3.5. Simply, when the main effects are analyzed, this study reveals that Azerbaijani parents' demographic characteristics do not influence their overall engagement in their young children's education. Since the overall ANOVA result was not significant, neither Pairwise Comparison nor Post-Hoc analysis was examined or reported.

However, the same Factorial ANOVA showed statistical evidence for the interaction effect. These are cross-over interactions that the means cross over each other in different situations as indicated in Table 6. Only significant results are reported in Table 3.6.

The interaction effect was significant for the IVs of the child's gender and the marital status, $F(1,283) = 3.96$, $p < 005$. The interaction effects of age, number of children, and employment status as when combined and analyzed separately from other IVs indicated significant results $F(1, 283) = 3.89$, $p < 005$. Likewise, similar results were reported for the IVs of educational level and the number of children $F(1, 283) = 4.27$, $p < 005$.

To figure out which specific interactions in the levels of the given IVs influence the DV, focused tests of interactions are needed which can be done by separate two-way and three-way ANOVA analysis in SPSS. The results for separate ANOVA for the interaction effects by using Univariate Analysis are shown in Table 3.7.

The focused ANOVA results for the IVs with interaction effects revealed that single parents of female children have shown a higher level of engagement than the other parents $F(1, 356) = 6.71$, $p < 005$ as shown in Table 3.7. Similarly, parents

TABLE 3.6 Interaction Effect Results of the Factorial ANOVA (N = 360)

Variable	df	Mean Square	F	Sig.
Child's Gender*Marital Status	1	150.48	3.96	.048
Age*Number of Children*Employment Status	1	147.67	3.89	.050
Educational Level*Number of Children	1	162.15	4.27	.040

TABLE 3.7 Focused ANOVA Results for Each Group of Interaction Effect (N = 360)

Variable			df	M	SD	Mean Square	F	Sig.
Child's Gender* Marital Status			1			260.96	6.71	.010
Female	Single			30.50	4.81			
	Married			24.93	5.94			
Male	Single			25	6.23			
	Married			26.58	6.53			
Age*Number of Children*Employment Status			1			159.28	4.06	.045
≤ 33	≤ 2	Unemployed		26.63	6.32			
		Employed		24.1	6.05			
	> 2	Unemployed		26.15	5.93			
		Employed		27.59	6.74			
> 33	≤ 2	Unemployed		26.31	6.09			
		Employed		26.30	6.01			
	> 2	Unemployed		25.35	6.65			
		Employed		23.25	6.61			
Educational Level*Number of Children			2			131.91	3.38	.035
< High School	≤ 2			22.50				
	> 2			27.90				
High School	≤ 2			26.91				
	> 2			25.33				
University and above	≤ 2			25.33				
	> 2			25.08				

who are above 33 years of age and employed with more than two children were found to show higher levels of family engagement $F(1, 352) = 4.06$, $p < 005$ in their young children's education. Furthermore, parents with less than a high school degree with more than two children in their families showed greater engagement than the rest of the participants; $F(1, 354) = 3.38$, $p < 005$. The rest of the interaction effects did not yield significant differences in DV when tested separately. Only statistically significant results are illustrated in the table.

Discussion and conclusion

There were two main objectives of this chapter. First providing detailed information about the parent involvement; in other words, family engagement, practices in Azerbaijan, and second, investigating the Azerbaijani parent's level of engagement in their young children's education as well as the influences of their demographic characteristics on their engagement. The first issue was addressed in the first part of the chapter. The following paragraphs will discuss the results of the investigation and provide implications and suggestions based on the current situation of parent involvement as explained and the results of the empirical study.

This study results showed that Azerbaijani parents' level of engagement was at an average level. Of course, the ideal level of family engagement is desired, particularly for its benefits for the young children themselves. When the results per each item analyzed, it is clear that the level of their involvement in parent training programs or workshops at their child's school to improve their skills to help their child's learning. The results also found a low level of engagement about voluntary help to improve their child's school and their participation in decision-making processes. Thus, it is suggested that the structured parent involvement programs should be developed to provide more parent training programs and workshops as well as invite the parents to join the decision-making process, particularly about the school improvement and advocacy for the school. The parent programs should also encourage parents to voluntarily help the schools to improve. The parents should be informed that the education of their children can get better if they can contribute to their educational settings in different ways and according to their talents, capacities, and opportunities. These voluntary bits of help might be arranged at the beginning of each year together with the parents as practiced in almost all developed countries.

The results also revealed that there are no statistical results to make it evident the influence of demographic characteristics of the participants on their engagement overall. However, three results showed marginal influence when analyzed separately in terms of their interaction effects suggesting that single parents of female children have shown a higher level of engagement than the other participants. Likewise, parents who are older and employed with more than two children were found to show higher levels of family engagement in their young children's education. More to the point, parents with less than a high school degree with more than two children in their families showed greater engagement than the rest of the participants. These results are inconsistent with the other studies mentioned previously.

Although there were no significant main effects found in the study, there are several implications to be drawn. For example, the results showed that there was no difference between fathers and mothers concerning their engagement. It contrasts with many other studies in other contexts. However, when interacting with their marital status variable, single mothers had slightly higher level of scores for their level of engagement. Another interesting point is the participants of this study. The results also showed that when the participants' age, marital status, and the number of children in the household are combined, participants with these attributions had slightly higher scores for their engagements. Further, interestingly, although there were no main effects of participants' educational level and the number of children on their when analyzed in combination with all other demographic characteristics, the results indicated parents with the lowest educational level and more children at home showed higher level of engagement than other groups, and that is totally in contrast with the other studies in the field. Based on the results, parent involvement programs should not be limited to only mothers. Father involvement is also the current trend in ECE as they are also reporting to be engaged in the Azerbaijani context. However, it is suggested that the involvement activities should show flexibility in terms of the schedule since it is seen that single and unemployed parents are showing a better level of engagement implying that the other parents might not be able to find enough time to be involved. These schedules might be arranged by the school together with the parents. Parent involvement programs should not underestimate the potentials of parents with lower educational backgrounds. Thus the parent involvement programs should be designed in a comprehensive way to target all parent groups with different demographic characteristics.

There were a few limitations in this study. First, the participants were recruited from only public schools in Baku. Second, there were no enough studies that were done in the same context that led to limited comparisons. The third limitation was that the study relied on the parents' self-report. Therefore, further research should be done with parents from different types of schools and different regions of Azerbaijan. There needs to be more research to be done with parents as well as teachers and other stakeholders such as the administrators to get more information on the matter. It is also critical to investigate the barriers of family engagement and parental efficacy for involvement to understand the source of this conservative result in Azerbaijan. More to the point policymakers should be aware of the family engagement and value it to integrate as the part of regulations of the education system. Conferences, handbooks, and other initiatives might help to increase this awareness. Teacher training should also integrate more parent involvement content to quip the pre-service and in-service teachers with the needed knowledge, skills, and dispositions. In conclusion, Azerbaijan is constantly making efforts to improve its young children's education, but it should be noted that the families are also significant part of the education and no families should be left behind.

References

AzEdu Education Portal. (2019). Retrieved from http://azedu.az/az/news/19989

Azerbaijan Muellimi Newspaper. (2019). Retrieved from www.muallim.edu.az/news.php?id=4034

Azerbaijan State Institute for Professional Development of Educators. (2017). Retrieved from www.arti.edu.az/az/newsd/26-tahsil-institutunun-taskilatciligi-ila-quot-3-va-4-yasli-usaqlarin-maktabaqadar-tahsila-calb-olunmasi-quot-layihasi-carcivasinda-talim-kecirilir

Azerbaijan Vision. (2020). *Look at the future*. Retrieved from https://president.az/files/future_az.pdf

Baker, M., & Milligan, K. (2016). Boy-girl differences in parental time investments: Evidence from three countries. *Journal of Human Capital*, *10*(4), 399–441. doi:10.1086/688899

Epstein, J. L., Sanders, M. G., Simon, B. S., Salinas, K. C., Rodriguez, J. N., & Van Voorhis, F. L. (2002). *School, family, and community partnerships: Your handbook for action*. Retrieved from www.gpo.gov/fdsys/pkg/ERIC-ED467082/pdf/ERIC-ED467082.pdf

Exemplary Charter of General School. (2010). Retrieved from www.tipii.edu.az/noduploads/document/mumi-tahsil-muassisasinin-pedaqoji-surasi-haqqinda.pdf

Exemplary Charter of Preschool Education Institution. (2009). Retrieved from www.e-qanun.az/framework/24394

The First Specialized Report on Children's Rights of the Commissioner for Human Rights (Ombudsman) of the Republic of Azerbaijan. (2010). Retrieved from www.legislationline.org/download/id/7102/file/Azerbaijan_Ombudsman_Report_Children_rights_2010_en.pdf

Fleischmann, F., & Haas, A. D. (2016). Explaining parents school involvement: The role of ethnicity and gender in the Netherlands. *The Journal of Educational Research*, *109*(5), 554–565. doi:10.1080/00220671.2014.994196

Fuller, K. (2017). *Examination of parental involvement in relation to a child's academic success*. (Doctoral diss.), Auburn University, Auburn. Retrieved from https://etd.auburn.edu/handle/10415/5811

Gehlbach, H. (2015). *Family engagement survey*. Retrieved from www.panoramaed.com/family-school-relationships-survey

General Education Law. (2019). Retrieved from www.e-qanun.az/framework/42543

Hung, C. L. (2005). Family background, parental involvement and environmental influences on Taiwanese children. *The Alberta Journal of Educational Research*, *51*(3), 261–276.

Katzev, A. R. (1994). *The effects of the family context and parent involvement on perceptions of children's school achievement* (Doctoral diss.), Oregon State University, Corvallis. Retrieved from https://ir.library.oregonstate.edu

Law on Rights of a Child. (1998). Retrieved from www.e-qanun.az/framework/3292

McQuiggan, M., Megra, M., & Grady, S. (2017). *Parent and family involvement in education: Results from the national household education surveys program of 2016*. Report No. 2017-102. Washington, DC: U. S. Department of Education.

Ministry of Education. (2015). *The handbook for principals of preschool educational institutions*. Baku: Tehsil Instutu.

Ministry of Education of the Azerbaijan Republic. (2019). Retrieved from https://edu.gov.az/az/page/418/7331

Muijs, D. (2011). *Doing quantitative research in education with SPSS* (2nd ed.). Thousand Oaks, CA: Sage.

NAEYC. (2020). *Organization information*. Retrieved from www.naeyc.org/about-us

National Center for Family and Community Connections with Schools. (2002). *A new wave of evidence: The impact of school, family, and community connections on student achievement, Southwest educational development laboratory*. Retrieved from www.sedl.org/connections/resources/evidence.pdf

Preschool Education Law. (2019). Retrieved from www.e-qanun.az/framework/35791

SABER Country Report. (2018). Retrieved from http://wbgfiles.worldbank.org/documents/hdn/ed/saber/supporting_doc/CountryReports/ECD/SABER_ECD_Azerbaijan_Country_Report_2018.pdf

State Statistical Committee. (2019). Retrieved from www.stat.gov.az/source/education/

State Strategy on Development of Education. (2013). Retrieved from https://president.az/articles/9779

Statutes of Pedagogical Council of Preschool Education Institutions. (2012). Retrieved from www.e-qanun.az/framework/24394

Tartori, V. (2018). Parent involvement in education among Albanian parents. *IIUM Journal of Educational Studies*, *6*(1), 38–55. doi:10.31436/ijes.v6i1

Tekin, A. K. (2011). Parent involvement revisited: Background, theories, and models. *International Journal of Applied Educational Studies*, *11*(1), 1–13.

Tekin, A. K. (2016). Parental perceptions of life context variables for involvement in their young children's education. *Education, 3–13*, *44*(3), 353–366. doi:10.1080/03004279.2015.1059870

UNESCO Institute for Statistics. (2017). *Education and literacy. Country profile: Azerbaijan*. Retrieved from http://uis.unesco.org/en/country/az?theme=education-and-literacy

United Nations (UN) Population Division. (2020). *Country profile: Azerbaijan*. Retrieved from www.un.org/en/development/desa/population/index.asp

Yagublu, V. (2012). Səmərəli Məktəb Modelində Məktəb-Valideyn Münasibətləri. *Azerbaijan Muellimi Newspaper*. Retrieved from www.anl.az/down/meqale/az_muellimi/2012/iyul/253579.htm

Zedan, R. F. (2011). Parent involvement according to education level, socio-economic situation, and number of family members. *Journal of Educational Enquiry*, *11*(1), 13–28

4

PARENTAL INVOLVEMENT IN EARLY CHILDHOOD EDUCATION IN BELARUS

Natallia Bahdanovich Hanssen and Volha Mamonka

Introduction

Over the past few decades, there has been an ongoing focus on the importance of parental involvement in early childhood education (ECE). The amount of parental involvement research, especially in ECE, has increased exponentially. The research literature indicates that the quality of parental involvement in ECE can significantly benefit children's learning, self-esteem and attitudes towards lifelong learning (Ceglowski &Bacigalupa, 2002; Kocyigit, 2015; Legankova, 2017). Furthermore, numerous studies have demonstrated positive links between parental involvement and their children's academic, learning, social and behavioural outcomes (Hill et al., 2004; Hill & Tyson, 2009; Hill, Tyson, & Bromell, 2009; Murray, McFarland-Piazza, & Harrison, 2015; Winder & Corter, 2016).

Despite the existence of considerable knowledge about the importance of parental involvement in ECE internationally, paradoxically, little research has been conducted in this area in Belarus. In Belarus, the research literature on parental involvement in ECE has been explored in the small number of studies. These investigations have focused on informing policy and practice about the *general* descriptions of parental involvement and how parental involvement should be brought into all educational contexts (Chechet & Korosteleva, 2004; Chechet, 2017; Legankova, 2017; Mamonka, 2008; Nikonova, 2016; Pozdeeva, 2015; Zhuk, 2017). Currently, there are no empirical studies on parental involvement directly concerning the clarification of the implications of parental involvement in ECE, nor are there in-depth studies of the characterisation, importance and efficacy of parental involvement in Belarus. However, Mamonka (2008), Chechet (2017) and Nikonova (2016) note that successfully building relationships with families strengthens the quality of ECE, increasing the effectiveness of the children's academic performance

DOI: 10.4324/9780367823917-4

and social outcomes as well as children's general well-being and their enjoyment of learning. Thus, it is obvious that there is a need to understand the nature of parental involvement in Belarus and achieve a more in-depth understanding of how parental involvement should be facilitated and developed.

Conceptualisation of parental involvement

To better understand parental involvement, the conceptual framework must be clarified. Internationally, there are numerous definitions of parental involvement, but primary focusing on families with school-aged children, defining parental involvement as 'parents' interactions with schools and with their children to promote academic success' (Hill et al., 2004, p. 1491). In the ECE context, parental involvement is the active participation of parents in all aspects of their children's social, emotional and academic development and success (cf. Hill et al., 2009; Murray et al., 2015; Persson & Tallberg Broman, 2017). In addition, parental involvement concerns numerous aspects, such as parental expectations about their children's social and academic future; the extent to which they become involved in social and educational activities in and out of the preschool; and the frequency with which parents are involved in communicating with the preschool (Hill et al., 2004, p. 149; Kocyigit, 2015; Uusimäki, Yngvesson, Garvis, & Harju-Luukainen, 2019). Parental involvement may also be explained as participation in preschool governance, involvement in the development of educational standards – or educational plans and programmes for ECE (Murray et al., 2015).

In Belarus, parental involvement is defined in various ways. According to Mitrosh and Kukhoreva (2012), parental involvement is the joint activity of preschool teachers, children and parents for planning and organising activities to achieve certain results in maintaining comfortable conditions for forming the motivation to learn, for the children's successful self-realisation and their social and academical development. Bezrukova (1994), for instance, suggests that parental involvement can be defined as 'the pedagogical integration of parents', here establishing the connection and relation between parents, children and preschool staff in promoting school readiness. Parental role thus includes exposing their children to educationally stimulating activities and experiences and fostering their educational aspirations. One strength of this definition of parental involvement is that parental involvement can maximise learning and cognitive attainment in enhancing academic outcomes and improving children's skills in particular areas. Here, the development of parental involvement as collaborative relationships with a wide variety of families can be evaluated from the perspective of academic performance of the children (Hanssen, 2017).

Several researchers have claimed that the notion of the 'pedagogical integration' of parents is broader compared with 'parental involvement and interaction' (Cakharevich & Legankova, 2010; Chechet, 2017; Legankova, 2017; Nikonova, 2016; Pozdeeva, 2015; Zhuk, 2017). However, we assume that 'integration' can be interpreted as a process of parental 'assimilation' in ECE. Such kind of parental involvement can be characterised by rigid formalism without adequate room for parents' new ideas and interest in their rights of codetermination. This can mean that parental involvement is envisioned as something fixed, unable to be revised. The repercussion is that an opportunity to create an equal, active, meaningful and caring partnership and community supporting children's holistic development throughout the ECE years may be weakened.

In sum, there are a variety of complex definitions of parental involvement in ECE. The terminological confusion complicates any attempt to reach a consensus regarding common terminology and common meaning (Chechet, 2017; Legankova, 2017; Nikonova, 2016; Pozdeeva, 2015). Therefore, there can be considerable variation and uncertainty among ECE practitioners and families in developing and maintaining strong family – ECE partnerships.

Belarusian educational policies related to parent involvement

To understand the conditions of the Belarusian context regarding parental involvement, an exploration of the ECE system, basic values and legislative framework were scrutinised and are briefly presented.

The main political, social and economic task of the Republic of Belarus is a comprehensive protection of childhood, family and motherhood. Moreover, Belarus bases its policy on the creation and improvement of a high-quality national education system, and ECE is among the state's priorities (World Data on Education [WDE], 2011). Inclusion is an overarching principle for all education in Belarus, but the country is in an initial phase towards achieving a more inclusive form of education (Hanssen, 2018). The main legislative documents that regulate activities in the field of education are based on the Constitution of the Republic of Belarus (1994), The United Nations Convention on the Rights of the Child (1990), the Law on Child's Rights (1993) and the Code on Education in the Republic of Belarus (CE) (2011). The national ECE mandate is specified in the CE Art. VII, Chapters 18–21. The documents describing the principles behind ECE in the country are the common curriculum is *The educational programme of preschool education* (Ministry of Education of the Republic of Belarus [MOE], 2019a) and *Educational standards for preschool education* (MOE, 2012).

Societal development in Belarus has led to the building and development of preschools; with this, the enrolment of children in the preschool system has increased significantly. Preschool coverage is estimated at 96.8% for children aged 3–6 and 67.2% in rural areas. However, the rate of children aged 0–3 participating in ECE is under 1%; this may relate to the structure of the parental leave system in Belarus. Parents who want to care for their children under three years at home are eligible for a parental leave and allowance offered by the government. This system can explain the reason why children under three years do not participate in ECE and are usually introduced to preschool at three years of age (CE, 2011; MOE, 2012, 2019b).

In general, Belarusian preschools are classified as nurseries, kindergartens, health resort nurseries and kindergartens, special preschool institutions and preschool child development centres. Moreover, there are several other forms of preschool education, including evening groups, adaptation groups, weekend groups, and school preparation groups (CE, 2011, Art. 145; MOE, 2019b). The period of ECE is determined by the legal representatives of the children (i.e., the parents decide when the child starts going to kindergarten). At the same time, the ECE educational programme runs up to five years and 10 months and can be increased by a year for medical reasons or for legal reasons (parents together with the medical commission decide whether the child is ready to go to school or should stay another year in preschool).

In Belarus, there is a provision that the parent committee [*родительский комитет, roditelskij komitet*] is a self-governing body of preschool. The position of the parent committee is regulated through the CE (2011) and approved by the MOE (2011). The parent committee is actively encouraged to collaborate with ECE educators to ensure that the learning experiences of children are meaningful (CE, 2011, Art.146). Moreover, the parent committee aims at strengthening the bond between family and ECE educators, gives assistance in creating conditions for the children's ECE and involves the parental community in the activities of the preschools. However, the parent committee cannot influence issues related to raising funds to support preschool activities (MOE, 2011). Nevertheless, a weakness is that issues that committee mandates mostly are centred around the maintenance of practical concerns and the arrangement of celebrations [*prazdniki*] rather than educational goals (Mamonka, 2008a, 2008b).

The primary language used in preschools is Russian although Lithuanian and Polish groups are also found (National Statistical Committee of the Republic of Belarus [Belstat], 2019; MOE, 2019b). On the requests of parents, the preschool establishments organised Belarusian-language groups. This is relevant because Belarus is bilingual – it has two state official languages, Russian and Belarusian.

Given that the system of education in Belarus is on its way towards inclusion, parental involvement in ECE for families with children with special educational needs is given a great deal of attention. Parents can individually or in consultation with the preschool apply for an assessment of their child's needs (Hanssen, 2018). Based on a psychological, medical and educational assessment at a regional centre – the Correction and Development Training and Rehabilitation Centre (DC) – the child's need for special educational needs assistance is assessed. In collaboration with parents, the DC advises what educational programme and preschool are better suited for their child. Parents have the right to refuse this decision (CE, 2011, Art. 279; Art. 265; Hanssen, 2018).

As indicated, the Belarusian ECE policy and laws emphasise the importance of families in children's ECE. The following position statement outlines 'The state and family are legally competent contributors to high-quality preschool education' (CE, 2011, Art. 141). All steering documents include parents (the legal representatives of the child) as a part of the ECE and determine parental involvement in the educational processes and experiences of their children. The CE orients ECE educators and parents towards a joint partnership directed at children's development and education (CE, 2011, Art. 59). Moreover, the CE (2011) highlights the parental committee as an effective strategy for cooperation with ECE administrators, educators and the community to encourage meaningful parental involvement in children's early education.

However, the policy documents do not clearly specify further parental rights, responsibilities and involvement in the development of educational goals and standards. Thus, a space for various parental involvement strategies is provided, resulting in an unsystematic variety of individual ways of involvement without a common understanding (Hanssen & Hansèn, 2017). The general unclear basis of policies and law may impede stable and lasting dispositions for parental involvement and can be challenging for all parties, particularly when anticipating what kind of parental interactions with preschools, ECE educators and even communities can be provided. Thus, at the governance level, clear policies are needed to develop and organise a strong, supportive, respectful and meaningful involvement of parents in ECE.

Parental involvement in practice

Given the emphasis on parental involvement in ECE in law and policy, it is important to note that all laws and policy are designed to be milestones and should provide a choice of options in practice. The question of how these directives realistically guide and shape parental involvement in practice must be addressed.

Parental involvement in practice began to develop when the educational model 'step-by-step' was first used to promote parental involvement (Mitrosh & Kukhoreva, 2012). The adopted Belarusian model 'first step' is still experimental and provides opportunities for involving families and educators in all stages of ECE. According to Mitrosh and Kukhoreva (2012), parental involvement is related to four constructs: meetings, consultations, projects and social networks on the individual, collective and informational levels. Through this model, parents together with preschools are involved in joint activities aimed at the projecting, planning, organisation and implementation of parent – teacher communication regarding the quality of the children's social and academic development. However, little is known about the various ways in which parents become involved. On the one hand, ECE administrators and educators emphasise how important it is for the programme to be realised in practice. On the other hand, the model is neither specified in the CE (2011) nor adopted in ECE common curriculum education (MOE, 2019a). There is, however, a noticeable absence of parental involvement in administrative and decision-making processes. Combined with the fact that this model is still experimental, this probably contributes to the Belarusian system maintaining a lack of clear strategies regarding parental involvement in ECE (Hanssen & Hansèn, 2017).

As previously mentioned, Belarus is working towards the development of inclusive ideology and acceptance of diversity; parental involvement in ECE for families with children with SEN is hence given a great deal of attention. However, several authors state that parental involvement for parents with children with SEN still is founded on experts' knowledge, with training being given to parents to 'teach' them about the developmental and educational needs of their children (Hanssen, 2018; Mamonka, 2008). As such, parents are not always seen as equal, competent and potential resources who can contribute and create subjects; rather, they are seen as 'learners'. This one-sidedness in parental involvement contributes to an increase in asymmetry, and expert dominance may lead to the risk of violating the parents as active meaning-making subjects, inhibiting the mutual equality and collaboration between parents and ECE educators and administrators. As a result, parents often do not want to 'learn' and withdraw themselves from involvement, arguing that ECE is teacher's task. Thus, there is a need to recognise that parents have a crucial role in aiding ECE, and their view of involvement as an *equal responsibility to cooperate* is an important basis for the utilisation of productive and effective strategies that can encourage meaningful parental involvement in ECE (Hanssen, 2017, 2018; Legankova, 2017; Mamonka, 2008a, 2008b; Nikonova, 2016).

Parental involvement in ECE teacher education

Considering parental involvement as a meaningful resource and power in ECE practice depends on the method of preparing teachers for working with preschool children. To provide a pedagogical activity in Belarusian preschools, relevant and specific professional competence is required. Preschool teacher education in Belarus is provided by colleges and teacher-training schools as forms of specialised secondary education (SSE), including a general education component and professional component within chosen specialisation (Hanssen, 2018; WDE, 2011). Additionally, preschool teacher education is also given by universities as a bachelor's degree. According to MOE (2019b), 62.3% of preschool teachers have formal training at a university level, 35.2% have SSE training, and only 2.5% have general secondary education (assistant, called a nanny, who is responsible for the sanitary-hygienic care of children). Still, 27.1% of preschool teachers lack formal training at a university level.

On both levels, preschool teacher education is linked to a strict core curriculum structure and the disciplinary epistemological core of developmental psychology and general and ECE pedagogy. Moreover, the curriculum provides discipline named 'the organisation of interaction between the teacher and the preschoolers' families. This discipline aims to deepen preschool teachers' theoretical knowledge and practical skills in the field of family pedagogy, interaction of family and social education is compulsory to attend. However, the discipline is studied only in the fourth year and for only one semester. Preschool teacher education provides a useful means for depicting, influencing and forming the knowledge base of future ECE teachers, who, in turn, appeal to knowledge domains and position themselves as professional, knowledgeable agents in ECE practice, especially for parental involvement (Hansen & Hansèn, 2017). However, the focus on parental involvement in ECE teacher education does not have a strong profile, and on its own, this discipline gives a very poor basis for the development of thoughtful partnerships with parents. As such, the possibility of practitioners' parental involvement knowledge foundation may be seriously undermined by this development. Clearly, the consequence has been that a personally oriented and arbitrary approach of preschool teachers towards parental involvement has emerged, thus maintaining an obscure and nonsustainable way for the active involvement of families in their child's education. Hence, the preschool teacher's education plays a crucial role in preparing future preschool teachers to meaningful cooperate with parents and enhance the children's well-being.

Conclusion

This chapter's starting point was to explore parental involvement in ECE in the Belarusian context. As argued, Belarus has developed a relatively clear parental involvement policy. However, there are challenges with the parental involvement in ECE on policy, educational and practical level. An unclear conceptualisation of parental involvement (on the policy level) complicates any attempts to reach a consensus regarding common understanding what parental involvement is and which kinds of frameworks are necessary for the development of parental involvement in Belarusian ECE. On the educational level, the focus on parental involvement in ECE teacher education gives a very poor basis for the development of thoughtful partnerships with parents.

On the practical level, parental involvement is still experimental, but opportunities are provided for involving families and educators in ECE. Nevertheless, the unclearness on the policy and educational levels has led to creation of a parental involvement system, which is mainly regulated by the ECE educators. As such, parents have to comply with the structures and expectations provided. Thus, one-sided perspective tends to restrict parents' ability to choose, reflect and influence (Hanssen, 2018).

The main reasons behind those developments may stem from the fact that country's specific history, and political and cultural positions, after the entire legacy of the Soviet Era, still can be characterised as deeply rooted system that generates a perception of uniformity and dependence on authorities. Tearing apart the old system is not so easy while building a new structure is just as difficult task, as a new structure takes time to erect.

As a summary, we point to several suggestions. First, we recommend that Belarus increase its focus on parental involvement when it comes to the voices of parents as a way to maximise holistic child development. The voices of parents and their possibilities to influence the content and forms of ECE and participate in the activities of ECE are vital. Therefore, at the policy-document level, it is necessary to clarify and describe parental involvement as a form of equal cooperation and partnership, with examples being given of mutual responsibilities and ways of working towards fruitful parental involvement.

Second, to enhance the quality of parental involvement, an increased emphasis should be placed on the preparation of preschool staff, ensuring they are qualified to provide a supportive educational partnership with parents. By strengthening students' competencies in parental involvement while simultaneously developing students' expertise within parental involvement, future practitioners can better provide effective strategies when communicating with and involving families.

Finally, more research is needed to contribute to parental involvement in ECE. Future research should seek to understand the conceptualisation of parental involvement, theoretically substantiating the process of parental involvement and revealing its significance, work directions and the most effective forms of work towards successful parental involvement in ECE.

Broadly, this chapter is an initial attempt to invite for a dialogue among practitioners, politicians, educators and researchers to discuss which kinds of frameworks are necessary for the development of parental involvement in Belarusian ECE.

References

Bezrukova, V. S. (1994). *Integration processes in pedagogical theory and practice* (In Russian). Retrieved from http://elar.rsvpu.ru/handle/123456789/6963

Cakharevich, A. A., & Legankova, O. V. (2010). *Working with family as one of priority spheres of activity of preschool education institutions* (In Russian). Retrieved from http://elib.bspu.by/handle/doc/2500

Ceglowski, D., & Bacigalupa, C. (2002). Four perspectives on childcare quality. *Early Childhood Education Journal, 30*(2), 87–92. doi:10.1023/A:1021245017431

Chechet, V. V. (2017). *Relevant problems of family pedagogics (on the material of research of domestic scientists in pedagogics), social and psychological-pedagogical help for family: Experience, problems, prospects* (In Russian). Retrieved from http://elib.bspu.by/handle/doc/29593

Chechet, V. V., & Korosteleva, T. M. (2004). *Family and preschool institution: Interaction in the interests of a child. Workbook for teachers of preschool institutions* (In Russian). Retrieved from http://elib.bspu.by/handle/doc/14100

Code on Education in the Republic of Belarus. (2011). Retrieved from www.pravo.by/main.aspx?guid=6361

Constitution of the Republic of Belarus. (1994). Retrieved from http://president.gov.by/en/constitution_en/

Hanssen, N. B. (2017). Preschool staff relationships with children with language difficulties: A comparative study in Belarusian and Norwegian preschools. *European Journal of Special Needs Education, 33*(3), 366–381. doi:10.1080/08856257.2017.1314112

Hanssen, N. B. (2018). *Special educational needs in Norwegian and Belarusian preschools* (Doctoral diss.), Nord University, Bodø.

Hanssen, N. B., & Hansèn, S. E. (2017). Special educational needs activities for children with language difficulties: A comparative study in Belarusian and Norwegian preschools. *Education Inquiry, 31*(4). doi:10.1080/20004508.2017.1380486

Hill, N. E., Castellino, D. R., Lansford, J. E., Nowlin, P., Dodge, K. A., Bates, J. E., & Pettit, G. S. (2004). Parent academic involvement as related to school behavior, achievement, and aspirations: Demographic variations across adolescence. *Child Development, 75*, 1491–1509.

Hill, N. E., & Tyson, D. F. (2009). Parental involvement in middle school: A meta-analytic assessment of the strategies that promote achievement. *Developmental Psychology, 3,* 740–763.

Hill, N. E., Tyson, D. F., & Bromell, L. (2009). Parental involvement in middle school: Developmentally appropriate strategies across SES and ethnicity. In N. E. Hill & R. K. Chao (Eds.), *Families, schools, and the adolescent: Connecting research, policy, and practice* (pp. 53–72). New York: Teachers College Press.

Kocyigit, S. (2015). Family involvement in preschool education: Rationale, problems and solutions for the participants. *Educational Sciences: Theory & Practice, 15*(1), 141–157. doi:10.12738/estp.2015.1.2474

The Law on Child's Rights. (1993). Retrieved from http://law.by/document/?guid=3871&p0=V19302570e

Legankova, O. V. (2017). *Features of preschool children's idea of a perfect parent* (In Russian). Retrieved from http://elib.bspu.by/handle/doc/32640

Mamonka, V. V. (2008a). *Forms of organisation of help for the family educating a preschool child with intellectual insufficiency* (In Russian). Retrieved from http://elib.bspu.by/handle/doc/5477

Mamonka, V. V. (2008b). Influence of family on socialization of preschool child with the peculiarities of psycho-physical development. *Age Regularities of a Personality's Socializing,* 131–133 (Collection of theses, Bel. State Ped. University named after M. Tank, editorial board: N. Starzhinskaya [and others]; L. Kandybovich, scientific Ed., In Russian).

Mitrosh, O. I., &Kukhoreva, N. N. (2012). *Forms of cooperation of preschool educationinstitution and family in the conditions of the educational model "the first step"* (In Russian). Retrieved from http//elib.bspu.by/handle/doc/12486

Ministry of Education of the Republic of Belarus (MOE). (2011). *Approval of the regulations on the pedagogical council of the institution of preschool education and the parent committee of the institution of preschool education.* Minsk, Belarus: Author. Retrieved from www.pravo.by/pdf/2011-84/2011-84%28088-111%29.pdf

Ministry of Education of the Republic of Belarus (MOE). (2012). *Educational standards for preschool education.* Minsk, Belarus: Author. Retrieved from http://edu.gov.by/sistema-obrazovaniya/doshkolnoe-obrazovanie/normativnye-pravovye-akty/postanovleniya/

Ministry of Education of the Republic of Belarus (MOE). (2019a). *The educational program for preschool education.* Minsk, Belarus: Author. Retrieved from https://pravo.by/upload/docs/op/W21934601p_1569618000.pdf

Ministry of Education of the Republic of Belarus (MOE). (2019b). *The system of preschool education in the Republic of Belarus.* Minsk, Belarus: Author. Retrieved from https://edu.gov.by/en-uk/sistema-obrazovaniya/preschool-education/the-system-of-preschool-education-in-the-republic-of-belarus/

Murray, E., McFarland-Piazza, L., & Harrison, L. J. (2015) Changing patterns of parent–teacher communication and parent involvement from preschool to school. *Early Child Development and Care, 185*(7), 1031–1052. doi: 10.1080/03004430.2014.975223

National Statistical Committee of the Republic of Belarus. (2019). Retrieved from www.belstat.gov.by/

Nikonova, L. E. (2016). *Organization of interaction between teacher and the family of a preschool child* (In Russian). Retrieved from http://elib.bspu.by/handle/doc/17727

Persson, S., & Tallberg Broman, I. (2017). Early childhood education and care as a historically located place – the significance for parental cooperation and the professional assignment. *Nordic Journal of Studies in Educational Policy*, *3*(2), 189–99. doi:10.1080/200 20317.2017.1352440

Pozdeeva, T. V. (2015). *Pedagogical bases of interaction between teachers and parents in educating humaneness in children of preschool age* (In Russian). Retrieved from http://elib.bspu.by/handle/doc/24567

The United Nations Convention on the Rights of the Child. (1990). *The United Nations convention on the rights of the child*. Retrieved from www.ohchr.org/en/professionalinterest/pages/crc.aspx

Uusimäki, L., Yngvesson, T., Garvis, S., & Harju-Luukainen, H. (2019). Parental involvement in ECEC in Finland and in Sweden. In S. Garvis (Ed.), *Nordic families, children and early childhood education* (pp. 81–99). Switzerland: Springer Nature.

Winder, C., & Corter, C. (2016). The influence of prior experiences on early childhood education students' anticipated work with families. *Teaching and Teacher Education*, *55*, 133–142. doi:10.1016/j.tate.2016.01.005

World Data on Education. (2011). *Belarus: International bureau of education*. Retrieved from www.ibe.unesco.org/en/document/world-data-education-seventhedition-201011

Zhuk, A. A. (2017). *Preparing future teachers for the interaction with family* (In Russian). Retrieved from http://elib.bspu.by/handle/doc/26285

5
PARENTAL INVOLVEMENT IN CROATIAN EARLY CHILDHOOD EDUCATION

Challenges and opportunities

Adrijana Višnjić Jevtić

Introduction

Changing paradigms about children and childhood as well as the position of the child in contemporary society resulted in understanding and respecting children's perspective and child role as an active participant in one's learning. Historically, childhood has been in the focus of the scientific public. Previously mentioned led to a re-examination the children's well-being and the importance of learning environment. Responsibility for providing a stimulating environment for the development and learning of children belongs to adults.

Children are in touch with different social communities that are affecting their learning and development. It is undeniable that the most important role belongs to their family, followed by early childhood education (ECE) settings. ECE settings should be considered as a complementary to familial upbringing. Therefore, cooperation between families and ECE settings is a prerequisite for the child's well-being.

Policy framework for parental involvement

Scholars (Hornby, 2000; Crozier, 2012; Shaw, 2014) cite the Plowden Report (1967) as a milestone in understanding the relationship between families and educational institutions. The Plowden Report (1967) highlighted research findings on the positive correlation between parental involvement in children's education and children's literacy. Because of these results, various forms of parental involvement emerge with a view to improving children's achievement. Johnston (1996) problematizes this approach by stating that the frequency of involvement is not always associated with an increase in parental interest in education, but rather a result of greater engagement by educational professionals.

DOI: 10.4324/9780367823917-5

Ten years before the Plowden Report was published, in former Yugoslavia, cooperation between families and kindergartens was regulated by the Kindergarten Act (1956). ECE had a legal obligation to assist parents in the upbringing of their children. All subsequent legal acts in the field of ECE, in addition to other aspects of its work, also regulated parental involvement (Act on Social Care for Preschool Children, 1981; Program Orientation of Early Childhood Education, 1991; Act on Preschool Education, 1997). Contemporary policy documents follow those directions. *National curriculum for early and preschool education* (2014) highlighted a partnership with parents. It maintains continuity in access to parents as associates in ECE. It is understandable that parental access in the documents varied depending on the position parents had in relation to educational institutions. However, it is important to highlight that just emphasizing the importance of this relationship stands for positive shift in the parental involvement. Although the state has ensured a roll in education policies for parental education, the legislation alone is insufficient for parents and teachers to truly act as partners and associates.

Previous research on parental involvement

Researchers (i.e., Maleš, 1994, 1996; Petrović-Sočo, 1995; Hornby, 2000; Epstein, 2001; Keyes, 2002; Sandberg & Vuorinen, 2008; Ljubetić, 2014; Visković & Višnjić Jevtić, 2017a) try to define the term *cooperation* in relations between families and educational institutions. Analysis of these definitions shows that the majority of authors focus on collaboration as a relationship where the emphasis is on communication of parents and teachers, exchange of information, and joint efforts to achieve a common goal. Some authors (i.e., Maleš, 1996; Clarke, Sheridan, & Woods, 2010; Hujala, Turja, Gaspar, Veisson, & Waniganayake, 2009) highlighted achieving optimal child development as a common goal for parents and teachers. It could be discussed if achieving child's development is a goal for cooperation or an outcome of it. Višnjić Jevtić (2021) concludes that parent–teacher cooperation is a process based on mutual communication, support, shared responsibility, and joint activities in order to achieve optimal child development.

Although this chapter is discussing parental involvement, it is necessary to clarify multiple terms used to describe relationship between parents and teachers. The term "parental involvement" can be considered trough the level of parental activity. Goodall and Montgomery (2014) see parental involvement as inactivity of parents. According to the same authors, involvement signifies the dominance of the educational institution, and therefore does not represent the relationship of equal participants. Contrary to that, Igo (2002) and Morgan (2017) see parental involvement as an active process, assuming parental responsibility for all activities connected with the care and education of their child. Bleach (2015) has pointed out a need to separate parental involvement in the care and education of their children from actual involvement in the ECE institutions. In doing so, it emphasizes the multiplicity of parenting roles, such as creating a home environment/family curriculum consisting of fostering the cognitive, social, and cultural development of the child, transferring values and shaping children's attitudes toward education. This parenting role cannot be passive involvement and concerns solely with the care and education of one's child. By acting on values and attitudes toward education, parents influence educators who in return influence society. Therefore, it is a multiple interaction.

In addition to the term parental involvement, Croatian scholars mostly use terms cooperation and partnership with parents, while terms teacher–parent partnership, parental engagement, and participation can be used as well. Some scholars (Christenson & Sheridan, 2001; Patrikakou, 2016) point out that involvement, partnership, collaboration, engagement, and participation are unambiguous terms and may be used as synonyms.

In Croatia, research about parental involvement has been started in the 1990s. Regardless of the importance of the aforementioned topic, just a few academics were dedicated to the family–school partnership. Maleš (1994) and Visković and Višnjić Jevtić (2017a, 2017b) researched parents' and teachers' perspectives on parental involvement while Maleš, Kušević, and Širanović (2014) gave the children's perspective. Though the lack of research is evident, they cover perspectives of everyone involved in the process of cooperation. Those studies also have given us an insight into perspectives on the parental involvement in Croatia. The results of the aforementioned research were following world trends in understanding the (importance) family–school relationships.

Teachers' education for parental involvement

Educational policies give teachers framework and/or guidelines for parental involvement. Therefore, ECE settings and teachers may be considered responsible to maintain satisfactory, mutual relationships with parents (Višnjić Jevtić, 2021). Contemporary research (Epstein & Sanders, 2006; Warren, Noftle, Ganley, & Quintanar, 2011; De Bruïne et al., 2014; Björk & Browne-Ferrigno, 2016; Hindin & Mueller, 2016; Sadownik, Aasen, & Visnjic Jevtic, 2019) emphasizes the teachers' competence for cooperation with parents as a prerequisite for achieving this relationship. It is questionable whether educational system gives teachers opportunities to get competencies for working with parents.

Višnjić Jevtić (2021) determinates teachers' competence for working with parents. She states that teachers' competence for working with parents may be described as a construct of:

- knowledge (on strategies and techniques for a more effective parental involvement, various family dynamics and functions, working with parents, constraints which hinder cooperation, support systems which the society provides to families),
- skills (communication, active listening, organization, and cooperation), and
- attitudes (toward parents and cooperation with parents).

Eraut (2003) made a distinction between terms *to be competent* and *to have competences*. *To be competent* implies excellence in the field. *To have competences* refers to someone's capability to do something.

Teachers' education gives them initial competences for becoming teachers. Educational reform of higher education in Croatia recognized the importance of family–school relationships, so they include subjects on parental involvement in their programs. Croatian early childhood teachers should have at least a bachelor's degree in ECE. There is a possibility to get a master's degree in ECE, but it is not compulsory. However, many teachers continue their education on the master level. There is no systematic study on reasons for continuing education, but it can be assumed that they would like *to be competent* instead of just *have competences*.

Study programs of Croatian Universities[1] show that the three higher education institutions (Faculty of Humanities and Social Sciences in Osijek, Faculty of Humanities and Social Sciences in Split and Faculty of Teacher Education in Zagreb) have compulsory subjects which aim to acquaint students with the knowledge and skills in the field of parental involvement. The Department of Teacher Education of the University of Zadar offers an elective course within the field. The University of Juraj Dobrila in Pula, the Department of Teacher Education of the University of Zadar, and the Faculty of Teacher Education in Rijeka offer similar content in the compulsory subject *Family Pedagogy*.

Almost all programs address this issue within the framework of other subjects – mostly pedagogical and psychological. It is understandable that due to the scope of other content within these subjects, content intended to enhance the competence of the cooperative educator cannot be considered enough to acquire this type of competence. According to the Act on Preschool Education (2013), bachelor and master students can work as teachers in ECE. It is possible that teachers who continue their education on graduate studies gain additional knowledge in the field. Since the minimum requirement for employment is the bachelor's degree in ECE, only those programs were discussed as the foundation of teachers' competence for working with parents.

Education for parental involvement has been the part of ECE teacher education for almost 15 years. It may be assumed that all teachers working in the ECE institutions have required level of competence for maintaining satisfactory relationship with parents, whether they were educated for it or they become competent through their professional experience. According to Eraut (2003), competence may be the outcome of both – initial education and ones acquired abilities.

Challenges to parental involvement

Parental involvement is susceptible to social and organizational changes. With each change, the number of factors influencing this relationship increases. Some of these factors contribute to parental involvement while others present challenges. If the challenges are perceived in a negative way, then they may turn into obstacles. Granata, Mejri and Rizzi (2016) identified factors that may cause obstacles in parental involvement. These factors are interpersonal (starting point is interpersonal characteristic participants in process), cultural (background, culture) and structural (organization, lack of support for the cooperation of the educational, political and economic system). Most authors (i.e., Davis-Kean & Eccless, 2005; Clarke et al., 2010; Olender, Elias, & Mastroleo, 2010) highlighted (inter)personal factors as the greatest challenge for parental involvement.

The challenges are an integral part of parent–teacher relationship. Barring denial does not improve relationship but widens the gap between the parties involved. Identifying challengeable factors can contribute to a more successful parental involvement. In order to reduce the possible challenges, parents and teachers should understand the factors that cause barriers to their relationship.

Method

The aim of the research conducted during the spring and the summer of 2018 was to find whether ECE teachers see cooperation with parents as the challenge or the opportunity. Presuming their responsibility and competence for working with parents, it was predicted that they can manage challenges in cooperation; they are competent for maintaining reciprocal relationship with parents, and they organized a variety of mutual activities for parents. To answer research questions, students of ECE conducted semi-structural interviews with participants.

Given that the research sought to gain insight into the teachers' understanding of cooperation, possible challenges, and activities in cooperation, it was justified to use a participatory paradigm in research (Guba & Lincoln, 2005; Bognar, 2012). It is assumed that teachers have a complete image of the relationship with the parents; therefore, they provide the most comprehensive insight into the research subject.

Participants

There were 180 (N=180) early childhood teachers who participated in the interviews. All participants were women with 1–40 years of professional experience. The youngest participant was 23 and the oldest was 60 years old. Most participants have a bachelors' degree (91.2%, f=146). Other participants have a master's degree (18.8%, f=34).

Interview

The interview initially consisted of 10 questions, although the final number of questions varied depending on the participants' willingness to answer. Starting from the assumption that a good interview is one in which the researcher allows the respondent to express himself freely while simultaneously sticking to the topic of the interview (Dornyei, 2007), the questions were not strictly defined.

The interview process was conducted during the spring and the summer of 2018. The interview was conducted in the personal contact of the ECE students with the participants. Although this is a survey where it is impossible to guarantee the anonymity of the participants, the participants are guaranteed that their identity will remain known only to the researcher. Each participant was assigned a code to ensure the anonymity of the participant during the presentation of the results. Interviews were conducted at the time specified by the participants and lasted from 20 to 30 minutes. Participants had opportunity to give their own introspections, and to reflect on the topic of the research while answering questions. At the end of the interview, the interviews were transcribed and coded.

Results

Rapley (2001) considers two approaches to analyzing interviews – interview results as a source (explaining the reality of how the interviewee sees them independently of the interview) and interview results as a topic (a joint construction of the interviewer and the interviewee's reality). For the purposes of this chapter, the results were approached as a topic in the construction of the issue that was the subject of the interview. Based on Morris's (2015) stages of interview analysis, the recordings of the interviews were transcribed; testimonials of key importance were identified and coded.

Analyzing interviews as topics that are relevant to the subject of the research determines the *definition of cooperation with parents, most performed forms of cooperation,* and *challenges to cooperation*. Defining cooperation with parents was crucial in order to gain insight into what participants meant by the term *cooperation*. The most of the participants (57,2%, f=103) consider cooperation as sharing information between parents and teachers and all activities involving both – parents and teachers (43.3%, f=78). Almost all participants (91.1%, f=164) discussed cooperation in relation to the child's well-being.

Participants are generally positive to cooperation and aware of the importance of it. Some of participants' comments:

> P5: *Working with parents is a common way of finding out how to be as successful as possible in the child's care and education.*
>
> P78: *Cooperation gives us possibility to reconcile the educational activities – the ones from the parental home and the kindergarten. We both received useful information about the child and developed common understanding of the child's well-being.*

Most participants showed a positive approach to cooperation. They highlighted the importance of information and mutual activities. In relation to most performed forms/activities, they mentioned more than one form. The answers were coded according to present forms, but also by active/passive role of parents in listed activities. Active role of parents included, i.e., communication, gatherings, parents' involvement in different type of activities; while passive role suppose activities where parents are present but without real involvement (Višnjić Jevtić, 2021). Although workshops and collecting materials presume parents' activities, those

TABLE 5.1 Codes and frequencies of data

Role of parents	Codes	f
Passive	Teacher–parents' meetings (group, individual)	180
	Informing (web pages, notice boards)	180
	Festive shows	180
	Workshops	164
	Collecting materials	147
Active	Parents' involvement in group activities	102
	Parents' involvement in institution activities	83
	Parents as partners in curriculum development	12

activities are usually organized by teachers. Parents are supposed to be active in those activities, but mostly, they don't influence them. Table 5.1 shows the codes and frequencies of participants' answers.

There were other activities mentioned (i.e., e-portfolios, open day, social media groups) but they were considered as a part of the aforementioned activities.

During the interviews, participants shared their thoughts about challenges they faced in cooperation with parents. Participants stated teacher–parents' meeting (31%, f=58) and individual consultations (27.7%, f=50) as the most challenging. Only few of them (6.7%, f=12) stated that there are no challenges in cooperation with parents. While they discussed challenges, they expressed fear from unpredictable situations:

> P18: *I feel uncomfortable during individual consultations because I don' know what questions parents will ask.*
>
> P87: *I find the new forms of cooperation challenging, the ones I didn't try before. I also find meetings difficult, especially if there are parents of a similar profession, they have huge expectations and they are more demanding.*
>
> P89: *I remember my first year in the kindergarten. I ran the teacher-parents' meeting and I was afraid. I didn't know parents; they didn't know me. I was terrified: What if they ask me something and I wouldn't know the answer???*
>
> P136: *. . . it is a challenge when you must inform the parent about some problems. There is fear of their* (parents') *reaction.*

Teachers highlighted challenges of teacher–parents' meeting because they need a lot of preparation (. . . *you have to read a lot, to be interesting to parents.*) or because they feel uncomfortable in public speeches (. . . *I don't like to speak in front of a group of people.*). Some of the participants mentioned that although it is great to have a parent in the room, as a part of everyday activities, they find her/him as a disturbance. One of the participants finds new communicational technology as a disturbance because there is no limit for using it, so teachers should be available even in their private time.

Most of the participants (90%, f=162) consider challenges from the teachers' perspectives – what they find challenging. Contrary to that, some participants thought about parents' perspectives. They feel worried about information transfer (i.e., *we try to inform them* (parents) *by writing notes on the notice board. That information sometimes stays unread, so they miss some important information.*) or absence of two-way communication (i.e., *At the meetings we don't have an opportunity to appreciate all families, so we just generalize. And we talk. Parents listen. It is one-way communication. And it isn't cooperation.*).

All participants mentioned the importance of preparation for establishing successful cooperation. Most of them (68.3%, f=123) mentioned education, either initial education or long-life learning, as the most important preparation. One of them (P97) concluded:

> . . . *you repeat some things, gather information, materials, incentives, and if there is any public speech, practice it in front of the mirror. Also, prepare yourself to be able to answer possible questions. In front of your parents, you use terms that are familiar to them and you don't seem to know-it-all.*

Discussion

Previous research shows that, mostly, cooperation is seen as the process of informing, communication and mutual activities (Epstein, 2001; Pianta, Kraft-Sayre, Rimm-Kaufman, Gercke, & Higgins, 2001; Fitzpatrick, 2012; Vuorinen, Sandberg, Sheridan, & Williams, 2014; Morgan, 2017). Participants in this study also confirm those findings. It is interesting that although participants mentioned the need for parents' support through different types of activities (meetings, consultations), they didn't find the support as a part of the cooperation definition. It is also interesting that no one mentioned responsibility or respect as a part of the cooperation. While many authors (i.e., Pianta et al., 2001; Keyes, 2002; Sandberg & Vuorinen, 2008) highlighted respect and responsibility as key terms in establishing cooperation, it seems that practitioners who participated in the interviews didn't find that important. It may be concluded that participants discussed cooperation from the position of parents' needs, without considering parents' possible contribution. Hornby (1989) stated that everyone involved in the teacher–parents' cooperation should communicate and give information to each other. But he also mentioned different levels of parental involvement based on their needs (i.e., support) or contributions (i.e., involvement in educational activities). This approach gives parents the possibility to be actively involved in cooperation, not just passively receive or deliver tasks.

Participants in the presented study follow the aforementioned trend – they all conduct those forms of activities where the parents have a passive role. Meetings or workshops may be considered as forms where the activity of everyone involved is needed. Still, it is questionable whether the parents are active while teachers describe activities, organize tasks, talk about curriculum, and most importantly, present *their* (teachers') expectations of parental involvement. Fritzell Hanhan (2008) stated that even if there is a communication, it is one-way communication, directed from teachers to parents. McAllister Swap (1993) points out that there are active roles of the parents. Parents could not only assist in activities but also advocate for children and professionals, decision makers, and problem solvers by engaging on various committees. It is interesting that no one of the participants mentioned parental involvement in managing ECE institutions even though, by the law, parents are members of ECE institution boards. Only one member of the board may be a parent, so it is possible that none of the interviewed had that experience for now. Besides, managing institutions is the responsibility of principals and teachers who may not have insight into these activities.

Cooperation is a reciprocal process. Following that, possible obstacles in cooperation are reciprocal as well. Participants in the study highlighted challenges that may lead to obstacles. Interestingly, most of them pointed challenges caused by parental behavior in challenging situations. Participants worried whether the parents are interested in cooperation. Participants also mentioned that they feel evaluated by parents, especially when the parents are involved in classroom activities. Prior and Gerard (2007) discussed what cooperation really means – it is supposed to be mutual informing, but parents' staying in institutions may be considered as a hindrance to the work of the teachers. Miretzky (2004) is questioning the real role of parents in these *unequal interactions*. He stated that parents are just visitors who participate in place and time appropriate for teachers.

From the participants' perspective, it seems that even though they did not mention responsibility, they are aware of it. They pointed the need for preparation, so they can be professional, interesting, supportive, and educative. Therefore, they are taking responsibility for establishing successful cooperation with parents. Still, there is space for improvement, especially in the reciprocity.

Research presented in the chapter shows that teachers see cooperation as informing, communication, and providing different types of activities. They didn't find sharing responsibilities or mutual respect part of the cooperation. Participants mostly conduct activities where parents are inactive. Possibly because they are afraid of unpredictable situations, so they feel better if they have control. The most common forms of cooperation are teacher–parents' meetings. At the same time, these forms are the most challengeable. Subsequently, teachers may not really want to organize those activities but are obligated by the curriculum.

Findings presented in this chapter give insight into practitioners understanding of parent–teachers' cooperation as well as their opinion about possible challenges. However, some limitations should be noted. One limitation was that the sample was not representative of the population. Another concerned research method. Although the conducted research answered the problem and the goal of the research, results could have been different if there had been just one person collecting data. They could have had different communicative skills and styles, so it could have affected the results. Nevertheless, the research provided the basis for possible new research that would remedy these shortcomings in its implementation.

Conclusion

Teacher–parents' cooperation represents part of everyday life in Croatian ECE institutions. Educational policy documents stated the importance of partnership with parents. Still, there are just a few researchers dealing with this subject. Although theory and policy put family–school relationships as the pillar of educational work, especially in ECE institutions, educational practices vary.

Croatian teachers meet challenges related to cooperation with parents. Regardless, they are positive in relation to parents. Teachers make opportunities to enhance the relationship with parents through different activities. Despite unequal position in their mutual relationships, teachers are willing to take responsibility for maintaining those relationships. Offering passive roles to parents, they probably guard their professional positions. Their professionalism could be seen in preparing themselves to meet parents' expectations toward the cooperation. Willingness to learn and develop professionally gives teachers opportunity to overcome possible challenges. ECE institutions should share responsibility for teachers' professional growth. The competent teacher could establish a reciprocal relationship with parents, founded on mutual support and responsibility with an active role of everyone involved.

Note

1 The education of ECE teachers in the Republic of Croatia is organized within the six universities:

   a) University of Osijek, Faculty of Humanities and Social Sciences
   b) Juraj Dobrila University in Pula, Faculty of Education
   c) University of Split, Faculty of Humanities and Social Sciences
   d) University of Rijeka, Faculty of Teacher Education
   e) University of Zadar, Department of Teacher Education
   f) University of Zagreb, Faculty of Teacher Education.

References

Björk, L. G., & Browne-Ferrigno, T. (2016). Parent-school involvement in Nordic countries: A cross-national comparison. *International Journal of Pedagogies and Learning, 11*(2), 103–117. doi:10.1080/22040552.2016.1227251

Bleach, J. (2015). Supporting Parents. In M. Reed & R. Walker (Eds.), *A critical companion to early childhood* (pp. 228–239). London: Sage.

Bognar, B. (2012). Pedagogija na putu prema pluralizmu znanstvenih paradigmi i stvaralaštvu. In N. Hrvatić & A. Klapan (Eds.), *Pedagogija i kultura* (pp. 100–110). Zagreb: Hrvatsko pedagogijsko društvo.

Christenson, S. L., & Sheridan, S. M. (2001). *School and families: Creating essential connections for learning*. New York: The Guilford Press.

Clarke, B. L., Sheridan, S. M., & Woods, K. E. (2010). Elements of healthy family – school relationships. In S. L. Christensen & A. L. Reschly (Eds.), *Handbook of school – family partnership* (pp. 61–79). London: Routledge.

Crozier, G. (2012). *Researching parent-school relationships*. British Educational Research Association Online Resource. Retrieved from www.bera.ac.uk/publication/researching-parent-school-relationships

Davis-Kean, P. E., & Eccless, J. S. (2005). Influences and challenges to better parent-school collaborations. In U. E. N. Patrikakou, R. P. Weissberg, S. Redding, & H. J. Walberg (Eds.), *School–family partnerships for children's success* (pp. 57–76). New York: Teacher College Press.

De Bruïne, E. J., Willemse, T. M., D'Haem, J., Griswold, P., Vloeberghs, L., & van Eynde, S. (2014). Preparing teacher candidates for family – school partnerships. *European Journal of Teacher Education, 37*(4), 409–425. doi:10.1080/02619768.2014.912628

Dornyei, Z. (2007). *Research methods in applied linguistics*. Oxford: Oxford University Press.

Epstein, J. L. (2001). *School, family, and community partnerships: Preparing educators and improving schools*. Boulder, CO: Westview Press.

Epstein, J. L., & Sanders, M. G. (2006). Prospects for change: Preparing educators for school, family, and community partnerships. *Peabody Journal of Education, 81*(2), 81–120.

Eraut, M. (2003). *Developing professional knowledge and competence*. London: Falmer Press.

Fitzpatrick, A. (2012). Working with parents in early years service. In M. Mhic Mhathúna & M. Taylor (Eds.), *Early childhood education and care: An introduction for students in Ireland* (pp. 262–274). Dublin: Gill and Macmillan.

Fritzell Hanhan, S. (2008). Parent-teacher communication: Who's talking? In G. Olsen & M. L. Fuller (Eds.), *Home-school relations: Working successfully with parents and families* (pp. 104–126). Boston: Pearson.

Goodall, J., & Montgomery, C. (2014). Parental involvement to parental engagement: A continuum. *Educational Review, 66*(4), 399–410. doi:10.1080/00131911.2013.781576

Guba, E. G., & Lincoln, Y. S. (2005). Paradigmatic controversies, contradictions, and emerging confluences. In N. K. Denzin & Y. S. Lincoln (Eds.), *The Sage handbook of qualitative research* (pp. 191–215). Thousand Oaks, CA: Sage.

Granata, A., Mejri, O., & Rizzi, F. (2016). Family–school relationship in the Italian infant schools: Not only a matter of cultural diversity. *Springer Plus, 5*(1), 1874. doi:10.1186/s40064-016-3581-7

Hindin, A., & Mueller, M. (2016). Assessing and understanding teacher candidates' dispositions toward and knowledge of parent involvement. *The Teacher Educator, 51*, 9–32.

Hornby, G. (1989). A model for parent participation. *British Journal of Special Education, 16*(4), 161–162.

Hornby, G. (2000). *Improving parental involvement*. London: Bloomsbury Academic.

Hujala, E., Turja, L., Gaspar, M., Veisson, M., & Waniganayake, M. (2009). Perspectives of early childhood teachers on parent-teacher partnerships in five European countries. *European Early Childhood Education Research Journal, 17*(1), 57–76. doi:10.1080/13502930802689046

Igo, S. (2002.). Increasing parent involvement. *Principal Leadership, 3*, 10–12.

Johnston, C. (1996). Addressing parent cognitions in interventions with families of disruptive children. In K. S. Dobson & K. D. Craig (Eds.), *Advances in cognitive-behavioral therapy* (pp. 193–209). Thousand Oaks, CA: Sage.

Keyes, C. R. (2002). A way of thinking about parent/teacher partnerships for teachers. *International Journal of Early Years Education, 10*(3), 177–191.

Ljubetić, M. (2014). *Od suradnje do partnerstva obitelji, odgojno-obrazovne ustanove i zajednice.* Zagreb: Element.
Maleš, D. (1994). Suradnja između roditeljskog doma i škole. In P. Aračić (Ed.), *Obitelj u Hrvatskoj – stanje i perspektive* (pp. 287–300). Đakovo: Nadbiskupski ordinarijat.
Maleš, D. (1996). Od nijeme potpore do partnerstva između obitelji i škole. *Društvena istraživanja, 5*(1), 21, 75–88.
Maleš, D., Kušević, B., & Širanović, A. (2014). Child participation in family-school cooperation. *CEPSJ: Center for Educational Policy Studies Journal, 4*(1), 121–136.
McAllister Swap, S. (1993). *Developing home-school partnerships: From concepts to practice.* New York: Teachers College Press.
Ministarstvo znanosti, obrazovanja i sporta. (2014). *Nacionalni kurikulum za rani i predškolski odgoj i obrazovanje* [National curriculum for early and preschool education]. Zagreb: Author.
Miretzky, D. (2004). The communication requirements of democratic schools: Parent teacher perspectives on their relationships. *Teachers College Record, 106*(4), 814–851.
Morgan, N. S. (2017). *Engaging families in schools: Practical strategies to improve parental involvement.* London: Routledge.
Morris, A. (2015). *A practical introduction to in-depth interviewing.* London: Sage.
Olender, R. A., Elias, J., & Mastroleo, R. D. (2010). *The school-home connection: Forging positive relationships with parents.* Thousand Oaks: Corwin Press.
Patrikakou, E. N. (2016). Contexts of family – school partnerships: A synthesis. In S. M. Sheridan & E. Moorman Kim (Eds.), *Family-school partnerships in contexts* (pp. 109–120). Cham: Springer.
Petrović-Sočo, B. (1995). Ispitivanje stavova roditelja o suradnji s dječjim vrtićem. *Društvena istraživanja, 18–19*(4–5), 613–625.
Pianta, R. C., Kraft-Sayre, M., Rimm-Kaufman, S., Gercke, N., & Higgins, T. (2001). Collaboration in building partnerships between families and schools: The national center for early development and learning's kindergarten transition intervention. *Early Childhood Research Quarterly, 16,* 117–132.
Plowden Report. (1967). Retrieved from www.educationengland.org.uk/documents/plowden/plowden1967-1.html
Prior, J., & Gerard, M. (2007). *Family involvement in early childhood education: Research into practice.* Clifton Park, NY: Thomson Delmar Learning.
Programsko usmjerenje odgoja i obrazovanja predškolske djece [Program orientation of early childhood education]. (1991). *Glasnik Ministarstva kulture i prosvjete RH 7-8/91.* Retrieved from https://www.maliprijatelji.com.hr/images/akti/Programsko_usmjerenje_odgoja_i_obrazovanja_predskolske_djece.pdf
Rapley, T. J. (2001). The art(fulness) of open-ended interviewing: Some considerations on analysing interviews. *Qualitative Research, 1*(3), 303–323.
Sadownik, A. R., Aasen, W., & Visnjic Jevtic, A. (2019). Norwegian and Croatian students of undergraduate kindergarten teacher education programs on their professional development and conditions for it. *Universal Journal of Educational Research, 7*(3A), 14–27. doi:10.13189/ujer.2019.071303
Sandberg, A., & Vuorinen, T. (2008). Preschool – home cooperation in change. *International Journal of Early Years Education, 16*(2), 151–161. doi:10.1080/09669760802025165
Shaw, S. (2014). History of education. In H. Cooper (Ed.), *Professional studies in primary Education* (pp. 17–35). Thousand Oaks: Sage.
Visković, I., & Višnjić Jevtić, A. (2017a). Teachers' opinion on the possibilities of collaboration with parents. *Croatian Journal of Education, 19*(1), 117–146.

Visković, I., & Višnjić Jevtić, A. (2017b). Development of professional teacher competences for cooperation with parents. *Early Child Development and Care, 187*(10), 1569–1582. doi:10.1080/03004430.2017.1299145

Višnjić Jevtić, A. (2021). Collaborative relationships between preschool teachers and parents as a prerequisite for the development of culture of communities of upbringing. In A. Višnjić Jevtić & I. Visković (Eds.), *Challenges of collaboration – development of teachers' professional competences for collaboration and partnership with parents* (pp. 77–112). Zagreb: Alfa.

Vuorinen, T., Sandberg, A., Sheridan, S., & Williams, P. (2014). Preschool teachers' views on competence in the context of home and preschool collaboration. *Early Childhood Development and Care, 184*(1), 149–159. doi:10.1080/03004430.2013.773992

Warren, S. R., Noftle, J. T., Ganley, D. D., & Quintanar, A. (2011). Preparing urban teachers to partner with parents and communities. *The School Community Journal, 21*(1), 95–112.

Zakon o dječjim vrtićima [Kindergarten Act]. (1956). Narodne novine 25/56.

Zakon o društvenoj brizi o djeci predškolskog uzrasta [Act on Social Care for Preschool Children]. (1981). Narodne novine 28-397/81.

Zakon o predškolskom odgoju i obrazovanju [Act on Preschool Education]. (1997). Narodne novine 10/1997.

Zakon o predškolskom odgoju i obrazovanju [Act on Preschool Education]. (2013). Narodne novine 94/13.

6
PARENTAL INVOLVEMENT IN CZECH REPUBLIC

Towards a partnership approach?

Martina Kampichler

Introduction

The involvement of parents in the education of their children has been strongly promoted by international organisations such as the EU and the OECD (e.g. OECD, 2006, 2012; European Commission, 2015), as a remedy for equalising educational differences among children with high and low socioeconomic status. At the same time, a growing number of works challenge the basic prerequisite of this view on the effectiveness of parental involvement, that is, the assumption that parents and teachers interact as equal partners. These works (e.g. Lareau, 1987; Lareau & Horvat, 1999; Vincent, 2001, 2017; Van Laere, Van Houtte, & Vandenbroeck, 2018) point out the heterogeneity of parents, their socioeconomic positioning, their understanding of their children's education and their involvement in it and emphasise their different ways and possibilities of getting involved in their children's education. As these works show, a promotion and practice of parental involvement that remains unaware of such differences and related (power) imbalances carries the risk of reproducing and actually deepening those social inequalities it is supposed to tackle (e.g. Vincent, 2017). Bearing these critiques in mind, this chapter examines how parental involvement is understood, dealt with and put into practice in the Czech Republic.

The current functioning of the ECE system in the Czech Republic and the way parental involvement is understood, developed over the last 30 years, among others, in relation to the aftermath of the state-socialist educational system. Therefore, before dealing with the current approach to parental involvement in the Czech context, this chapter starts out with a more general introduction to the Czech ECE system, featuring a short historical contextualisation and a concise overview of the relevant transformations in the last three decades.

DOI: 10.4324/9780367823917-6

Transformation and system context of ECE

The most important features of the state-socialist education system were its unification and homogeneity as well as the way it was instrumentalised to accomplish socialist/communist goals through systematic and purposive pedagogical work. This system featured early education and care service institutions (*jesle*) for children from zero to three years old, and pre-school institutions (*mateřské školy*) for children from three to six years old (Rýdl & Šmelová, 2012).

Parental involvement was a central feature of the state-socialist system and built on two basic assumptions: first, the necessity to reconcile and unify family and institutional education, and to achieve the desired educational effects; and second, that the family needed the help of professional, institutionalised care services to successfully manage the systematic and efficient education of pre-school children and their preparation for school. Pre-schools were supposed to take the lead in educational matters, define the relevant educational goals and provide the parents with the necessary methodological guidance. Hence, the role of parents within this system was subordinate, and the central actor in the educational process was the pre-school teacher. Equipped with the relevant (socialist) expert knowledge, she was expected to guide the parents towards fulfilling socialist educational goals (Jírová, 1982, pp. 9–12). In this sense, the actual role of parents was often reduced to that of a facilitator between teacher and child, solving problems that could impair efficient education, related for example to the child's attendance or behavior (Rabušicová, 2009, p. 319). The central institution for the interaction of pre-schools with the parents was a kind of parent-teacher association (*Sdružení rodičů a přátel škol* – Association of parents and friends of the school), which had to be established at every school and worked as a communication tool between pre-school and parents. Furthermore, not only parents' evenings, individual meetings, and celebrations, but also individual visits to the family were organised. They aimed at presenting and enforcing socialist pedagogy to align the parents' educational efforts accordingly (Keřková, 1982, pp. 53–75).

After the end of state socialism in 1989, this system started to transform. One central feature of the transformation during the 1990s was its familisation (e.g. Saxonberg, 2014), which, together with demographic developments, led to important capacity reductions. In contrast to the early care facilities, which were largely closed down, the pre-school facilities remained the first (voluntary) level of the education system as well as a recognised institution with widespread impact (Kuchařová & Svobodová, 2006). However, the leading role of the family in the child's education was emphasised and democratic principles and the idea of free choice promoted.

To this effect, pre-school facilities received comprehensive conceptual and organisational freedom, which became part of the headmaster's responsibilities. The period from 1990 to 2004 was dominated by the individualisation and democratisation of pre-school pedagogy. The central state-socialist curriculum documents were abolished and replaced with a very generally formulated guideline. This led to great conceptual freedom of the individual pre-school facilities, and the different ways to approach this work on the part of the headmasters produced large differences in the public[1] facilities' programmes and pedagogical approaches and hence their quality. The sources for this conceptual work differed greatly. While many headmasters continued to draw on the state socialist programme and method documents and tried to adapt them to the changed social and political situation, others found inspiration in established alternative programmes (such as Waldorf and Montessori pedagogy) or in newer programmes (e.g. step by step). (Bečvařová, 2003; Koťátková, 2014b).

Accordingly, the handling of parental involvement differed substantially, with new – more participative and cooperative – ways of dealing with and involving parents emerging in those facilities inspired by traditional alternative and newer pedagogical approaches (cf. Rabušicová, 2004b, who presents the example of the step-by-step programme). Those facilities, which continued by adjusting the former state socialist programmes, however, rather lacked new inspiration in this regard. The obligation to establish "Associations of parents and friends of the school" was abolished, which lead either to the dissolving of these groups or to their re-creation as citizens' associations (MŠMT, 2000).

Parental involvement in key steering documents

Finally, the growing quality differences led to the development of a single curriculum document, with a single conception of ECE for public pre-school facilities, which came into effect as part of the Educational Act passed in 2004 (Bečvařová, 2003; Koťátková, 2014b): In 2005, the Ministry of Education, Youth and Sports issued the Framework Education Programme for Preschool Education (FEP), specifying the main requirements, conditions and rules for the institutional education of children of pre-school age. While the Educational Act outlines only the basic rights (e.g. for information, for counselling services and commenting) and duties (such as ensuring the child's regular attendance and informing the school in relevant matters) of parents in relation to schools and educational facilities, the FEP defines the relationship between family and ECE facility and the task of ECE within this relationship as complementary to family education (MŠMT, 2018, pp. 6–7):

> *The task of institutional pre-school education is to complement and support family education and, in close relation to it, to help provide the child with an environment with sufficient versatile and adequate incentives for their active development and learning. Pre-school education meaningfully enriches the child's daily program during their pre-school years and provides the child with professional care. It seeks to build the first educational steps of a child on a well-thought-out, professionally supported and humanly and socially valuable basis, and to ensure that the time spent in kindergarten is a joy, a pleasant experience and a source of good and reliable foundations for their later life and education.*

The detailed understanding of parental involvement in the FEP is formulated as an ideal case benchmark. The FEP defines parental involvement as one of the conditions of pre-school education: The relationship between parents and ECE facility should be characterised by mutual trust and openness, goodwill, understanding, respect and openness for co-operation, based on a partnership approach. In case of interest, parents have the possibility to get involved in the planning and realisation of the pre-school facility's programme. The facility staff should track the needs of the family and the children, try to understand them and comply with them. They should inform the parents on regular basis about the child's progress and learning and co-ordinate their educational approach with the parents. The pre-school facility should support and help family education, by providing information and consultancy, but at the same time respect the family's privacy and avoid unrequested advice (MŠMT, 2018, pp. 34–35). Hence, the Czech FEP departs from a partnership approach, but at the same time requires the ECE facility to respect and work with differences among parents (which however are not further elaborated).

Since September 2007, this document is binding for those pre-school facilities that are part of the network of schools and educational facilities (MŠMT, 2019a). The large majority of these facilities are public (91.5 percent in the school year 2018/19[2]) and the rest are founded by private entities (including churches, for-profit and non-profit organisations), but are also co-funded by central state grants. Additionally, over the last 10 years, a limited alternative pre-school market has emerged, which consists of private entities fully funded by parental fees. These facilities are not part of the network of schools and educational facilities and therefore offer more space for alternative pedagogical approaches. These are often used as marketing tools to target specific segments of parents that also have the resources to fund this type of ECE service (Kampichler, Dvořáčková, & Jarkovská, 2018).

Apart from the Educational act and the Framework programme, there are further current strategic policy documents, relevant for the Czech ECE system, like the *Strategy for Education Policy of the Czech Republic until 2020*, the preparatory documents for the new strategy 2030+ and the long-term plans 2015–2020 and 2019–2023. The strategy 2020 presents a strengthening of the co-operation between parents and the school environment as part of the measures for improving the accessibility and quality of pre-school education and this is substantiated in the long-term plan 2015–2020, which presents related measures to be financed from EU funds (such as parental involvement in the facility's activities as well as in the planning of the pre-school's programme). However, these planned activities are not related to a comprehensive plan, how parental involvement is understood and should be supported and further developed. The current long-term plan 2019–2023 includes no more references to parental involvement and the preparatory document for the new Strategy 2030+ features only a very narrow and specific understanding of parental involvement, which exclusively targets parents with a low socio-economic status and Roma. In this sense, it employs mainly social policy measures – such as case management supporting the whole family in their given situation, parental education and strengthening of parenting competences – but also the reduction of economic barriers (relief from pre-school fees or free lunches). Apart from the fact that this understanding of parental involvement approaches only a certain part of parents, it also raises the question of whether it is in accordance with the partnership approach to parental involvement outlined in the FEP.

Research on parental involvement in ECE

Pedagogical research on parental involvement in ECE over the last three decades has mainly focused on different approaches to characterise parents and their relationship with the ECE facility, dealing with questions such as *how do parents perceive pre-schools, how do they relate to the facility and how do they present and accomplish their interests?*

The majority of this research does not exclusively focus on pre-school facilities, but rather deals with data from both pre-schools and elementary schools. In this regard the research discusses and explores the transformed – more active role – of parents in the educational system in general, related to the theoretical transition towards a participative and partner approach (cf. Rabušicová & Pol, 1996a, 1996b), as it is grounded in the Educational act and the FEP. Later works examine to what extent these theoretical possibilities are actually put into practice by parents and in what ways (e.g. Rabušicová, Čiháček, Emmerová, & Šeďová, 2003; Rabušicová, Šeďová, Trnková, & Čiháček, 2004, Rabušicová, 2004a; Trnková & Číháček, 2003). These works identify different roles parents take on in their interaction with the educational facility, identifying four main types: parents as clients, partners, citizens and as a problem.

Particular forms of parental involvement, their frequency as well as perception by parents and teachers, were examined in a survey carried out for the OECD report *National report on the state of early childhood education and childcare for pre-school children in the Czech Republic* (MŠMT, 2000). However, these particular forms of parental involvement (such as meetings, consultations, celebrations, parental participation in the pre-school facility, events organised by parents and so own) are neither further examined, theoretically reflected, developed, nor examined in the published academic research. However, the documentation of such forms of parental involvement and what kind of role they play in the context of different pedagogical approaches in particular facilities is a popular topic for bachelor's theses in the field of ECE.

Parental involvement in teacher education

The relevant qualification for working as a pre-school teacher in the Czech Republic can be obtained in three different ways: high school specialisation (ISCED 3A), vocational school training (ISCED 5A) as well as in the form of a bachelor university study program (ISCED 5) (Opravilová, 2007, pp. 1055–1057). For historical reasons, the majority of pre-school teachers attained their qualification at the high school level[3] and only in recent years, related to discussions on the further professionalisation of pre-school teachers, the bachelor study programme gains in importance. The three educational levels differ mainly with regard to the scope, detail and theoretical backing of the relevant subjects.

Parental involvement is mainly dealt with in subjects on pre-school, special and social pedagogy. These subjects present parental involvement in the context of the relevant legal documents (the Educational act, pre-school related regulations and most importantly, the FEP) and deal with the practical side of parental involvement such as the teacher's duties in relation to the parents, the necessary competences and principles for a successful co-operation with the parents, or how to successfully organise and realise a parent-teacher interview. Furthermore, they present general principles of the functioning of the ECE-facility which support parental involvement, such as an organisational and spatial openness of the facility, which allows parents to join their children, the organisation of parent-teacher interviews, the involvement of parents in the facility's planning, programme and evaluation as well as particular ways of informing parents (e.g. notice boards, web pages, magazines, special events and celebrations organised for the parents, events organised in co-operation with the parents) (Syslová & Grůzová, 2019).

Furthermore, pre-school teacher training features subjects that specialise on the family as a social institution in general (predominantly on the bachelor's level), like the *Sociology of the Family* or *Family Care and Education*. These subjects focus mainly on introducing the students to the functions of the family, socialisation processes, different parental styles as well as understanding the family and parenthood in the context of current social changes and developments and in this sense can help the pre-school teacher to develop a better understanding of the situation of parents.

Relevant course literature dealing with these points includes for example: Rabušicová et al., 2004; Opravilová, 2016; Horká & Syslová, 2011; Čapek, 2013; Koťátková, 2014a).

Parental engagement in practice

The ways parental involvement is actually put into practice in particular ECE facilities differ importantly among various types of facilities, mainly depending on the programme and pedagogical orientation of the given facility. The differences among the particular facilities show also the wide range of possibilities for parental involvement, which the framework programme allows for. To exemplify how differently parental involvement is handled in practice, in the following I will shortly present how six ECE facilities deal with parental involvement. The data for this characterisation were gathered in the course of the research project Diversification of pre-school education in the Czech Republic (GA16–18940S) in the years 2016 and 2017.

In this project, we chose six ECE facilities offering childcare services for children aged three to six years. We selected three public facilities, with high, medium, and low parental demand (based on the number of applications per place offered), and three private facilities offering their services at high, medium, and low prices (in the context of our city of research). These different types of ECE facilities do not mirror the share of these different types in the overall offer of ECE services in the city of research, but they are thought to delimit the range of currently available services and hence show the current system's inner diversity. With the exception of the forest nursery school, all of them are part of the network of schools and educational facilities and hence have to apply the Framework Education Programme for Pre-school Education.

Public high-demand facility

One of the central features of this facility is a basic openness towards parental involvement: The parents and the pre-school teacher meet before the children start pre-school, and the adaption programme for new children (at the beginning of the year) is very flexible and fully adaptable to the needs of the children and the family. In general, parents have access to the facility whenever they want to join; if they wish to do so, they can spend the day with their child at pre-school. The facility organises regular parent-teacher interviews, but the teachers are also available for spontaneous talks (e.g. in the morning or in the evening, usually when parents pick up their child directly in class). There are several celebrations during the year (such as common work in the facility's garden) and the parents are encouraged to get involved in the facility's programme, as well as to organise events on their own (e.g. a sleep-over in the pre-school). The interviewed parents perceive the facility's approach as special and exceptional compared to other public facilities.

Public medium-demand facility

Parental involvement in this facility is mainly realised in the form of regular celebrations and events the parents can join in the course of the year (Christmas, Easter, end of the school year). There are no regular parent-teacher interviews and information is mainly passed on to the parents when they pick up their children and ask for it. At the same time the parents of this facility seem to be satisfied with this approach and see their involvement rather related to situations, when particular problems (on the side of the teacher or the child) arise. At the same time, however, the headmistress of this facility complained about the lack of involvement and interest on the side of the parents, arguing that the parents expect the pre-school to do all the educational work to prepare their children for school.

Public low-demand facility

This facility is located nearby an excluded Roma locality; hence, it provides an example of how parental involvement becomes intertwined with – and, as a result potentially reduced to – certain ways of tackling of social inequalities (as emphasised in the Strategy 2030+ preparatory document, presented earlier). The facility puts special emphasis on parental involvement. The example of this facility, however, shows how the intertwining of parental involvement with specific ways of tackling social inequalities threatens the principle of equal partnership and mutual respect in parental involvement, raising questions like *On what terms does social 'inclusion' take place through pre-school facilities? What does it actually mean for the children and their parents? Do we talk about equalizing opportunities to fulfil the child's individual potential or rather normalizing and assimilating children and their parents into pre-defined paths?* In this sense, it points also to the importance of reflecting power relations and potentially different positions of parents and facility staff in parent–ECE-facility relations.

Private high-price facility

In this facility, the parent–pre-school relationship is characterised best as a client-service provider relationship. The facility provides a broad range of information and feedback for the parents – such as a Facebook group, where photos and videos are posted on regular basis, a pie chart with development milestones available at the child's locker, parent-teacher interviews on regular basis and information about the child on daily basis (when the parents pick up their child). Furthermore, the facilities organise different kinds of events and celebrations around the year. At the same time, the facility offers a broad range of activities for the children, allowing the parent to 'outsource' some of their duties (e.g. speech development training, various sports).

Private medium-price facility (a forest pre-school)

Parental involvement in this facility is both, a central component of the ECE facility's conception and programme and a central criterion for the parents. The parents are expected to get involved and at the same time expect this involvement and see it as a way to be part of their child's ECE life. Every family takes over a certain task (e.g. to provide drinking water on one day), the programme welcomes parental involvement (parents may join during the day, realise their own ideas for the programme) and provides open spaces, where parents can meet, socialise and share – usually parents stay on the premises of the forest pre-school for some time in the morning and in the afternoon, to chat with each other and with the facility's staff. Moreover, the facility provides parent-teacher interviews and twice a year written feedback for each child.

Private low-price facility

This facility is basically quite open to parental involvement, offering for example a special form of parent-teacher interviews and parental tutorials. However, similarly as in the case of the public medium-demand facility, also here, the facility's headmaster talked about a lack of interest on the part of the parents in getting more involved with the ECE facility.

Final thoughts

On a theoretical level, parental involvement in the Czech Republic is basically understood as a partnership between parents and the ECE-facility. However, putting this approach into practice is complicated by several points:

Despite this theoretical emphasis on partnership, the decisive role and responsibility in the Czech understanding of parental involvement seems to be ascribed to the parents. In this regard, the parents, their characterisation and understanding have been in the centre of research interest so far. Pedagogical research hardly examines how parental involvement is actually contextualised in the ECE facility's approach, and hence not only a question of parental initiative or certain fixed parental roles but also a mutual process. Understanding parental involvement as a mutual process helps to see the importance of two points, which could further (but also hinder) the development of parental involvement in ECE in the Czech context:

1) The system prerequisites for a basic openness for parental involvement in average public facilities: In these facilities, teachers often have to work in overcrowded classes with up to 28 children and most of the time one teacher has to handle these big groups on their own. This situation leaves only very little space for individual interaction with the parents. According to the current plans, on the long run, the number of children in classes should be reduced to a maximum of 20 and the time of two teachers per class should be extended to at least 2.5 h per day. Still, the question is, whether the current public system prerequisites actively support the realisation of the vision of parental involvement outlined in the FEP.
2) The recent policy focus on parental involvement as a remedy to inequalities in the educational system and the related focus on families with a low socio-economic background and especially Roma, carries the risk of creating a dual understanding and practice of parental involvement, turning partnership into a principle of exclusion instead of inclusion: While in certain ECE facilities the partnership with and involvement of (middle-class) parents is more and more established as a way of not only taking part but also co-creating the ECE life of children in accordance with the educational values of their parents, parental involvement for parents coming from low socio-economic and Roma backgrounds takes on a different meaning. In their interactions with the ECE facility, they often dispose only a very limited agency to develop, articulate or accomplish their own child-rearing ideas, choices or individual notions of parental involvement (in the sense of a partnership approach) – e.g. to seek and actively choose ECE services that function according to their own ideas of what is best for their child and get involved according to their own needs and priorities. Rather, things often work the other way around: the public ECE facility enforces specific ideas, content and extent of parental involvement among the Roma parents.

Concerning the latter point, the recognition of parental involvement as a mutual process also means reflecting and working with power relations among ECE facilities and parents with different socioeconomic positionings, diverse understandings of their children's education and their involvement in it as well as different ways and possibilities of getting involved in their children's ECE. These topics, however, currently lack not only in pedagogical research but also in teacher training.

Notes

1 Under the term "public" we subsume preschool facilities founded by the state, a region, municipality or a confederation of municipalities, funded by this founding entity and central state grants.
2 When it comes to the number of children inscribed, the share is even bigger, amounting to 96 percent of the children attending public facilities (cf. MŠMT, 2019a).
3 Under state socialism, the number of nursery schools started growing quickly and there was a lack of qualified teachers. Therefore, a high school specialisation was introduces and the qualification requirements lowered. Only in the 1970 a dual system for the training of pre-school teachers was launched, with a relevant university program mainly aimed at the training for potentially pre-school headmasters (Opravilová, 2007, p. 1054).

References

Bečvářová, Z. (2003). *Současná mateřská škola a její řízení*. Praha: Portál.
Čapek, R. (2013). *Učitel a rodič: Spolupráce, třídní schůzka, komunikace*. Praha: Grada.
European Commission. (2015). *Education & training 2020: Schools policy. A whole school approach to tackling early school leaving*. Brussels: Author.
Horká, H., & Syslová, Z. (2011). *Studie k předškolní pedagogice*. Brno: Masarykova Univerzita.
Jírová, M. (1982). Společenský význam výchovy dítěte v předškolním období. In L. Bělinová, M. Jírová, & A. Keřková (Eds.), *Mateřská škola spolupracuje s rodinou* (pp. 9–12). Praha: Statní pedagogické nakladatelství.
Kampichler, M., Dvořáčková, J., & Jarkovská, L. (2018). Choosing the right kindergarten: Parents' reasoning about their ECEC choices in the context of the diversification of ECEC programs. *Journal of Pedagogy, 9*(2), 9–32. doi:10.2478/jped-2018-0009
Keřková, A. (1982). Pomoc socialistické společnosti při výchově dítěte. In L. Bělinová, M. Jírová, & A. Keřková (Eds.), *Mateřská škola spolupracuje s rodinou* (pp. 53–75). Praha: Statní pedagogické nakladatelství.
Koťátková, S. (2014a). *Dítě a mateřská škola: Co by měli rodiče znát, učitelé respektovat a rozvíjet*. Praha: Grada.
Koťátková, S. (2014b). Jak se mateřských škol dotýkaly transformační a kurikulární změny? *Pedagogická Orientace, 24*(4), 583–597. doi:10.5817/pedor2014-4-583
Kuchařová, V., & Svobodová, K. (2006). *Síť zařízení denní péče o děti předškolního věku v ČR*. Praha: VÚPS.
Lareau, A. (1987). Social class differences in family-school relationships: The importance of cultural capital. *Sociology of Education, 60*(2), 73. doi:10.2307/2112583
Lareau, A., & Horvat, E. M. (1999). Moments of social inclusion and exclusion race, class, and cultural capital in family-school relationships. *Sociology of Education, 72*(1), 37. doi:10.2307/2673185
Ministerstvo školství, mládeže a tělovýchovy (MŠMT). (2000). *Národní zpráva o stavu předškolní výchovy, vzdělávání a péče o děti předškolního věku v České republice*. Praha: Author.

Ministerstvo školství, mládeže a tělovýchovy (MŠMT). (2018). *Rámcový vzdělávací program pro předškolní vzdělávání (úplné znění k 1. lednu 2018)*. Praha: Author.
Ministerstvo školství, mládeže a tělovýchovy (MŠMT). (2019a). *Preschool education, MŠMT ČR*. Retrieved from www.msmt.cz/areas-of-work/preschool-education
OECD. (2006). *Starting strong II: Early childhood education and care*. Paris: OECD.
OECD. (2012). *Starting strong: Early childhood education and care, 3, a quality toolbox for early childhood education and care*. Paris: OECD.
Opravilová, E. (2007). Teacher education in the Czech Republic. In R. S. New & M. Conchran (Eds.), *Early childhood education: An international encyclopedia* (Vol. 4, pp. 1053–1058). London: Praeger Publishers.
Opravilová, E. (2016). *Předškolní pedagogika*. Praha: Grada.
Rabušicová, M. (2004a). Kapitola 7 – Mateřská škola a rodiče: Případová studie. In M. Rabušicová, K. Šeďová, K. Trnková, & V. Čiháček (Eds.), *Škola a (versus) rodina* (pp. 106–121). Brno: Masarykova Univerzita.
Rabušicová, M. (2004b). Postavení rodičů jako výchovných a sociálních partnerů školy (shrnutí některých výsledků z výzkumného projektu). *Pedagogika, 54*(4), 326–341.
Rabušicová, M. (2009). Rodiče a škola. In *Pedagogická encyklopedie* (p. 319). Praha: Portál.
Rabušicová, M., Čiháček, V., Emmerová, K., & Šeďová, K. (2003). Role rodičů ve vztahu ke škole – empirická zjištění. *Pedagogika, 53*(3), 309–328.
Rabušicová, M., & Pol, M. (1996a). Vztahy školy a rodiny dnes: Hledání cest k partnerství (1. část). *Pedagogika, 46*(1), 49–61.
Rabušicová, M., & Pol, M. (1996b). Vztahy školy a rodiny dnes: Hledání cest k partnerství (2. část). *Pedagogika, 46*(2), 105–116.
Rabušicová, M., Šeďová, K., Trnková, K., & Čiháček, V. (2004). *Škola a (versus) rodina*. Brno: Masarykova Univerzita.
Rýdl, K., & Šmelová, E. (2012). *Vývoj institucí pro předškolní výchovu (1869–2011)*. Olomouc: Univerzita palackého v Olomouci.
Saxonberg, S. (2014). *Gendering family policies in post-communist Europe: A historical-institutional analysis*. Basingstoke: Palgrave Macmillan.
Sylsová, Z., & Grůzová, L. (2019). *Spolupráce Rodiny a MŠ*. Powerpointová prezentace v rámci předmětu Předškolní pedagogika.
Trnková, K., & Čiháček, V. (2003). Možnosti prosazování zájmů rodičů ve škole. *Pedagogická Orientace, 13*(2), 22–38.
Van Laere, K., Van Houtte, M., & Vandenbroeck, M. (2018). Would it really matter? The democratic and caring deficit in "parental involvement". *European Early Childhood Education Research Journal, 26*(2), 187–200. doi:10.1080/1350293x.2018.1441999
Vincent, C. (2001). Social class and parental agency. *Journal of Education Policy, 16*(4), 347–364. doi:10.1080/0268093011-54344
Vincent, C. (2017). "The children have only got one education and you have to make sure it's a good one": Parenting and parent – school relations in a neoliberal age. *Gender and Education, 29*(5), 541–557. doi:10.1080/09540253.2016.1274387

7
PARENTAL INVOLVEMENT IN EARLY CHILDHOOD EDUCATION IN DENMARK

Katharina Jacobsson

Introduction

For several years, Early Childhood Education and Care (ECEC) has been of global interest (Karila, 2012) with Early Childhood recognised as a critical period in human development (Gregoriadis, Grammatikopoulos, & Zachopoulou, 2018). Parental involvement has been considered an essential part of education for several decades (Christenson, 2004; Hornby & Lafaele, 2011) and it is shown to be positive for children of all ages (Cox, 2005). In Denmark, like many other countries, children are exposed to multiple different environments, like their home and childcare institutions. Although these two contexts can be viewed both separately and in relation to each other, they are considered structurally connected through the child (Røn Larsen, 2017). The Danish social pedagogical tradition focuses on collaboration between parents and teachers, with the purpose of supporting children's opportunities for learning, development and well-being (Andenæs & Haavin, 2018). According to Sylva, Melhuish, Sammons, Siraj-Blatchford & Taggart (2004), educator-parent and educator-child relationships can be seen as essential ingredients for improving children's development, both socially and emotionally. International research shows that partnerships vary across family socio-cultural backgrounds (Daniel, 2015). This chapter hence discusses the Danish ECEC model and parental involvement in ECEC in Denmark. It aims to show the intentions in Danish steering documents for ECEC and parental involvement and how it is implemented in preschool teachers' education in Denmark, how parental involvement is facilitated and how it can be improved.

Denmark is located in the north of Europe and has high living standards compared with the rest of the world. The population is estimated at 5.823 million and the population density at about 138 per square kilometre, according to Danish Statistics (2018). The country covers an area of 43,094 square kilometres consisting

DOI: 10.4324/9780367823917-7

of the Jutland peninsula and 406 islands. It also comprises two additional self-governing municipalities and five regions, each covering several municipalities. The Ministry for Social Affairs is responsible for the Social Service Act and has the primary responsibility for ECEC facilities, while the Ministry of Education is responsible for the act on primary and lower secondary education. ECEC generally includes facilities for children younger than the compulsory school age. In Denmark, all children between the ages of six months and six years have the right to a full-time place at an early-childhood centre. Compared with other EU countries, this is quite unusual – only Denmark, Finland, Sweden and Slovenia offer full-time places for children of about one year of age (Juhl, 2018). Children's participation in ECEC is not compulsory, but the participation rate is among the highest in the EU (European Commission/EACEA/Eurydice/Eurostat, 2019).

Overview of Danish ECEC

The Danish ECEC system includes nurseries (children from ½ to three years old) and nursery school (children from three to five years old), but most children between ½ a year and six years old are enrolled in day care (age-integrated settings). In addition to this, children can take part in the system through home-based provision, but only a small percentage rely on this (Juhl, 2018). During 2018, 69,855 children between 0 and two years old were enrolled in municipal and independent day-care facilities. For those between three and five years old, 154,773 were enrolled in such facilities, and 32,435 children were enrolled in the municipal childminders' scheme. Of all children, 98 per cent attend some form of early childhood education centre and/or care centre (Statistics Denmark, 2018). According to Winther-Lindqvist and Svinth (2017), 38 per cent of these children spend about eight hours a day, sometimes more, in an ECEC centre. Centres are often open from 6.30 a.m. to 5.00 p.m. Monday to Friday, but there are no specific legislative demands regarding opening hours under ECEC, except that the service should be available every weekday. However, the Day Care Act requires that opening hours consider the purpose of ECEC and meet local needs for flexible childcare (The Ministry of Children and Social Affairs, 2018). Early childcare centres vary in size and organisation, but in general, children spend three to four hours a day playing outside in a playground, and they also take part in daily adult-initiated activities. Staff at day-care centres also include assistants both with and without teacher education (Winther-Lindqvist & Svinth, 2017). Danish teachers require a bachelor-level education in care provision and supporting development (Ministry of Higher Education and Science, 2017).

Key steering document for ECEC in Denmark

Since 2004, all Danish ECEC centres have had to base children's education on a curriculum according to six themes: Personal development; Social skills; Communication and language; Body, Senses and motion; Culture, Aesthetics and society and Nature, Outdoor and formation (Ministry of Children and Social Affairs, 2017). The 2016 ECEC agreement, *Stærke dagtilbud – alle skal med I fællesskabet* (Strong ECEC settings – everyone must form part of the community), was passed by the Danish Parliament (the Folketing) in 2018 and established a new statutory framework for developing the curriculum with the purpose of improving the quality of ECEC in Denmark. A new curriculum was introduced on 1 July 2018, which municipalities and ECEC centres are required to implement by 1 July 2020. The new regulatory framework includes the following principles: 1) providing a common pedagogical foundation with crucial elements constituting the understanding and approach to work on children's well-being; 2) establishing a pedagogical environment throughout the day, including routines; 3) developing a curriculum which relates to vulnerable children and cooperation with parents and the surrounding community to facilitate children's learning; and 4) establishing an evaluation culture in ECEC settings (Ministry of Children and Education, 2020).

Educators are required to accommodate the following points when they are working with children (Ministry of Children and Education, 2020, § 8): Play, A childhood- where being a child has its own value, Formation and childhood perspectives, Learning, Children's communities, Educational learning environment, Parental co-operation, Children in exposed positions and Coherence in transitions.

ECEC institutions design their curriculum based on a national framework; however local curricula should account for local characteristics such as the interests of specific groups of children. Education is prioritised in every situation, at breakfast and during play and outdoor walks for example. Staff should give children opportunities to direct daily events and stimulate them to develop their understanding of democracy (Ministry of Children and Education, 2020). Institutions should continually adapt to the needs of society and families (Garvis & Ødegaard, 2017). ECEC in Denmark has traditionally been child-centred with an emphasis on the values of respecting children's democratic rights and the right to play (Jensen, 2009; Winther-Lindqvist, 2017). Sommer (2019) highlights a globalised, transnational educational agenda as a specific challenge. Learning plans, pedagogy and practice have been influenced by professional theory set domestically, but globalisation and transnational influence can, according to (Røn Larsen (2017) and Sommer (2019), put pressure on day-care teachers to provide a more school-like education for children. Despite pressure on the Danish model to start children's education earlier, Sommer (2019) points out that Danish state policy documents refer to fundamental principles from the Nordic/Danish model with regards to professional themes in the Day Care Act (Ministry of Children and Social Affairs, 2017).

ACEA (European Commission/EACEA/Eurydice/Eurostat, 2019), ECEC settings should divide children into groups of 11–12 with 3–4 teachers/day-care assistants assigned to each group. Groupings may vary from setting to setting. The Danish ECEC system falls under the responsibility of the Ministry for Children and Social Affairs. Municipalities pay about 75 per cent of the cost of ECEC and parents account for the rest. The ministry is responsible for the curriculum and overall regulation. Social approaches state that services are also intended for children in need of additional support for learning and care due to disability. The caring approach focuses on children's need to be taken care of during the time their parents are working. These purposes are used in both day-care and family day-care centres (Jensen & Iannone, 2018). The guidelines for admission to ECEC centres are based on local conditions and needs. Municipalities take decisions regarding siblings, how children are assigned to groups, the geographical location of ECEC centres and provisions for children with special needs. Parents can state a preference for a specific ECEC setting. Municipalities are obliged to inform parents about application deadlines and take their preferences of ECEC centre into account (Ministry of Children and Social Affairs, 2018).

Research about parental involvement in practice

In ECEC, there is an expectation on professional educators in preschool to manage partnerships with parents and collaborate with them to make a positive difference in children's social and intellectual development (Morrow & Malin, 2004). Different terms have been given to parental involvement, such as 'parental collaboration', 'positive relations' and 'partnership', and the concept seems to represent both formal and informal connections between parents and professionals (Røn Larsen, 2017). Parental involvement is also described as motivated parental behaviour and attitudes to influence children's educational well-being (Christenson, 2004). Involvement includes activities in school, at home and in the community (Epstein, 1995).

Parental involvement and collaboration between parents and educators can represent a strong and important relationship with the aim of achieving shared goals for the benefit of a child (Pirchio, Tritrini, Passiatore, & Taeschner, 2013). According to Dencik (1999), both parties have a responsibility to contribute to children's socialisation, and dual socialisation is useful due to their participation in both home life and childcare. Preschools that can provide multiple forms of parental cooperation tend to have the highest parental attendance. A culture of cooperation in which educators are open-minded and can identify with parents' perspectives can be an excellent way of fostering good relations with them (Sandberg & Vuorinen, 2008). Parents and educators can have different thoughts about the child's needs and their separated positions can be positive in the way that the children's needs are monitored from the two horizons (Smitdh, 2017).

Røn Larsen (2017) argues that parental authority to evaluate the quality of childcare can prevent educators from fostering parents' understanding. Brix and Jensen (2009) notes that parents with no experience in the field of education or in participating in their child's education have difficulties supporting them and collaborating with teachers. Schmidt (2017) mentions that ideally cooperation between educators and parents should relate to daily, coexisting and competing considerations, practices and ways of thinking about learning and well-being, but that norms and values in relation to parents' obligations are not locally defined within individual day care, which can be an obstacle to cooperation. The researcher points out that parenting is often categorised by educators on the basis of culturally charged norms and values, for example that they judge a home learning environment to be either strong or weak. Hornby and Lafaele (2011) describe barriers to parental involvement in terms of class, ethnicity, gender and economic and political structures.

A survey of informal parental involvement (EVA, 2018) summarises six areas in which teachers can work to create collaboration with parents:

1) *The daily exchange of knowledge*. Pick-up and drop-off situations create a daily exchange of knowledge about children and their everyday lives. These situations make it possible to talk about what is working and what is difficult about cooperation and how a child's day has been. 2) *Induction and acclimatisation to day care*. Presents an opportunity for collaboration between staff and parents in the form of meetings. 3) *Individual family talk*. This can facilitate an equal dialogue between parents and educators about subjects that do not arise in daily communication. This type of conversation should take place about once a year, or more often if there is a need for it. 4) *Social arrangements*. Koushols and Berliner (2013) recommend that day-care centres work to make children the focus of social activities within families, including theatres, galleries and related exhibitions. Researchers argue that these informal arrangements are essential to overall cooperation between parents and educators. 5) *Voluntary work*. This can include participating in excursions or inductions for new parents and children. Problems can arise when parents become too involved in pedagogical activities resulting in a lack of clarity over the roles of parents and educators. 6) *Digital communication*. This kind of communication allows parents to connect with their children's daily lives. Jensen, Brandi, Kousholt, Berliner, Holm, Rasmussen, and Friis-Hansen (2012) shows that leaders and educators at day-care centres emphasise: 1) the build-up of a transparent and equal dialogue with parents, 2) fast action when there are challenges to a child's well-being, 3) ongoing information about activities and 4) creating a clear distinction between the roles of educators and parents. According to Højholt, Larsen and Stanek (2007), parental cooperation is perceived as a challenge, and teachers think that it takes time away from working with children. Researchers have shown that parents have the interest of their own child in mind, unlike teachers who must focus on both individual children and the rest of a group (Højholt, Larsen & Stanek, 2007). Peters (2010) points to the value of educators listening to parents' perspectives and being more aware of barriers that can prevent their engagement in their child's development at preschool.

Røn Larsen (2017) also notes the dilemmas and challenges concerning parental collaboration in childcare. Parents can be seen as both consumers of day-care services and participants in the ongoing assessment of the quality of childcare centres, which includes the work of educators who have a responsibility to deliver a learning environment and activities with which parents are satisfied. Røn Larsen (2017) shows that parents' authority in evaluating the quality of childcare services can impede educators from fostering their understanding (2017). Brix and Rosendal Jensen (2009) articulate that parents without experience in education or in participating in their child's learning are not always able to support it. Ejrnæs and Monrad's (2013) quantitative research examined the relationship between the attitudes of parents and teachers concerning pedagogical issues in day-care centres. Their results show that the attitudes of the two groups were similar on a wide range of questions, while both were internally divided in much the same way over others. The researchers argue that existing approaches to welfare professions need to be modified to account for the empirical evidence of the diversity of attitudes of professionals as well as the similarity between those of professionals and parents. Marschall (2019) notes that a collaboration between educators and parents requires them to meddle in each other practices with the purpose to explore and understand everyday aspects of children's life.

Method

In this study, content analysis is used to identify specific characteristics of the chosen documents. Qualitative content analysis is one of several qualitative methods available for analysing and interpreting data (Schreier, 2012). Content analysis is used to examine patterns and structures in text and to classify data (Gray & Densten, 1998). Content analysis was conducted on steering and policy documents regarding Danish ECEC, steering documents for preschool teacher education in Denmark – from six university colleges. The following research questions were explored: How are parental involvement expressed into steering documents for Danish ECEC and steering document for preschool teacher's education? How appears parental involvement in practice and is it possible to find ways to improve it? Preschool teachers, pedagogues and educators have been used synonymously in the text.

Theoretical approach

Epstein (2010) suggests six major types of parental involvement that includes different forms of involvement based on the theory of overlapping spheres of home, school and community influences that shape children's learning and development. The framework can be a possibility to help educators to develop more comprehensive programs of the school and family partnerships and also helps researchers locate their questions and results in ways that inform and improve practice (Epstein, 1987; Connors & Epstein,1995; Epstein & Sanders, 2000; Epstein et al., 2018). By analysing data, this type examines forms of parent involvement in family-school partnership found in documents and previous research. The typologies can be described as follows: *Parenting*, creating a supportive home environment for a child as a learner; *Communicating*, dialogue between parents and educators about a child's education; *Volunteering*, parental participating in education activities; *Learning in-home*, parents supporting curriculum-related activities, Decision-making – including parents' and family members from all backgrounds as representatives in the school board, *Community*, integrating community resources to support learning (Epstein, 2010). In this study the purpose was to examine the intention about parents' involvement and collaboration with preschool teachers expressed in steering documents for ECEC and ECEC teacher education.

Results

Key steering documents on parents' role in ECEC

Danish child and family policy is based on the principle that family is the foundation of a child's upbringing and that children's living conditions are mainly the responsibility of parents (Ministry of Children and Social Affairs, 2017). Formal parental involvement in ECEC is regulated by policy documents and legislative acts, which contain stipulations about parents' cooperation with day-care staff. The steering document requests that day-care educators cooperate with parents to promote children's well-being, learning, development and formation in the course of a safe childhood (Ministry of Children and Social Affairs, 2018).

Both municipal and independent day-care facilities must create a parent board with the power to make decisions in essential matters concerning conditions for children. A parent board is not required by private facilities operating by agreement with a local authority (Ministry of Children and Social Affairs, 2018). The members of parent boards are parents elected by and amongst those of the children attending the day-care centre. The Social Service Act defines parental influence in the following areas: 1) principles governing the work of the daily day-care facility, such as educational methods and activities, cooperation between parents and the day-care facility and cooperation with others; 2) principles governing the use of the budgetary framework, which means that the parent's board must adopt principles to apply to purchases relating to children, in particular toys, materials, furniture and other expenses such as summer camps; and 3) recommendations to the local authority concerning the employment of staff.

Parent boards must be given access to the necessary information to provide a strong basis for their recommendations, for example, member participation in job interviews during staff recruitment (Ministry of Children and Social Affairs, 2017). A business plan should be provided as a vital tool in dialogue and collaboration between parents and members of staff, as well as to the local town or city council. It can also be used as a basis to evaluate the performance of day-care facilities (OECD, 2000). The national curriculum states that cooperation between parents and educators should be based on local traditions and the needs of individual families. Educators have to provide a planning document describing how cooperation with parents on children's learning will be arranged (Ministry of Children and Social Affairs, 2018). Strong day-care offer for every child is a policy document that states the responsibilities of families to give children a good childhood. Furthermore, it denotes day-care centers as partners that will work together with parents to create a good life for children (Ministry of Children and Social Affairs, 2017).

It mentions that early intervention in terms of support can ensure better school results. The three themes included in the policy document are: 1) increased flexibility; 2) better learning, comfort and a coherent childhood and 3) high-quality service subjects and transparent leadership. The document focuses on systematic, evidence-based work as a way to give parents influence over learning environments. Collaboration between professionals and parents includes learning activities and support for children when they require it. In addition to the national curriculum, The Danish Folketing passed an amendment (1 July 2019) to strengthen Danish language and culture for children in marginalised areas. It states that it is mandatory for all children between the ages of one and two to attend an ECEC centre or regulated home-based setting 25 hours every week free of charge (Ministry of Children and Social Affairs, 2020). The Starting Strong report (OECD, 2012) emphasises that the curriculum and learning standards are essential to ensuring even quality services across ECEC settings, supporting staff by giving them guidance on how to improve teaching strategies and helping parents make informed choices and better understand child development. Parents should be regarded as partners, and recent OECD reports (2015, 2017) point out that teacher-parent collaboration is vital to ensure quality teaching and learning.

When using Epstein's (2010) theory of six types of involvement, Table 7.1 illustrates forms of involvement, examples from steering documents, challenges and possibilities and suggested improvements connected to the types of involvement.

TABLE 7.1 *Six types of involvement*

Involvement	Sample topics from steering documents	Challenges and/or possibilities connected to the types of involvement	Suggested improvements connected to the types of involvement
Parenting	Early intervention in terms of support can ensure better development for the child. Collaboration between professional and parents includes learning activities and support for children when they require it.	The educators could create a clear distinction between the roles of educators and parents.	Create good relationships with the parents systematically. Achieve shared goals – parents and pedagogues.
Communication	Educators have to provide a planning document describing how cooperation with parents will be	Daily cooperation between educators and parents is ideal but norms and values in relation to parents	Use the different perspective that the parents and the institution have regarding the children's needs –

(Continued)

TABLE 7.1 (Continued)

Involvement	Sample topics from steering documents	Challenges and/or possibilities connected to the types of involvement	Suggested improvements connected to the types of involvement
	arranged in line with the local curriculum.	obligations are not defined within individual day care, which can be hindering for the cooperation. The daily meeting in the tambour gives good possibilities for pedagogues and parents to share knowledge about children's day at preschool and home.	to give a more precious knowledge about the children. Personalised communication can be a way to create or warn preschool environment for parents, pedagogues and children, and a key to empowering partnership.
Voluntary work	..that day care educators cooperate with parents to promote children's well-being, learning, development and formation in the course of a safe childhood.	Informal arrangements are essential to overall cooperation between parents and educators. Problems can arise when parents get too involved in pedagogical arrangements.	Arrange meetings between parents. 'New parents' could be given tutoring guide from more experienced parents.
Learning at home	When children leave preschool, there can be two years of difference in their social, speaking and emotional skills. This difference is related to the children's social family background.	Parents with no experience in the field of education or in participating in their child's education have difficulties supporting them and collaboration with teachers.	Conduct meetings with parents and discuss how the preschool work and how the parents can support the child. Workshops for parents to give them possibilities to understand the goals in the curriculum.
Decision making	Principles governing the use of the budgetary framework, which means that the parent's board must	The preschool teachers must take into account the parent's need and preferences when making decisions	Try to incorporate parents more in decision-making. Establish regular communications with parents to get

Involvement	Sample topics from steering documents	Challenges and/or possibilities connected to the types of involvement	Suggested improvements connected to the types of involvement
	adopt principles to apply to purchases relating to children's in particular toys, materials, furniture and other expenses. Recommendation to the local authority concerning the employment of staff	about their children. The preschool teachers must be aware of barriers that can prevent parents' engagement in their child's development at preschool.	in touch with their ideas, suggestions and questions about all things that affect them and their child.
Collaboration with the community	The municipality must establish the municipality's framework for day-care facilities, including any priority initiatives in this area.	Community counsellors may collaborate with preschool teachers to see if or how they can be involved to help families or preschool.	Identify community resources to assist children and families, if it is needed.

Parental involvement in ECEC teachers' education curricula

Parental involvement is included in the curricula for pre-teacher education in Danish universities. The following goals as shown in Table 7.2 are outlined in the bachelor course specification under the heading Profession and Organisation (Ministry of Higher Education and Science, 2017).

TABLE 7.2 *Goals from the national curriculum in which parental cooperation is mentioned* (Ministry of Higher Education and Science, App. 2, 2017).

Area	Knowledge goals The student has knowledge about:	Proficiency goals The student can:
Competence area 1: Childhood, culture and learning	–	–
Competence area 2: Profession and organisation	Parent cooperation and parent involvement in relation to the child's development	Plan and prepare parent cooperation based on the needs of the individual child and the well-being, learning and development of the group of children

(Continued)

TABLE 7.2 (Continued)

Area	Knowledge goals The student has knowledge about:	Proficiency goals The student can:
Competence area 3: Relation and communication	Dialogue and professional communication	Communicate in a nuanced, precise and comprehensible manner with children, families and colleagues
Competence area 4: Tension between parenting capital and educational practice	Incorporation of children's and parents' perspectives in development and change processes	Incorporate the ideas and creativity of children and parents as part of pedagogical development and change processes

Table 7.3 shows examples from the curriculum for preschool teacher's education in which parental involvement is mentioned in goals for the education.

TABLE 7.3 *Examples from the six universities' knowledge and proficiency goals*

Knowledge goals	Proficiency goals
Professional collaboration	Communicate and collaborate professionally with parents, colleagues, teachers and relevant parties
Incorporating children's and parent's perspectives in development and change processes	Incorporate the ideas and creativity of children and parents as part of pedagogical development and change processes
Parental cooperation and involvement in relation to the development of children and adolescents	Plan and prepare parent cooperation from the starting point of the well-being, learning and development of the individual child
Communication relevant to the profession, argumentation and collaboration	Communicate and collaborate professionally with parents, colleagues, teachers and other relevant parties
Coordinate cooperation and innovative processes that involve children, parents and other professions	Coordinate development projects
Take into account children's and parents' perspectives in improvement processes	Use parents' ideas in daily pedagogical work

The literature and research articles connected to competence area 2 taken from one university included books on the following subjects: dilemmas and possibilities of parental involvement and different social backgrounds – different pedagogical practice. The literature discusses tensions between parenting capital and educational practice. With regard to competence area 3, the literature deals with communication and relations and the importance of competence to meet the family.

Area 4 contains a focus on change processes and research on pedagogical ideas. Parental involvement is a part of this.

Discussion

This chapter has provided an overview of Danish ECEC settings and how parental involvement is expressed in steering documents and practice. The study shows how parental involvement is treated in ECEC steering documents for day-care centres and ECEC teachers' education curricula and gives some examples of pedagogical implications. The present study shows that the Danish steering documents for ECEC have a strong focus on parental involvement. Recent strengthened legislation in Denmark, the Day Care Act from 2018, has presented new stipulations that highlight the need for cooperation with parents and emphasise collaboration to promote children's well-being, learning, play, development and formation in the course of a safe childhood. Day Care facilities are required to create parent boards, which have the power to make decisions on educational methods and activities and local budgets. Educators must also include in the local curriculum how they will cooperate with parents to facilitate children's learning. The expectations of collaboration can consist of high quality and important relationships to achieve common goals for the benefit of children.

Epstein's six types of parental involvement could be identified in data. Parental engagement can in practice present class, gender, ethnicity and economic barriers *(Parenting)*. It also shows that both shared and different ways of supporting the children can be useful and that problems can appear when parents become too involved in pedagogical activities. The families' background can be hindering or affecting *(Parenting & Learning in-home)*. The result points out that daily communication during pick-up and drop-off situations can give possibilities to exchange knowledge about the children. There is a need for good quality in communication and also an understanding of parent´s different agendas *(Communication)*. When the parents participate at the day-care during social activities, it is essential to build up relations between parents and educators *(Volunteering)*.

The result also revealed that parents' authority in evaluating the quality at preschool could affect the educators not to challenge the parents' and undermine conflicts *(Decision-making)*. To assist children and their family, the community counsellors have to establish communication with preschool teachers to investigate needs *(Collaboration with the community)*.

The result shows that educators are responsible for establishing a relationship with parents in support of the goals of children's development and well-being. However, sometimes they feel that this involvement takes time away from working with children. The study shows that not all parents can support the child in a way that is expected from the pedagogues. The study has illustrated that parental involvement is a complex phenomenon consisting of both dilemmas and possibilities.

Parental involvement is visible in both the national curriculum of the Bachelor in Social Education and the six universities' educational curricula for preschool teacher education (in both theory and practical training). The steering documents for preschool teacher education indicate knowledge goals connecting to Epstein's types of Parenting, communication, and decision-making.

In summary, there is a different way of how parents can be involved in their child's development and education. It also shows some difficulties in cooperation. This study demonstrates various ways of parental involvement that is expressed as intentions in national public documents and how the preschool teacher education curricula deal with the knowledge is of parent cooperation. A new theme of parental involvement emerged in the data, and it was found in the goals from the national curriculum and in the preschool teacher education curriculum. It could be like improvement processes and coordinating pedagogical development projects.

Limitations and areas for future research

There were limitations in this study that have to be mentioned. First, Epstein's (1995) theory shows that utilising the six types of involvement can increase parental involvement in practice. In this study, the types were used to explore what forms of parental involvement that was mentioned in steering documents and what kind of possibilities and challenges that appear in practice. Second, the researcher failed to provide an operational definition of improvement processes in the study. Research needs to be conducted to ascertain how these processes can be operationalised in practice. Preschool pedagogues must be more used to meet educational learning situations and improve the child, focusing on collaboration in improvement processes with parents and the community.

The complex issue partnership between parents and pedagogues and how the two parts perceive their work concerning children's development needs more research. Multiple forms of parental involvement and families' circumstances could be discussed in practice and at preschool teacher education to better understand hindering factors from enabling cooperation between parents and preschool teachers. The intention of educational curricula from university college could be to investigate in practice during the lessons for the students. The teacher education and skills development for preschool teachers can create possibilities to integrate more of improvement processes in cooperation with parents and community. Research collaboration with students – by action research – could be a way to improve and get more knowledge about how parental involvement in both education and practice could be understood. In-service teachers also need more knowledge and skills to be able to integrate with parents and to be able to tutor students in practice.

References

Andenæs, A., & Haavind, H. (2018). Sharing early care: Learning from practitioners. In M. Fleer & B. van Oers (Eds.), *International handbook of early childhood education* (pp. 1483–1502). New York: Springer.

Brix, D., & Jensen, N. R. (2009). Efforts and models of education for parents: The Danish approach. *Social Work & Society*, 7(2), 199–218.

Christenson, S. L. (2004). The family-school partnership: An opportunity to promote the learning competence of all students. *School Psychology Review*, *33*(1), 83–104.

Connors, L. J., & Epstein, J. L. (1995). Parent and school partnerships. In M. H. Bornstein (Ed.), *Handbook of parenting* (Vol. 4, pp. 437–458). Mahwah, NJ: Lawrence Erlbaum Associates, Inc.

Cox, D. (2005). Evidence-based interventions using home-school collaboration. *School Psychology Quarterly*, *20*(4), 473–497.

Daniel, G. (2015). Patterns of parent involvement: A longitudinal analysis of family-school partnerships in the early years of school in Australia. *Australasian Journal of Early Childhood*, *40*(1), 119–128.

Danish Statistics. (2018). *News and publications about childcare institutions*. http://www.dst.dk/en.Statistik/emner.levevillkaar

Dencik, L. (1999). *Børn af familie i det postmoderne samfund* [Children and families in the post-modern society]. Copenhagen: Hans Reitzels Forlag.

Ejrnæs, M., & Monrad, M. (2013). Profession, holding og habitus: Forholdet mellem pædagogers og forældres holdningen til pædagogiske spørgsmål i daginstitutioner [Profession, attitude and habitus: The relationship between educators 'and parents' attitudes to pedagogical issues in day care institutions]. *Dansk Sociologi*, *24*(3), 63–83.

Epstein, J. L. (1987). Toward a theory of family-school connections: Teacher practices and parent involvement. In K. Hurrelman, F. Kaufmann & F. Losel (Eds.), *Social intervention: Potential and constraints* (pp. 121–136). New York: DeGruyter.

Epstein, J. L. (1995). School/family/community partnerships. *Phi Delta Kappan*, *76*(9), 701.

Epstein, J. L. (2010). School/family/community partnerships: Caring for the children we share. *Phi Delta Kappan*, *92*(3), 81–96.

Epstein, J. L., & Sanders, M. G. (2000). Connecting home, school, and community. In M. T. Hallinan (Ed.), *Handbook of the sociology of education* (pp. 285–306). Boston: Springer.

Epstein, J. L., Sanders, M. G., Sheldon, S. B., Simon, B. S., Salinas, K. C., Jansorn, N. R, & Williams, K. J. (2018). *School, family, and community partnerships: Your handbook for action*. Corwin Press.

Ertmann, B., Gundelach, S., Andersen, J., Madsen, L., & Rasmussen, K. (2008). *Myter og realiteter om forældresamarbejde i dagtilbud*. FOA Fag og Arbejde.

European Commission/EACEA/Eurydice/Eurostat. (2019). *Key data on early childhood education and care in Europe*. Eurydice and Eurostat Report. Luxembourg: Publications Office of the European Union.

EVA. (2018). *Forældresamarbejde i dagtilbud* [Parental cooperation in day care]. Copenhangen: Danmarks Evalueringsinstitut.

Garvis, S., & Ødegaard, E. E. (Eds.). (2017). *Nordic dialogues on children and families*. London: Routledge.

Gray, J. H., & Densten, I. L. (1998). Integrating quantitative and qualitative analysis using latent and manifest variables. *Quality and Quantity*, *32*(4), 419–431.

Gregoriadis, A., Grammatikopoulos, V., & Zachopoulou, E. (Eds.). (2017). *Professional development and quality in early childhood education: Comparative European perspectives*. Dordrecht: Springer.

Højholt, C., Larsen, M. R., & Stanek, A. (2007). *Børnefællesskaber: Om de andre børns betydning. At arbejde med rummelighed og forældresamarbejde* [Child communities: About the importance of other children. To work with inclusiveness and parent collaboration]. Copenhagen: Forlaget Børn & Unge.

Hornby, G., & Lafaele, R. (2011). Barriers to parental involvement in education: An explanatory model. *Educational Review*, *63*(1), 37–52.

Jensen, B. (2009). A Nordic approach to early childhood education (ECE) and socially endangered children. *European Early Childhood Education Research Journal*, *17*(1), 7–21.
Jensen, B., Brandi, U., Kousholt, D., Berliner, P., Holm, A., Steiner Rasmussen, O., & Friis-Hansen, M. (2012). *Vidensbaseret indsats over for udsatte børn i dagtilbud –modelprogram. Statusrapport 3. Modelprogram – Midtvejsanalyser* [Knowledge-based efforts towards vulnerable children in day care model program. Status report 3. Model program – Mid-term analyses]. Copenhagen: Institut for Utdannelse og Pædagogik (DPU), Aarhus Universitet.
Jensen, B., & Iannone, R. L. (2018). Innovative approaches to continuous professional development (CPD) in early childhood education and care (ECEC) in Europe: Findings from a comparative review. *European Journal of Education*, *53*(1), 23–33.
Juhl, P. (2018). Early childhood education and care in Denmark: The contested issue of quality in children's everyday lives. In S. Garvis (Ed.), *International perspectives on early childhood education and care: Early education in the 21th century* (pp. 42–53). London: Routledge.
Karila, K. (2012). A Nordic perspective on early childhood education and care policy. *European Journal of Education*, *4*(1), 584–595.
Kousholt, D., & Berliner, P. (2013). *VIDA-forskningsrapport 3-modelprogram Forældreinddragelse*. København: Aarhus Universitet.
Marschall, A. (2019). Children's well-being – A joint effort? Collaboration about children's well-being across the contexts of family life and kindergarten. In S. Phillipson & Garvis, S. (Eds.), *Teachers' and families' perspectives in early childhood education and care: Early childhood education in the 21st century* (Vol. 2, pp. 47–57). London: Routledge.
Ministry of Children and Social Affairs. (2016). *Stærke Dagtilbud – Alle Børn Skal Være med i Fællesskabet* [*A strong day care offer – all children must be a part of the community*]. Christiansborg, Copenhagen: The Danish Government.
Ministry of Children and Social Affairs. (2017). *Bekendtgørelse af lov om dag-, fritids- og klubtilbud m.v. til børn og unge* [The Day Care Act]. Christiansborg, Copenhagen: The Danish Government. https://www.retsinformation.dk/documents?dnr=1326&t=dagtilbud
Ministry of Children and Social Affairs. (2018). *Den styrkede pædagogiske læreplan* [The strengthened pedagogical curriculum]. Copenhagen: The Danish Government.
Ministry of Children and Education. (2020). *Dagtilbudsloven, LBK nr 1326 from 09/09/2020* [The Day Care Act]. https://www.retsinformation.dk/eli/lta/2020/1326
Ministry of Higher Education and Science. (2017). BEK nr 354 from 07/04/2017. https://www.retsinformation.dk/eli/lta/2017/354
Morrow, G., & Malin, N. (2004). Parents and professionals working together: Turning the rhetoric into reality. *Early Years*, *24*(2), 163–177.
Nationalencyklopedin. (2019). *Nationalencyklopedin*. Malmö: NE Nationalencyklopedin AB.
OECD. (2000). *Early childhood education and care: An overview of developments in OECD countries*. Paris OECD Publishing.
OECD. (2012). *Starting Strong III. A quality toolbox for early childhood education and care*. Paris: OECD Publishing.
OECD. (2015). Starting strong IV: Monitoring quality in early childhood education and care. Paris: OECD Publishing. doi:10.1787/97892642335-en
OECD. (2017). Starting strong 2017: Key OECD indicators on early childhood education and care. Paris: OECD Publishing. doi:10.1787/9789264276116-en
Peters, S. (2010). *Literature review: Transition from early childhood education to school*. Report commissioned by the Ministry of Education. Wellington: Ministry of Education.

Pirchio, S., Tritrini, C., Passiatore, Y., & Taeschner, T. (2013). The role of the relationship between parents and educators for child behaviour and wellbeing. *International Journal about Parents in Education*, 7(2), 145–155.

Røn Larsen, M. R. (2017). Collaboration between child care and parents: Dilemmas and contradictory conditions in the institutional arrangement of child care. In C. Ringsmose, & G. Kragh-Müller (Eds.), *Nordic social pedagogical approach to early years* (pp. 219–236). Cham: Springer.

Sandberg, A., & Vuorinen, T. (2008). Preschool-home cooperation in change. *International Journal of Early Years Education*, 16(2), 151–161.

Schmidt, L. S. K. (2017). *Pædagogers samfundsmæssige roller i forældresamarbejde* [Educators' societal roles in parent collaboration]. Sorø: Center for Pædagogik, Professionshøjskolen Absalon.

Schreier, M. (2012). *Qualitative content analysis in practice*. London: Sage.

Sheridan, S., & Williams, P. (Eds.). (2018). *Undervisning i Förskolan: En Kunskapsöversikt* [*Teaching in preschool: A literature review*]. Stockholm: Skolverket.

Sommer, D. (2019). Early childhood education (ECE) in the Nordic countries: Universal challenges to the Danish model-Towards a future ECE paradigm. In S. Garvis, H. Harju-Luukkainen, S. Sheridan, & P. Williams (Eds.), *Nordic families, children and early childhood education* (pp. 193–212). Cham: Palgrave Macmillan.

Statistics Denmark. (2018). *Living conditions: Children and staff*. Copenhagen, Denmark.

Sylva, K., Melhuish, E., Sammons, P., Siraj-Blatchford, I., & Taggart, B. (2004). *The effective provision of pre-school education (EPPE) Project: Findings from pre-school to end of key stage 1*. Nottingham: Department for Education and Skills.

Winther-Lindqvist, D. A. (2017). The role of play in Danish child care. In C. Ringsmose & G. Kragh-Müller (Eds.), *Nordic social pedagogical approach to early years: International perspectives on early childhood education and development* (Vol. 15). Cham: Springer.

Winther-Lindqvist, D. A., & Svinth, L. (2017). *Early childhood education and care (ECEC) in Denmark*. Oxford: Routledge.

8
PARENTAL PERSPECTIVE IN THE FINNISH EARLY CHILDHOOD EDUCATION CONTEXT

Karoliina Purola, Heidi Harju-Luukkainen and Jonna Kangas

Introduction

There are four steering documents that guide the Finnish Early Childhood Education and Care (ECEC) sector: (1) Act on Early Childhood Education and Care (540/2018); (2) FNAE – National Core Curriculum for Early Childhood Education and Care (Finnish National Agency for Education, 2018); (3) FNBE – National Core Curriculum for Pre-Primary Education (Finnish National Board of Education, 2016), and (4) Guidelines and recommendations for evaluation of the quality of early childhood education and care (Finnish Education Evaluation Centre, 2018). The first two documents guide the work for children under the age of six, and the third applies to work with children during the preschool year. Preschools in Finland are under the Basic Education Act (628/1998), but are mostly managed by ECEC centres. The fourth guide sets the indicators to evaluate the ECEC provision from different perspectives. These three first documents were prepared in collaboration with specialist educators from the field and included ECEC specialists, researchers, trade union representatives, and administrators. The responsibility for ECEC on the national level lies with the Ministry of Education and Culture; on the local level it is the municipalities that are responsible for arranging the different ECEC services and ensuring their quality and supervision. The Finnish ECEC is based on an integrated approach supporting children's well-being through care, education, and teaching, the so-called educare model where learning through play has centre stage (see Kangas, Ojala, & Venninen, 2015).

The cooperation (also called the partnership, parental involvement or parental collaboration) with the parents is highlighted in the Finnish ECEC steering documents. An entire chapter in the national core curriculum is devoted to discussing parental participation and its implementation. According to the National Core Curriculum for ECEC (Finnish National Agency for Education FNAE), the aim for

DOI: 10.4324/9780367823917-8

the partnership cooperation is in meeting the needs of the child to ensure their growth, development, and learning. The previous Finnish National Curriculum Guidelines for Early Childhood Education and Care (STAKES, 2005) emphasised parent-teacher cooperation as a partnership. Within this document, the partnership between ECEC teachers and parents is defined by such terms as, "trust, respect, and equality . . . and parental knowledge" (Alasuutari, 2010, p. 150). It is claimed that the partnership aspect of cooperation was changing the role of parents to that of clients. This claim raised concerns over challenges in developing such parent-teacher cooperation and the processes associated with the cooperation (Vlasov & Hujala, 2016).

The new Core Curriculum (FNAE, 2018) discusses cooperation and parental participation from a new perspective. Today the teachers are obligated to offer parents an opportunity to participate in designing and evaluating the educational programme regularly, as well as joining the process for creating, implementing, and assessing their child's personal curriculum for early education. They can do this through a document that is reflected on and revised by teachers and parents in a joint meaning-making process (Uusimäki, Yngvesson, Garvis, & Harju-Luukkainen, 2019; FNAE, 2018).

The Finnish Education Evaluation Centre (FEEC) presents the new quality indicators for ECEC to guide municipalities and ECEC provisions (2018). The FEEC has listed several indicators for parental participation. These indicators measure how the municipalities and teachers guide and inform parents about the forms of education and the goals and objectives of the pedagogy. The guidance from municipalities is important for families to be able to choose the right ECEC service for their child. For example, they would have to decide if they want full day, half-day or up to 20 hours per week at ECEC, family day care; parents have the right to choose the amount, location and level of education. In the FEEC's indicators, teachers and supporting teachers' ability to plan and execute the transition phase from home to school is evaluated where children's experiences of safety and belonging are highly valued. Finally, quality indicators point out that parents have a right to participate in designing, planning, implementing and assessing the daily education with teachers. Therefore, we may conclude that the recent steering documents in Finland oblige teachers and ECEC provisions to create a framework for parental participation and highlight the mutual planning and assessment of a child's educational plan.

In this chapter, we take a closer look at research connected to parental participation, and how teacher training programmes take this into consideration in the course contents. After that, we turn our focus towards how this partnership is conducted in practice and finally take a critical perspective on future developmental objectives on the field of ECEC and parental collaboration.

Research connected to parental participation

Early childhood education between ages 1 and 5 is voluntary in Finland. Parents can choose if they would like to put their child into an early childhood education facility or care for their child at home. Early childhood services are offered in a wide range of settings. Parents may choose an ECEC service for their child among multiple options: full day, half-day, or needed days per week. Parents can also choose between an ECEC centre and family day care, and further between public and private organisers. In practice, the municipality offices for ECEC offer their support for parents to make these decisions. After starting the ECEC, the responsibility of cooperation moves from the administrative level to the ECEC centre's teachers and director where the demand for collaborative participation requires expert collaboration skills as well as understanding and respect from the teachers (see closer Uusimäki et al., 2019). Not all parents have equal opportunities to participate. According to Lammi-Taskula and Siippainen (2018), those parents who work night shift had fewer opportunities to participate in ECEC parents' conferences, special events, and conversations in comparison to those parents who worked traditional hours in Finland.

Parental participation in ECEC has been under the governance of the Ministry of Social and Health Affairs until the year 2012. After that, it was transformed under the governance of Ministry of Education and Culture. This has had its natural effects on both the research conducted and the terms used in the literature. Onnismaa (2010) studied the Finnish steering documents from 1967 to 1999. In those previous documents, according to Onnismaa (2010), parents were considered as weak participants who needed help and guidance, whereas the children were seen as capable individuals. The assumption is that weak parents may reflect negatively on the cooperation between teachers and parents. Since the governance of ECEC has moved under the Ministry of Education and Culture, the view on parental partnership has changed. Further, parents have become more involved in the process of creating steering documents.

Collaboration between ECEC and parents can be viewed from different perspectives. According to Alasuutari (2010), the challenge in this collaboration is to agree on the interpretation of participation for both teachers and parents. Mahmood (2013) also studied collaboration and noted that teachers can find this collaboration challenging if the roles and responsibilities of the cooperation have not been clearly stated in steering documents and practice. The teachers' professional skills and level of education have been found to affect the formation of a successful collaboration with parents; thus, teachers need expert skills to develop collaboration skill regarding parental cooperation (Chan & Ritchie, 2016; Mahmood, 2013; Uusimäki et al., 2019). Hakyemez-Paul, Pihlaja, and Silvennoinen (2018) conducted a study with a sample of 287 Finnish ECEC teachers. According to the results, the professionals have in general a positive attitude towards parental involvement. Further, the participants stated that difficulties in parental involvement are often caused by poor parental motivation, and a lack of time on the part of both teachers and parents. A deeper analysis revealed that these positive attitudes were somewhat superficial, and ECEC teachers wanted to restrict education to institutions, and regard parents as passive. These attitudes teachers have can be viewed from many perspectives. In their study Venninen and Purola (2013) identified three different ways to characterise teachers' attitudes concerning parental participation in ECEC;

these were (1) the professional, (2) the customer, and (3) the partnership perspective. In the professional perspective, the ECEC professional takes an expert role in discussions with parents. From the customer perspective, parent satisfaction is the driving force. The challenge for ECEC teachers from the customer perspective might be that the expertise, responsibility and experience of the child lie with the parents. The partnership perspective includes the two previous perspectives. The teacher who acquires the partnership standpoint seems to have best opportunities to cooperate successfully with parents.

An International Parent-Professional Partnership research study conducted by Hujala, Turja, Gaspar, Veisson, and Waniganayake (2009) focused on the contemporary challenges of parent-teacher partnerships in early childhood education from a cross-cultural perspective. The purpose of the research was to examine parent-teacher partnerships in ECEC services in five countries: Estonia, Finland, Lithuania, Norway, and Portugal. The survey questionnaire focused on teachers' views of parents' involvement in ECEC facilities. According to the results, there were differences in teachers' approaches to parent-teacher partnerships from one society to another as well as within each country. Parents also differed in their capacity to develop and maintain partnerships with teachers. There were differences in the professional status of the teachers in each country, which were connected to the parents' role in the parent-teacher partnerships in ECEC services. According to Vlasov and Hujala (2017), ECEC services maintain a central role in supporting families with young children. How this partnership between families and service providers is conducted and understood is dependent on the political, societal and cultural changes in a national context. Therefore, the teachers' interpretation of the collaboration is not the only determinant; there may be many other societal factors that influence the success of this collaboration.

Cooperation with parents as a subject in Finnish teacher training programmes

The cooperation between parents and teachers depends on teachers' professional skills and quality (Uusimäki et al., 2019; Alasuutari, 2010; Mahmood, 2013). Parental participation follows the professional practices and knowledge of educational goals. In teacher education, students are trained in curriculum work, interaction with children, and the development of educational practices. Above that, Finnish teacher education aims to promote the critical thinking and reflection skills of future teachers so that they can not only follow educational policies and practices but also act as active agents to change them (Niemi, Toom, & Kallioniemi, 2016). All these depend on the quality of teacher education (Mahmood, 2013). Finnish teacher education focuses on the pedagogical thinking processes and capabilities to design, implement, document, evaluate and critically reflect on the processes of teaching and learning. In Finland teacher training aims to give teachers toolboxes to cope with an unknown future (Seikkula-Leino, Satuvuori, Ruskovaara, & Hannula, 2015). Parental participation has been a topic among other cooperative and multiprofessional practices in teacher training programmes. This approach views teaching as a dynamic and dialogic profession with much networking and joint work. Researchers around the world have highlighted a need to move from traditional teacher-dominated practices towards dialogic and dynamic spaces of cooperation that include engagement with parents (see Chan & Ritchie, 2016; Lastikka, 2019).

Finnish ECEC teachers are trained in universities and are qualified with a bachelor's degree in Education. Their training programme focuses on the learning and development of children, and the curriculum and subjects of teaching within the educational context. Cooperation with parents is covered in courses in which students familiarise themselves with the plan for a child's development and learning. The diversity of different families is also addressed as part of the teacher training programme. Some universities collaborate with parental organisations and organise specialised lectures on how to put this parental partnership into practice.

In order to gain a better understanding of the contents in teacher education connected to parental participation, we conducted a brief content analysis of eight universities' curriculums in Finland that offer Baccalaureate programmes in early childhood education. We analysed the curriculums to identify 'key features' of each document that we wanted to examine (see Williams, 2007). The searches were done on concepts around parental collaboration, partnership or other keywords that were connected to this area of interest (see Leedy & Ormrod, 2001). The searches were done in both concepts of studies and objectives of studies. This curriculum analysis provides an overview comparison among the different universities' concepts and learning objectives in the education programmes in the area of parental collaboration (see Table 8.1).

According to the results of this content analysis, the university curriculums have quite a few mentions of the concepts of 'parents' and 'family', but more emphasis has put on the concept of 'professional co-operation'. In fact, 'parental participation' is hardly mentioned in any of the curricula. The curricula have more mentions of the concepts itself than learning objectives in studies, and there is some variation among the universities.

Partnership in practice

Cooperation has multiple functions and can take on different forms during the child's ECEC according to the steering documents (FNAE, 2018; FNBE, 2016). The initiation of cooperation is the role of the ECEC teachers, and requires expert collaboration skills in meeting families with understanding and respect (see for instance Uusimäki et al., 2019; Alasuutari, 2010; Mahmood, 2013). The child's everyday learning and development experiences that are shared with parents, or creating a trusting environment between the parents and teachers are important. These interactions are especially important in challenging situations, where for example there is a concern about the child's well-being. The observations parents and the teachers make and share with each other forms the basis for a perception of the child's overall well-being and positive development. These occasions where these matters are discussed thoroughly are held two or three times a year during an ECEC education plan conversation. In these conversations, it is important to have an open and positive dialogue between parents and teachers to support the child's learning and development, particularly in meetings when a translator may be needed so that both parties can understand one another. This is important when special support is identified for a child, and the parents must meet with the child support team. Educational and support plans are described in more detail within the national core curriculum. Cooperation is also crucial during transitional phases, whether the child begins the ECEC, he/she enters the next level in ECEC, or is transferred to year one of primary school. The municipal ECEC steering documents guide these transitional phases rather closely. For instance, in

TABLE 8.1 *Parental collaboration as objectives and concept of studies in teacher education programmes*

	Mentions in general by concept					Mentions in concept versus objectives	
	Number of mentions of					Number of mentions in	
	Parent or parental	Family	Home	Professional cooperation	Parents' participation	Concept in studies	Learning objective in studies
University of Helsinki (2018–2020)	0	1	0	4	0	5	0
University of Turku (2019–2020)	5	3	0	7	0	13	2
University of Jyväskylä (2017–2018)	2	10	0	6	1	13	6
University of Eastern Finland (2019–2020)	7	1	1	7	0	12	4
Lapland University (2015–2017)	4	4	2	8	1	5	14
University of Oulu (2018–2020)	1	0	0	1	0	2	0
Åbo Akademi University (2019–2020)	1	0	0	1	0	2	0
University of Tampere (2017–2019)	1	3	0	4	0	4	4

Kirkkonummi (municipality in Finland) all families are offered a first discussion at home. Parents are also invited to the day-care centre with the child for a week or two so that the child becomes familiar with the teachers, other children and the premises. This gives the parents an opportunity to take part and support the child's participation and share and discover what she/he likes and wants.

Many parents in ECEC are involved in parental association voluntary work. Parent associations in ECEC provisions are held by voluntary parents in preschools. The associations organise different programmes, collect funds at different events and with the help of these are able to finance trips or provide other needed materials. Through these local associations, parents have a way to influence the programme more on a practical level. Often these local associations are organised under the main national parents' associations called Suomen Vanhempainliitto and Förbundet Hem och Skola i Finland r.f., for the Swedish and Finnish language preschools and schools. These two parent organisations collaborate as a central association organising local parent associations in schools and preschools. The central associations provide a variety of projects and information in different forms for both parents and teachers. They also work with policymakers across the country. The goal of this work is to strengthen a positive dialogue between parents and early childhood and school environment as well as bring forth parents' voices. The associations have a functional status in the society, and they employ several full-time specialists. Further, both of the associations are members in Nordic parental collaboration association called NOKO (Nordiska föräldraorganisationernas samarbete inom Nordisk Kommitté) and are also taking part in the meetings of European Parents' Association (EPA). The national associations collaborate with the teacher education departments and organise lectures where the parent and preschool or school collaboration is highlighted (more about the association work can be found from www.hemochskola.fi and www.vanhempainliitto.fi).

Future developmental objects

Though there is an understanding that parents have an important role in children's upbringing, there seems to be very little research on this area, especially in Finland. Even though the latest curriculum for ECEC in Finland (FNAE, 2018) highlights the collaboration with parents, this has not yet been transferred yet to the steering documents or contents of different teacher education programmes. This is a clear developmental object for the future since teachers need expert skills for this collaboration (Chan & Ritchie, 2016; Mahmood, 2013; Uusimäki et al., 2019).

Following the Act on ECEC in Finland (540/2018) and the National Curriculum (FNAE, 2018), parents should be included in developing the ECEC curriculum, environment and practices together with the children and teachers. In practice, this would need a more developed digital solution, which is encouraged to be used and developed. For example, all necessary contact information as well as curricula, locations and developmental goals for municipal education can be found online. A challenge lies with keeping parents up to date on their children's everyday activities at the ECEC centre, and the delivery of children's learning processes and outcomes. These learning processes are difficult to document even for teachers, because of the nature of multidimensional learning and participation of children in ECEC in Finland (Rintakorpi & Reunamo, 2017). Different tools for pedagogical documentation such as digital portfolios to enhance parental participation have been developed in Finland during the past decade; they have been partly funded by the government (Purola & Smeds, 2018).

The FEEC (2018) has begun to gather information from municipalities on how well the ECEC quality indicators are met, and these results point to the need for further teacher training on parental participation. The results also indicate how parental participation and structures in day-care centres should be developed in different locations, as they are not all the same.

These findings indicate that the Finnish steering documents highlight parental participation in ECEC, and the teaching of parental participation in teacher education is important. The latest research on multicultural families in Finnish ECEC suggests that teachers need more training on how to cooperate with different kinds of parents and in difficult situations (Hakyemez-Paul et al., 2018; Lastikka, 2019). There is a very limited research into parents' view on parental participation in Finland, and more study is required before parental participation can be enhanced further in Finnish ECEC.

References

Act on Early Childhood Education and Care. (540/2018). Retrieved from www.finlex.fi/fi/laki/alkup/2018/20180540

Alasuutari, M. (2010). Striving at partnership: Parent – practitioner relationships in Finnish early educators' talk. *European Early Childhood Education Research Journal, 18*(2), 149–161.

Basic Education Act. (628/1998). Retrieved from www.finlex.fi/en/laki/kaannokset/1998/en19980628.pdf

Chan, A., & Ritchie, J. (2016). Parents, participation, partnership: Problematising New Zealand early childhood education. *Contemporary Issues in Early Childhood, 17*(3), 289–303.

Finnish Education Evaluation Centre. (2018). *Guidelines and recommendations for evaluating the quality of early childhood education and care* (J. Vlasov, J. Salminen, L. Repo, K. Karila, S. Kinnunen, V. Mattila, T. Nukarinen, S. Parrila, & H. Sulonen, Eds.). Retrieved August 12, 2019, from https://karvi.fi/app/uploads/2019/03/FINEEC_Guidelines-and-recommendations_web.pdf

Finnish National Agency for Education. (2018). *The national core curriculum for early childhood education and care*. Retrieved from https://www.julkari.fi/bitstream/handle/10024/75535/267671cb-0ec0-4039-b97b-7ac6ce6b9c10.pdf?sequence=1

Finnish National Board of Education. (2016). *National core curriculum for pre-primary education 2014*. Helsinki: Author.

Hakyemez-Paul, S., Pihlaja, P., & Silvennoinen, H. (2018). Parental involvement in Finnish day care – what do early childhood educators say? *European Early Childhood Education Research Journal, 26*(2), 258–273. doi:10.1080/1350293X.2018.1442042

Hujala, E., Turja, L., Gaspar, M. F., Veisson, M., & Waniganayake, M. (2009). Perspectives of early childhood teachers on parent – teacher partnerships in five

European countries. *European Early Childhood Education Research Journal, 17*(1), 57–76. doi:10.1080/13502930802689046
Kangas, J., Ojala, M., & Venninen, T. (2015). Children's self-regulation in the context of participatory pedagogy in early childhood education. *Early Education and Development, 26*(5–6), 847–870.
Lammi-Taskula, J., & Siippainen, A. (2018). Vanhempien vuorotyö, lasten hyvinvointi ja yhteistyö vanhempien kanssa varhaiskasvatuksessa [Parents' shift work, wellbeing of the children and cooperation with parents in early childhood education]. *Yhteiskuntapolitiikka, 83*(4), 422–426.
Lastikka, A. L. (2019). *Culturally and linguistically diverse children's and families' experiences of participation and inclusion in the Finnish early childhood education and care.* Helsinki: Unigrafia. Retrieved from http://urn.fi/URN:NBN:fi-fe2019102835162
Leedy, P., & Ormrod, J. (2001). *Practical research: Planning and design* (7th ed.). Upper Saddle River, NJ: Merrill Prentice Hall; Thousand Oaks: Sage.
Mahmood, S. (2013). First-year preschool and kindergarten teachers: Challenges of working with parents. *School Community Journal, 23*(2), 55–85.
Niemi, H., Toom, A., & Kallioniemi, A. (Eds.). (2016). *Miracle of education: The principles and practices of teaching and learning in Finnish schools.* Rotterdam: Springer.
Onnismaa, E. L. (2010). *Lapsi, lapsuus ja perhe varhaiskasvatusasiakirjoissa 1967–1999* [Child, childhood and family in early childhood education documents]. Helsinki: Helsingin yliopisto.
Purola, K., & Smeds, K. (2018). Huoltajien kokemukset ja osallisuus digitaalisten portfolioiden kehittämisessä ja kokeilemisessa [Parents' experiences and participation in development and experiment of digital portfolio]. In K. Smeds (Ed.), *Diggaa mun digimatkaa – Digga min digiresa – digitaaliset portfoliot varhaiskasvatuksen pedagogisen toimintakulttuurin kehittämisessä.* Report. Retrieved from https://indd.adobe.com/view/9ce1fc00-a197-48e0-851f-c0d88ee6b402
Rintakorpi, K., & Reunamo, J. (2017). Pedagogical documentation and its relation to everyday activities in early years. *Early Child Development and Care, 187*(11), 1611–1622.
Seikkula-Leino, J., Satuvuori, T., Ruskovaara, E., & Hannula, H. (2015). How do Finnish teacher educators implement entrepreneurship education? *Education + Training, 57*(4), 392–404.
STAKES. (2005). *Finnish national curriculum guidelines for early childhood education and care.* Retrieved from e_vasu (julkari.fi)
Uusimäki, L., Yngvesson, T. E., Garvis, S., & Harju-Luukkainen, H. (2019). Parental involvement in ECEC in Finland and in Sweden. In S. Garvis, H. Harju-Luukkainen, S. Sheridan, & P. Williams (Eds.), *Nordic families, children and early childhood education: Studies in childhood and youth* (pp. 81–99). Cham: Palgrave Macmillan. doi:10.1007/978-3-030-16866-7_5
Venninen, T., & Purola, K. (2013). Educators' view on parents' participation on three different identified levels. *Journal of Early Childhood Education Research, 2*(1), 48–62.
Vlasov, J., & Hujala, E. (2016). Cross-cultural interpretations of changes in early childhood education in the USA, Russia, and Finland. *International Journal of Early Years Education, 24*(3), 309–324.
Vlasov, J., & Hujala, E. (2017). Parent-teacher cooperation in early childhood education – directors' views to changes in the USA, Russia, and Finland. *European Early Childhood Education Research Journal, 25*(5), 732–746.
Williams, C. (2007). Research methods. *Journal of Business and Economic Research, 5*(3), 65–71.

9
EDUCATIONAL PARTNERSHIP
Parental collaboration in German ECEC settings

Emely Knör

The idea of educational partnership in German preschools

Collaboration with parents or families in preschools is described both internationally and nationally as one of the three central standards for early childhood education and care (ECEC), alongside direct pedagogical work with children and networking with other institutions (Cloos & Karner, 2010; Fröhlich-Gildhoff, 2013a, 2013b; Fröhlich-Gildhoff, Kraus, & Rönnau, 2006; Textor, 2006). In Germany, this consensus prevails between the normative requirements of Social Code Book Eight, almost all curricula of the federal states (Roth, 2010; Textor, 2006; Viernickel & Schwarz, 2009), as well as by the scientific discourse on ECEC (Kasüschke & Fröhlich-Gildhoff, 2008; Viernickel, 2006; Wolf, 2006).

In the German context, the concept of parental work is obsolete, as it implies an interpretation of an asymmetrical relationship. It is being increasingly replaced by the terms cooperation with parents or "Erziehungs- und Bildungspartnerschaft" (educational partnership), which refer to the basic relationship of (equal) cooperation (Fröhlich-Gildhoff, 2013b). To guarantee the welfare of the child, it is necessary for parents and teachers to share information in the interest of the child and to promote its development (Fröhlich-Gildhoff, Pietsch, Wünsche, & Rönnau-Böse, 2011). Especially the accelerated social and societal change and their effects on the coexistence lead to increasing pressure and burden on parents. The demand that both important reference systems of children (home and preschool) cooperate closely and support each other in the interest of the children is confirmed (Fröhlich-Gildhoff, 2013b). In supporting parents, preschools have a key role by acting in a way that complements the families (Friederich, 2011). The low-threshold accessibility of parents in ECEC institutions and the acceptance of teachers by parents as supporters and advisors can contribute to raise sensibility for and perception of parental education. (Rönnau & Fröhlich-Gildhoff, 2008; Thiersch,

DOI: 10.4324/9780367823917-9

2006). Furthermore, collaboration with parents is especially important for a living culture of welcome because of the families' different cultural and socio-economic backgrounds.

The concept of the educational partnership has positive connotations (Fröhlich-Gildhoff et al., 2011). But the fundamental asymmetrical parent–teacher relationship has received limited reflection (Cloos & Karner, 2010). Competition and mutual recriminations lead to asymmetries and power relations that merit consideration (Cloos & Karner, 2010; Fröhlich-Gildhoff, 2011).

Responsibilities of ECEC in Germany

In contrast to many other countries, ECEC in Germany is part of the child and youth welfare service, not the school system. The legal basis for ECEC is regulated at three levels: the national level, the federal level, and the local level. Only general guidelines are set at the national level (Schreyer & Oberhuemer, 2017). The federal states are required to implement these guidelines at the federal level. Detailed specifications on content are defined. The local level is obliged to implement the federal state-specific requirements. Consequently, the ECEC system is decentralized and considerably heterogeneous at the local level (Schreyer & Oberhuemer, 2017).

Parental collaboration in steering documents

Book Eight of the Social Code – Services for Children and Young People (*Sozialgesetzbuch, SGB VIII – Kinder- und Jungendhilfe*) defines the general objectives, for example, the right of the child to development and education (SGB VIII, §1). According to the law, ECEC in Germany has to adapt to the needs of children and their families, in both pedagogical and organizational respects (Schreyer & Oberhuemer, 2017). Family upbringing and education should be supported and supplemented by ECEC to help parents to reconcile family and work (SGB VIII, §22). The parents are to be involved in important decision-making processes in the ECEC setting (Schreyer & Oberhuemer, 2017).

The Social Code Book Eight is a central law in Germany, but in regard to further steering documents, the decentralized system in Germany has an impact on the content and obligation. Examining steering documents in terms of collaboration with parents in Germany, two types of documents emerge as the main focus. On the one hand, the national common framework and on the other hand the 16 curricula of the federal states.

In 2004 the Conference of Ministers of Culture and Youth (Jugendministerkonferenz/Kultusministerkonferenz [JMK], 2004) adopted the *Common Framework for Early Education*. This nationwide document is not mandatory but provides guidance for the development of curricula in the federal states between 2003 and 2008 (Schreyer & Oberhuemer, 2017). Regarding parental collaboration, a partnership between parents and teachers is emphasized. Parents should be involved in important matters of the institution. Regular communication with, as well as information and educational offers for parents, is recommended.

At the federal level, the aspect of parental collaboration is considered in most *curricula* of the federal states, for example, the *orientation plan for education and training for ECEC institutions in Baden-Württemberg* (Ministerium für Kultus, Jugend und Sport Baden-Württemberg [KM BW], 2011), the *Bavarian education and upbringing plan for children in daycare institutions up to school enrolment* (2016), and *Berlin educational program for daycare centers and childcare* (2014) (Viernickel, Nentwig-Gesemann, Nicolai, Schwarz, & Zenker, 2013). It is unambiguous that the ECEC is increasingly and consistently seen as a task in which families have to be intensively involved (Viernickel et al., 2013). Therefore, the development of an educational partnership between parents and teachers is considered necessary (Viernickel & Schwarz, 2009). The curricula of the federal states differentiate this aspect in various respects. In terms of content, the educational partnership can be summarized in five categories: *acclimatization, exchange with parents, transparency of the pedagogical work, participation and codetermination of parents*, and *offers for parents* (Viernickel & Schwarz, 2009).

In terms of a child's *acclimatization* to the preschool, different demands are placed on teachers. In addition to accompanying the family during the process of settling in, there are also admission interviews. Furthermore, parents should be supported in the process of deciding on a suitable institution, using public relations, hospitations, and information evenings as examples. The regular *exchange with parents* is characterized by daily conversations in passing. Annual individual parent meetings, to discuss the development of the child and parent evenings are part of this exchange. Thus, joint aims and contents of the pedagogical work can be developed in cooperation. The educational work should be *transparent for the parents*. Teachers have to ensure that the provision of all necessary information is up to date. Furthermore, teachers have to guarantee that language barriers do not cause problems and that the information is understandable for everyone. Documentation, weekly schedules, and other documents serve as methodical access. *Co-determination and participation of parents* should be ensured in all aspects of the pedagogical work (concept development, annual and project planning). This presupposes clear information about the possibilities of the parents. In cooperation with parents, this aspect is of particular importance. A regular questioning of parents for evaluation purposes and well-managed complaints management is desirable. Preschools should provide *offers for families*, as their extended area of responsibility includes the advisory and supportive function for families. For example, parenting courses, discussion groups, parent counseling, targeted involvement of fathers, parents with disabilities, and grandparents can be named. If the setting of the institution is not able to provide this offer itself, teachers have to recommend the parents to an appropriate offer.

Summarizing the curricula of the federal states postulates the need for an educational partnership. Cooperation between parents and teachers is for the benefit of the child and is characterized by respect, trust, openness, and appreciation.

Parental collaboration in ECEC teacher education

When teacher training shifts into focus, not only a decentralized picture of responsibility emerges but also different training paths. In Germany, for a long time, training at professional schools and vocational colleges for social pedagogy was the only way to become a preschool teacher (Wahle, 2009). About 15 years ago, university courses of study on early childhood education were increasingly developing (Wahle, 2009). Looking at the content of the parental collaboration in the curricula of the two educational pathways, a very similar picture emerges as already described in the steering documents.

For the bachelor's degree, there are internal university module manuals that control the contents of the course of study. Most of the module manuals of the Bachelor's degree "Pedagogy of Early Childhood Education" name parental collaboration (Fröhlich-Gildhoff et al., 2011). However, the depth of content differs, and the allocation of credit points suggests that the topic is hardly relevant.

School-based education is regulated by curricula in each federal state. The majority of the curricula establish a link to parental collaboration, but mostly as a cross-cutting subject (Friederich, 2011). Only three of the curricula contain separate relevant modules. Due to a certain amount of freedom in the interpretation of the curricula and an individual focus of each school, it remains ambiguous what and how much is taught concerning collaboration with parents. Thus, it has to be declared that the results only partially reflect the great importance and complexity of the topic (Friederich, 2011).

In conclusion, the issue of parental involvement should become an even stronger part of education and training. There is obvious potential for development (Friederich, 2011; Fröhlich-Gildhoff et al., 2006; Viernickel et al., 2013). For example in methodological competencies, such as resource-oriented conflict discussion, requirement analyses but also the examination of one's attitude (Friederich, 2011; Fröhlich-Gildhoff et al., 2011).

The implementation of the educational partnership in ECEC settings

Due to the country-specific differentiation of the educational partnership between teachers and parents, a heterogeneous variety of practical implementations emerges. Fröhlich-Gildhoff et al. (2011) categorize five different aspects.

(1) Information includes, for example, the first parental contact before admitting a child to preschool (admission interview, home visits), written information about daily routines, parents' evenings in general, and especially the conversations in passing. (2) Another aspect is the exchange and close cooperation regarding the development of the child. Regular developmental discussions based on a previously documented observation are an important aspect of the exchange and a central starting point for collaboration. Furthermore, jointly designed transition processes such as the transition from the family to the preschool and also the later transition

from preschool to primary school are significant. (3) The educational partnership aims to provide parents with the opportunity to participate in the decision-making process of the preschool. By participating in parents' councils or the development of the concept, the parents can have a voice in various aspects of the preschool. (4) Active participation in the preschool can be implemented through a wide range of possibilities. Parents are directly involved in the daily or specific activities. These include the organization of festivities, guest visits, participation in everyday life, for example as a reading mentor or in a parents' café or through a parents' newspaper. (5) Preschools have the responsibility of supporting families. Part of this is the provision of parental education. In this way, parents are supported in their parenting skills. Among these are targeted offers, such as consultation hours, topic-specific parents' evenings, or courses. Parents' courses, in particular, are increasingly being introduced into preschools and are conducted by teachers in cooperation with external specialists.

The implementation of these different forms in practice is valued and organized very variably in the preschools. Nevertheless, a unilateral tendency can be identified in pedagogical practice. Most of the implemented methods seem to be one-sided ways of informing parents (Viernickel et al., 2013). Frequently mentioned are conversations in passing individual parent meetings and regular parents' evenings (Fröhlich-Gildhoff et al. 2006; Gragert, Peucker, Pluto, & Seckinger, 2008; Viernickel et al., 2013). Nevertheless, the conversations in passing as well as regular meetings about the child's development are important for the continuous assurance of successful collaboration and should by no means be neglected (Fröhlich-Gildhoff, 2013b). According to Fröhlich-Gildhoff (2013a, 2013b), the professionalism in these possibilities of the educational partnership is shown in the respective interaction and the adaptation of the offer to the needs of the target group. The adaptation is necessary, because parents are not a homogeneous group, considering the great heterogeneity of life situations and the variety of parenthood.

The active participation of parents is a far less used form of the educational partnership (Viernickel et al., 2013). Active participation seems often neither intended nor welcome (Hachfeld, Anders, Kuger, & Smidt, 2016). Only the planning and designing of festivities is used for this purpose. Everyday activities, concept development, thematic work, or participation in decision-making processes are far less-used opportunities. Innovative possibilities for exchange or cooperation, for example, parents' cafés, regulars' tables, or information in different languages are also very rarely found (Viernickel et al., 2013). The involvement of parents in the work of the preschool or the use of the preschool as a place of residence or communication is rarely realized (Gragert et al., 2008).

A tendency that deserves a positive declaration is the development of family centers. The motivation was the recognition that parents have needs and wishes that preschool alone is unable to meet (Friederich, 2011). Besides, families often live separately from their family of origin, which results in a lack of support from the family association (Friederich, 2011). With the help of family centers, families will become socially integrated and in this way a network and social structures will be created to facilitate exchange and solidarity (Weiß, 2007). Parental education offers such as open counseling, topic-related parents' evenings, and offers to strengthen parenting skills are increasingly offered (Tschöpe-Scheffler, 2006). This process of developing German preschools into family centers is still in its first stages and will require further development in the coming years.

Research on parental involvement in Germany

The research field on parental involvement in ECEC in Germany has a rather small amount of results to declare. Below some selected research efforts in Germany will be presented.

So far, there is little empirically proven knowledge about the effects of collaboration between professionals and parents on child development. One reason is the complexity of proving the effects of collaboration between parents and teachers on child development (Friederich, 2011). Child development is influenced by many factors. The German scientific discourse in this area usually draws on international studies, such as the Head-Start Project.

Larger studies include parental involvement as one aspect of their research but define their superficial research interest differently (Friederich, 2011), for example, the two large studies by Fröhlich-Gildhoff et al. (2006) and Viernickel et al. (2013). They investigated the collaboration of teachers and parents in ECEC institutions. Fröhlich-Gildhoff et al. (2006) interviewed 1,147 parents and pedagogical staff from 146 preschools on the background, forms, and contents of cooperation in a quantitative study. Viernickel et al. (2013) conducted a quantitative survey of 1,237 professionals as part of their study "Keys to Good Education, Upbringing and Care." On a qualitative level, they conducted 15 in-depth group discussions with preschool teams, in which the topic of collaboration with families was of particular importance. Fröhlich-Gildhoff (2013b) summarizes the findings of both studies in terms of three aspects: the importance of the teachers' attitudes and basic orientations, the orientation toward the needs of the target group and the lack of necessary basic conditions.

The attitude of the teachers is repeatedly cited in the scientific discourse as an important factor for a successful educational partnership (Friederich, 2011; Fröhlich-Gildhoff, 2011; Fröhlich-Gildhoff et al., 2006). In contrast to parents, the attitude of teachers is characterized by professionalism, impartiality, and openness (Friederich, 2011). Nentwig-Gesemann et al. (2011) have further differentiated the concept of professional attitude. A professional attitude refers to concrete patterns of orientation, in the sense of ethical–moral value orientations, norms, interpretation models, and beliefs that guide actions. Furthermore, the image of the child and the individual professional role and self-image is essential. Thus, the attitude of the teachers forms the foundation for behavior, the structuring of practice, and pedagogical relationships. This professional attitude needs to be developed through training, supervision, and reflection (Thiersch, 2006). Fröhlich-Gildhoff et al. (2006) were able to demonstrate the importance of this attitude when working with parents in their study. For successful collaboration, a changed and reflected attitude of teachers toward parents is necessary. Cooperation that was characterized by competition and fear of contact could, with the help of a changed and strengthened self-image of the teachers, broaden the view from the individual child to the entire family. Teachers recognized that they should reach out to the parents as professionals and orient themselves toward their strengths and interests. Even parents with less motivation or reservations about collaboration accept the teachers' counseling offers if they are actively addressed by the teachers in a purposeful, continuous, and appreciative manner (Fröhlich-Gildhoff et al., 2011).

The forms of collaboration already described (conversations in passing, individual development meetings, regular parents' evenings, festivities) require a systematic needs analysis in their implementation. According to Fröhlich-Gildhoff (2013a), this is the only way to create a suitable offer for the parents. If the target group-specific offers are implemented systematically and reflectively, a positive effect for families with a migration background, in particular, can become apparent. Therefore, it is necessary to approach parents in a culturally sensitive manner and to offer low-threshold services, such as joint encounter events. Furthermore, Fröhlich-Gildhoff et al. (2006) identified teachers as the most important contact persons for educational questions after (spouses) partners. Parents would like special support especially in questions of child development, upbringing, and the observation of possible behavioral problems.

The teachers interviewed at Viernickel perceived the continuous cooperation with parents as an overload in terms of time, structure, and organization. The necessary basic conditions for coping with these challenges are partly not available. On the one hand, the topic receives too little attention in education and further training (Friederich, 2011; Fröhlich-Gildhoff et al., 2006; Viernickel et al., 2013). On the other hand, teachers do not have the necessary time to prepare the cooperation with parents (Viernickel et al., 2013).

Some studies that focus on a certain partial aspect or a specific target group of collaboration with parents (Hachfeld et al., 2016). Lokharde (2013), for example, examined the motives of families with a migration background to using an ECEC institution. A total of almost one-third of all parents surveyed cited collaboration with parents as an obstacle to use an ECEC institution before the age of three. All of the groups with a migration background surveyed indicated cooperation with parents as a qualitative barrier with a higher probability. Neither the generation of immigration nor the parents' education played a role. Tietze et al. (2013) could state similar results. Half of all Turkish and Russian mothers with an immigrant background state that they would give their two-year-old child to an ECEC setting if the cooperation between parents and teachers were better. In contrast, only 17% of all German mothers agree.

Future perspectives and development tendencies of parental involvement

Parental collaboration is of particular importance in Germany, but the educational partnerships in ECEC are heterogeneous. The pedagogical work is distinguished by one-sided implementations and reservations toward active collaboration of parents. The further development of the educational partnership in Germany requires an increased implementation of collaboration with parents in teacher training and further education. Theoretical curricula (Friederich, 2011; Fröhlich-Gildhoff et al., 2011) have to be included in education and thus better prepare teachers for the assignment of the educational partnership. Besides, the research will be responsible for examining the implementation of the educational partnership in terms of its effect on the child. In contrast, there is still the possibility of self-evaluation of preschools, which can contribute to further development. Furthermore, it seems desirable to further promote the development of family centers. It is possible to establish a successful educational partnership between parents and preschool and to positively support the child in its development.

Textor (2015) looks ahead to the future and describes the developmental tendencies in the following years toward less sustainable relationships between parents and teachers. Accordingly, the reason is the increasing number of full-day care from the first year of life. Consequently, parents have less time to attend preschool events, not to mention to actively participate. Conversations in passing will only be possible to a limited extent, as teachers will work in shifts and therefore the respective contact persons will no longer be available at drop-off and pick-up times. Furthermore, teachers are progressively becoming the main educators of children. Therefore, the question arises how an equal educational partnership can be possible in such a situation. Competition, feelings of guilt, envy, criticism on the side of the parents, as well as conflicts of loyalty on the side of the children are seen by Textor (2015) as possible consequences. In conclusion, it is possible to assume that the educational partnership that has developed in recent decades will change. Presumably, the need for family education and educational counseling will increase. In any case, it will be necessary for purposes and concepts to adapt to the changing situation of families. Needs analyses will follow as an inevitable consequence.

References

Bayerisches Staatsministerium für Arbeit und Soziales, Familie und Integration & Staatsinstitut für Frühpädagogik. (2016). *Der Bayerische Bildungs- und Erziehungsplan für Kinder in Tageseinrichtungen bis zur Einschulung* (7th ed.). Berlin: Cornelsen Scriptor.

Cloos, P., & Karner, B. (2010). Elternarbeit oder Erziehungspartnerschaft? Zum Programm eines veränderten Elternbildes. In P. Cloos & B. Karner (Eds.), *Erziehung und Bildung von Kindern als gemeinsames Projekt. Zum Verhältnis familialer Erziehung und öffentlicher Kinderbetreuung* (pp. 169–189). Baltmannsweiler: Schneider-Verlag Hohengehren.

Friederich, T. (2011). *Zusammenarbeit mit Eltern – Anforderungen an frühpädagogische Fachkräfte*. Munich: WiFF.

Fröhlich-Gildhoff, K. (2013a). Kooperation von Familien und familienergänzenden Einrichtungen. In M. Stamm & D. Edelmann (Eds.), *Handbuch frühkindliche Bildungsforschung* (pp. 357–372). Wiesbaden: Springer.

Fröhlich-Gildhoff, K. (2013b). Die Zusammenarbeit von pädagogischen Fachkräften und Eltern im Feld der frühkindlichen Bildung, Betreuung und Erziehung. *Bildungsforschung*, *10*(1), 11–25.

Fröhlich-Gildhoff, K., Kraus, G., & Rönnau, M. (2006). Gemeinsam auf dem Weg. Eltern und ErzieherInnen gestalten Erziehungspartnerschaft. *Kindergarten heute*, *10*, 6–15.

Fröhlich-Gildhoff, K., Pietsch, S., Wünsche, M., & Rönnau-Böse, M. (Eds.). (2011). *Zusammenarbeit mit Eltern in Kindertageseinrichtungen. Ein Curriculum für die Aus- und Weiterbildung*. Freiburg: FEL.

Gragert, N., Peucker, C., Pluto, L., & Seckinger, M. (2008). *Ergebnisse einer bundesweiten Befragung bei Kindertagesstätten: Zusammenfassung für die teilnehmenden Einrichtungen*. Munich: DJI.

Hachfeld, A., Anders, Y., Kuger, S., & Smidt, W. (2016). Triggering parental involvement for parents of different language backgrounds: The role of types of partnership activities and preschool characteristics. *Early Child Development and Care*, *186*(1), 190–211.

Jugendministerkonferenz/Kultusministerkonferenz (JMK). (2004). *Gemeinsamer Rahmen der Länder für die frühe Bildung in Kindertageseinrichtungen*. Retrieved from www.bildungsserver.de/Bildungsplaene-fuer-Kitas-2027-de.html

Kasüschke, D., & Fröhlich-Gildhoff, K. (2008). *Frühpädagogik heute: Herausforderungen an Disziplin und Profession*. Cologne: Link.

Lokharde, M. (2013). *Hürdenlauf zur Kita: Warum Eltern mit Migrationshintergrund ihr Kind seltener in die frühkindliche Tagesbetreuung schicken*. Berlin: Sachverständigenrat deutscher Stiftungen für Integration und Migration.

Ministerium für Kultus, Jugend und Sport Baden-Württemberg (KM BW). (2011). *Orientierungsplan für Bildung und Erziehung in baden-württembergischen Kindergärten und weiteren Kindertageseinrichtungen*. Retrieved from http://kindergaerten-bw.de/site/pbs-bw-new/get/documents/KULTUS.Dachmandant/KULTUS/Projekte/kindergaerten-bw/Oplan/Material/KM-KIGA_Orientierungsplan_2011.pdf?attachment=true

Nentwig-Gesemann, I., Fröhlich-Gildhoff, K., Harms, H., & Richter, S. (2011). *Professionelle Haltung/Identität der Fachkraft für die Arbeit mit Kindern unter drei Jahren*. Munich: DJI/WiFF.

Rönnau, M., & Fröhlich-Gildhoff, K. (2008). *Elternarbeit in der Gesundheitsförderung. Angebote und Zugangswege unter besonderer Berücksichtigung der Zielgruppe "schwer erreichbare Eltern"*. Stuttgart: Landesgesundheitsamt.

Roth, X. (2010). *Handbuch Bildungs- und Erziehungspartnerschaft. Zusammenarbeit mit Eltern in der Kita*. Freiburg: Herder.

Schreyer, I., & Oberhuemer, P. (2017). Germany – key contextual data. In P. Oberhuemer & I. Schreyer (Eds.), *Workforce profiles in systems of early childhood education and care in Europe*. Retrieved from www.seepro.eu/English/pdfs/GERMANY_Key_Data.pdf

Senatsverwaltung für Bildung, Jugend und Wissenschaft. (2014). *Berliner Bildungsprogramm für Kitas und Kindertagespflege*. Weimar: Das netz.

Textor, M. R. (2006). *Erziehungs- und Bildungspartnerschaft mit Eltern: Gemeinsam Verantwortung übernehmen*. Freiburg: Herder.

Textor, M. R. (2009). *Elternarbeit im Kindergarten. Ziele, Formen, Methoden*. Norderstedt: Books on Demand GmbH.

Textor, M. R. (2015). *Vom Erziehungspartner zum Haupterzieher: Neue Anforderungen an die Elternarbeit*. Retrieved from www.kindergartenpaedagogik.de/fachartikel/elternarbeit/elternarbeit-grundsaetzliches-ueberblicksartikel/2317

Thiersch, R. (2006). Familie und Kindertageseinrichtung. In P. Bauer & E. J. Brunner (Eds.), *El- ternpädagogik: Von der Elternarbeit zur Erziehungspartnerschaft* (pp. 80–105). Freiburg: Herder.

Tietze, W., Becker-Stoll, F., Bensel, J., Eckhardt, A. G., Haug-Schnabel, G., Kalicki, B. . . . Leyendecker, B. (Eds.). (2013). *NUBBEK. Nationale Untersuchung zur Bildung, Betreuung und Erziehung in der frühen Kindheit.* Weimar: Verlag das netz.

Tschöpe-Scheffler, S. (2006). *Konzepte der Elternbildung – eine kritische Übersicht* (2nd ed.). Opladen: Budrich.

Viernickel, S. (2006). *Qualitätskriterien und -standards im Bereich der frühkindlichen Bildung und Betreuung.* Remagen: Ibus.

Viernickel, S., Nentwig-Gesemann, I., Nicolai, K., Schwarz, S., & Zenker, L. (2013). *Schlüssel zu guter Bildung und Betreuung – Bildungsaufgaben, Zeitkontingente und strukturelle Rahmenbedingungen in Kindertagesstätten.* Retrieved from www.gew.de/Binaries/Binary96129/Expertise_Gute_Bildung_2013.pdf

Viernickel, S., & Schwarz, S. (2009). *Schlüssel zu guter Bildung, Erziehung und Betreuung.* Retrieved from www.google.com/url?sa=t&rct=j&q=&esrc=s&source=web&cd=1&ved=2ahUKEwi8jNHK_c3dAhWC_SwKHcFtAhAQFjAAegQIBBAC&url=https%3A%2F%2Fwww.nifbe.de%2Fpdf_show.php%3Fid%3D226&usg=AOvVaw3ovcyumayh-xqtgDJbpE7V

Wahle, M. (2009). Berufsausbildung im Umbruch: Das Beispiel der beruflichen Ausbildung von Erzieherinnen und Erziehern. In T. Blech & M. Wahle (Eds.), *Erzieher-in-Ausbildung auf dem Prüfstand: Beiträge zur aktuellen Reformdebatte* (pp. 78–94). Bochum and Freiburg: Projekt-Verlag.

Weiß, H. (2007). Was brauchen Kinder und ihre Familien? *Frühförderung interdisziplinär. Zeitschrift für Praxis und Theorie der frühen Hilfe für behinderte und entwicklungsauffällige Kinder, 2,* 78–86.

Wolf, B. (2006). Elternarbeit. In L. Fried & S. Roux (Eds.), *Pädagogik der Frühen Kindheit* (pp. 168–172). Weinheim: Beltz.

10
PARENTAL INVOLVEMENT IN EARLY CHILDHOOD EDUCATION IN GHANA

Francis R. Ackah-Jnr

Introduction

Early childhood education (ECE), generically described as services for the care and education of children from birth to age 8 (Bredekamp, 2011; UNESCO, 2008), is a critical policy and practice. In Ghanaian context, ECE refers to the timely provision of a range of services that promote the survival, growth, development, and protection of young children from birth to 8 years (ECCD Policy, 2004). Formal ECE programmes serve five main age categories of children: (1) crèches cater for children under 2 years, (2) day-care centres for the age group 2–3 years, (3) nurseries for children aged 3–4 years, (4) kindergartens for children aged 4–5 years, and (5) primary 1 to 3 for children aged 6–8 years, which are part of the Basic Education system (Ackah-Jnr, 2016). ECE programmes are designed for varied purposes, including enrichment-oriented programmes to foster cognition, socialisation, and development of children, and compensatory/intervention programmes to address perceived "gaps" in children's development and background. Due to the interconnected familial relationships or kinship in Ghana, extended family members, parents and community are all involved in a child's ECE. Parent involvement in ECE is thus an important practice, founded on traditional collective and interdependent cultural beliefs and values that the socialisation, learning and well-being of children are a shared, collaborative, and communal responsibility. The Government of Ghana however remains the chief promoter, leveraging parental involvement in ECE.

Steering documents on parental involvement in Ghana

Positioned in a unique socio-cultural and eco-political Ghanaian context, parent involvement is guided by a set of international policies and best practices, and national policies and legal frameworks that aim to strengthen parents' motivation and contributions to quality ECE. The 1992 Constitution (Government of Ghana [GOG], 1992) is the major document on parent involvement. Section 28(c) stipulates

> parents [must] undertake their natural right and obligation of care, maintenance and upbringing of their children... [including ECE] ... in the interests of the children.

According to the Children's Act 560 (GOG, 1998), parental duty and responsibility is paramount to children's education. Pursuant to Section 6(3),

> every parent has rights and responsibilities whether imposed by law or otherwise towards his child which includes the duty to provide good guidance, care, assistance and maintenance ... the child's survival and development [and education].

In furtherance, sub-part 3(47) of the Children's Act 560 states:

> a parent or any other person who is legally liable to maintain a child ... is under a duty to supply the necessities of health, life, education ... for the child
>
> *(p. 17).*

The Early Childhood Care and Development ([ECCD], GOG, 2004) policy states that parents will be actively involved in ECE. Their involvement is a strategic principle and process to enhance the survival, growth, development, and protection of all children aged 0–8. According to the ECCD Policy, the concept of parent involvement in ECE will be broadened to embrace parent participation, which respects and strengthens the parent's role in the child's development and establishes linkages between the home, early childhood programmes and children's transition into the primary school.

Broadly, the community, families, and parents are instrumental to sustaining ECE and are expected to support parent involvement through:

> the contribution of labour to build facilities; (2) provision of equipment and play things; (3) provision of food for children; (4) contribution towards the payment of salaries of caregivers (they may be allowed to pay in kind) and any other cost that may be necessary.
>
> *(ECCD Policy, 2004)*

Other supporting documents are: The 2008 Education Act 778, Section 1(2), confers responsibility on parents to ensure children attend free and compulsory Basic Education, including 2-year ECE (GOG, 2008). Parent failure is punishable by law, "unless the parents cannot genuinely afford to educate the child" (p. 5). As per the 2014 Child and Family Welfare Policy (GOG, 2014), Strategy 3.2,

> parents . . . shall retain primary responsibility for the welfare of their children and for the provision of basic needs such as [early childhood] education . . . support for the child's socialisation and identity development.
>
> *(p. 16)*

The Ghana Inclusive Education Policy ([GIEP], MOE, 2015) identifies parents as key ECE planners who must be actively engaged in meeting children's needs, especially those with disability and learning challenges. Parental involvement shall include multifaceted roles:

> parents are expected to participate in school-related decisions . . . collaborating with teachers . . . set realistic goals for their children . . . fulfil their home-school obligations . . . meet the needs of their child . . . are obliged to fulfil their part of the role. . . [*and*] failure shall be tantamount to shirking of responsibility and denial of the child's fundamental human rights
>
> *(p. 23)*.

Consistent with the 2015 Ghana's Sustainable Development Goal 2: Achieve Universal Primary Education, parent involvement is a supportive environment and a quality issue. The recent Pre-Tertiary Education Bill (GOG, 2019) reinforces the obligation and criticality of parents to inclusive ECE of all children. Like the 2015 Education Bill (GOG, 2015) and the 2006 Disability Act (715) (GOG, 2006), the Pre-Tertiary Education Bill (GOG, 2019) stipulates

> parents shall take advantage of inclusive education facilities to send a child with special needs to the appropriate education facility or make a request for the provision of an appropriate education facility.
>
> *(p. 15)*.

The National Council for Curriculum and Assessment (NaCCA) through the National Inspectorate Board (NIB) enjoins parents through homework and assessment policies and guidelines to hold schools, headteachers, and teachers accountable for their roles in implementing the National Pre-Tertiary Education Curriculum Framework ([NPTECF], MOE, 2018). The Ghana Education Strategic Plan ([ESP], 2018–2030) recommends effective community engagement in education to promote a culture of learning and social accountability (MOE, 2018).

Research base on parental involvement in ECE in Ghana

Parent involvement in education literature is evolving and becoming enriched in Ghana. Most research generally focus on parent involvement across the education level such as primary, junior high and secondary schools (Ackah-Jnr, 2009; Chowa, Ansong, & Osei-Akoto, 2012; Donkor, 2010; Donkor, Issaka, & Asante, 2013; Nyarko, 2011; Pryor & Ampiah, 2004). There are a few specific studies related to parent involvement in ECE (Ackah-Jnr, 2016; Ackah-Jnr & Appiah, 2011; Obeng, 2012; UNICEF, 2011; Wolf, Aber, & Behrman, 2018; Wolf & McCoy, 2019; Wolf, 2020; Yaro, 2015).

Ackah-Jnr and Appiah (2011) identified parent involvement in early intervention programmes and child-rearing practices as a catalyst for effective ECE. Parents were seen as important collaborators and their shared responsibilities at the home and school contribute to children's progress, prevention of risks and disabilities and attainment of educational goals. Yaro (2015) examined how parents with low formal education in a rural community are involved in children's ECE learning. Study results showed parent mentorship and engagement in local business transactions were learning and evaluation contexts fostering children's math competence; parents perceived giving and receiving correct change-mediated children's math learning; and parents considered their involvement in children's math as an instigator of children's future success. Parents saw increased time spent on academic activities improved children's success within an exam-centric socio-cultural context, but parents' low education affected their effective involvement in children's math learning.

Wolf et al. (2018) conducted a teacher-training intervention programme across public and private kindergartens serving children aged 4–6 years in six districts of the Greater Accra Region. They tested the additional impact of parental awareness meetings on the programme, e.g. encouraging parent-teacher and parent-school communication meetings. While generally the intervention improved teaching, classroom quality and school readiness, the parenting awareness meetings did not result in improved teaching quality and positive child outcomes, suggesting a negative impact of parent engagement in ECE.

In a qualitative study, involving education officials, ECE principals and teachers, Ackah-Jnr (2016) found enhanced parental involvement as a recurrent expectation for promoting inclusive quality ECE for all children. Parents are expected "to reinforce children's learning, including those with disability at home" and "provide effective care, attention and requisite support" for their education (p. 151). Ackah-Jnr stated parent involvement serves as reinforcement and a bridge to strong home-ECE setting, important resources and partners. Examining parent investments in children's home learning and school readiness outcomes across five developmental domains at the start of ECE, Wolf and McCoy (2019) found parent socioeconomic status, directly and indirectly, influenced parents' pathways of investment and that involvement was the primary mechanism enhancing children's school readiness skills but did not predict executive function.

Nyarko (2011) identified specifically that mothers' school involvement correlates more positively with student academic performance than that of fathers. It is unsurprising because as heads of families, fathers must cater for the families' needs. They often go to work; hence they delegate attending of school meetings and other events to mothers. The level of involvement at home and school depended on the child's gender.

Ghanney's (2017) study of rural early childhood centres found structural parent involvement in school governance through School Management Committee (SMCs) but specific socio-economic factors such as financial constraints and corporal punishment practices limited parent participation in most school activities. Donkor (2010) identified that parents appreciated the value of education, but poor supervision of homework led to children's poor performance. Parents spend more time on their jobs than with children at home, and their involvement occurred mostly through parent-teacher association (PTA) meetings, which served as the sole conduit for interacting with the school.

Chowa et al. (2012) found that Ghanaian parents were involved in children's schooling and education, but generally to a lower extent. There was high involvement level in school, e.g. attending PTA meetings and at home, e.g. discussing expectations with their children and ensuring homework is done, but many parents never assisted children directly with homework. In another study, Chowa, Masa, and Tucker (2013) revealed parent involvement is a bidimensional construct comprising home-school activities and that academic performance is a function of the involvement type. Whereas home-based parent involvement was associated positively with academic performance, school-based parent involvement had a negative association.

Other studies focus broadly on community participation in early childhood and school activities. UNICEF (2011) reported that some non- governmental organisations (NGOs) provide training and awareness to parent teacher associations (PTAs) to enhance parent engagement in ECE. According to CREATE (2010), community members with shared responsibilities, including parents, PTA members and other stakeholders can work collaboratively with teachers and schools to enhance regular attendance of children who irregularly attend or drop out of school. Pryor and Ampiah (2003, 2004) found most parents in a rural community were indifferent, uninterested or dissatisfied with their children's education. Parents assume that the child's schooling is unsupportive of their farming careers. Other socio-economic factors, including poverty, personal priorities, and self-interest accounted for parents' limited or non-involvement in their children's learning activities (Pryor & Ampiah, 2003, 2004).

Treatments or attentions to parental involvement in ECE teacher education

Evidence on treatments of parent involvement in ECE teacher education is a mixed bag. Significantly, all universities, colleges of education and other institutions such as the National Nursery Teachers' Training Centre (NNTTC) in Ghana engaged in preparing teachers and developing early childhood programmes identify the essence of parental involvement and have some designated or related courses on it in their curricula or programmes for teachers.

Practically, there are weak content treatments or attentions to parent involvement in ECE teacher education curricula and research. Across higher education institutions, parent involvement is treated as either a course or course content. There is usually a three or four credit-hour single course taught as part of the on-campus, distance, sandwich or online education programme for early childhood (EC) teachers. Further analytic review of the Teacher Education programmes of two pioneer universities of education, University of Cape Coast (UCC), Cape Coast and University of Education, Winneba, shows parent involvement is taught to EC teachers as a three or four credit-hour single, separate course a semester in sandwich and regular ECE certificate, diploma or degree programmes. This forms a negligible part of about 135 or 64 credit hours teacher trainees are expected to complete for the award of Bachelor or Diploma in ECE respectively at the UCC (see Department of Basic Education [DBE], n.d). The credit allocation to the course on parent involvement in the yet to be implemented Master of Philosophy in ECE is minimal. Pre-service teachers in other education programmes may take courses emphasising parental involvement that relates to the broader goal of child growth, learning and development, and survival.

Seven Colleges of Education in Ghana that offer diploma or degree in Basic Education focus on ECE; hence they treat parent involvement as part of the programme for pre-service teachers as a two or three credit-hour course. In ECE Teacher Education, treatments of parent involvement are theoretically oriented with limited or no opportunities for pre-service teachers to practise course knowledge, skills, and strategies during their training programmes. Teacher-centric didactic approaches are used, so EC pre-service teachers play passive roles in the teaching and learning process and only have opportunities to practise acquired knowledge and skills when they are faced with reality after completing their study programme.

In ECE teacher education programmes, another minimal treatment of parent involvement is evident in related courses such as early childhood special education, managing and supervision of EC centres, and contemporary issues and ethics in ECE (DBE, n.d). These related curricula courses at the DBE treat parent involvement as content topics. In the course, managing and supervision of EC centres, parent involvement is treated as an administrative task or function headteachers should practise effectively in ECE settings.

A survey of undergraduate research projects, master's and doctoral theses, at the College of Education, UCC, on ECE and areas of emphasis show little or non-existing attentions to issues of parent involvement. Almost all postgraduate research on parent involvement were conducted by students or educators studying in universities abroad (e.g. Ackah-Jnr, 2016; Ghanney, 2017; Yaro, 2015). Among the research projects and theses submitted to the Department of Basic Education, UCC, that runs ECE programmes, parent involvement is not considered a topical research issue. This may be no different from other universities and colleges in Ghana that run similar ECE programmes. In terms of the education level, research on parent involvement focuses more on junior high and secondary schools (Chowa et al., 2012; Donkor, 2010) or community participation (Pryor & Ampiah, 2004) but a few are specifically related to ECE (Ackah-Jnr, 2016; Obeng, 2012; Wolf & McCoy, 2019; Wolf, 2020; Yaro, 2015). There are limited studies on contextual factors affecting parents' involvement and lack of distinctive policies on parent involvement in ECE like the Family-School Partnerships Framework in Australia and the No Child Left Behind in the USA that enjoins schools to have written parent involvement policies and school-parent compacts, describing how parent should be involved in schools and how they will take part in improving children's achievement. Little research exists on how parents view their role in their children's early schooling, or how parent-teacher relationships may shape classrooms (Wolf, 2020). Additional research is needed to explore parent involvement in Ghana, particularly where parents have shown to value early education (Bidwell, & Watine, 2014). Attentions to parent involvement in ECE teacher education are somewhat hotch-potch, reflecting limited application, practicality, and value of parent involvement in ECE.

Parental engagement in practice in ECE

Parent engagement takes different but interrelated forms in practice. Research (Ackah-Jnr, 2016; Ackah-Jnr & Appiah, 2011; Chowa et al., 2012; ECCD Policy, 2004; MOE, 2015; Wolf, 2020; Wolf & McCoy, 2019; Yaro, 2015) shows parent engagement is multidimensional comprising home, school and community activities that support children's learning and well-being. According to the Ghana ECCD Policy (2004), parent engagement includes the contribution of labour to build facilities; provision of equipment and play materials; and provision of food for children. The MOE-GIEP (2015) similarly articulates that participating in school-related decisions, collaborating with teachers and attending to home-school obligations as three involvement responsibilities of parents. Wolf and McCoy (2019) reported at-home stimulation activities, at-home resources for learning and school engagement are essential forms of parent engagement. Chowa et al. (2012) found parent school-based activities include (1) attendance at PTA meetings; (2) communication with their child's teacher and counsellor; (3) attendance at school events; and (4) volunteerism at school. In home-based processes, parents (1) checked their children's homework, (2) talked to their children about what they learned in school, (3) talked about expectations for their children's school work and (4) talked about what their children learned in school. Attending PTA meetings are the main source of engagement, but their effectiveness is conditioned on schools' commitment to provide formal parent engagement programmes (Dampson, 2010).

Wolf (2020) identified that parents perceived their involvement in ECE as a mutual responsibility of teachers and parents. Yet parents felt it is all about child caring and ensuring their children's basic necessities are met, including nutrition, cleanliness and payment of school fees, and less so in supporting children's educational experiences through engaging in enrichment or educational activities. Other parents had never been to the child's school and rarely interacted with their child's teacher, which made teachers frustrated that parents did not invest much in their children's learning and development. According to Dampson (2010), parent ECE engagement includes volunteering at school, communicating with teachers and other school personnel, assisting in academic activities at home, and attending school events, meetings of PTAs, and parent-teacher conferences. Parent support includes reading activities and informal meetings with teachers to discuss children's progress. Dampson concluded that while homework is the most interactive activity, not many parents have time and appropriate techniques to support children. The prevalent parent involvement activities thus mirror Epstein's (2018) typologies of involvement.

Community members and organisations make further contributions to create home and school conditions supporting children's learning and parent leadership in ECE (UNICEF, 2011). Some NGOs offer training support to teachers and parents to enhance their roles in ECE. Prominent community members, including opinion leaders such as chiefs, MPs and doctors serve as resource persons in ECE settings (Ackah-Jnr, 2009). There are community or district-led ECE committees that also make material, financial and human contributions to support ECE (ECCD Policy, 2004; UNICEF, 2011).

Parental engagement involves the multiple modalities for communicating with parents (Ackah-Jnr, 2009; Epstein, 2018; Wolf et al., 2018) that are respectful, ongoing and promote positive relationships. These include communication channels for connecting parents, families, schools and communities. Such two-way and open communication—home to school and school to home—involves newsletters, home visits, open days, parent groups, fundraising activities and face-to-face interactions (Ackah-Jnr, 2009; Epstein, 2018). Community education, personal contacts, emails and other emerging technologies can be used to engage families.

Generally, parents support ECE settings that are highly curriculum-centred and focus on English-only policy. Parents with low education levels are less engaged in their children's math learning at home (Yaro, 2015). Others are not engaged since they were less confident in communicating with teachers or due to lack of knowledge of the school system and their own negative educational experiences. Ackah-Jnr (2016) reported that most parents, especially those of children with disability, did not provide adequately for or engaged in their children's ECE, except a few enlightened parents. Some parents saw involvement as interference (Dampson, 2010) or felt free ECE in Ghana absolves them from responsibilities (Ackah-Jnr, 2016).

Multiple contextual factors influence parent engagement, including language, education level, gender, time, poverty, school leadership, socio-economic status, value of ECE, staff attitudes and cultural influences (Ackah-Jnr, 2016; Chowa et al., 2012; Dampson, 2010; Donkor, 2010; Ghanney, 2017; Wolf & McCoy, 2019; Wolf, 2020; Yaro, 2015). Traditional culture, Donkor et al. (2013) found to have the most influence on parents' support and engagement in their children's education as strong cultures may be rigid and difficult to adapt. Misunderstanding between parents and school staff arising from corporal punishment practices

(Ghanney, 2017) and expectations and aspirations of parents influence engagement (Ackah-Jnr, 2016; CREATE, 2010).

Developing parental engagement and collaboration in Ghana

Not all parents and families have the background knowledge, skills and disposition to engage in ECE. Ways deemed important to developing parental engagement and collaboration are:

Education and encouragement: Educate and encourage parents to get involved in their children's education and support learning and achievement by showing interest and concern for children's learning and progress, and communicate parents' expectations for success (CREATE, 2010). Parent education programmes can augment child care, education, and rearing practices (ECCD Policy, 2004). Education can ensure parents overcome impressions that their engagement is no longer required to secure inclusive quality ECE (Ackah-Jnr, 2016; UNICEF, 2011). Educate parents consistently about their effective roles in ECE (UNICEF, 2011). The role of teachers and ECE centres must be delineated.

Capacity building: Empower parents to ensure they have knowledge and skills or dispositions to foster their parenting contribution. Training ECE practitioners, including parents through a national integrated ECCD capacity building programme, is a key strategy to foster behavioural changes (UNICEF, 2011). Parents require more intensive training (Wolf et al., 2018) and appropriate educational packages to improve their capacities and abilities (ECCD Policy, 2004). Specific training for parents, especially those of children with disability, can focus on understanding the disabling condition, managing self-care activities and behaviour (Ackah-Jnr & Appiah, 2011). Capacity building of PTAs and SMCs (UNICEF, 2011) and advocacy and training of PTAs is needed to foster active engagement (Obeng, 2012). The capacity of teachers and ECE centres needs to be developed so that they can promote meaningful relationships and involvement of parents.

Multifaceted two-way communication: Communicating effectively is the basis for a strong relationship with parents. As a first step towards increasing engagement, ECE settings can adopt multifaceted two-way communication strategies such as newsletters, home visits, open days, fundraising and face-to-face interactions to communicate with and engage parents (Ackah-Jnr, 2009; Epstein, 2018). In communicating with parents, the language should be clear and respectful of the sensibilities and background of parents. ECE settings should equally pay attention to parents' views and receive their feedback on issues.

Parent engagement policy: Policies at the ECE and system levels are vital (Ackah-Jnr, 2016; Ghanney, 2017; Wolf & McCoy, 2019) to harmonise formal parent engagement through PTAs and SMCs or community-led committees and informal engagements. Policies articulating stakeholders' roles and responsibilities to support quality ECE are needed (Ackah-Jnr, 2016). Policies should have explicit approaches to engage parents and acknowledge their voice. For Ghanney (2017), such policies should reflect contextual differences or dynamics between both ECE governance structures and key engagement players, especially parents.

To improve parent engagement in home-ECE activities, researchers (e.g. Ackah-Jnr, 2009; Dampson, 2010) based on Epstein's (2018) work identified six key strategies: (1) providing parenting support (2) communicating with parents (3) providing a variety of volunteer opportunities (4) supporting learning at home (5) encouraging parents to be part of decision making in schools and (6) collaborating with the community.

Parental engagement for their children's learning and general well-being and its partnership with teachers, schools and community in Ghana

Parent engagement for children's learning and general well-being occurs in partnership with ECE stakeholders, including teachers, schools and the community. For parents, this means taking opportunities in the everyday interactions they have with their children and with teachers and schools to support children and to connect learning at home and community. For teachers and schools, this entails modalities and activities they use to connect and work with parents, and to build their capacity and motivate them for effective engagement. Parent partnership with the community reflects involvement of various community structures and organisations in the decision-making process, governance and leadership, or activities of ECE settings. Community groups and other parents contribute towards creating conducive environment for teaching and learning or mobilising resources for effective ECE. These engagement forms show that the immediate and larger community partners with parents for holistic education and development of children.

A UNICEF (2011) country case study in Ghana shows kindergarten parents reported infrequent individual interaction with teachers, which indicates limited opportunities for addressing parenting practices. Wolf (2020) reported that teachers' communication with parents focused more frequently on their children's concerns and needs rather than positive feedback about children. Obeng's (2012) study indicates a lack of parent involvement or support for EC teachers, especially from parents of children with special needs. These parents and others without children with disability did not actively engage with teachers because of "lack of motivation or reluctance to actually get involved" in ECE (Ackah-Jnr, 2016, p. 152). Further though capitation grants for all children and feeding programmes in selected schools are available to support poor parents, yet some parents did not take advantage of such programmes to engage meaningfully in their children's ECE.

Wolf and McCoy (2019) applied a cognitive stimulation model to understand how parent investment/ engagement affects children's school readiness and development in Ghana. They found parent investment occurs in partnership with ECE settings and schools in three ways: at-home stimulation activities (e.g. reading, stories and counting), at-home resources for learning (e.g. the number of books in the household), and school engagement (e.g. attend PTA meeting and school event).

They concluded that households' socioeconomic and educational levels (e.g. the number of books in the household) directly affect and can predict the extent of parental engagement.

Other studies show NGOs and other education agencies, as part of the larger community, provided capacity building programmes to PTAs and SMCs to encourage parental support and involvement in early childhood and school planning (UNICEF, 2011). District-level ECE committees received support to enhance their role in bringing local-level stakeholders, including parents together for planning and communication related to ECE (ECCD, 2004; UNICEF, 2011). Parent engagement for children's well-being and learning and its partnership with the community is evident in the connections between ECE services and all forms of input and contributions by the community services. Different services, including formal ECE, out-of-school, and health services, work as a continuum of services that is reassuring of parents and can meet the needs of young children.

Conclusion

Parent involvement in ECE is best practice. Significantly, it is important for promoting children's learning and well-being. As a right, responsibility and obligation, and a collective legal and social activity for parents and the community, parent involvement is supported by key steering documents that seek to enhance the contributions of both parents and community for quality ECE. Despite local research and attentions to parental involvement in ECE teacher education curricula and research are limited. Practically, engagement involves "actual" participation, investment, contribution and modalities or broad spectrum of home-ECE centre activities that parents engage in to foster their children's education, socialisation and development. Education, policy development, capacity building and effective two-way communication in addition to Epstein's (2018) six strategies are important to promoting parent involvement. More positively, parent involvement as a collective responsibility occurs in partnership with teachers, schools and community.

References

Ackah-Jnr, F. R. (2009). *School-community partnership in basic education*. Cape Coast: My Redeemer Lives Publishers.

Ackah-Jnr, F. R. (2016). *Implementation of inclusive early childhood education policy and change in Ghana: Four case sites of practice* (Doctoral thesis), Griffith University, Brisbane, Australia. Retrieved from http://hdl.handle.net/10072/367710

Ackah-Jnr, F. R., & Appiah, J. (2011). Early intervention as a catalyst for effective early childhood education in Ghana: How can this work? *Ife Psychologia, 19*(1), 226–239.

Bidwell, K., & Watine, L. (2014). *Exploring early education programs in peri-urban settings in Africa: Final report*. New Haven, CT: Innovations for Poverty Action. Retrieved from https://www.poverty-action.org/sites/default/files/publications/final_ecd_report_full.pdf

Bredekamp, S. (2011). *Effective practices in early childhood education: Building a foundation*. Upper Saddle River, NJ: Pearson Education Inc.

Chowa, G. A., Ansong, D., & Osei-Akoto, I. (2012). Parental involvement and academic performance in Ghana. *Youthsave Research Brief*, 12–42.

Chowa, G. A., Masa, R. D., & Tucker, J. (2013). The effects of parental involvement on academic performance of Ghanaian youth: Testing measurement and relationships using structural equation modelling. *Children and Youth Services Review*, *35*(12), 2020–2030.

CREATE. (2010). *Typologies of drop out in Southern Ghana*. CREATE Ghana Policy Brief 1. Retrieved from http://www.create-rpc.org/pdf_documents/Ghana_Policy_Brief_1.pdf

Dampson, G. (2010). Parental involvement in homework for children's academic success. A study in the Cape Coast municipality. *Academic Leadership: The Online Journal*, *8*(2), 30.

Department of Basic Education. (n.d). *Bachelor and diploma of ECE programmes*. Unpublished manuscript, University of Cape Coast, Ghana.

Donkor, A. K. (2010). Parental involvement in education in Ghana: The case of a private elementary school. *International Journal About Parents in Education*, *4*(1), 23–38.

Donkor, A. K., Issaka, C. A., & Asante, J. (2013). Cultural practices and education in Ghana: The effects of traditional culture on parental involvement in education. *Research on Humanities and Social Sciences*, *3*(7), 110–120.

Epstein, J. L. (2018). *School, family, and community partnerships: Preparing educators and improving schools*. New York: Routledge.

Ghanney, R. A. (2017). A case study of teacher involvement that affect parental involvement in basic education in rural Ghana. *World Journal of Educational Research*, *4*(1), 1–13.

Government of Ghana. (1992). *The 1992 constitution of the republic of Ghana*. Accra: Ghana Publishing Company.

Government of Ghana. (1998). *Children's act 1998 (Act 560)*. Accra: Government of Ghana. Retrieved from http://www.unesco.org/education/edurights/media/docs/f7a7a002205e07fbf119bc00c8bd3208a438b37f.pdf

Government of Ghana. (2004). *Early childhood care and development (ECCD) policy*. Accra: Government of Ghana.

Government of Ghana. (2006). *Persons with disability act 2006 (Act 715)*. Accra: Government of Ghana. Retrieved from https://sapghana.com/data/documents/DISABILITY-ACT-715.pdf

Government of Ghana. (2008). *Ghana education act 2008 (Act 778)*. Accra: Government of Ghana.

Government of Ghana. (2014). *Child and family welfare policy 2014*. Accra: Ministry of Gender, Children and Social Protection. Retrieved from https://www.mogcsp.gov.gh/mdocs-posts/child-and-family-welfare-policy/

Government of Ghana. (2015). *Education bill 2015*. Accra: Ministry of Education. Retrieved from https://educationghana.org/download/education-bill-2015/?wpdmdl=19108&refresh =61263ded26fdb1629896173

Government of Ghana. (2019). *Pre-tertiary education bill 2019*. Accra: Ministry of Education.

Ministry of Education. (2015). *Ghana Inclusive education policy (GIEP)*. Accra: GES/MOE. Retrieved from 2006 https://sapghana.com/data/documents/Inclusive-Education-Policy-official-document.pdf

Ministry of Education. (2018). *Education strategic plan (ESP) 2018 to 2030*. Accra: MOE.

Ministry of Education. (2018). *National pre-tertiary education curriculum framework (NPTECF) 2018*. Accra: Ministry of Education.

Nyarko, K. (2011). Parental school involvement: The case of Ghana. *Journal of Emerging Trends in Educational Research and Policy Studies*, *2*(5), 378–381.

Obeng, C. S. (2012). Children with disabilities in early care in Ghana. *International Journal of Early Childhood Special Education*, *4*(2), 50–63.

Pryor, J., & Ampiah, J. G. (2003). *Understandings of education in an African village: The impact of information and communication technologies*. Report on DFID Research Project Ed2000-88. Retrieved from https://core.ac.uk/download/pdf/7052384.pdf

Pryor, J., & Ampiah, J. G. (2004). Listening to voices in the village: Collaborating through data chains. In K. Mutua, & B. B. Swadener, (Eds), *Decolonizing research in cross-cultural contexts: Critical personal narratives* (pp. 159–178). Albany, NY: State University of New York Press.

UNESCO. (2008). *The EFA global monitoring report*. Retrieved from http://unesdoc.unesco.org/images/0015/001547/154743e.pdf

UNICEF. (2011). *Evaluation of UNICEF's early childhood development programme with focus on Government of Netherlands funding (2008–2010):* Ghana country case study report. New York: UNICEF. Retrieved from http://www.unicef.org/evaldatabase/files/ECD_Ghana_Final.pdf

Wolf, S. (2020). "Me I don't really discuss anything with them": Parent and teacher perceptions of early childhood education and parent-teacher relationships in Ghana. *International Journal of Education Research*, *99*, 101525.

Wolf, S., Aber, J. L., & Behrman, J. R. (2018). *The impacts of teacher training and parental awareness on kindergarten quality in Ghana*. Preliminary results brief. New Haven, CT: Innovations for Poverty Action.

Wolf, S., Aber, J. L., Behrman, J. R., & Tsinigo, E. (2019). Experimental impacts of the "quality preschool for Ghana" interventions on teacher professional well-being, classroom quality, and children's school readiness. *Journal of Research on Educational Effectiveness*, *12*(1), 10–37. https://doi.org/10.1080/19345747.2018.1517199

Wolf, S., & McCoy, D. C. (2019). Household socioeconomic status and parental investments: Direct and indirect relations with school readiness in Ghana. *Child Development*, *90*(1), 260–278.

Yaro, K. (2015). *Parental involvement in children's mathematics learning: A case of a rural community, Ghana* (Master's diss.), University of British Columbia, Vancourver, Canada. Retrieved from https://hdl.handle.net/2429/52871

11

PARENTAL INVOLVEMENT IN EARLY CHILDHOOD EDUCATION IN HONG KONG

Critical analysis of related policies

Aihua Hu

Introduction and background

Historically, Chinese parents have been highly involved in their children's education, influenced by the traditional belief that education is crucial for a better life (Ho, 1995) and success (Cheung & Pomerantz, 2011). However, this involvement was previously confined to home-based involvement in the form of supervising home assignments in Hong Kong (HK), especially before 1985. The importance of parental involvement was not recognized by the government and not mentioned in any education policies until the 1990s, when the positive evidence of having parents involved in their children's education was internationally reported. As a result, the government initiated different measures to gradually involve parents at different levels of education (Ng, 2007).

In Hong Kong, early childhood education (ECE) and care is provided by three types of preprimary institutions, namely, childcare centers providing service to children from birth to three years of age, kindergartens cum child-care centers admitting children aged two to six years, and kindergartens offering services to children aged three to six years. They were initially under the supervision of different government departments. In the late 1990s and early 2000s, the government planned and implemented the harmonization of childcare centers and kindergartens (Education and Manpower Bureau, 2003)[1]. Under the harmonization scheme, all kindergartens cum childcare centers and schools with kindergarten classes are classified as kindergartens and subject to the same requirements, registered under Education Ordinance, while the Social Welfare Department regulates childcare centers under the Child Care Services Ordinance.

The focus of this chapter is kindergartens and ECE refers to kindergarten education. At present, most kindergartens operate on a half-day basis, with some offering

DOI: 10.4324/9780367823917-11

whole-day service. All preprimary institutions in Hong Kong are privately run, but they must register under either the Education Ordinance or Child Care Service Ordinance. Kindergartens are categorized as non-profit-making kindergartens and private independent ones depending on their sponsors which can be either voluntary agencies or private enterprises. Seventy-five percent of kindergartens are non-profitmaking (Research Office Legislative Council Secretariat, 2019). Parents must pay for ECE whichever institution they choose. Low-income families can apply for fee waiving under the Kindergarten and Child Care Centre Fee Remission Scheme. Furthermore, some kindergartens and kindergartens cum childcare centers receive direct subsidies from the government under the Free Quality Kindergarten Education Scheme, and they are called *aided preprimary institutions*. Ninety-seven percent of non-profit-making kindergartens are aided preprimary institutions (Research Office Legislative Council Secretariat, 2019).

ECE is regulated by different government policies. Four government policy documents are chosen for analysis in this chapter. These are the Operation Manual for Pre-primary Institutions (Version 2.0), the Kindergarten Education Curriculum Guide, Performance Indicators: Kindergartens, and the Administration Guide for the 2017–2018 School Year. They have been chosen for the following reasons: First, according to the Operation Manual, all the policies should be complied with by all the preprimary institutions except those in the Administration Guide, which is specifically for aided preprimary institutions, although others can refer to it (Education Bureau & Social Welfare Department, 2019). As such, they all have a direct influence on how preprimary institutions should be operated across Hong Kong. More importantly, in one way or another, they all provide guidelines on how parental involvement should be operationalized and practiced in kindergartens. Moreover, all of them are updated policies. Except for the Administration Guide, which is provided only in traditional Chinese, all the documents have English versions.

Preservice ECE teacher education is conducted at different levels and at different tertiary institutions, subject to the approval of the Education Bureau. There are no territory-wide curriculum guides for the institutions to refer to in constructing their training courses/curriculums. They usually refer to the Kindergarten Education Curriculum Guide in this regard. At the same time, the Education Bureau provides respective program frameworks for institutions' reference in designing their teacher education programs. In the frameworks, the key objectives, performance outcomes, and practicum requirements of the training programs are set out. The program frameworks are devised in collaboration with the program providers, drawing reference from the principles and recommendations of Kindergarten Education Curriculum Guide. Institutions have their professional autonomy in developing ECE programs with their own features under the frameworks. As a result, learning goals related to parental involvement are in line with what is stated in the Kindergarten Education Curriculum Guide.

Aims of the chapter

The literature review on parental involvement at the ECE level in Hong Kong for this chapter indicates that researchers in Hong Kong focus more on how to develop and/or validate tools to study parental involvement (e.g., Lau & Rao, 2012; Phillipson & Phillipson, 2010), home–school collaboration (Lau & Ng, 2019), parental involvement and transition (e.g., Tao, Lau, & You, 2019), parental involvement and influential factors (Hong Kong Council of Social Service, 2010), and the power relations in parental involvement (Ng & Yuen, 2015). What is missing in the literature is an investigation of how government policies stipulate parental involvement. Examining government policies is part of examining the societal perspective, where the state apparatus – in the form of laws, statutory instruments, and institutionalization of practices – influences local practices (Hedegaard, 2009). This chapter will add to the literature on parental involvement in Hong Kong from this perspective. In addition, although residents in Hong Kong are predominantly of Chinese descendants (92% of a population of 7.38 million; Census and Statistics Department, 2017), it is becoming increasingly diverse due to an increasing number of immigrants. It is important to examine how parents of different ethnic backgrounds are expected to become involved in their children's education at the policy level.

The aims of this chapter are threefold. First, the chapter aims to critically interrogate how parental involvement is stipulated and discussed in different government documents through critical policy analysis. Second, it intends to advocate for some changes through connecting the analysis with existing empirical findings and government self-report practices. The third aim is serving as a foundation for a further empirical study.

Qualitative content analysis

Qualitative content analysis is used to analyze the collected documents because it "allows researchers to understand social reality in a subjective but scientific manner" by exploring "the meaning underlying [a] physical message" (Zhang & Wildemuth, 2009, p. 1). Questions raised by Edmondson (2000) for critical policy analysis (CPA) are adapted as guiding questions for the analysis (see Table 11.1). CPA is used to understand how the policies have rendered parents of different social economic and ethnic backgrounds "active" or "uninvolved" in their children's kindergarten education (Young, 1999).

Two types of parental involvement (home- and kindergarten-based involvement) are also used to present findings of the second guiding question. School-based involvement refers to the practices that require parents to have actual contact with the school, such as participating in parent–teacher meetings and volunteering in school events and activities (the term *kindergarten-based involvement* is used to describe this), while *home-based involvement* comprises the practices that take place at home and are related to children's learning development, such as supervising

TABLE 11.1 Guiding questions for data analysis adapted from Edmondson (2000)

1. How is parental involvement defined in Hong Kong according to the policies, and what are policymakers' goals and values?
2. What and how are parents involved in their children's kindergarten education as stipulated in the policies?
3. Who stands to benefit and who is left out in the involvement process?

TABLE 11.2 *Overview of the analyzed policies*

Policy	Issued by	Applies to	Major functions[2]
Operation Manual for Pre-primary Institutions	Education Bureau and Social Welfare Department, 2019	All preprimary institutions	To provide a comprehensive guide for understanding the statutory requirements and the respective requirements of the Social Welfare Department and Education Bureau in regulating childcare centers and kindergartens
Kindergarten Education Curriculum Guide prepared	Curriculum Development Council, 2017	Pre-primary institutions that offer education to children aged two to six years	To provide a curriculum framework for kindergartens
Performance Indicators: Kindergartens	Education Bureau, 2017b	Kindergartens	To provide a reference for self-evaluation and external assessment
Administration Guide for the 2017–2018 School Year	Education Bureau, n.d.	Aided pre-primary institutions and reference for non-aided ones	To guide kindergartens on administration work

children's home assignments and discussing school with children (Ho, 1995). Beyond what has been discussed in Ho's work, more varieties of home- and kindergarten-based involvement are discussed in this chapter since the policies offer more suggestions on the activities. Table 11.2 gives an overview of the policies to be analyzed in this chapter.

Findings and discussion

In this section, the findings are organized to answer the three questions listed earlier. Government reports on measures the government and kindergartens have taken to advocate and promote parental involvement, as well as empirical research on parental involvement in Hong Kong, are considered to elaborate on and support the findings and discussion.

Definition and goals of parental involvement stated in the policy and the embedded values

In all the policies, there is no clear definition of parental involvement. However, in one way or another, all the policies have mentioned how parents should and can be involved in their children's education. The two approaches taken by the government to promote parental involvement are home–school cooperation schemes and parent education. The requirements of what and how parents should be involved in their children's kindergarten education take departure from these two approaches. They also indicate that parental involvement is multidimensional, with a wide range of parental practices, taking place both at home and in school (Desforges & Abouchaar, 2003; Fan & Chen, 2001). This is detailed in the next section.

It is evident from the policies that the government has realized the importance of parental involvement. Policies also advocate regarding parents as partners instead of just participants in the education of future generations. For example, the Operational Manual states, "In order to promote children's learning, parent participation is an essential element" (Education Bureau & Social Welfare Department, 2019, p. 59), and "Institutions should establish a good partnership with parents" (p. 80); in Curriculum Guide, it says, "Quality kindergarten education relies on collaboration among school, family and community in which all stakeholders have close communication and cooperation" (Education Bureau, 2017a, p. 14), and "parents are close partners of school" (p. 97). More importantly, the importance has been upheld in practice. The Committee on Home–School Co-operation was established in February 1993 to promote home–school cooperation through various measures, one of which is to disburse grants to schools that have ideas for innovative approaches to improving home–school cooperation and enhancing parent education (Committee on Home-School Co-operation, n.d.).

The common goal of parental involvement across the policies is to provide quality education and care to children in Hong Kong, and thus, achieve the goal of laying a good foundation for their whole-person development (Education Bureau, 2017a). Quality education and whole-person development are keywords for almost all kindergarten-related policies. However, there are no definitions of quality education. Nevertheless, the government established a Quality Education Fund to finance projects that promote quality education in Hong Kong. In addition, the Performance Indicators for kindergartens have made it clear what quality education entails in terms of what indicators are included. More importantly, parental involvement is one of the indicators to assess the quality of kindergarten education. At the same time, the Curriculum Guide clearly articulates what quality kindergarten education entails and how it can help achieve whole-person education:

> Quality kindergarten education should be aligned with primary and secondary education in laying a firm foundation for the sustainable learning and growth of children, fostering in children a balanced development in the domains of ethics, intellect, physique, social skills and aesthetics, thus achieving the goal of whole-person education.
>
> *(Education Bureau, 2017a, p. 8)*

As stated in the Curriculum Guide, the core value is "childcentredness," and the essential principle is "understanding and respecting the unique developmental patterns of every child" (Education Bureau, 2017a, p. 10). Collaboration with family is among the five guiding principles in curriculum design.

Home- and Kindergarten-based parental involvement

The analysis of the four policies has indicated that parents are regarded as (close) partners of the school, and they have been assigned to different roles. In the Operation Manual, parental involvement is seen as essential for children's learning; parents are depicted as service recipients in that they should be informed and consulted for approval, assistant in that they should assist in activities, partners in the care and education of children, and advisors who can provide suggestions. It also gives recommendations on how to involve parents. In the Administration Guide, parents are described as children's role models and the most important educators, able to make a significant difference in enhancing children's learning at school and promoting their development via support and involvement in their children's kindergarten education.

The Curriculum Guide describes that parents should be involved in their children's kindergarten education, with the roles of clients who have the right to be informed, home educators who can provide care and guidance, assistants to help with organized kindergarten activities, and stakeholders who can make suggestions on decision-making and vote or participate in the election of parent managers on the School Management Committee (SMC). The Curriculum Guide sees parents as children's first teachers and close partners of schools from different perspectives.

Juxtaposed with these roles assigned to parents, the policies have stipulated which parents should be involved and how. The presentations of findings and discussion of parental involvement below are based on Ho's (1995) classification according to the locus of involvement.

Home-based parental involvement

The forms of home-based involvement are not directly mentioned. Instead, they are expressed in how parent education, organized by the government and kindergartens, can serve the purposes of home-based involvement. According to the analyzed policies, home-based involvement takes different forms, from parents helping their child complete home activities to supporting children's home assignments, and engaging in parent–child reading to helping their children form and keep good life and learning habits, cultivating different abilities and skills, and fostering good morals. For example, in the Curriculum Guide, it says that parents should "take the initiative to express their concern and support to their children and listen to children's sharing of their anecdotes at school" (Education Bureau, 2017a, p. 88), "help children develop positive values and attitudes and adapt to the changes at school" (p. 89), and help "progressively develop children's self-care abilities" (p. 94). In the Administration Guide, it states that kindergartens should assign some tasks for children to do at home, with parents helping as needed (Education Bureau, n.d.). As mentioned in the opening paragraphs, home-based parental involvement, especially in terms of academic learning, has a long history. Moreover, HK parents have a high sense of responsibility for their child's education (Lam, Ho, & Wong, 2002). Most parents are highly cooperative in helping their children with learning-related activities.

To achieve home-based parental involvement, all the policies have explicitly or implicitly suggested how to help parents understand child development and set developmentally appropriate expectations, and thus, provide appropriate assistance in their children's learning and development. Kindergartens are asked to provide parent education and establish a platform for parents to communicate about all aspects of kindergarten education. At the same time, the government offers seminars and workshops and creates and maintains websites (e.g., Smart Parent Net) to provide relevant materials and information to parents, ranging from how to read with their children to how to help their children form good habits. Parents are encouraged to attend workshops and seminars held by the kindergarten to determine the challenges their children will meet in the transition and how to help them (Education Bureau, 2017a). Although the government has provided useful materials and information, as well as workshops and seminars on parent education and parenting, and there is a choice of an English version, most workshops and seminars offered by either the government or kindergartens are conducted in Cantonese, which has left out non-Cantonese-speaking parents, including those who speak Mandarin, while most written and/or online materials and information are offered in Chinese, leaving out parents with no knowledge of Chinese written language.

Kindergarten-based parental involvement

According to some scholars, parents' participation in children's learning at home is not enough; involvement in school can help enhance the school quality.

Kindergarten-based parental involvement is relatively new, since most Chinese parents perceive that the management and leadership of a school's affairs should rest with the teachers, and parents would like to be "distant assistants" (Fan & Chen, 2001). The four policy documents all directly or indirectly suggest what and how to implement kindergarten-based involvement. In general, all the involvement falls into the forms described later.

Home–school communication emerged as the most frequently reported school-based involvement practice. All the policy documents make clear that schools should take responsibility for establishing different communication channels to have regular and frequent contact and communication with parents. The Curriculum Guide states that the purpose of communication is "to enhance mutual understanding and gather information about children's lives both at home and at school" (Education Bureau, 2017a, p. 97) To summarize the suggested communication channels, they include contacting individual parents when they are escorting their children to and from the institutions every day, telephone contacts, office interviews, home visits, parent newsletters, and teacher–parent meetings. The empirical findings of Lau and Ng (2019) confirmed that kindergartens use the suggested ways to communicate with parents. Moreover, the verbs used in these policies are "inform, involve, arrange, invite, provide, encourage," and the subjects are either teachers or kindergartens, which indicates that the communication is usually one way; that is, parents are informed and involved instead of parents taking initiatives. Although the Curriculum Guide states that teachers gather information about children's lives at home, teachers are the ones to take the initiative. This is in line with what empirical studies have found. Parents in Hong Kong take a relatively passive role in most school-based involvement (Ho, 2003; Pang, 2011).

Volunteering/assisting is a common feature of kindergarten-based parental involvement. Frequent volunteer tasks include teaching/teaching assistant, administrative, and activity/ceremony assistance. The Operation Manual suggestions include "inviting parents to volunteer in the activities of the institutions, such as assisting in decorating the premises during festivals, compiling parent newsletter, leading special activities, conducting occupation introduction, designing activities, etc." (Education Bureau & Social Welfare Department, 2019, p. 81). In terms of volunteering as a teaching/teaching assistant, it is thought that some parents have the expertise to enrich and enhance the curriculum. For example, the Curriculum Guide states that parents can assist schools in the implementation of the curriculum and provide opinions regarding the planning and implementation of the curriculum, which facilitates the sustainable development of schools (Education Bureau, 2017a). For non-Chinese-speaking (NCS) parents, being activity/ceremony assistants means involvement in all, one, or some of the processes of planning, preparing, and implementing the activities/ceremonies (Education Bureau, 2017a). The Curriculum Guide further suggests encouraging parents who understand both Cantonese and other languages to be a bridge of communication to facilitate exchange between teachers and NCS parents.

According to the four policies, the third form of kindergarten-based involvement is participating in parent activities organized by kindergartens, such as class observation, theme talks, workshops and seminars, open days, and family picnics. In Performance Indicators, it is stated that kindergarten should serve as a platform for parents to meet and support each other and obtain relevant information on community resources, especially in the case of NCS parents (Education Bureau, 2017b).

All the above types of kindergarten-based involvement are covered in the four policies with different wordings. However, what is missing is parents' participation in decision-making. The Curriculum Guide states that parents can make suggestions on making kindergarten-based decisions. Ng (2007) finds that parent representatives are always marginalized by other members in the school board in Hong Kong, while Lau and Ng (2019) find that Chinese parents rarely engage in the management of kindergartens or undertake active school-based involvement in general.

Some stand to benefit with the underprivileged being left behind

Coupled with the requirements and expectations of parents from government policies, the government invites professionals, such as ECE specialists, social workers, and psychologists to conduct workshops and seminars for parents, with kindergartens also conducting parent education seminars, which are helpful to parents in different ways. In addition, as mentioned earlier, kindergartens also hold different workshops, seminars, and sharing meetings for parents to learn from experts and each other on how to help their children with preprimary education.

According to empirical research findings (e.g., Lau, 2014; Lau & Li, 2011; Lau & Ng, 2019), parents' lack of time has been identified as a barrier to participating in general school activities across different kindergartens. It is a common practice that most parents need to supervise their children's home assignments/activities. In addition, many children participate in extracurricular activities after school and during weekends. Hence, it is difficult for many parents to participate in kindergarten activities. Thus, many choose not to be involved in kindergarten-based activities, and they are *voluntarily left out*. Nevertheless, there are some full-time working parents who want to be involved but cannot, which I term *involuntarily left out*. This type of left out is because of socioeconomic status.

The other type of involuntarily left out is due to language barriers. As mentioned previously, there are some non-Cantonese-speaking parents. Although there is some information, workshops, and seminars provided in English, at both government and kindergarten levels, most workshops and seminars are conducted in Cantonese, which also leaves out parents who speak Mandarin. What is more, there are non-Cantonese-speaking parents who do not understand English or are illiterate. As such, they are left out not only from most kindergarten-based parental involvement but also in terms of obtaining information on their children's kindergarten life.

The power relation between teachers and parents puts parents in a secondary position in home–school cooperation. According to Ng (2017), there is still a phenomenon whereby "teachers regard themselves as experts and professionals and maintain control over parents" (p. 268), which also makes it difficult for parents to have equal status when it comes to participating in their children's education. Moreover, according to the empirical research of Ho and Kwong (2013), most parent volunteers serve as auxiliary support for school activities. Although they are involved in tasks like serving as instructors of interest groups and producing teaching aids and materials, this requires specific knowledge and skills, which limits the participation of some parents: "In Hong Kong, it is usually reported that the ethnic minority parents experience barriers like language ability, hesitation in meeting strangers, custom obeisance, etc. which discourage their involvement in schools" (Hong Kong Council of Social Service, 2010, p. 7).

Conclusion and implications

All the important policies on ECE recognize the significance of parental involvement and stipulate how parental involvement should be conducted, providing explicit directions on what parents should do and how kindergartens should help parents. Hong Kong parents are involved in different aspects of their children's ECE, from being informed about what is going on to volunteering and giving suggestion. However, at the practical levels, there are still some real-life problems and barriers that make it difficult for some parents to get involved in their children's ECE.

This study has practical implications for developing and modifying the existing government policies on parental involvement. The policies emphasize kindergartens' role and responsibility to engage, involve, and educate parents. Parents are regarded as knowing almost nothing about how to educate their children or how to become involved in their children's kindergarten education. As such, I have argued that policy should recognize parents' competences and encourage them to take initiatives in home – school cooperation and regard them as equal partners who have some knowledge about the education of their children and how to involve themselves in their children's education. Some parents have expertise that kindergartens can make use of (Lau & Ng, 2019). In addition, there is a need to construct a territory-wide curriculum guide for kindergarten preservice teacher education. It is not enough for kindergarten teacher education institutions to construct their training courses/curriculum by referring to the kindergarten Curriculum Guide. More importantly, it should indicate how future teacher should be prepared to meet parents in a good way.

For teacher education institutions, beyond offering courses on home–school cooperation, it will be effective to integrate home–school partnership instruction and activities into field experiences, allowing preservice teachers to interact with parents. This will enhance their perceptions of comfort and competence in working with families (Morris & Taylor, 1998). In addition, teacher training in Hong Kong needs to focus on skills that enable educators to better communicate and work with parents from diverse backgrounds and address concerns about facilitating parents' all-round involvement (Lau & Ng, 2019). Moreover, teacher education programs need to educate teachers who are better prepared to work with busy parents, who represent the great majority of Hong Kong parents (Lau, Li, & Rao, 2011).

At a practical level, both government and kindergartens can take some measures. When it comes to the time constraints that are stopping parents from being involved in their children's ECE, government could subsidize employers to give parents of kindergartners at least a couple of hours or a half day off work to engage in kindergarten-based activities at least once a month. The existing community centers could also be employed to organize small-scale workshops and seminars for the neighborhood, so parents do not need to spend time traveling. Moreover, at least English translation if not translation to other languages should be provided if workshops or seminars are given in Cantonese. In addition, tailor-made workshops and seminars for parents of different ethnic groups in their language will be helpful for them. Although family background appears to be a powerful determinant of parental involvement, when an effort is made, most parents are found to have the potential to devote time and effort at home or in school (Ho, 2002).

The practice whereby different governmental departments, and especially the Education Bureau, offer workshops, seminars, and information on different websites about how to parent at home and cooperate with schools is good. Waanders, Mendez, and Downer (2007) found that parents who are confident in their ability to promote their children's academic achievement are more likely to have higher levels of home–school partnership than those who are not. However, some parents are voluntarily and/or involuntarily left out of attending the workshops and seminars because of either time constraints or language barriers. Since Hong Kong is increasingly becoming a diverse society, it would be ideal to provide information, workshops, and seminars in different languages. If this is impossible, English versions should be provided to reach more parents. In addition, some ethnic minorities are illiterate. As a result, oral presentations are important to them. The organizers of workshops and seminars should make good use of the Centre for Harmony and Enhancement of Ethnic Minority Residents (CHEER) to help with interpretation/translation services.

It is important that kindergartens serve as the meeting place for parents to share experiences and obtain support from other parents and professionals and provide opportunities for recently immigrated parents to become involved in their children's education. Kindergartens should make good use of CHEER to help facilitate NCS parents' communication with other parents and teachers. Beyond the implications for policymaking or policy modification, teacher education, and kindergarten practices, this analysis has laid a foundation for constructing a survey with closed and open-ended questions for further empirical research on what parents are involved in and how, as well as what they think of their involvement in their child's ECE in reality.

Notes

1 It was called the Education and Manpower Bureau before July 2007; it is now the Education Bureau.
2 The functions are direct quotes from the policies.

References

Census and Statistics Department. (2017). *2016 population by-census thematic report: Ethnic minorities.* Retrieved from www.censtatd.gov.hk/press_release/pressReleaseDetail.jsp?charsetID=1&pressRID=4354

Cheung, C. S. S., & Pomerantz, E. M. (2011). Parents' involvement in children's learning in the United States and China: Implications for children's academic and emotional adjustment. *Child Development, 82*(3), 932–950. doi:10.1111/j.1467-8624.2011.01582.x

Committee on Home – School Co-operation. (n.d.). *About CHSC.* Retrieved from https://chsc.hk/show_content.php?act_id=1&lang_id=1&c_id=1764&category_id=2

Desforges, C., & Abouchaar, A. (2003). *The impact of parental involvement, parental support and family education on pupil achievement and adjustment: A literature review.* London: Department for Education and Skills.

Edmondson, J. (2000). *America reads: A critical policy analysis.* Delaware, MD: International Reading Association; Chicago, IL: National Reading Conference.

Education and Manpower Bureau. (2003). *Harmonisation of pre-primary services.* Education and Manpower Bureau Circular No. 20/2003. Retrieved from www.edb.gov.hk/attachment/en/edu-system/preprimary-kindergarten/harmonisation-of-preprimary-services/background/embc03020e.pdf

Education Bureau. (2017a). *Kindergarten education curriculum guide: Joyful learning through play balanced development all the way.* Retrieved from www.edb.gov.hk/attachment/en/curriculum-development/major-level-of-edu/preprimary/ENG_KGECG_2017.pdf

Education Bureau. (2017b). *Performance indicators: Kindergarten.* Retrieved from www.edb.gov.hk/attachment/en/edu-system/preprimary-kindergarten/quality-assurance-framework/performance-indicators-pre-primary-institutions/PI_KG_EN.pdf

Education Bureau. (n.d.). *Kindergarten administration guide (version 1.0).* Retrieved from www.edb.gov.hk/attachment/en/edu-system/preprimary-kindergarten/free-quality-kg-edu/Admin%20Guide%20Chi%201718%201.0.pdf

Education Bureau & Social Welfare Department. (2019). *Operational manual for pre-primary institutions (version 2.0).* Retrieved from www.edb.gov.hk/attachment/en/edu-system/preprimary-kindergarten/overview/Operation_Manual_eng.pdf

Fan, X., & Chen, M. (2001). Parent involvement and students' academic achievement: A meta-analysis. *Educational Psychology Review, 13*(1), 1–22.

Hedegaard, M. (2009). Children's development from a cultural-historical approach: Children's activity in everyday local settings as foundation for their development. *Mind, Culture, and Activity, 16*(1), 64–82.

Ho, E. S. C. (1995). Parent involvement: A comparison of different definitions and explanations. *Education Journal, 23*, 39–68.

Ho, E. S. C. (2002). *Home-school-community collaboration: From theory, research to practices.* Hong Kong: The Chinese University Press.

Ho, E. S. C. (2003). Students' self-esteem in an Asian educational system: Contribution of parental involvement and parental investment. *The School Community Journal, 13*(1), 65–84.

Ho, E. S. C., & Kwong, W. (2013). *Parental involvement on children's education: What works in Hong Kong.* Springer Briefs in Education. Singapore: Springer.

Hong Kong Council of Social Service. (2010). *Parent involvement for children's educational advancement a comparison between the Chinese and the ethnic minority parents in Hong Kong research report.* Retrieved from www.hkcss.org.hk/uploadfileMgnt/0_2014612145312.pdf

Lam, C. C., Ho, E. S. C., & Wong, N. Y. (2002). Parents' beliefs and practices in education in Confucian heritage cultures: The Hong Kong case. *Journal of Southeast Asian Education, 3*(1), 99–114.

Lau, E. Y. H. (2014). Chinese parents' perceptions and practices of parental involvement during school transition. *Early Child Development and Care, 184*(3), 403–415. doi:10.1080/03004430.2013.792258

Lau, E. Y. H., & Li, H. (2011). An overview of research on parental involvement in early childhood education and its implication. *Hong Kong Journal of Early Childhood, 10*(2), 31–37.

Lau, E. Y. H., Li, H., & Rao, N. (2011). Parental involvement and children's readiness for school in China. *Educational Research, 53*(1), 95–113. doi:10.1080/00131881.2011.552243

Lau, E. Y. H., & Ng, M. L. (2019). Are they ready for home-school partnership? Perspectives of kindergarten principals, teachers and parents. *Children and Youth Services Review, 99*, 10–17. doi:10.1016/j.childyouth.2019.01.019

Lau, E. Y. H., & Rao, N. (2012). Exploring parental involvement in early years education in China: Development and validation of the Chinese early parental involvement scale (CEPIS). *International Journal of Early Years Education, 20*(4), 405–421.

Morris, V. G., & Taylor, S. I. (1998). Alleviating barriers to family involvement in education: The role of teacher education. *Teaching and Teacher Education, 14*(2), 219–231.

Ng, S. W. (2007). The chronological development of parent empowerment in children's education in Hong Kong. *Asia Pacific Education Review, 8*(3), 487–499.

Ng, S. W. (2017). The evolving roles of parents in the process of developing home-school relationships in Hong Kong: Issues and challenges. In T. Tse & M. Lee (Eds.), *Making sense of education in post-handover Hong Kong: Achievements and challenges* (pp. 180–198). London: Routledge.

Ng, S. W., & Yuen, W. K. G. (2015). The micro-politics of parental involvement in school education in Hong Kong: Ethnocentrism, utilitarianism or policy rhetoric! *Educational Review, 67*(2), 253–271. doi:10.1080/00131911.2013.868786

Pang, I. W. (2011). Home-school cooperation in the changing context: An ecological approach. *The Asia-Pacific Education Researcher, 20*(1), 1–16.

Phillipson, S., & Phillipson, S. N. (2010). The involvement of Hong Kong parents in the education of their children: A validation of the parents' attributions and perception questionnaire. *Educational Psychology, 30*(6), 625–649. doi:10.1080/01443410.2010.496900

Research Office Legislative Council Secretariat. (2019). *Statistical highlights: Pre-primary education in Hong Kong.* Retrieved from www.legco.gov.hk/research-publications/english/1718issh33-pre-primary-education-in-hong-kong-20180628-e.pdf

Tao, S. S., Lau, E. Y. H., & You, H. M. (2019). Parental involvement after the transition to school: Are parents' expectations matched by experience? *Journal of Research in Childhood Education, 33*(4), 637–653. doi:10.1080/02568543.2019.1653409

Waanders, C., Mendez, J. L., & Downer, J. T. (2007). Parent characteristics, economic stress, and neighborhood context as predictors of parent involvement in preschool children's education. *Journal of School Psychology, 45*(6), 619–636. doi: 10.1016/j.jsp.2007.07.003

Young, M. D. (1999). Multifocal educational policy research: Toward a method for enhancing traditional educational policy studies. *American Educational Research Journal, 36*, 677–714.

Zhang, Y., & Wildemuth, B. M. (2009). Qualitative analysis of content. In B. Wildemuth (Ed.), *Applications of social research methods to questions in information and library science* (pp. 308–319). Westport, CT: Greenwood Publishing Group.

12
FROM INSTITUTIONAL DOMINANCE TO PARENTAL INVOLVEMENT

Models of working with families in Hungarian Kindergartens

Anikó Varga Nagy, Sándor Pálfi and Eleonora Teszenyi

Introduction

In many 'first world', industrialised countries, there is a curricular and legislative expectation that professionals in early childhood settings work together with families in the care and education of young children. This collaboration reflects the cultural, social, economic and political circumstances of each country. This is no different in Hungary. The majority of early childhood education and care (ECEC) takes place in state-funded kindergartens for children between the ages of three and six and is compulsory from the age of three (Ministry of Human Resources, 2011). This directly influences how relationships between kindergartens and families develop. Although fee paying private provision is starting to gain impetus, parents, on the whole, are not seen as consumers, who pay for a service, but stakeholders who have a vested interest in shared governance through developing reciprocal relationships with ECEC institutions: families influence how their children's kindergarten operates and the kindergarten influences the lives of its families. (When using the term parents throughout this chapter, we are referring to both biological parents and any other primary care givers.)

This chapter will discuss:

- the legislative requirements and theoretical background that frame the work between kindergartens and families,
- the paradigmatic shift between practice during the socialist regime and today,
- five distinct models of ECEC institutions engaging with families,
- how parental involvement is addressed as part of the kindergarten pedagogue training programmes.

The chapter concludes with identifying some directions of travel in strengthening relationships with all families and developing ways of working towards partnership, rather than involvement.

DOI: 10.4324/9780367823917-12

The legislative and theoretical frame for parental involvement in Hungary

In Hungary, the National Public Education Act (Ministry of Human Resources, 2011) lays down the operational principles and legislative requirements for educational and care practices in all state-funded and state-run institutions from kindergartens to secondary schools. Article 3, paragraph 1 states that at the centre of public education are the children, pupils and students, pedagogues and parents, whose rights and responsibilities 'form a coherent unit' (p. 2). (The term 'pedagogue' is used as a collective terminology throughout for primary and secondary school teachers and kindergarten pedagogues or early childhood educators, as they may be known more widely.) Parents and educational institutions share the responsibility for the care and education of children. The foundation of this shared responsibility and its activities are 'trust and the professional credibility and integrity of the pedagogues and the institutions' (Ministry of Human Resources, 2011, pp. 2–3, paragraph 2). This legislation is predicated on the idea that the partners in their shared roles respect one another and the child's progress is also seen as a shared achievement.

The legislative framework for kindergarten education and care is outlined in the Hungarian government's decree, the National Core Programme for Kindergarten Education (Ministry of Human Resources, 2018). The Core Programme identifies three fundamental roles that kindergartens fulfil: the protection and safeguarding of children, a nurturing role that enables the development of children's personality and supporting children's social development through the various processes of socialisation. While each kindergarten adheres to its principles and requirements, they are also expected to personalise the Core Programme by writing their own pedagogical programmes to suit their local cultural contexts. Alternatively, kindergartens can apply and adopt a programme that is already designed and available, for example, the Complex Preventative, Montessori or Play-Movement-Communication Programmes (Molnár, Pálfi, Szerepi, & Varga Nagy, 2015). Interestingly, out of all the readily available early childhood programmes, it is only the 'Step-by-Step' kindergarten programme that puts parent partnership in the centre of its pedagogical design (Deliné, 1997).

Beyond the relevant articles of the National Public Education Act (Ministry of Human Resources, 2011) discussed earlier, more detail on the expectations of engaging with families is provided in the various sections of the Core Programme. In the 'introduction' one of its core principles is outlined: the care and education of children is the prime responsibility of the parents (Ministry of Human Resources, 2018). In the implementation of this principle, the cornerstone of engagement is the respect for human rights and the rights of all children (Pálfi, Rákó, Varga Nagy, & Teszenyi, 2019).

In the 'image of the child' section of the Core Programme (Ministry of Human Resources, 2018), it is emphasised that the 'development of the personality of the child' (p. 2) is to be supported by a child-centred and inclusive approach. This inclusivity ensures that children are accepted and valued for who they are, together with what they bring from their home environment. Pedagogues are expected to take into consideration the various forms of parenting children experience and how this influences the development of their personality traits. By keeping their own approaches consistent with family practices, pedagogues are to ensure continuity for children between the institution and home. It is widely a parental expectation that pedagogues take on the role of a parent while their children are in institutional care. This includes adopting the sensitive, caring behaviours of parents and also ensuring the continuity of love expressed towards the child, which provide both physical and emotional security for young children (Bakonyi & Szabadi, 1971; Antal & Zsubrits, 2015).

The section on the 'image of the kindergarten' outlines the foundations on which the relationship between the institution and the families is built: families have priority in their children's lives and the 'institution plays a *complementary* role in caring for and educating young children from the age of three until they start school' (Ministry of Human Resources, 2018, p. 2). It is made very clear that kindergarten pedagogues must take account of children's prior experiences. Young children's curiosities, interests and motivations first develop within a family context and as they enter an institution, their world expands. Kindergarten provision must build on the child's sensitivities and openness to the outside world so that their attachment to their families and to their own country along with their developing sense of social responsibility can be nurtured. These attachments will influence how they navigate and find their place in the wider world later in their lives.

In the 'resource implications' section of the Core Programme (Ministry of Human Resources, 2018) the expectations are set for a pleasant working environment for kindergarten pedagogues as well as an appropriate space for parents, where they can talk privately with the pedagogues about their children. The significance of effective relationships and shared engagement between the institution and families is also emphasised. It is only with families that the Ministry of Human Resources (2018) expects kindergartens to develop these high intensity relationships. Ways to develop and nurture relationships are not specified in the Core Programme; instead, kindergartens and the families are encouraged to develop these together.

Over the past 15 years, there have been several studies examining the relationship and its effectiveness between families and institutions (Christenson & Reschly, 2009; Roffey, 2012; Cottle & Alexander, 2014; Goodall & Montgomery, 2014; Daniel, 2015; Grundmeyer & Yankey, 2016; Murray et al., 2018) and these provide some theoretical framing for working with families in Hungary, too. Studies in school contexts are numerous (Imre, 2019; Podráczky, 2012); however, there is a paucity of research on parental involvement in the kindergarten context. Instead, some discussion papers are available to provide examples of what might be considered as 'good practice' (Varga Nagy, 2017, 2018). Although useful, these are not backed up by empirical evidence.

Studies on parental motivation for choosing a particular kindergarten highlight a number of factors that influence decision-making. Török's (2004) survey is significant in that it is the first large-scale study after the fall of the socialist regime in 1989 that consults with parents. After the end of the Soviet dominance, in the mid-80s to early 90s, the government's attention turned to early childhood care and education and the first national kindergarten curriculum was introduced in 1996. This also coincided with parents being given their rights to choose early childhood provision for their children. Török (2004) found that parents selected kindergartens based on their geographical location and on how much they liked the kindergarten pedagogue who would be looking after their children. This is echoed in a small-scale study a decade later by Teszenyi and Hevey (2015), who additionally found that kindergarten's local pedagogical programmes, reputation and recommendation were also key decision-making drivers. Examining the reasons why parents might choose a kindergarten for their children, Szilágyiné Szemkeő (2008) in her research identified (i) security, (ii) love expressed for the children, (iii) views of other parents, (iv) the physical environment and (v) consistency of morals and values between the home and the institution as most influential in their decision-making. Jaskóné Gácsi and Stóka's (2014) study focuses on parental expectations of kindergartens and their findings confirm that for 42% of the parents the security of their children is the priority. Beyond this, parents want friendly, harmonious, family-like environments. Twenty-six per cent of parents have the expectation that their children can play freely in the kindergarten and that their social and emotional development is supported. According to Campbell-Barr, Georgeson, and Varga (2015), Hungarian kindergarten provision is characterised by unstructured play, unconditional love and child-centredness. What is highlighted in the findings of the studies outlined earlier is that 'the personal' matters to parents when it comes to institutional care for their children. This includes what pedagogues personally can offer their children and the environment this care takes place in. It could be argued that positive relationships between pedagogues and families, and attachments between children and their pedagogues lay the foundations for co-operation and parental involvement in early childhood care and education institutions in Hungary.

These secure foundations could make way for innovative practices in the way institutions engage with their families. Török (2005) claims that parents' contributions can potentially enrich the work and life of an institution and he argues that there is a need for more family-friendly events and programmes and for a kindergarten to become the hub of its local community. He also warns that with school readiness on the parents' (and the government's) agenda, kindergartens can potentially be under significant pressure to prioritise preparation for school in their education provision. This, in turn, can alter the power balance between the institution and families. Murray et al.'s (2018) comparative tri-national study confirms that the schoolification agenda influences the relationship and the nature of parental involvement in ECEC settings, but they also acknowledge that institutions in Hungary are beginning to take the needs of families into consideration as they are making attempts to forge more equal relationships. This shift in their approach is significant when considered in the context of the country's socio-political heritage. This is explored in more detail in the subsequent section.

The paradigmatic shift between practice during the socialist regime and today

Working with families has been significantly influenced by the changing political landscape in Hungary and it has undergone a significant paradigm shift after the fall of the dictatorship in the 1990s. Parental involvement remains a critical contemporary issue, and this section outlines the changes in approaches and thinking that Hungarian kindergartens have experienced as the political system gradually moved from socialism to market economy.

Educating and re-educating parents was an expectation of educational institutions in the politically charged climate of the Soviet domination. Its aim was to reinforce the 'socialist man ideal' and for everyone to achieve it. A child was desired to acquire a socialist personality where individualism was to be tamed and 'made able to serve the community's needs' (Millei, 2011, p. 42). As an educational institution, a kindergarten was positioned as powerful in its relationship with parents (Földesi, 1957). One of the training handbooks used at the time asserted that families should not educate children for the moment but for the future. They were to educate their children to become a well-rounded future citizen of the society of the time, who would live for the collective (Millei, 2011). Families were urged to recognise that an egocentric person, the product of an individualistic upbringing typical of a capitalist society, could not find happiness in a socialist society. Parents were helpless in the face of an institution that was regarded as superior and dictated what would happen. They only gained entry to an institution on special occasions (formal parents' evening, celebratory events), had no access to their children's classroom and often only managed a brief exchange with a pedagogue about their children along the corridors.

In the transitional period, during the 1990s, an interesting phenomenon appeared: scarred by the dictatorial approach kindergartens had employed, parents tried to take back full control for their children's lives while in the care of a kindergarten. Small groups of parents in many kindergartens across the country engaged in extreme compensatory behaviour for the loss of their authority over their child and dictated to pedagogues what they could and could not do with their children (whether they can take their children outside or not, how long their children could sleep, etc.). At the end of each day, these parents checked what exactly happened and held pedagogues accountable for their actions. This reversal of roles saw parents acting in the same authoritarian way as kindergartens had previously done so. As a result, some kindergartens had lost some confidence in their pedagogic approach and were steered towards meeting parental wishes more than the needs of children in their care.

In the past 25 years, policy makers have made conscious efforts to introduce legislation that enables trust to be re-established between families and institutions. This required a complete re-tune of attitude from both parties. In today's practice, the shift in thinking and approaches to involve parents in their children's early learning is particularly noticeable. The individual needs of families are gradually gaining more attention and institutions have adopted a more family-friendly approach, where not only the parents but also the whole family are invited to get involved. Parents and pedagogues together are involved in the care and education of children and the institutions' holistic approach considers the child, first and foremost, in the context of his family. Support offered to parents is more aligned with the preferences and wishes of families and parents are no longer viewed as 'outsiders' looking in, but 'insiders' taking part in the life of a kindergarten.

One of the benefits of this paradigm shift for the children is better co-ordinated, better attuned processes of socialisation, which can potentially avoid any conflict (and its negative impact) between the families and the institution. Fundamental to working with families effectively is the kindergarten's desire to learn about the cultural practices of each family, which may differ from accepted societal norms. Kindergartens, as educational institutions, are well placed to strengthen and develop communities and to become the cultural hub for their localities (particularly in cases where there are no other establishment to fulfil this role). Pedagogues' inclusive approach must ensure that they accept and value difference (unlike the socialist approach that expected everyone to be the same) and enable local traditions to flourish and a strong sense of belonging to develop (Varga Nagy & Molnár, 2019).

Five distinct models of working with families

More parent-friendly, family-centred approaches are becoming widespread across the public education sector in Hungary. There is greater focus on the individual needs of families, and institutions seek to find innovative ways of engaging parents in many aspects of the life of a kindergarten (Korintus, Villányi, Mátay, & Badics, 2004). The various forms of parental involvement practice currently reflect both the post-Soviet heritage, which is formal and authoritarian, and some more modern, somewhat innovative approaches. The five models of parental involvement presented later describe established current kindergarten practices. Brief explanations of the experiences of parents, children and kindergarten pedagogues are provided for each of the five models listed in Table 12.1.

The first model 'Parents and Spectators' harps back to the power dynamics of the socialist times, and parents are passive recipients of all interaction (Silova, Piattoeva, & Millei, 2018). Practice represented by this model typically invites families into the kindergarten where children are put 'on display'; they give a well-rehearsed performance that showcases their skills. These high-stake events encourage competition, and evidence 'child-centredness' profoundly misinterpreted: the child IS in the centre but under duress. It raises serious questions about respect for the rights of the child as outlined in the UNCRC (Pálfi et al., 2019).

In the second model, 'Parents as Organisers', the baton is handed to parents to organise institution-wide events to involve all families (i.e., charity ball, International Children's Day). These parents also want to impress, and they draw heavily on the generosity of families to support the planned event (with donations of raffle prizes, cakes and their time). The aim of these events is often to nurture local or

TABLE 12.1 Outline of the five parent involvement models.

INVOLVEMENT MODEL	PARENT'S experience	CHILD's experience	KINDERGARTEN PEDAGOGUE's experience
1. **Parents as Spectators**	Invited as guests to watch their children's performance; Use this as an opportunity to check their child's progress against peers and form an opinion on the quality of the pedagogues' work; End of year, leavers' celebratory events, children's performances at government or local authority events are very significant in a family's life;	The feeling of being on display; Pressure and expectation to perform well to an audience; Sense of competition between groups and individual children; No choice, compliance expected;	Bearing the responsibility of organising a high-stake event on the basis of which they will be judged; Institution wide events generate comparison between groups; Misinterpreted child centredness: children are the centre of attention, but events follow the adult's agenda;
2. **Parents as Organisers of Events**	Responsibility for organising an institution-wide event; Allocate tasks in the preparation and the management of the event on the day; Contribute with resources; financially support the event;	The sense of being entertained by a spectacular, theatrical event; Take part in activities in an orderly manner (they cannot spoil a carefully planned event that runs to an agreed script); These events are meant for the children, it is meant to serve their needs.	Working together with a small executive parent group; Aim to 'dazzle' the families attending the event to make a good impression; Use the events to nurture folk and local tradition; Has the intention of strengthening the local community;

INVOLVEMENT MODEL	PARENT'S experience	CHILD's experience	KINDERGARTEN PEDAGOGUE's experience
3. **Parents as Volunteer Labourers**	Willingness to improve their child's wellbeing in an improved environment; Volunteers own labour (often using specialist skill) to contribute to the maintenance of the kindergarten; Models community engagement to children;	Improved, aesthetically more pleasing environment, safer equipment; Greater range of resources;	Identify jobs to be done and put out call to parents and the local community; Ensure safety of equipment and environment for children; Improved relationship with volunteering parents, gratitude for contributions;
4. **Nurturing & Educating Parents**	Greater sense of trust towards pedagogues; A possible sense of inadequacy; Better informed of child related issues; Enhanced parenting skills; Improved personal support network;	Experience of better parenting; Primary care giver's improved relationship with the pedagogue strengthens the child's secondary attachments; Greater emotional security; Sense of continuity of care;	More in-depth knowledge and greater understanding of parents' circumstances; Advice tailored to individual needs to fill gaps in parenting skills; Greater sense of working towards a shared aim; Organising information events for parents on topics of child health, psychology, nutrition . . . etc. with the intention of educating parents;

(Continued)

TABLE 12.1 (Continued)

INVOLVEMENT MODEL	PARENT'S experience	CHILD's experience	KINDERGARTEN PEDAGOGUE's experience
5. **Active Involvement**	Greater level of interest and opportunities for participation in the child's learning; A sense of commitment to enhancing children's curriculum experiences; Greater understanding of the institution's value systems; The joy of sharing skills, talent and experiences;	Positive sense of shared experience through the presence of parents/grandparents (intergenerational activities); Greater variety in learning experiences, broadened perspectives; Enriched curriculum that is culturally relevant to the child;	Conscious efforts to involve families in their child's learning, facilitating inter-generational events; Planning and organising for regular parent involvement; Enhanced breadth of curriculum; Unique opportunities to gain insights to family practices, skills and competences of parents;

folk tradition, to bring seasonal festivals to the kindergarten (i.e., Harvest Festival, Advent, Sports Day) or to engage families in sport or leisure activities (Bakonyi & Karczewicz, 2016). Although these events are meant to serve the children's needs, this involvement model is again adult centred.

The roots of 'Parents as Volunteer Labourers' model go back to the 'Communist Saturdays' of the Soviet times, where parents contributed to the upkeep of local parks, walkways and public spaces (today this is largely fulfilled by people on community service). The economic reason for kindergartens to involve families in this volunteering capacity is the shortage in central funding (Pálfi, 2006). In the interest of safety and aesthetic appeal, kindergartens have to rely on the generosity of parents who are willing to offer their skills and some materials (i.e., painting, decorating rooms, making furniture) to maintain play equipment and the physical environment.

The fourth model demonstrates kindergartens' attempts to involve parents through nurturing and educating them. The aim of this is two-fold: to provide personalised parenting support to individual parents (Miller, 2010), and to inform parents of child-related issues, such as health, nutrition, development or child psychology. While the former could be seen as sensitive support, the latter reflects the idea that kindergartens feel that parents need to be educated. The topic of information events, and which expert is invited to give a talk, is determined by the kindergarten based on what they judge as most important for parents to know.

The fifth, 'Active Involvement' model represents practice where kindergarten pedagogues make conscious efforts to involve families in their children's learning. The physical presence of parents within an institution strengthens the idea that families and kindergartens share an aim in working together in the interest of children's wellbeing and progress (Varga Nagy & Molnár, 2019). While pedagogues regard the activities they plan for children pedagogically superior, they also see the value in what parents and grandparents add to the curriculum to enhance their children's and grandchildren's learning (Sykes, 2018). These could be, for example, cooking, bread, jam or lace making, weaving or caring for animals. Parental contributions are planned into daily activities on a regular basis (typically once a month) and, parents getting involved together with their children serves as a positive model for the future promoting sustainability (Varga Nagy et al., 2017).

Although not exhaustive, these five models capture the currently existing and most dominant involvement patterns between early childhood institutions and families in Hungary. The models may be seen to potentially serve as a tool for reflection and self-evaluation that could feed into individual kindergarten's cycle of developmental and action planning.

During the transitional period after the collapse of the Soviet regime, any attempt to innovate in engaging with families appeared hesitant, because, at the time, it lacked pedagogical backing from the government and the kindergartens themselves. Much has changed since then; however escaping the deeply engrained political heritage is difficult. In practice, kindergartens may employ more than one model to involve their families depending on the purpose of the engagement. What the five models given earlier suggest is that, whichever ways kindergartens choose to engage with families, their aim appears to be to assert their own values in their engagement with families and to determine the way in which families may contribute to the life of the kindergarten (or indeed their children's lives at kindergarten). True reciprocity in their relationship remains questionable and the direction of involvement is still dominated by the institution.

Working with families from disadvantaged backgrounds

Compulsory kindergarten attendance age was reduced from five to three in September 2015 (Ministry of Human Resources, 2012) for reasons of early intervention and with the aim to provide equal opportunities for all children, particularly for those from disadvantaged backgrounds and living in extreme poverty. Bognár (2016) defines 'disadvantage' as families having low-economic status as a result of limited access to paid work.

As a result of this new legislation, 95% of three-year-olds access kindergarten provision in Hungary which meets the European Union target of 95% of four-year-olds to attend kindergarten by 2020 (Széll, 2014). Early intervention is to provide appropriate support for the youngest of children at an early age to minimise the effects of socio-economic deprivation. With support, they settle into kindergartens, develop the skills and competencies that are essential for successful completion of compulsory education. The aim is to reduce drop-out rates for primary-aged children (6–14), which currently stand at 11% (Varga Nagy & Molnár, 2019; Bognár, 2016).

As mentioned earlier, the Core Programme stipulates that pedagogues adjust their approaches to individual families' ways of life, their customs and habits, which is particularly important with families of low socio-economic status. To be able to offer sensitive and relevant pedagogic support, kindergarten pedagogues need to find out about the circumstances and prior experiences of these families and work with the specificities of children's everyday experiences (Lazzari, Vandenbroeck, & Peeters, 2013). Some parents may find it more difficult to engage because they themselves had never accessed kindergarten provision or maybe their experience was negative or traumatic. Others may feel inferior compared to other parents and feel relegated or relegate themselves to the periphery of all kindergarten action. Whatever the reason may be, it is the pedagogues' responsibility to find the right approach to communicate and engage with these parents. Parental involvement may take a different shape from what was described in the five models earlier. There have been examples of tapping into specific and sometimes specialised skills of parents from ethnic minority or low socio-economic status (Rákó, 2014). Parents can be invited to teach young children their craft, such as basket weaving, carving wooden utensils or teaching children their traditional folk songs. Being involved in the kindergarten's life in the presence of their own children has the potential to help those low status children being accepted by their peer groups. Organised kindergarten-wide family events can also serve to involve and educate low socio-economic status families: to help them appreciate quality time spent together and to understand the value of shared experiences that strengthen bonds between parents and children. These events can also improve community cohesion.

Since September 2018 social co-workers have been appointed by Family Support and Child Welfare Centres to support kindergartens in their work with families from disadvantaged backgrounds, which brings a new perspective to developing relationships between institutions and families. The social co-workers are fully embedded in the daily life of a kindergarten. They take part in events organised by the institution for families, carrying out safeguarding duties, and they also work with parents both on an individual basis and in groups to provide advice and support, for example, on child rearing or overcoming difficulties within the family. They are supported in their role by the kindergarten's nominated social work co-ordinator (Department of Social and Child Welfare Services, 2018).

Pre-service training for working with families

In an increasingly diverse and fast changing society, good workforce preparation is critical to meet the challenges of effective partnership working with families. Although in many countries in Europe the qualification level of early childhood educators is under level six (OECD, 2006), in Hungary kindergarten pedagogue training is at bachelor level. In preparation for working with parents, during the three-year programme trainees develop theoretical understanding of what impact a child's socio-cultural background has on the learning and teaching processes: they learn to identify key components of disadvantage and compensatory measures. Trainees are introduced to the legislative framework for safeguarding, and gain knowledge of early intervention programmes and support available to families within the various systems. Among the key pedagogical competences in relation to working with families are: effective communication and co-operation with families, relevant professionals and agencies, respectful and unbiased relationships between the family and institution, professional conduct with children and families, keeping abreast with research in family pedagogy, and innovative ways of engaging with parents.

Developing skills to work with families is also part of the trainees' practice during the final eight to ten-week placement. They need to demonstrate their abilities to work co-operatively with parents and families as this forms part of their final practical assessment. During short placements (two weeks in each semester of an academic year) the focus is on applying pedagogical theory to practice that focuses on engaging with children, not their parents. Creating more opportunities to engage with parents in real-life contexts is an area for development for the placement programme designed for trainee pedagogues.

Bachelor-level pre-service training is in line with the wide reaching aim to professionalize the workforce (Oberhuemer, 2005). However, these processes of professionalization would ideally extend to in-service training so that parental partnership could be included in continuous professional development programmes for those pedagogues who are already working in ECEC institutions.

Conclusions and ways forward

Because early childhood care and education is considered a sociological, rather than a political issue in Hungary, the role of parents in their child's kindergarten life is less of a focus for education policy (Török, 2005). We started this chapter by stating that in state-funded ECEC provision, parents are not viewed as service users. However, the image of kindergartens as service providers, developed in the 1990s, seems to persist, which places obstacles in the way of significant development in how kindergartens work with families. Currently, institutional, rather than parental initiation, dominates as evidenced in the five models of involvement, and this continues to reflect the power imbalance between parents and kindergartens. Practice in Hungary moved from institutional dominance in the Soviet times to the power balance changing in favour of parents through the appearance of service provider approach in the transitional period. What is missing today is an approach that strikes a balance between the two and equalises parent-pedagogue partnerships. The five models outlined in this chapter reflect 'involvement' between kindergartens and families: involvement, that is rooted in a compensatory approach, where pedagogues make up for what might be considered as deficit in children's home education provided by their parents. Therefore, the priority in Hungary is to work towards a partnership model, where both partners feel empowered and privileged to work together in their children's care, nurture and education in these formative years. There is a need to redefine 'partnership' and for pedagogues and parents to develop a shared sense and understanding of what this way of working means.

The Ministry of Human Resources (2012) affords kindergartens a high degree of autonomy in Hungary; therefore, the Core Programme provides the legislative underpinning for such developments to take place. A new model would need to reflect forms of collaboration that best suits the needs of local cultures and circumstances and is most supportive of both families and pedagogues (Kovács, 2015). The developmental trajectory for Hungary is to explore ways of transforming the involvement model(s) into a partnership model, where true reciprocity between families and institutions is established. Pedagogues need to develop sensitivities towards parent initiation rather than responding or reacting to what they may regard as parental need. Kindergartens need to keep the child's interests at the centre of their work, have realistic expectations of parents and consider their starting points for collaboration so that they can move forward together in an enabling manner. There will be challenges along the way but the benefits for all stakeholders involved would be a worthwhile investment for the future.

References

Antal, B., & Zsubrits, A. (2015). Az óvodapedagógus gyermekszemmel [The kindergarten pedagogue through the eyes of a child]. *Óvodai Nevelés, 4,* 16–19.

Bakonyi, A., & Karczewicz, Á. (2016). Szülők és óvodapedagógusok együttműködése [Co-operation between parents and kindergarten pedagogues]. In *Az óvodapedagógusok nagykönyve [Kindergarten pedagogues' handbook]* (pp. 203–229). Budapest: Neteducatio.

Bakonyi, P., & Szabadi, I. (1971). *Az óvodai nevelés programja [The care and education programme of kindergartens].* Budapest: Tankönyvkiadó.

Bognár, M. (2016). *Combating dropout: The state and potential of second chance schools in Hungary.* Retrieved from https://fszk.hu/wp-content/uploads/2016/04/Dropout_in_HU_en.pdf

Campbell-Barr, V., Georgeson, J., & Varga, A. N. (2015). Developing professional early childhood educators in England and Hungary: Where has all the love gone? *European Education, 47*(4), 311–330. doi:10.1080/10564934.2015.1100451

Christenson, S., & Reschly, A. L. (2009). *Handbook of school-family partnerships.* London: Routledge.

Cottle, M., & Alexander, E. (2014). Parent partnership and "quality" early years services: Practitioners' perspectives. *European Early Childhood Education Research Journal, 22*(5), 637–659. doi:10.1080/1350293X.2013.788314

Daniel, G. (2015). Patterns of parent involvement: A longitudinal analysis of family – school partnerships in the early years of school in Australia. *Australasian Journal of Early Childhood, 40*(1), 119–128. doi:10.1177/183693911504000115

Deliné, F. K. (1997). Lépésről lépésre óvodafejlesztő program. *Hajdúböszörmény, Családok bevonása az óvodai életbe*, 183–214.

Department of Social and Child Welfare Services. (2018). *Szakmai ajánlás az óvodai és iskolai szociális segítő tevékenység bevezetéséhez* [*Recommendations for the introduction of social support activities in kindergartens and primary school*]. New Delhi: Ministry of Human Resources.

Földesi, K. (1957). *Nevelő munka az óvodában* [*Care and education in kindergartens*]. Budapest: Tankönyvkiadó Vállalat.

Goodall, J., & Montgomery, C. (2014). Parental involvement to parental engagement: A continuum. *Educational Review, 66*(4). Retrieved from https://www-tandfonline-com.libezproxy.open.ac.uk/doi/full/10.1080/00131911.2013.781576

Grundmeyer, T., & Yankey, J. (2016). Revitalizing the school-parent partnership: A participatory action research study using virtual parent-teacher conferences. *The International Journal of Learning: Annual Review, 23*(1), 1–13. doi:10.18848/1447-9494/CGP/1-13

Imre, N. (2019). *Az iskola és a szülő közötti együttműködés lehetőségei*. Retrieved from https://ofi.hu/publikacio/az-iskola-es-szulo-kozotti-egyuttmukodes-lehetosegei

Jaskóné Gácsi, M., & Stóka, G. (2014). Mit várnak el a szülők az óvodától? [What do parents expect from kindergartens?]. *Módszertani Közlemények, LIV*(2), 1–14.

Korintus, M., Villányi, G., Mátay, K., & Badics, T. (2004). *Gyermekeink gondozása és nevelése* [*The care and nurture of our children*]. Corvinus Kiadó. Retrieved from www.google.com/search?q=Gyermekeink+gondoz%C3%A1sa+%C3%A9s+nevel%C3%A9se+2%C3%B6%C3%B64&rlz=1C1GCEV_enGB865GB865&tbm=isch&source=iu&ictx=1&fir=-PLGcYAsZSNDiGM%253A%252CFlnerLP8keHr6M%252C_&vet=1&usg=AI4_-kQIvUoSXxLqclKjmHvCfl60V3BTtA&sa=X&ved=2ahUKEwjY_sS54IrmAhWKUBUIHYQWBmwQ9QEwBHoECAoQCQ#imgrc=PLGcYAsZSNDiGM:

Kovács, E. (2011. *"Legyen jobb a gyerekeknek!" Biztos Kezdet Programok alapelvei. ["Doing It Better For The Children!" The Basic Principles of the Sure Start Programme]In: Labáth Ferencné (editor)Hátrányos helyzetű 3-7 éves korú gyermekek integrált óvodai nevelése. A Biztos Kezdet Óvodai program háttértanulmányai 1*. Budapest: Educatio Ltd.

Lazzari, A., Vandenbroeck, M., & Peeters, J. (2013, July 10). *The early years workforce: A review of European research and good practices on working with children from poor and migrant families*. Background Paper. New York: Transatlantic Forum on Inclusive Early Years.

Millei, Z. (2011). Governing through early childhood curriculum, "the child", and "community": Ideologies of socialist Hungary and neoliberal Australia. *European Education, 43*(1), 33–55. doi:10.2753/EUE1056-4934430103

Miller, S. (2010). *Supporting parents: Improving outcomes for children, families and communities*. London: McGraw-Hill Education.

Ministry of Human Resources. (2011). *2011. Évi CXC törvény a nemzeti köznevelésről* [*National public education act, 2011, XCX*]. Washington, DC: Author.

Ministry of Human Resources. (2012). *Act CXC of 2011 on public education, paragraph 8*. Retrieved from https://eacea.ec.europa.eu/national-policies/eurydice/content/legislation-29_en

Ministry of Human Resources. (2018). *Government decree on the national core programme for kindergarten education*. Budapest: Author.

Molnár, B., Pálfi, S., Szerepi, S., & Varga Nagy, A. (2015). Kisgyermekkori nevelés Magyarországon [Early childhood education in Hungary]. *Educatio, 3*, 121–128.

Murray, J., Teszenyi, E., Varga, A. N., Pálfi, S., Tajiyeva, M., & Iskakova, A. (2018). Parent-practitioner partnerships in early childhood provision in England, Hungary and Kazakhstan: Similarities and differences in discourses. *Early Child Development and Care, 188*(5), 594–612. doi:10.1080/03004430.2018.1438422

Oberhuemer, P. (2005). Conceptualising the early childhood pedagogue: Policy approaches and issues of professionalism. *European Early Childhood Education Research Journal, 13*(1), 5–16. doi:10.1080/13502930585209521

OECD. (2006). *Starting strong II: Early childhood education and care.* Paris: OECD. doi:10.1787/9789264035461-en

Pálfi, S. (2006). A globalizáció hatása a Magyar óvodákra [The effect of globalization on Hungarina kindergartens.]. In *Globalizációs ismeretek.* Hajdúböszörmény: Galenos Alapitvany.

Pálfi, S., Rákó, E., Varga Nagy, A., & Teszenyi, E. (2019). Children's rights in Hungary in early childhood education and care. In *The Routledge international handbook of young children's rights* (pp. 354–365). London: Routledge.

Podráczky, J. (Ed.). (2012). *Szövetségben: Tanulmányok a család és az intézményes nevelés kapcsolatáról.* Budapest: ELTE Eötvös Kiadó.

Rákó, E. (2014). Egy hátránykezelő óvodai program tapasztalatai [Experiences of a kindergarten programme addressing disadvantage]. *Szociálpedagógia [Social Pedagogy], 1*(2), 5–10.

Roffey, S. (2012). *School behaviour and families: Frameworks for working together.* London: Routledge.

Silova, I., Piattoeva, N., & Millei, Z. (Eds.). (2018). *Childhood and schooling in (post)socialist societies: Memories of everyday life* (1st ed.). Cham: Palgrave Macmillan.

Sykes, G. (2018). Intergenerational communities: The young and the old together. In *Young children and their communities: Understanding collective social responsibility* (pp. 70–85). London: Routledge.

Széll, K. (2014). *Az OECD az oktatásról – adatok, elemzések, értelmezések [The OECD about education – Data, analysis and interpretation]* (Körképek Az Oktatásról, pp. 1–96). Budapest: Oktatáskutató és Fejlesztő Intézet.

Szilágyiné Szemkeő, J. (2008). Óvodások és kisiskolások szüleinek intézményválasztási motivációi [Parental motivation for choosing kindergartens and lower primary schools]. *Új Pedagógia Szemle, 2.*

Teszenyi, E., & Hevey, D. (2015). Age group, location or pedagogue: Factors affecting parental choice of kindergartens in Hungary. *Early Child Development and Care, 185*(11–12), 1961–1977. doi:10.1080/03004430.2015.1028391

Török, B. (2004). *A gyermeküket óvodáztató szülők körében végzett országos felmérés eredményei [The findings of the national survey with parents whose children attend kindergartens].* Budapest: Felsőoktatási Kutató Intézet.

Török, B. (2005). Óvodák és szülők [Kindergartens and parents]. *Education, 4,* 787–804.

Varga Nagy, A. (2017). *Családi nevelés 2 [Family pedagogy].* Debrecen: Didakt Ltd.

Varga Nagy, A. (2018). *Családi nevelés 3 [Family pedagogy].* Debrecen: Didakt Ltd.

Varga Nagy, A., & Molnár, B. (2019). Nevelési mintázatok roma családok körében [Patterns of care in Roma families]. In *Így kutatunk mi [This is how we research].* Debrecen: Kapitális Ltd.

Varga Nagy, A., Molnár, B., Pálfi, S., & Szerepi, S. (2017). Education for sustainability in the Hungarian kindergartens. In *Early childhood education and care for sustainability: International perspectives.* London: Routledge.

13
CHILDREN'S PARTICIPATION IN PARENT MEETINGS IN LIGHT OF THE HISTORY OF PRESCHOOL POLICY DOCUMENTS IN ICELAND

Kristín Dýrfjörð and Guðrún Alda Harðardóttir

Introduction

In recent decades, the importance of collaboration between families and preschools has been widely acknowledged, including in policy papers such as national laws, curriculum and regulations in Iceland (OECD, 2019) and internationally (Geinger, Vandenbroeck, & Roets, 2014). According to Janssen and Vandenbroeck (2018), critical analyses of parental involvement are almost non-existent. However, national perspectives are often entwined within the curriculum and pedagogical traditions. Participation between parents and preschool is not researched much in Iceland, with one of the few articles written addressing the power relationship in such partnership. The findings indicate that preschools constantly face a dilemma concerning power and roles when it comes to partnerships between families and preschool (Einarsdóttir & Jónsdóttir, 2017). In the study, however, the children's roles, perspective and voices are silent.

Children have become increasingly active agents in the preschool research community, with their voices listened to, and their perspectives sought (Hreiðarsdóttir & Dýrfjörð, 2019). At the same time, children still tend to be viewed as vulnerable and unable to participate in meaningful discussions and decisions in their preschools and lives. That view can be seen, for example, in the regulation of children's bodies during mealtimes (Ryberg, 2019) and what activities they may choose to do in preschools (Hreinsdóttir & Davvíðsdóttir, 2012). Despite talk about democracy within preschools and even in the curriculum, it may not always be children's lived reality.

A related, ongoing debate concerns children's participation in parent meetings, with perspectives ranging from the view that it is unacceptable (Jensen & Jensen, 2008) to the belief that it is both desirable and unquestionable (Markström, 2008). We favour the latter viewpoint and consider children to be both capable and essential practitioners in parent meetings. We, however, acknowledge that parents sometimes may need meetings with teachers without children present.

In this chapter, we describe an innovative project where teachers in one preschool developed parent meetings in cooperation with five-year-old children. We examine how the teachers experienced the connections between meeting preparations and children's empowerment and democracy. Habermas' (2007) theories on democracy and empowerment provide the foundation for this part of our chapter. We give an overview of the general development of parental involvement in public policy documents concerning preschools in Iceland in recent decades as a backdrop. At last, we discuss the project bearing in mind the development of the Icelandic preschool policy documents.

The Icelandic context

Preschool attendance in Iceland is almost universal. Children start preschools around 18–24 months old, with the gap from parental leave (nine months) covered by family daycare. According to Statistics Iceland (2017), around 97% of 2.5–6-year-old children and approximately 80% of children 1.5–2 years old attend preschools. All preschools have full-day classes, and most children attend school for around 7.5–8 hours daily (Statistics Iceland, 2017). Municipalities primarily finance and manage the preschool system; private preschools are funded in the same way as public ones. All parents pay fees on a sliding scale based on their income, ultimately contributing 12%–15% of the costs of running preschools (Icelandic Association of Local Authorities, 2011). Iceland's early childhood education system is not divided by children's age, and the same laws and rules apply to all children younger than six years old. For example, the same standards for the curriculum and teacher education apply for all age groups under six years old.

Iceland policies on parental involvement in preschools

Iceland made its first laws concerning preschools in 1973 (no. 29/1973) with the primary aim to clarify responsibility for who would finance the building of preschools. A provision in article 19 concerned preschool principal's responsibility to establish a conversation between homes and preschools on children's well-being. In 1976 the laws were amended, and new parts related to both pedagogy and staff were added (no. 112/1976). These articles on parental collaboration in the first two sets of laws on preschools were followed in Iceland's first national curriculum guidelines. The curriculum promoted all kinds of parental involvement, such as transition periods at the beginning of children attendance, parent meetings, and parent and educator collaboration on projects, was promoted (Ministry of Education, 1985). The curriculum guidelines gave warnings about how parents' different social situations and statuses could affect their opportunities to collaborate with preschools and emphasized that understanding the home situation could provide teachers with insights into children's behaviours and emotions. The document viewed preschools as both saviours and specialists that had the responsibility to help and support parents in their role. In 1991, an entirely new set of laws was passed (no. 48/1991), declaring that attending preschools (playschools, as in the laws) was the right of the child. A later amendment to the law added that preschools were the first step in Iceland's educational system. The law stated that the role of preschools was to give children the best possible educational opportunities in collaboration with parents and homes. Preschool children's parent associations in every municipality were also supposed to participate in elected political committees. With entirely new laws from 2008 (90/2008) and following national curriculum guidelines, this view is strengthened.

> Children's wellbeing at preschools is inseparable from the welfare of their family and home. Parents' attitudes and contributions to preschool activities are an essential factor in the comprehensive overview of children's welfare and wellbeing. When children go to school for the first time, parents and preschools embark on collaboration in which concern for children's welfare is the main objective. Preschool teachers and other personnel are to show different family forms of understanding and respect
> *(Ministry of Education, Science, and Culture, 2011, p. 48).*

An article in the most recent law on preschool (no. 90/2008) concerns parents' obligations to participate in the evaluation of preschools and to form parental legal councils for every preschool. The councils have a role in providing feedback and closely following the implementation of educational and other plans within their preschools. The act also stresses that the parent councils have a right to have a say in all significant changes within their preschools (The Preschools Act, 90/2008, article 11). In a survey conducted by the Ministry of Education, 92% of preschool principals in the country said that in their school the parental councils have been established and have set themselves a written code of conduct (Ministry of Education, 2016).

According to the development of policy documents of recent decades, parental involvement clearly has become essential to preschools. Parents' legal status has gradually strengthened through, for example, official parental committees with the power to agree to or disagree with preschool school curriculum and policies. Another noticeable change has occurred in the language used, switching from exclusively talking about parents to using the term families in more recent policies and laws.

According to a 2019 TALIS Starting Strong report (OECD, 2019), most preschools in Iceland invite parents to visit their schools and meet teachers before children begin attending. Parents are also offered meetings with principals and teacher to discuss the preschool methods and policies. According to a brochure published by the Reykjavík city preschools, parent meetings are usually held twice a year, almost always without children, but there are examples that children participate in the last meeting before they start primary school (Reykjavík, n.d.). It is common for a teacher to share learning stories and documentation with parents and ask parents for their views and knowledge. However, parents do not very actively exercise their rights to involve themselves in matters concerning the preschools. Hence, there is a need to promote parental cooperation in preschools, according to the report (OECD, 2019).

Our primary research focus is on the parent-teacher meeting; it is to say when a teacher meets individually with the parents of each child to discuss the child's life within the preschool. The first reference to formal parent/teacher meetings that we found in official documents was in the first national curriculum recommending interviews between parents and teachers (Ministry of Education, 1985). Over the next decades, the tone changed, going from being very one-sided and directive to be more collaborative. In 1999 using documentation in a parent, meetings were recommended in then-new official curriculum guidelines (Ministry of Education, 1999). Still, otherwise, the context has remained similar, as apparent in the 2011 curriculum guidelines stating:

> During regular interviews between parents and preschool teachers, opportunities arise to discuss children's wellbeing, education, and development at home and preschool. Parents know their children best and support their school attendance by giving valuable information which is the basis for children's education
> *(Ministry of Education, Science, and Culture, 2011, p. 33).*

Empowerment and democracy

The impact from The United Nation Convention on the Rights of the Child (UNCRC, 1989) can be seen at the National curriculum guidelines for preschool from 1999 and onwards. In the 1999 National Curriculum, the right of the child to be involved in matters related to both curriculum and evaluation of their school is an example of that (Ministry of Education, 1999). The last national curriculum guidelines include a chapter dedicated to democracy in preschools, where doing democracy is promoted (Ministry of Education, Science, and Culture, 2011). It states:

> Preschools should encourage equality and children's active participation in society by giving them opportunities to experience democratic working methods and relationships in everyday activities. In this way, they come to understand what democracy involves, learn democratic values and working methods, and develop civil consciousness. Children's intuition, experience, skills, and opinions should be respected, and their views taken into consideration when organizing preschool activities, thereby giving them opportunities to take part in decisions on tasks and work methods.
> *(Ministry of Education, Science, and Culture, 2011 p. 35)*

This description aligns with what Malaguzzi's (in Hoyuelos, 2013) postulates – that schools' single most important role is to create diverse opportunities for children to reflect on the importance of their democratic participation in their communities. Educational institutions should promote awareness of democratic thinking and actions (Hoyuelos, 2013). However, it is up to each preschool to decide how to translate those ideas into action and what to emphasize. Icelandic preschool teacher can look towards an example from a Danish preschool, in a report from EVA, a Danish national evaluating institute, says when parents ask teachers how their children's day was, the teachers are encouraged to respond, "Why don't we ask Lisa [child] how her day has been?", thereby involving the children and the parents in a dialogue (EVA, Danmarks Evalueringsinstitut, KL, & BUBL, 2017).

Harðardóttir (2014) used Habermas's (2007) definition of empowerment as an analytical tool within preschools. Harðardóttir categorized empowerment as

a) the mental status of individuals who are aware of their skills and the right to influence their circumstances;
b) the social status of individuals who have opportunities to influence their conditions; and
c) the changed emotional states of individuals who have acquired greater confidence in their own abilities and potential to control themselves and their situations.

To explain Harðardóttir, for example, drew up this picture; preschool children are provided with opportunities to influence the organization of the day in their preschools (social status). The children find that their views are respected, and they have the right to participate in decision-making (mental status). Consequently, they have a sense of recognition and increased confidence in their own abilities (emotional state).

Empowerment entails changes in both what individuals want and think they can do. However, for change to happen, schools need to be structured so that the individuals in each school involved feel that they are taken seriously and are given opportunities to participate in shaping their school communities in ways that matter, thereby forming cooperation based on democratically sound practices. Involving children in dialogue with both teachers and their families about their daily lives in preschools can be challenging. However, if no one dares to try new methods to work with children and families, nothing will change.

An innovative project – the preschool

The project we present took place in Aðalþing, a Reggio Emilia-inspired preschool in Iceland. From its founding in 2009, the preschool has based its pedagogy and curriculum on the writings of Malaguzzi in dialogue with Reggio Emilia's work on preschool education in which listening (through documentation) and democracy are core concepts (Rinaldi, 2006). The preschool has consistently taken various pedagogical steps to involve parents and promote democratic pedagogy.

Data were gathered by recording a critical dialogue among teachers reflecting on their participation in the project during the autumn of 2019. Points from teachers' professional meeting when they discussed this idea for the first time were also made available. The children and their parents had all left the preschool when we gathered data, and hence, were not interviewed about their experiences.

The story

In the winter of 2018–2019, three teachers in the oldest classroom (5–6 years old) with 30 children wanted to change the last parent meeting before the children's transition to primary school. The teachers wanted to give the children voices in how they saw their learning in preschool, how they had developed as persons and what memories they had of their time there. The teachers also knew that in primary school, the children would become active partners in parent meetings, so the teachers thought that it was important for the children to be prepared for and feel safe in their new reality. They wanted the children to feel both in power and empowered.

The beginning of the project

During a pedagogical meeting in February, the teachers discussed how they could change and develop the form of parent meetings practised so far. They wrote down the following questions and points:

We want to:

- Show the children the learning process.
- Ask children: What do you as a child want to be better at doing?
- Why do you wish so?
- What has gone well for you in preschool?
- What have you learned as a child in this school?
- What has been difficult for you?

At a teacher meeting, the teachers decided to discuss these questions with the children. The teachers would find a photo of each child when they started in the preschool. As a conversation starter, the teachers would show the children their photographs, along with some pedagogical documentation from the current winter on a television screen. The teachers predicted that this approach would allow the children to revisit the projects on which they had worked, and the documentation would aid and support their discussion. The teachers thought it was essential to display the documentation on a television screen, giving all the children the same visual access to the data, thus enabling the democratic process. Another goal for the teachers was to support the children's metacognition and facilitate their thinking about their thoughts and thinking process.

The teachers split the children into groups of four or five children who looked together at the pedagogical documentation. The teachers took notes at the meeting and discussed with the children. Afterwards, they split the children into groups of two or three to discuss the questions the teachers had put forwards during their meeting. In the smaller groups, the teachers led the discussions with questions such as: What do think you enjoy the most in preschool? What is difficult in preschool? What would you like to tell your parents about what we do here? The teachers wrote down what each child said.

Parent meetings

The parent meetings took place during school hours and lasted for 20–40 minutes, with most around 20 minutes. The meeting started with the teacher welcoming everybody and then giving the word over to the child. The child sat between parent and teacher in front of a TV screen with the photos the child had chosen on display. The teachers said they soon discovered that the children were excited, and some were on edge the day of the meetings, so the teachers early on planned to hold the meetings during the mornings. Consequently, the waiting period was bearable for the children, and they were more relaxed during the meetings. The children seemed to look forward to the meetings, and most said happily, "Today, it is my turn for a meeting". The children seemed to be very proud of their participation, and to enjoy the meetings, talking about themselves in preschool and what they had learned. Afterwards, most returned to the classroom running and waving their photos. One teacher stated, "It was like they had somehow grown; they became taller". The also gave an example of how a child took control of the meeting. The teacher was wrapping up the meeting when a child said. "I am not done, I have more to share", and kept on for a few more minutes sharing information.

During the parent meetings, the children discussed what they had decided during the small group discussions. Most talked about what they deemed to be their strengths, what they wanted to be better at, most enjoyed and had learned. The teachers found it remarkable that most children discussed their learning from a holistic perspective rather than mentioning individual learning goals and skills. Many children cited competences connected to self-help, independence and social competences. The teachers noticed emerging patterns. For example, many children mentioned being helpful, especially towards younger children on the playground. One teacher stated that she was surprised when a child who spoke very little Icelandic said, "'When I am outside, I am good at helping the younger children communicate.' The child gave an example, saying, if a child, for example, took a thing away from another child, she helped".

Teachers' discussion afterward – the next steps

The teachers discussed their experience related to the project. One teacher said that putting her thoughts into words during our dialogue prompted her to reflect in a new way on the project and what happened in it. She also saw the children's learning in a new way. The teachers viewed the discussions as opportunities for children to put their thoughts into words, encouraging them to think about thinking. One teacher added that how deeply the children thought about what they learned varied:

> I think we are introducing something new to the children, a new way of thinking and using their brain, that I, as a child, am not just asked about my learning goals once but again and again. Over time, it becomes a routine discussion between us within the school. But at the same time, I [the teacher] realize it is obviously different between individual children how deeply they think about the discussion. But I believe that voicing your experiences can promote thinking. It will provoke something bigger.

Evaluating the children's participation in the parent meeting project, the teachers identified merits that deserved further reflection and development. They decided that they wanted to start the discussions with the children in the autumn and ask the children what they liked to do, who their playmates were, at what things they excelled, what was difficult for them and whether they want to learn something new or more about another topic. The teachers wanted to see if they could use these discussions to decide both the learning goals for each child and as a red thread in the pedagogical planning of the preschool. At the time of the discussion with the researcher, the teachers had taken the first steps to form a pedagogy based on the children's interests.

Discussion

The development of parent meetings in Iceland displays historical changes. Initially, attention was paid to giving parents information about preschools and children's lives there and asking for specific information about children's home life. Over time, this approach changed to producing narratives about children for parents, such as pedagogical documentation, portfolios and learning stories. Although undeniably highly useful, these tools still miss children's voices and ownership. These documents convey teachers' power, tell about teachers' professional constructions of preschools and preschool children and present what teachers want to tell parents about life and learning in preschools. Teachers have almost omnipotent power to define and control the dialogue. The development of involving children in telling their own stories to parents has made a small power shift in parent meetings. Instead of one-way interviews delivering information, the meetings could focus on narratives the participants can discuss in conversation, moving towards three-dimensional dialogue – children connecting parents and teachers. In our project, this new approach to parent meetings was first applied with, five-year-old children. The teachers in Aðalþing have since deliberated at what age the children should be involved. When this was written, conclusion had not been reached.

We initially stated that children's participation in the life and organization of preschools often consists more of words than actions. However, many preschools have a will and are finding ways to change that reality, and some may even use the tips from the Danish preschool, asking parents to ask their children (EVA et al., 2017). In this project, we sought to highlight ways to create opportunities for children to have meaningful conversations with teachers and parents about their learning both daily and as part of systematic learning assessment. The conversations had the spirit of Habermas (2007) and Harðardóttir (2014), endorsing democracy and empowerment as guiding lights. Our project shows that when offered joint authority over situations and the power to do, children grab it. It is possible to create a situation where children experience that their views are respected, and they have the right to participate in decisions and discussions about themselves as emphasised in the United Nations Convention on the Rights of the Child.

Important distinctions exist between children describing their viewpoints and experiences and teachers putting themselves in children's shoes through, for example, documentation. Questions should arise about viewpoints and who has the power to tell the story. We know that whoever tells the story has power over the narrative and can direct and shape the story according to his or her interest. What is meaningful for the child is not always same as what is meaningful for the teacher. Many years ago, a teacher came into a room in Aðalþing, where children were stacking glasses on top of each other. The teacher presumed the children were counting and building a tower; she snapped a photo and did not think much of it. A few weeks later, she was going through her photos with group of children and came upon that photo, the children became very excited and wanted to have a close-up look and asked her to enlarge it. When the teacher asked them why and what was happening in the photo, they told her that they had caught a fly and were experimenting with how many glasses they needed to keep the fly prisoned – the same story with two possible narratives and a reminder of how important it is to listen to children.

We definitely recommend using different types of documentation in the dialogue between parents and preschool teachers regardless of children's involvement. Documentation opens a valuable window into preschools and helps parents understand what happens to individual children, between children and among them. If done well, documentation shows parents the learning opportunities that take place every day. However, we also want to point out that as in our case, making children owners, in control, of what happens in parent meetings can be a game changer. It makes teachers and, hopefully, parents see children's strengths and, as in this case, gives teachers new tools to both discover and organize learning opportunities. It helps construct learning opportunities and environments with children.

The national curriculum guidelines clearly acknowledge the importance of preschools as a tool and a place to promote democracy in children's lives. Working methods used in each preschool should promote democratic values that lead children to understand civil consciousness (Ministry of Education and Culture, 2011). Learning from this project and involving children in parent meetings seems to be one way to promote change, mainly if the information gathered during children's meetings is also used to plan the curriculum for both the class and the individual child. According to the 2019 TALIS Starting Strong report, there is a need to promote parental cooperation in Icelandic preschools (OECD, 2019) and the method used in Aðalþing could contribute to this necessary change. When preparing for this project the teacher there used examples from primary schools and from preschools abroad, hopefully, the project will be of some relevance even inspiration for a preschool teacher in other parts of the world as well as in Iceland.

References

Einarsdóttir, J., & Jónsdóttir, A. H. (2017). Parent-preschool partnership: Many levels of power, *Early Years*, *39*(2), 175–189. doi:10.1080/09575146.2017.1358700

EVA, Danmarks Evalueringsinstitut, KL, & BUBL. (2017). *Forældresamarbejde om børneperspektiver i læringsmiljøet*. Retrieved from www.eva.dk/dagtilbud-boern/foraeldresamarbejde-om-boerneperspektiver-laeringsmiljoeet?fbclid=IwAR0LRmoBzMXNw_ixU1RAUvmKcOm8P-fFrzAgEBbhUy4xdP2D2lC7Jsvjv8Q

Geinger, F., Vandenbroeck, M., & Roets, G. (2014). Parenting as a performance: Parents as consumers and (de)constructors of mythic parenting and childhood ideals. *Childhood, a Global Journal of Child Research*, *21*(4), 488–501.

Habermas, J. (2007). *Mellan naturalism och religion: Filosofiska uppsatser*. Gothenburg, Sweden: Daidalos.

Harðardóttir. (2014). *Námstækifæri barna í leikskóla: Tækifæri leikskólabarna til þátttöku og áhrifa á leikskólanám sitt [Children's learning opportunities in preschool]*. Háskóli Íslands, Iceland: Menntavísindasvið.

Hoyuelos, A. (2013). *The ethics in Loris Malaguzzi's philosophy and pedagogical work*. Reykjavík, Iceland: Ísalda.

Hreinsdóttir, A. M., & Davvíðsdóttir, S. (2012). Deliberative democratic evaluation in preschools. *Scandinavian Journal of Educational Research*, *56*(5), 519–537. doi:10.1080/00313831.2011.599426

Hreiðarsdóttir, A. E., & Dýrfjörð, K. (2019). Mat leikskólabarna á þátttöku í tilviksrannsókn. [Children assessment of participating in a case study.] *Netla – Veftímarit um uppeldi og menntun*. doi:10.24270/serritnetla.2019.34

Icelandic Association of Local Authorities. (2011). *Leikskólar – gjaldskrár – regular [Preschools, tariff, and regulations]*. Reykjavík, Iceland: Icelandic Association of Local Authorities.

Janssen, J., & Vandenbroeck, M. (2018). (De)constructing parental involvement in early childhood curricular frameworks. *European Early Childhood Education Research Journal*, *26*(6), 813–832. doi:10.1080/1350293X.2018.1533703

Jensen, E., & Jensen, H. (2008). *Professionellt föräldrasamarbete*. Stockholm, Sweden: Liber.

Lög um bygging og rekstur dagvistunarheimila [Act of law on building and running preschools] no. 29. (1973). *skoða öll login*. Retrieved from https://opinvisindi.is/bitstream/handle/20.500.11815/2040/skil%20skolastiga.pdf?sequence=1&isAllowed=y

Lög um byggingu og rekstur dagvistarheimila fyrir börn [Act of law on building and running preschools] no. 112. (1976). Retrieved from www.althingi.is/lagas/140a/1976112.html

Lög um leikskóla [Act of law on preschools] no. 48. (1991). Retrieved from www.althingi.is/altext/stjt/1991.048.html

Lög um leikskóla [Act of law on preschools] no. 90. (2008). Retrieved from www.government.is/menntamalaraduneyti-media/media/frettatengt2016/Preschool-Act-No-90-2008.pdf

Markström, A. M. (2008). Förskolans utvecklingssamtal: Ett komplex av aktiviteter i tid och rum [The parent – teacher meeting: A complex of activities in time and space]. *Educare*, *1*, 51–67.
Ministry of Education. (1985). *Uppeldisáætlun fyrir dagvistarheimili – markmið og leiðir*. Reykjavík, Iceland: Author.
Ministry of Education. (1999). *Aðalnámskrá leikskóla*. Reykjavík, Iceland: Author.
Ministry of Education. (2016). *Skýrsla mennta-og menningarmálaráðherra til Alþingis um framkvæmd skólastarfs í leikskólum skólaárin 2011–2012, 2012–2013, 2013–2014 og 2014–2015 [Report from the Ministry of Education to the Iceland parliament concerning preschools the school years 2011–2012, 2012–2013, 2013–2014 og 2014–2015]*. Reykjavík, Iceland: Alþingi Íslands.
Ministry of Education, Science, and Culture. (2011). *The Icelandic national curriculum guide for preschool*. Reykjavík, Iceland: Ministry of Education, Science, and Culture. Retrieved from https://reykjavik.is/sites/default/files/A_aln_mskr__enska.pdf
OECD. (2019). *Providing quality early childhood education and care: Results from the starting strong survey 2018*. Paris, France: TALIS OECD Publishing. doi:10.1787/301005d1-en
Reykjavík. (n.d.). *Fjölskylda og leikskóli – Handbók um samstarf [Family and preschool, handbook]*. Retrieved from https://reykjavik.is/sites/default/files/ymis_skjol/skjol_utgefid_efni/handbokumforeldrasamstarf_0.pdf
Rinaldi, C. (2006). *In dialogue with Reggio Emilia: Listening, researching and learning*. London: Routledge.
Ryberg, L. (2019). *Måltiden i förskolan – barns utrymme i kommunikation och handling* (Unpublished licentiate thesis), Gothenburg University, Gothenburg, Sweden.
Statistics Iceland. (2017). *Fewer children and staff in pre-primary schools*. Retrieved from www.statice.is/publications/news-archive/education/pre-primary-schools-2016/
The United Nations Convention on the Rights of the Child. (1989). Retrieved from https://downloads.unicef.org.uk/wp-content/uploads/2016/08/unicef-convention-rights-child-uncrc.pdf?_ga=2.252877185.945397406.1591653110–2069899867.1591653110

14
PARENTAL INVOLVEMENT IN EARLY CHILDHOOD EDUCATION IN JORDAN

Policy and practice

Fathi Ihmeideh and Ali Kemal Tekin

Introduction

Located in the Middle East, Jordan is a developing country with few natural resources and limited agricultural land. To meet the modern and future needs of technically qualified citizens, Jordan has paid much attention to the educational system as the decisive factor in producing the skills needed for economic development. In 2019, the population of Jordan was 10.1 million people who were predominantly Arab and Muslim, and 3.8 million of this population were children under the age of 15 (over 34.4% of the population) (Department of Statistics, 2019). Of these, nearly 30% were non-Jordanian, many of whom were refugees fleeing from armed conflicts in neighbouring countries such as Palestine, Iraq, and Syria.

The current educational system in Jordan consists of three stages administrated by the Ministry of Education (MoE): kindergarten education, basic education, and secondary education. Kindergarten education provides preschool education for children aged four to six. The kindergarten stage consists of two levels: Kindergarten 1 (KG1) for children aged four to five, and Kindergarten 2 (KG2) for children aged five to six. To date, this stage remains a non-compulsory part of the educational system. Kindergarten education is primarily run by volunteer organizations, charitable societies, and the private sector, but the MoE supervises it entirely. In the basic education stage, ten years of education is mandatory and free of charge for all Jordanian children from the age of six to 16. Following the compulsory stage, secondary education is two years of schooling organized for students who have completed the tenth grade. Once the students pass the General Certificate of Secondary Education Examination, known as *Tawjihi*, they can pursue higher education (Ministry of Education, 2002).

Jordan's enrolment rate for school-aged children is 95%, although it differs slightly between urban and rural areas (Business Optimization Consultants (BOC), 2011).

In Jordan, the vast majority of young children are cared for at home; the dominant view regarding child-rearing is that mothers are caregivers and fathers are providers (Abayad Research & Marketing Consultancy, 2003). Less than 3% of children aged from infancy to three years attend nurseries or day-care centres. Only 13% of children aged four to five have access to KG1, and 59% of those aged five to six years have access to KG2 (El-Kogali & Kraft, 2015).

In total, the gross enrolment ratio in pre-primary education is 27.14% at a number of 471,819, and there is no gender gap between girls (27.03%) and boys (27.24%) in terms of access (UNESCO, 2018). Almost 40% of Jordan is composed of school-aged children; however, the enrolment rate in pre-school education is not at a level that meets United Nations Sustainable Development Goal (SDG) 4.2, which concerns access to quality early childhood education (ECE) for all children (Tekin, 2019).

This chapter aims to provide a brief background about the status of parental involvement in ECE in Jordan and particularly to describe the efforts made by local, regional, and international organizations to establish parental involvement programmes in kindergartens. More specifically, the chapter addresses the following questions:

1   What are the most prominent efforts that are contributing to the development of parental involvement in the Jordanian ECE context?
2   What research has been done in the area of parental involvement in ECEC in Jordan?
3   To what extent does parental involvement in the Jordanian ECE context align with Epstein's parental involvement model?
4   How is parental involvement addressed in early childhood teacher education programmes?
5   How should parental engagement and collaboration be developed in the Jordanian ECE context?

Parental involvement in the Jordanian educational context

Over the last two decades, Jordan has made great strides in the field of parental involvement in education as a result of its great interest in the ECE sector. Since 1996, UNICEF's Jordan office has been working on the Better Parenting Programme (BPP), one of the largest parenting programmes in the country (UNICEF, 2009). Since the majority of young Jordanian children are cared for at home, UNICEF's BPP was initially designed to enhance parenting. The programme was implemented by thirteen national partners with the aim of improving parents' knowledge, attitudes, and behaviours related to caring for young children (Queen Rania Foundation, 2019). Jordan's BPP educates and trains parents of young children on how to provide their children with the best care possible and to create safer home environments for their children from birth to eight years old. Partners in six countries, including Jordan, developed strategies to motivate parents and caregivers to provide a stimulating, loving, and protective environment at home (Brown, 2000) by increasing parents' awareness and skills regarding children's health, nutrition, and growth. In 2003, the BPP was revisited and redesigned to provide a more holistic approach to ECD including issues such as child protection, abuse, and neglect (Brown, 2000).

In 1999, the Jordanian government made ECE a top priority. As a result, Her Majesty Queen Rania Al-Abdullah commissioned a team of Jordanian professionals to develop a National Early Childhood Development (ECD) strategy (National Team for Early Childhood Development, 2000). Parenting, from pregnancy to eight years, received a large share of this ECD strategy, which was launched in 2000 (MOE, NCFA, & UNICEF, 2000). The ECD strategy valued the role that parents play in their children's lives. In July 2003, the MoE, in coordination with the US Agency for International Development (USAID), launched Jordan's Education Reform for the Knowledge Economy (ERfKE) programme, which aimed to reform education in Jordan (MoE, 2004). This project was the first of its kind in the Middle East. In addition, the ERfKE project contributed to the emergence of parental involvement in ECE in Jordan. The ERfKE project included four key components, the fourth of which was related to ECE. Its aim was to improve ECE in Jordan through establishing high-quality ECE programmes and professionalizing teachers in the field (MoE, 2004). One of its components was parent and community participation and partnership to raise awareness and understanding of the importance of the early childhood stage. The action area of this component provided education to increase parents' understanding of the importance of high-quality early childhood experiences and to raise their awareness of their role as their children's first educators (MoE, 2004; World Bank, 2003).

The ERfKE project was implemented in two phases with the first phase known as ERfKE I. The second phase (ERfKE II) was characterized as an extension of ERfKE I and was designed to build on the successful outcomes and achievements of ERfKE I (Al-Hassan, 2018). Based on the project's outcomes, the MoE started (1) developing parental involvement programmes in some public kindergartens, and (2) increasing parental participation in children's learning (Kaga, 2007). To turn theory into practice, the joint MoE – USAID Parental Involvement Initiative (PII) aimed to (a) enable Jordanian parents to participate actively in the education of their children in kindergartens, (b) familiarize parents with the teaching methods used and the routine philosophy followed, (c) enhance the classroom environment by exploiting parents' experiences and expertise in facilitating children's learning (Kaga, 2007; UNICEF, 2009). The PII programmes had mothers and female family members volunteer in the classrooms to help kindergarten teachers. The PII programmes aimed to make parents partners in providing assistance in the education of children during the daily activities of the kindergarten classrooms to achieve the greatest benefit and educational development for kindergarten children. The MoE acknowledged the following achievements: (1) teachers were trained to build their capacity; (2) involving the parents inside the classroom had a positive effect on activating the learning process; (3) parents' attitudes and concepts towards early childhood were changed; (4) some kindergartens were refurbished well; and (5) several important documents were developed, such as developmental standards and indicators for early childhood and kindergarten learning outcomes (Roggemann & Shukri, 2010, p. 18).

By 2017, several other parenting programmes had emerged, such as the Child Safety Programme implemented by the Jordan River Foundation, the Parent Involvement Programme for public kindergartens at the MoE, and smaller programmes with various organizations such as the Children's Museum of Jordan. Thus, parental involvement programmes were expanded in Jordanian early childhood settings (Queen Rania Foundation, 2019).

Further, the 2016–2025 Human Resource Development (HRD) Strategy was launched in 2016 that included a whole component in early childhood education and development (ECED) (Queen Rania Foundation, 2019) and proposed raising parents' awareness and providing them with the necessary education and training to (1) improve training outreach to parents and other primary caregivers, and (2) mobilize families to better support learning and ECE at home and increase their involvement in their children's learning (National Committee for Human Resource Development, 2016). As a short-term extension of the HRD, the MoE also launched the Education Strategic Plan (ESP) 2018–2022, which includes raising parents' awareness of health, nutrition, and social protection (MoE, 2018).

Research context

Parental participation is a relatively recent phenomenon in the Jordanian educational context. Research in this field in Jordan was slightly delayed compared to that in many Western countries. Understanding parent-teacher relationships has been one of the main challenges that early childhood teachers have faced for a long time. Wreekat and Jeara (1994) conducted a study to examine the problems facing kindergarten teachers in Jordan and found that almost half of the teachers were concerned about the lack of parental participation and interest in their children's learning. Another study carried out by Abu Taleb (2000) indicated that kindergarten teachers in Jordan viewed parental engagement in their children's learning as one of the main sources of job stress they faced. Recently, research has focused more on the concept of parental involvement within the context of education in Jordan (e.g., Ihmeideh, Khasawneh, Mahfouz, & Khawaldeh, 2008; Fayez, Sabah, & Abu-Rudwan, 2011).

In the 2000s, the term parental involvement was introduced in research conducted in the Jordanian context (Ihmeideh, 2006; Ihmeideh et al., 2008; Fayez et al., 2011). Ihmeideh's (2006) study was the first to investigate the status of parental involvement in the context of literacy development. It examined the role of parental involvement in developing children's Arabic literacy skills. The study found that parents supported their children's literacy skills at home and valued the role of the home environment in the development of children's learning. In addition, parents were completely excluded from the school because there were no real opportunities for their involvement in young children's education despite their strong motivation to be involved, which is an essential aspect of successful school-family partnerships (Tekin, 2016).

Since parental involvement was limited and/or excluded from the kindergartens, researchers started exploring the obstacles to parental involvement in the Jordanian context. In an evaluative study, Ihmeideh et al. (2008) found that kindergarten principals' negative attitudes towards parental involvement appeared to be a major source of challenges as they were not always interested in welcoming it. In addition, kindergarten teachers were found to have negative perceptions of parents with respect to the skills needed to teach children. However, another study revealed that teachers' attitudes towards parental involvement were positive and that teachers' attitudes were more positive towards parental involvement in home-based activities than in school-based activities (Shehadah, 2012). In the same context, Alkraisha (2019) examined teachers' and parents' attitudes towards parental involvement in kindergarten daily programmes and revealed positive attitudes towards parental involvement among teachers and parents. Thus, parental involvement was no longer viewed as a luxury, but it had become the main component of early childhood programmes (Ihmeideh & Oliemat, 2015).

Another line of research was the evaluation of parental involvement programmes established in the Jordanian context. For instance, Al-Hassan and Lansford (2011) evaluated the BPP through an experimental study. They found that the BPP was beneficial for the parents who participated in the programmes as they improved their parenting knowledge and spent time playing with and reading books to their children. Another evaluative study about family literacy programmes that Ihmeideh (2014a) carried out indicated that parents who participated in family literacy programmes were more likely to promote their children's early literacy development than parents who did not participate. Regarding the effectiveness of parent involvement in such programmes, for instance, Ihmeideh and Oliemat (2015) evaluated five domains of parental involvement: planning, implementation, evaluation, children's extracurricular activities, and communication with kindergarten. Their study revealed that parent involvement in the domains of children's extracurricular activities and communication with kindergarten was effective, although family involvement in the domains of planning, implementation, and evaluation was ineffective.

As mentioned previously, the vast majority of parental involvement research conducted in Jordan has focused mainly on mothers as the children's primary caregivers, which is consistent with that of most other countries (Tekin, 2012). In light of the importance of fathers' roles in their children's learning and development, research into their involvement has started to emerge in Jordan. One study found that fathers' beliefs regarding involvement were higher than their practices, and their perceptions of their actual practices in kindergarten-based activities were low (Ihmeideh, 2014b). However, in a similar study on father involvement, Betawi, Abdel Jabbar, Al Jabery, Zaza, and Al-Shboul (2014) found that fathers had a moderate level of practice concerning their home-based activities although their perceptions of their actual home-based activities were low.

Epstein's six types of parental involvement model

The level of parental involvement in the Jordanian educational context has evolved as a result of the efforts of the MoE and the international agencies and organizations, and it is, to some extent, close to the levels set by Epstein's model of parent involvement, which is considered to be the one that is most widely used (Epstein, 1992, 1995). This is not surprising because the promotion of parental participation in Jordan has been supported by the efforts of international organizations and Western experts and researchers who developed parental participation programmes in their own countries.

In this model, Epstein and colleagues conceptualized parental involvement in six types of family-school relationships as follows: parenting, communicating, volunteering, learning at home, decision-making, and collaborating with the community. As Nathans and Revelle (2013) argue, Epstein's model of parental involvement highlights the importance of parents in their children's learning and development. Epstein's model provides schools with a structure to enable them to prepare more activities that involve parents in their children's education and development (Winters, 2002). A massive body of research conducted in the field of parental involvement explores home-school partnerships based on Epstein's model of the six types of parent involvement as this model is recognized as a more school-centred model in the area of parental involvement (Epstein, 2001; Nathans & Revelle, 2013). More recently, in a context similar to the Jordanian ECE context, Ihmeideh, AlFlasi, Al-Maadadi, Coughlin, and Al-Thani (in press) conducted a study to explore how Epstein's model of parental involvement aligned with the Qatari ECE context from different perspectives. The results showed that Epstein's model was being implemented since participants expressed high to moderate levels of involvement based on it.

One can conclude that the efforts made by the Jordanian government in supporting parental involvement in early years were linked to Epstein's six types in the following domains:

Parenting

This domain was addressed through UNICEF's BPP. The programme helped parents develop parenting skills and establish a home environment for children as students. One of ERfKE's main objectives was to expand and develop parenting programmes in Jordan to encourage parents to provide their children with nurturing environments and to facilitate the role of civil society organizations and local communities in providing services for early childhood programmes (ERfKE II, 2008). The MoE frequently offered parenting workshops and training programmes to increase parents' awareness of the importance of their role in children's health and safety and to help parents support their children's learning and deal with their children appropriately.

Communicating

This domain of involvement was addressed by keeping parents informed about their children's development and progress. The MoE emphasized that kindergartens should invite parents frequently to attend meetings with teachers. The MoE trained kindergarten principals and teachers on how to establish contact with parents in different ways (i.e., electronic communication, sending home children's work, newsletters, or any information about children's progress). The MoE asked kindergarten principals to increase parental involvement and to use "communicating" as a criterion to evaluate the effectiveness of the kindergarten.

Volunteering

This domain of participation was largely visible through the MoE's efforts to improve kindergartens in the country. The MoE trained principals and teachers on how to recruit mothers at kindergartens to be involved as volunteers for school performances. PPI programmes were expanded and the number of volunteers in the kindergarten classroom reached 5,000 mothers volunteering.

For instance, the ERfKE II document on early childhood development states that care must be taken to ensure that "the involvement of parents as volunteers must benefit children and should not merely serve to fill financial gaps" (ERfKE II, 2008, p. 2).

Learning at home

Parents always want to support their children's learning at home, which is traditionally common. In this case, this type of involvement was implemented extensively in the Jordanian educational context. In the parental involvement initiatives programmes implemented by the MoE within the ERfKE project, kindergarten teachers were trained on how to involve parents in their children's learning and how to implement the kindergarten daily routine. According to the National Kindergarten Curriculum implemented in public kindergartens, most public kindergartens send newsletters home to help parents understand what is going on in them. In the Jordanian context, the involvement of parents in this domain is considered to be the easiest since not all parents are able to be in the kindergarten classrooms, particularly parents who are employed and who have difficulty coming to school.

Decision-making

This type of involvement was not implemented in the way Epstein sets out. This could stem from cultural issues as schools are considered the main decision makers particularly when it comes to what and how children learn.

Collaborating with the community

This domain of involvement is defined as identifying and integrating resources and services from the community to improve school programmes (Epstein et al., 2002). It is notable that this type of participation has not been implemented in the Jordanian context to the extent suggested in Epstein's model. Despite this, personnel in some schools have made attempts to achieve this type of participation but in an unintended way. For instance, some kindergartens invited professionals (doctors, drivers, bakers, nurses, etc.) to take part in the children's kindergarten programmes and talk about their careers and experiences with the children. Collaboration with the community is also observed in some Jordanian kindergartens in which principals or teachers provide parents with newsletters about community health services or other related services.

It can be concluded that Epstein's model of parent involvement has been implemented in the Jordanian educational context to some extent and at different levels. While the model has been largely implemented in the first four domains, it is insufficient or almost non-existent in the last two.

Parental involvement in early childhood teacher education

In the late 1990s and the early 2000s as a result of interest in the field of ECE in Jordan, the Ministry of Higher Education and Scientific Research (MoHESR) established undergraduate programmes in ECE in a number of Jordanian public and private universities to prepare an adequate number of ECE specialists. These programmers consist of 132 credit hours of courses offered over four years. The practicum (fieldwork) is 12 hours and lasts a full semester (16 weeks). After reviewing the study plan of most Early Childhood Teacher Education Programme (ECTEP) in different universities in Jordan, we noted the following shortcomings:

- There are no specific courses on parental involvement in these programmes.
- Parental involvement principles are not integrated in other courses.
- There are a few courses about parenting. The courses tackle issues related to child-family relationships, parental styles, parenting roles, and responsibilities without paying particular attention to their involvement children's learning whether at home or school.
- Practicum courses do not require student teachers to collaborate with parents.

Although the importance of parental involvement in their children's education is acknowledged, the aforementioned do not improve pre-service teachers' skills to work with parents or to collaborate with them when they start to practice. The successful education of children requires collaboration between teachers and parents. To remedy the situation, teachers need to be prepared to provide clear strategies that parents can implement with teacher guidance.

Developing parental involvement and collaboration in the Jordanian context

Parents are considered to be the most important teachers in their children's lives. It is also a key element in the success of children in school. Thus, decision makers and policy-makers need to encourage parents to become more involved in their children's learning and development. As previously noted, the Jordanian government started paying more attention to the importance of parental efforts in young children's education. Despite the considerable rhetoric about the value of parental involvement in ECE, parental engagement and collaboration initiatives and programmes in children's learning are limited or implemented within a narrow range. Moreover, most parents do not benefit from these programmes as the benefits of parental involvement programmes do not reach most children in Jordan. There is also a lack of national initiatives, especially regarding the efforts of the private sector, to promote parental participation. Furthermore, pre-service and in-service teacher preparation programmes lack support for and the promotion of parental participation in early childhood teacher education institutions.

In light of the above, we propose several suggestions and recommendations to develop parental involvement in the Jordanian educational context.

- *Expanding parental involvement programmes*

It is important to expand parental involvement programmes (PIP) across the country to support parents' roles in their children's learning and development. PIPs should be established not only in public kindergartens but also in private schools and should also be distributed throughout all regions in order to increase parental involvement, improve parents' skills and knowledge, and ensure that all parents benefit from PIP services. PIPs should be fully supervised by the MoE and should be assessed periodically to determine their effectiveness.

- *Developing early childhood teacher education programmes*

Early childhood teacher education programmes (ECTEP) established at universities/colleges should offer courses related to home-school relations, parental involvement theory and practice, and effective methods of co-operation with parents. These courses can adequately prepare preservice teachers to work closely with parents and communities. Study plans and courses offered for student teachers in ECTEPs need to be reviewed to increase the their skills and practices in parental involvement in ECE. Empowering teacher education programmes to adequately train pre-service teachers is critical. Practicum courses in ECTEPs should ensure that student teachers communicate and collaborate with parents. ECTEPs should stimulate student teachers to reflect upon their concerns and assumptions about parental involvement and provide candidates with opportunities to develop a variety of skills and strategies in this regard.

- *Supporting parents in helping their children at home and in kindergarten*

The Jordanian MoE needs to engage parents in their children's education both at home and at school. This could be done by inviting parents to kindergartens to educate them by offering training sessions on how to help children at home and in school. Examples of these efforts could include, but are not limited to, the following: inviting parents to share information about their child's learning, sending parents evaluation reports so that they can track their children's progress and monitor areas in which they need assistance, identifying what type of support system parents have at home, etc. In line with this notion, there should be training programmes to improve principals' and teachers' skills regarding parental involvement and to help them learn about how to invite parents and to create a welcoming school atmosphere.

- *Offering activities to encourage parental engagement both at home and at school*

The MoE should design opportunities for parents to work closely with teachers and encourage parent engagement both at home and at school. Such opportunities could include planning sessions with parents to help parents develop strategies to enhance children's learning and development at home and school, developing and using a home-to-school communication system through a variety of methods, and involving parents in making decisions related to their children's learning.

- *Integrating the principles of parental involvement into the curriculum*

We recommend that the National Kindergarten Curriculum is re-developed to include activities that require more parental involvement. The curriculum should determine specifically the role of parents in each activity and include guidelines for teachers to help them learn how to get parents involved in kindergarten programmes, particularly in the planning, implementation, and evaluation domains.

Finally, it is important for all stakeholders (e.g. researchers, educators, parents, policymakers, and other people in the education field) to establish parental involvement programs in the Jordanian educational context and enhance its effectiveness to include not only the ECE stage but also the later stages of education.

References

Abayad Research & Marketing Consultancy. (2003). *Preliminary research on the male's perception of early child development*. Amman: Commissioned by UNICEF, Jordan (mimeo).
Abu Taleb, T. (2000). Sources of job stress as experienced by kindergarten teachers in Great Amman region. *Dirasat*, *27*(1), 187–200.
Al-Hassan, O. (2018). Developments of early childhood education in Jordan. *Early Years*, *38*(4), 351–362.
Al-Hassan, S., & Lansford, J. (2011). Evaluation of the better parenting programme in Jordan. *Early Child Development and Care*, *181*(5), 587–598.
Alkraisha, M. (2019). *Kindergarten teachers' and mothers' attitudes towards parents' participation in kindergarten daily program* (Unpublished M.A. diss.), Al-Isra University, Jordan.
Betawi, I., Abdel Jabbar, S., Al Jabery, M., Zaza, H., & Al-Shboul, M. (2014). Father involvement with three-to four-year olds at home: Giving fathers a chance. *Early Child Development and Care*, *184*(12), 1992–2003.
Brown, J. (2000). *Evaluation report of the better parenting project*. Amman, Jordan: UNICEF.
Business Optimization Consultants (BOC). (2011). *Official website in tribute for King Hussein of Jordan*. Retrieved from www.kinghussein.gov.jo/
Department of Statistics. (2019). *Jordan statistical report 2019*. Amman: Author.
El-Kogali, S., & Kraft, C. (2015). *Expanding opportunities for the next generation: Early childhood development in the Middle East and North Africa*. Washington, DC: World Bank.
Epstein, J. (1992). *School and family partnerships*. ERIC Document Reproduction Service No. ED 343-715. Baltimore, MD: Center on Families, Communities, Schools, and Children's Learning, Johns Hopkins University.
Epstein, J. (1995). School/family /community partnerships: Caring for the children we share. *Phi Delta Kappan*, *76*(9), 701–712.
Epstein, J. (2001). *School, Family, and Community Partnerships: Preparing Educators and Improving Schools*. Boulder, CO: Westview Press.
Epstein, J., Sanders, M., Simon, B., Salinas, K., Jansorn, N., & Van Voorhis, F. (2002). *School, family, and community partnerships: Your handbook for action* (2nd ed.). Thousand Oaks, CA: Corwin Press.
ERfKE II. (2008). *Component 4.1: Early childhood development*. Draft. Amman: MoE (mimeo).
Fayez, M., Sabah, S., & Abu-Rudwan, E. (2011). The state and level of involvement among Jordanian kindergarten parents and its relationship to teachers' efforts of outreach. *Contemporary Issues in Early Childhood*, *12*(3), 241–251.
Ihmeideh, F. (2006). *An investigation into the development of Arabic literacy in kindergartens in Jordan* (Unpublished Ph.D. diss.), University of Huddersfield, Huddersfield.
Ihmeideh, F. (2014a). The effectiveness of training program for kindergarten teachers to help family promote their children's early literacy development and its effect on children's progress. *Educational Journal*, *111*, 247–278.
Ihmeideh, F. (2014b). Giving fathers a voice: Towards father involvement in early years settings. *Early Child Development and Care*, *184*(7), 1048–1062.
Ihmeideh, F., AlFlasi, M., Al-Maadadi, F., Coughlin, C., & Al-Thani, T. (in press). Perspectives of family – school relationships in Qatar based on Epstein's model of six types of parent involvement. *Early Years*.
Ihmeideh, F., Khasawneh, S., Mahfouz, S., & Khawaldeh, M. (2008). The new workforce generation: Understanding the problems facing parental involvement in Jordanian kindergartens. *Contemporary Issues in Early Childhood*, *9*(2), 161–172.
Ihmeideh, F., & Oliemat, E. (2015). The effectiveness of family involvement in early childhood programmes: Perceptions of kindergarten principals and teachers. *Early Child Development and Care*, *185*(2), 181–197.

Kaga, K. (2007). *Jordan's strategies for early childhood education in a lifelong learning framework: UNESCO policy brief on early childhood*. ERIC Document Reproduction Service No. ED 497347. Retrieved from https://files.eric.ed.gov/fulltext/ED497347.pdf

Ministry of Education (MoE). (2002). *Towards a vision for a new education system*. Amman: Author.

Ministry of Education (MoE). (2004). *The development of education: National report of the Hashemite kingdom of Jordan*. Amman: Author.

Ministry of Education (MoE). (2018). *Education strategic plan 2018–2022*. Retrieved from http://planipolis.iiep.unesco.org/sites/planipolis/files/ressources/jordan_education_strategic_plan_esp_2018-2022.pdf

Ministry of Education, National Council for Family Affairs & UNICEF. (2000). *Early childhood development strategy in Jordan*. Retrieved from http://ncfa.org.jo:85/ncfa/sites/default/files/publications/early-childhood developmentstrategy-jordan.pdf

Nathans, L., & Revelle, C. (2013). An analysis of cultural diversity and recurring themes in preservice teachers' online discussions of Epstein's six types of parent involvement. *Teaching Education*, *24*(2), 164–180.

National Committee for Human Resource Development. (2016). *Education for prosperity: Delivering results. A national strategy for human resource development 2016–2025*. Retrieved from www.mohe.gov.jo/en/documents/national-hrd-strategy.pdf

National Team for Early Childhood Development. (2000). *Early Childhood Development strategy in Jordan*. Amman, Jordan: Author.

Queen Rania Foundation. (2019). *Parenting in Jordan: Findings from the QRF national early childhood survey 2015*. Amman, Jordan: Author.

Roggemann, K., & Shukri, M. (2010). *Active-learning pedagogies as a reform initiative: The case of Jordan*. Washington, DC: U.S. Agency for International Development.

Shehadah, S. (2012). *Teachers' attitudes towards parental involvement in the elementary public schools at Zarqa district* (Unpublished M.A. diss.), The Hashemite University, Jordan.

Tekin, A. K. (2012, September 8–9). *Father involvement in early childhood education*. Paper presented at ICER2012: Challenging Education for Future Change Conference, Khon Kaen University, Khon Kaen, Thailand, vol. 5, 739–751. doi:10.13140/2.1.4349.8883

Tekin, A. K. (2016). Parental perceptions of life context variables for involvement in their young children's education, *Education, 3–13*, *44*(3), 353–366. doi:10.1080/03004279.2015.1059870

Tekin, A. K. (2019). How to achieve quality early childhood education for all: Goal 4 of the United Nations sustainable development. *Journal of Sustainable Development Education and Research*, *3*, 71–80. doi:10.17509/jsder.v3i1.17173

UNESCO. (2018). *Data for sustainable development goals by country: Jordan*. Retrieved from http://uis.unesco.org/en/country/jo

UNICEF. (2009). *Jordan's early childhood development: Making Jordan fit for children* (Vol. 2). UNICEF MENA-RO Learning Series. Retrieved from www.unicef.org/jordan/jo_children_ecddocumentation2009en.pdf

Winters, W. (2002). Book review of school, family, and community partnerships: Preparing educators and improving schools, by Joyce Epstein. *Journal of Education for Students Placed at Risk*, *7*(4), 449–451.

World Bank. (2003). *Document of the world bank*. Report No: 25309-JO. Human Development Sector. Washington, DC: Author.

Wreekat, K. Y., & Jeara, Y. (1994). Problems faced by kindergarten teachers in Amman City and their relationship to some selected variables. *Muttah Journal for Research*, *9*(3), 49–76.

15
PARENTAL INVOLVEMENT IN ECE IN NORWAY

Alicja Renata Sadownik and Ruth Ingrid Skoglund

Introduction

Parental involvement in early childhood education (ECE) in Norway is currently framed by the *Act of Kindergarten* (2005, updated in 2008 and 2010) and the *Framework Plan for Kindergartens: Content and Tasks* (UDIR, 2017). The former is a legal document providing the law and thereby the general framework for the involvement of and collaboration with parents, while the latter document focuses on provisionally important tasks and the content of ECE. However, each ECE setting remains free to choose the ways and methods of implementing the tasks into its own practice provided the chosen methods do not contradict the general legal framework or the imposed content and tasks. Since parental involvement is described in Norwegian steering documents through the concepts of *collaboration* and *understanding* and the present versions of the documents do not explain these concepts sufficiently (Skoglund, 2019), we start with presenting a historical overview of meanings connected to *collaboration* and *understanding* in previous versions of the steering documents.

Principles of *understanding* and *collaboration*

The categories of collaboration and understanding with the child's home appeared in the first Kindergarten Act of 1975, which states that the ECE shall provide children with good development and activity possibilities in *close understanding* and *collaboration* with home. The meanings of "understanding" and "collaboration" are not directly defined. However, they first appear in the School Act 1848, where their meanings were related to the Lutheran State Church, and after the Second World War, they were linked to Human Rights and the Rights of the Child. This means that ECE and school *collaboration* and *understanding* with children's homes

DOI: 10.4324/9780367823917-15

build on Christian cultural heritage and international conventions and designate parents as those responsible for their children's upbringing and education. In light of this, the Kindergarten Act of 1975 obliges schools to establish understanding and collaboration with parents (NMER, 2007–2008).

The Kindergarten Act of 2005 continues to oblige ECE to develop *collaboration* and a *close understanding* with children's homes. At the time, however, the focus was not on upbringing, but to "safeguard the children's need for care and play, and promote learning and formation as a basis for all-round development" (NMER, 2005, section 1). The character of the ECE setting's *cooperation* and *close understanding* was, however, formulated as *assisting* (Norwegian: å bistå) the home in fulfilling the child's developmental needs, thus creating a good basis for the child's lifelong learning and participation in a democratic society (NMER, 2005, section 2a). Nevertheless, the home was primarily responsible for achieving these goals.

In the revised 2008 document, the adjective "close" was removed from the *understanding* between the ECE setting and the child's home (NMER, 2007–2008) this referred to changes made two years earlier to the curricula for ECEC: Framework Plan for Kindergartens Content and Tasks (NMER, 2006), and it could be interpreted as strengthening the kindergarten's position in facilitating the child's development and the societal mandate for kindergarten-based education of children (Skoglund, 2019). This can also be seen as the ECE's political response to an increasingly heterogeneous society, and thereby increasingly dissimilar family models, cultures, religions, and values.

The Framework Plan for Kindergarten Content and Tasks (NMER, 2006) was anchored in Christian and Humanistic values. Since 2006, some ECE settings have been allowed to omit the term "Christian values," but they are still obliged to promote values anchored in human rights and designated in the document as "fundamental" and "cornerstones of our culture." These values include the following: a sense of community, care for others, joint responsibility, respect for human value, and the right to be different. Moreover, human equality, equal opportunity, intellectual freedom, and tolerance are also specified (NMER, 2006, p. 7).

The right to establish an ECE setting under a peculiar religious umbrella, beyond Christian values, was completely legalized in 2010, and also impacted parental collaboration at the level of choosing a particular ECE setting that would represent religious values that better correspond to parental ones. It is, however, important to highlight that kindergartens with a Christian/Humanistic value base[1] are also supposed to be able to discuss these values with parents while respecting the child's and parents' integrity (UDIR, 2017, p. 29) and this includes non-religious families.

As mentioned earlier, opening up to religious diversity can be seen as ECE policy responding to an increasingly diverse society and modes of family life. Since encountering the *Other* often requires explaining things that are usually taken for granted, the Framework Plan for Kindergarten Content and Tasks published in 2006 explains the concepts of understanding and collaboration (NMER, 2006, pp. 9–10). These concepts are presented as covering different aspects of contact between the ECEC and the caregivers as well as facilitating understanding between both parties.

> Understanding means mutual respect and recognition of each other's responsibilities and tasks in relation to the child. Collaboration means regular contact during which information and reasoning is exchanged. Questions relating to the wellbeing and development of children shall be discussed, along with the pedagogical activities of the kindergarten. This collaboration shall make it possible to develop the mutual understanding needed to deal with dilemmas that may arise when the considerations of an individual child have to be seen within the context of the group of children.
>
> *(NMER, 2006, p. 9)*

The phrase "questions relating to the wellbeing and development of children shall be discussed" can also be seen as meeting the needs of a very diverse society. We believe this to be so since the child's well-being and development is something that every parent, caregiver, and professional wants for the child, even though these categories can be filled with completely different, culturally anchored meanings and associations. Nevertheless, starting collaboration with the assurance that both parties are focusing on the individual child's well-being seems to be good since many disagreements on how to make it happen can occur. This is why information about and reasoning for both pedagogical activities and parental doubts and anxiety are mentioned.

Further in the document, it is emphasized that the ECE setting and the home share joint responsibility for the child's well-being, which is why an open, trust-based collaboration between the two parties is so important. It also invites parental criticism and ensures that parents will feel confident when raising their concerns.

> Parents and the staff of kindergartens have a joint responsibility for the well-being and development of children. The daily collaboration between homes and kindergartens must built on mutual openness and trust. Parents must feel confident that they can raise the issues that concern them in relation to their children and their kindergartens, even if they involve criticism. Parents must be informed of the general duty of confidentiality of the staff, and their special duty of disclosure in relation to child welfare services.
>
> *(NMER, 2006, p. 10)*

When any of the dilemmas mentioned arises, it is the ECE setting that "must work to strike a balance between respecting parents' priorities and safeguarding children's rights and the fundamental common values to which kindergartens are committed" (NMER, 2006, p. 10). In other words, in the case of any dilemma the *collaborating parties* of the ECE setting and the home have to *understand* and accept "that kindergartens have a social mandate and particular values that the staff are committed to." However, "the staff are responsible for providing parents with the necessary information about the activities of the kindergarten, and the reasoning behind them and for inviting parents to participate" (NMER, 2006, p. 10). What kind of information is absolutely necessary and in which way it should be justified ("this is how we do things in Norway" or "this is what research shows is best for the child's health") is not stated. How parents can participate is also not specified, which again can lead to very different culturally anchored assumptions arising about what parental participation is.

Regardless of the level or character of the reasoning for the pedagogical work or understandings underlying parental participation, "parents must feel confident that their children are being noticed and respected, and that they are participating in a social environment that benefits them" (NMER, 2006, p. 10).

One of the child's benefits, in which parents also participate, is formulated in the 2008 update of the Kindergarten Act. Since 2008, it has included not only child's play, care, and (life-long) learning as the content of ECE collaboration with the home, but it also has included cultural formation (Norwegian: *danning*). This concept of cultural formation, which is also described as *bildung* or becoming, is, briefly, the child's self-creation through dialogical involvement with the cultural values represented by the community and educational institutions (Ødegaard & White, 2016; Ødegaard, 2015). Thus, cultural formation is not only the formation that is about cultural shaping or upbringing. *Danning* is not when the child is being formed exclusively by community values; rather it happens when the child's subjectivity and agency are seen and respected and this leads to individual self-creation. In other words, the child negotiates and dialogs with "imposed" values, and thereby creates him- or herself. The category of *danning* allows the child to create him- or herself at the intersection of very different cultures and values and sees all of them as resources and content for dialogical self-creation. Thus, *danning* removes the monopoly for forming the child from both the ECE and the parents and in a way "forces" them to agree that neither one of them has the power to define the child's identity, while both parties can and should enrich this process. This is how the child's general well-being for which caregivers and ECEC settings have joint responsibility is understood within the new concept of *danning*.

Provisional section 1 of the Kindergarten Act (2005) states that "the Kindergarten must, in collaboration and understanding with the home, safeguard the children's need for care and play, and promote learning and cultural formation as a basis for all-round development" (The Kindergarten Act, 2005, section 1). The present version for the Framework Plan for Kindergarten: Contents and Tasks (UDIR, 2017) re-writes this to include the concept of partnership and a translation of the Norwegian *danning* as "formative development" as follows:

> The Kindergarten shall work in partnership and agreement with the home to meet the children's need for care and play and promote learning and formative development as a basis for all-round development, cf. the Kindergarten Act, Section 1. The terms "home" and "parents" also extend to include other guardians. The kindergarten shall respect the parents' right to participate

and shall work in close co-operation and agreement with the parents, cf. the Kindergarten Act, Sections 1 and 4. The best interests of the child shall always be the primary consideration in all co-operation between the home and the kindergarten.

(UDIR, 2017, p. 29)

The partnership can be interpreted as a shared responsibility for the child's well-being and development. However, cooperation around this joint responsibility is framed by the ECE's social mandate that both parents and staff must acknowledge (UDIR, 2017, p. 29). In case of disagreement, both sides are asked indirectly to compromise as the document requires that both the ECE setting and the parents "seek to prevent the child from experiencing conflicts of loyalty between home and kindergarten" (UDIR, 2017 p. 29). But here again it is important to remember that the ECE setting is not supposed to compromise on its social mandate.

Collective and individual involvement

The same mandate, however, also expects the ECE setting to be sensitive to the expectations and wishes of parents, both as individuals and as a group. The implementation of the kindergarten's values and pedagogical practices should therefore be presented regularly at parents' council meetings and in coordinating committees. It is particularly important to build a mutual understanding and confidence between kindergartens and homes in this matter.

In both previous and provisional legal and steering documents, parental involvement is formalized in the collective bodies of the parents' council and the co-ordinating committee.

> The objective of the parents' council and the co-ordinating committee is to serve as active channels for maintaining contact between the parents and the kindergarten. The parents' council shall promote the common interests of the parents and help to ensure that the co-operation between the kindergarten and the parents results in a good kindergarten environment. The parents' council shall be asked to address issues of importance to the parents' relationship with the kindergarten. The parents' council must give its consent before parents' fees can be increased beyond the stipulated maximum. The co-ordinating committee shall be an advisory, communication-focused and co-ordinative body. The committee shall be asked to address issues of importance to the kindergarten's content and activities and to the relationship with the parents. The co-ordinating committee shall draw up an annual plan for the kindergarten. Other important matters include proposals on budgets or operational changes.

(UDIR, 2017, p. 30)

Individual parental collaboration can also be formalized as systematic and regular individual conversations with the caregivers of each child; however, the way this is implemented depends on local kindergartens and their leaders or owners. The steering document only mentions that "co-operation with the parents shall take place both at an individual level, with the parents of each child, and at a group level through the parents' council and the co-ordinating committee" (UDIR, 2017, p. 29).

Preparing teachers for parental collaboration

Since there are ECEC teachers who are responsible for making parental collaboration happen, the guidelines for their education are an interesting source to examine. In Norway, this is the National Guidelines for Kindergarten Teacher Education, which sets forth the objectives and content of initial ECE teacher education.

The parents/caregiver appear in the general description of the content, where it is stated that being a kindergarten teacher professional demands ethnical awareness about the social mission that the exercise of the profession has for children, colleagues, caregivers, and external collaborators (NMER, 2012, p. 5). The issue of parental involvement is focused on specifically in the second year of study, during which learning outcomes of practical training in in-service kindergartens also address leadership abilities and cooperation with children, staff, and parents (NMER, 2012, pp. 8–9).

Later, parental collaboration appears under the learning outcomes of various areas of knowledge that the kindergarten teacher should be introduced to. The Norwegian Kindergarten Teacher Education student is introduced to the following areas of knowledge: a) child development, play, and learning (*Barns utvikling, lek og læring* – BULL); b) society, religion, world view, and ethics (*Samfunn, religion, livssyn og etikk* – SRLE); language, text, and mathematics (*Språk, text og matematikk* – STM); art, culture, and creativity (*Kunst, kultur og kreativitet* – KKK), nature, heath, and movement (*Natur, helse og rørsle* – NHR), and leadership, co-operation, and developmental work (*Ledelse, samarbeid og utviklingsarbeid* – LSU).

Cooperation is mentioned as part of child development, play, and learning, and one of the general competences expected of the students is the ability to analyze and reflect critically on their own professional exercise in interactions with children, staff, and caregivers (NMER, 2012, p. 12). The area of society, religion, world view, and ethics includes basic thinking about ethical and philosophical issues and provides insight into different human views and perceptions of reality, which helps the students to reflect critically on their own practices, especially on the behavior or expectations the students take for granted when meeting children, personnel, and caregivers from diverse backgrounds (NMER, 2012, p. 13). The caregivers are also mentioned in the area of language, text, and mathematics with regard to the expectation of the students being able to participate actively and critically in professional kindergarten discussions connected to language, text, and mathematics and being able to discuss ethical and professional issues with personnel, caregivers, and external collaborators (NMER, 2012, p. 15). The last area of knowledge in which parents/caregivers are mentioned is leadership, co-operation, and developmental work, in which parental collaboration is seen as related to the leadership and cooperation skills of future teachers. The learning outcome of this area of knowledge is that the student can collaborate with colleagues, caregivers, and external collaborators in the child's best interest.

Research on teacher education

Since what is in the best interests of the child is seen differently from various culturally anchored value-positions, co-creating a joint understanding of this is challenging for both in-service teachers and students. Consequently, some universities and colleges have developed various interdisciplinary projects to help students deal with the challenges of a heterogenic society in the safe framework of drama-inspired training. *The Difficult Conversation* Project was conducted at the Western University of Applied Science for several years (Bakken, Carson, & Ohm, 2019), and it received very positive feedback from the students, who indicated the importance of linking theory and practice and developing pedagogical tact and empathy for parents from diverse backgrounds.

National evaluation involving the parental perspective

Norwegian ECEC research suffers from a lack of complex, large-scale studies on parental involvement. However, picking up children from ECE settings was researched and reported on in a master's thesis (Velde Lønning, 2016) that was written as part of GOBAN, a large, longitudinal ECE research project. Moreover, a user survey among parents is conducted annually throughout Norway (UDIR, 2018). Some qualitative studies have also been conducted that present the perspectives of migrant parents on ECE (Sadownik & Ødegaard 2018, Sadownik 2021, Sønsthagen 2018).).

Velde Lønnings's master's thesis (2016) reconstructs five aspects that were identified as influencing the quality of pick up. These included information, care, the child's well-being, staff competence, and physical surroundings. The parents participating in the study referred to information as news about their child and her/his day and the structure of the day. Care referred to staff attention to the child's expressions of what was said, and this was mentioned together with staff interaction with the child and their closeness. At pick up, the parents got an impression of the quality of the relationships between the staff and the child. By child's well-being, the parents referred to the child's joy of seeing the parent, which meant that they enjoyed pick up more than drop off. On the other hand, the children were sometimes tired at pick up, which presented some challenges in the interactions with both children and staff. The study also reports that pick up revealed the different levels of professional competences the various members of the staff had and that there were differences between ECE teachers and assistants. The last aspect mentioned referred to physical surroundings. The more spacious and practically organized the entrance areas were, the easier it was to talk during pick up. When these spaces were small, the parents concentrated on making space for other parents arriving for pick up (Velde Lønning, 2016). Pick up is important because it happens every day, and it can build basic trust in the setting, and parents do not hesitate to engage in more difficult discussions when necessary (Drugli & Onsøien, 2010; Glaser, 2018).

In Norway, drop off and pick up are the main basis for answering a user survey. This annual survey asks about the following dimensions of kindergarten practices:

1   outdoor and indoor spaces;
2   relationships between children and adults;
3   children's general well-being;
4   information flow;
5   child development;
6   parental participation;
7   drop off and pick up;
8   adaptation and beginning school;
9   general satisfaction.

Parents participate directly in some of these dimensions (i.e., parental participation, information flow, dropping off and picking up), while in others they must rely on their child's/children's experiences (relationships, general well-being, child development, adaptation, and beginning school) and the documentation and/or communications sent by the ECE settings. Thus, in terms of methodology, the accuracy, or validity, of these measurements is questionable.

The issue of parental involvement is operationalized in this survey in the parts about information and participation as dropping children off and picking them up. Practically, these are the eight survey questions or statements the parents respond to. We present the average response in Table 15.1. The Norwegian Directorate for Education and Training (UDIR, 2018) does not publish the percentages of parents who gave scores from 1 to 5; just the average scores are published, which are quite high.

The average responses indicate that the average parent is satisfied with the possibilities they have to collaborate and participate and also with the information they receive and the way the staff interacts with them. However, the parental survey does not reveal anything about non-average parents or the category of *understanding* underscored in the Kindergarten Act and Framework plan.

Some research among Somali mothers indicates that "getting used" to an institutionalized childhood and, thus, an institutionalized family life, is a big transition (Sønsthagen, 2018), while research conducted by others indicates that migrant parents from countries with institutionalized care struggle with *different* institutional practices. Sadownik (2017; Sadownik & Ødegaard, 2018) designates Polish migrant parents as those whose understanding of and trust in ECE settings depend strongly

TABLE 15.1 Parental participation

		Average response
1	The ECEC setting works to safeguard parental participation.	4.3
2	The ECEC setting takes my views into account.	4.4
3	I my experience, the parental meetings are useful.	4.1
4	I receive good information about how my child is doing in the ECEC setting.	4.3
5	I receive sufficient information about the content of the ECEC setting's program.	4.3
6	The ECEC setting is good at informing me about possible staff changes.	4.1
7	How satisfied or dissatisfied are you with the way the staff interacts with you when dropping your child off at the ECEC setting?	4.4
8	How satisfied or dissatisfied are you with the way the staff interacts with you when picking your child up from the ECEC setting?	4.3

on the argumentation strategies used by the ECE teachers who interact with these parents. The more professional (e.g., "small children sleep outside because it's good for their immunological systems") and the less "national" argumentation (e.g., "It's how we do it in Norway") is, the greater parental understanding of and trust in ECE setting practices. Another study of Polish parents (Sadownik, 2021) also shows parental skepticism of certain practices is rooted in their value positions; however, focusing on the child's perspective helped some of them to overcome their own value positions (e.g., traditional gender roles) and allow the child to develop her/his own personality and subjectivity. Simultaneously, assuming the perspective of the child helped them to stay in line with the social mandate of the ECE and prevent loyalty conflicts.

This shows, however, that the imposed understanding between ECE and the child's home, is rather one directional. The staff tend to meet parents from other countries, by informing them about the Norwegian way to "do ECE" and very seldom ask about the parents' point of view or about their cultural practices. Analogical results are reported by Sand (2014) and Drugli and Nordahl (2016) in relation to school-home cooperation.

What can be improved?

In our view, the categories of understanding, collaborating, and partnering between the home and the ECE setting should be explained more clearly and related to each other in both of the steering documents and in ECE teacher education so that ECE settings dealing with increased diversity do not have to guess or risk the unintentional involvement of biases in their interpretation of these concepts. All of these could be related to the concept of cultural formation (Norwegian: *danning*) in which the child's subjectivity and agency are highlighted. These would allow focusing on the child's perspective when having a dialog on the ECE setting and the home's understanding of the child's best interest. Moreover, in order to embrace all parental voices, and not only statistically average ones, we suggest publishing the exact scores of the parental survey. Finally, since so much money is being spent on conducting this survey, we also suggest improving its methodology so that the questions asked relate to practices that the parents either witness or participate in, thus avoiding having the parents "guess" what the ECE settings are doing based on the documentation they are sent. This would increase this survey's validity and prevent the ECEs from documenting educational facts for the sake of the survey.

Note

1 Section 1 of the Kindergarten Act states that kindergartens shall build on fundamental values in the Christian and humanist traditions such as respect for human dignity and nature, freedom of thought, compassion, forgiveness, equality and solidarity – values which exist in various religions and world views and which are entrenched in human rights law (UDIR, 2017).

References

Bakken, Y., Carson, N., & Ohm, M. (2019). The difficult conversation: Facilitating students' professional learning and development. *Universal Journal of Educational Research*, 7(3A), 40–49.
Drugli, M. B., & Nordahl, T. (2016). *Samarbeidet mellom hjem og skole. En oppsummering av aktuell kunnskap om hva som skaper et godt samarbeid mellom hjem og skole*. Oslo: Utdanningsdirektoratet.
Drugli, M. B., & Osnøien, R. (2010). *Vanskelige foreldresamtaler – gode dialoger*. Oslo: Cappelen Damm akademisk.
Glaser, V. (2018). *Foreldresamarbeid: Barnehagen i et mangfoldig samfunn*. Oslo: Universitetsforlag.
Norwegian Ministry of Education and Research [NMER]. (2005). *Act no. 64 of June 2005 relating to kindergartens (The Kindergarten Act)*. Retrieved January 1, 2020, from www.regjeringen.no/en/dokumenter/kindergarten-act/id115281/
Norwegian Ministry of Education and Research [NMER]. (2006). *Framework plan for the content and tasks of kindergarten*. Retrieved September 27, 2019, from www.regjeringen.no/globalassets/upload/kd/vedlegg/barnehager/engelsk/frameworkplanforthecontentandtasksofkindergartens.pdf
Norwegian Ministry of Education and Research [NMER]. (2007–2008). *Ot. Prp Om lov om endringer i barnehageloven* [Proposition of law on changes in kindergarten act]. Retrived January 17, 2020, from www.regjeringen.no/no/dokumenter/otprp-nr-47-2007-2008-/id506030/
Norwegian Ministry of Education and Research [NMER]. (2012). *Retningslinjer for barnehagelærerutdaning*. Retrieved September 27, 2019, from www.regjeringen.no/globalassets/upload/kd/rundskriv/2012/nasjonale_retningslinjer_barnehagelaererutdanning.pdf
Ødegaard, E. E. (2015). Glocality in play: Efforts and dilemmas in changing the model of the teacher for the Norwegian national framework for kindergartens. *Policy Futures in Education*, 14(1), 42–59.

Ødegaard, E. E., & White, E. J. (2016). Bildung: Potential and promise in early childhood education. In M. Peters (Ed.), *Encyclopedia of educational philosophy and theory*. Springer: Singapore. doi:10.1007/978-981-287-532-7

Sadownik, A. R. (2017, July 6). *Polish parents developing trust to the Norwegian kindergarten*. Conference presentation at European research Network on Parents in Education, University of Roehampton, London.

Sadownik, A. R. (2021). Princes (don't) run in the mud. Tracing child's perspectives in parental perception of cultural formation through outdoor activities in Norwegian ECEs. In L. T. Grindheim, H. V. Sørensen, & A. Rekers-Power (Eds.), *Outdoor learning and play: Pedagogical practices and children's cultural formation. vol. 34*. Cham: Springer. doi: https://doi.org/10.1007/978-3-030-72595-2_4

Sadownik, A. R., & Ødegaard, E. E. (2018). Early childhood education and care in Norway: Cultural historical context, new regulations and perceived quality. In S. Garvis, S. Phillipson, & H. Harju-Luukainen (Eds.), *International perspectives on early childhood education and care: Early childhood education in the 21st century* (Vol. 1, pp. 143–153). London and New York: Routledge.

Sand, S. (2014). Foreldresamarbeid- vitenskapelige eller kulturelle praksiser? *Barnehagefolk*, 2, 44–49.

Skoglund, R. I. (2019). Anerkjennelse i samarbeid mellom barnehage og foreldre – en utfordring! I R. I. Skoglund & I. Åmot (Red.), *Anerkjennelsens kompleksitet i barnehage og skole* (Utg.2. s.187–211). Oslo: Universitetsforlaget.

Sønsthagen, A. G. (2018). "Jeg savner barnet mitt": Møter mellom somaliske mødre og barnehagen. *Nordic Journal of Comparative and International Education*, 2(1), 55–71. doi:10.7577/njcie.2289

UDIR [Directorate for Education and Training]. (2017). *Framework plan for kindergartens: Content and tasks*. Retrieved September 27, 2019, from www.udir.no/globalassets/filer/barnehage/rammeplan/framework-plan-for-kindergartens2-2017.pdf

UDIR [Directorate for Education and Training]. (2018). *Foreldreundersøkelsen i barnehager – resultater*. Retrieved January 2, 2020, from www.udir.no/tall-og-forskning/statistikk/statistikk-barnehage/foreldreundersokelsen-i-barnehager-resultater/

Velde Lønning, K. (2016). *Foreldrenes opplevelse av hentesituasjonen i barnehagen knyttet til kvalitet* (Master thesis), Department of Early Childhood Education, University of Stavanger. Retrieved January 2, 2020, from https://uis.brage.unit.no/uis-xmlui/handle/11250/2401521

16
THE STATE OF PARENT INVOLVEMENT IN EARLY CHILDHOOD EDUCATION

Case of Oman

Ali Kemal Tekin, Laila Al-Salmi and Maryam Al-Mamari

Introduction and background

As proposed by Bronfenbrenner's Ecosystemic Theory, parents are located in the immediate environment of the child; thus they are central to their development in all aspects including their learning and education (Bronfenbrenner, 1979). The parents' role in young children's educational lives is constantly evolving in the chronosystem as family dynamics are subject to change. For example, children were seen as economic and social wealth before the twentieth century, and fathers were seen as the breadwinners, while mothers were responsible for caring for and raising children and other domestic work. However, starting from the early twentieth century and particularly after World War II, both family roles and dynamics underwent major changes. For instance, more mothers started to work as full-time employees and more fathers started to do a share of domestic work including child-rearing. Several social movements such as women's rights, children's rights, and even workers' rights also had impacts on these changes. Nuclear and even single-parent families have also become common phenomena creating more demand for daily care and education for young children outside households. Thanks to globalization, no nation is immune to these changes.

Regardless of sociocultural differences, the status of young children around the globe has been going through these changes as children are constantly in interaction not only with their physical but also social milieux, and their learning mainly takes place during these interactions with their sociocultural elements including their parents who are seen as their first educators as proposed by Vygotsky (1978). Policymakers and practitioners have been trying to respond to these changes by accommodating appropriate services that have been revised constantly to meet the needs of children and families. First, many ECE settings were established by either public or private entities. Second, appropriate practices such as parent involvement

DOI: 10.4324/9780367823917-16

have been integrated into early childhood programs to make early education more effective and contribute to the lives of the coming generations.

There are four main beneficiary groups in ECE: young children, families, communities, and governments. First, young children reap benefits for their development. Besides, families benefit as their young children learn many real-life skills earlier. Then, communities advance because children with early education become better functioning, more productive individuals in society. Finally, governments spend less money on individuals who face difficulties in their later lives such as drug abuse, family dysfunction, dropping out of school, unemployment thanks to the resilience skills and problem-solving capacities they developed as children in ECE that provide them with greater potential to recover faster and more efficiently from difficulties. Hence, these four groups are expected to work collaboratively in young children's education to attain goals successively. This collaboration is critical particularly in the family–school context; in other words, parental involvement in ECE is essential in all contexts. Although parents' involvement in their young children's education is a relatively new research area, it is widely acknowledged that parents play a vital role in their children's education (Tekin, 2016). Parents are seen as founts of knowledge for making changes in children's lives and education (Moll, Amanti, Neff, & Gonzalez, 1992). Therefore, involving parents in their children's education is inevitable and beyond dispute (Tekin, 2019a). This also applies to the Omani context where the government's ambitious development goals are in place to meet United Nations Sustainable Development Goals 4.2 by 2030 concerning the quality of early education, and parent involvement is a critical aspect of this goal (Tekin, 2019b). Hence, the aim of this study was to understand the state of parent involvement in ECE settings by focusing on current practices and challenges as reported by school administrators. The authors also attempted to provide solutions and suggestions to improve parent involvement in ECE in the Omani context.

Omani context

Oman is located on the southeastern Arabian Peninsula and is a member of the Gulf Cooperation Council (GCC). Its population is 4,647,402 and among this population, 58.20% are Omani and 41.80% are expatriates (National Center for Statistics and Information, 2020). Its citizens and residents are predominantly Muslims. According to the World Bank (2019), its GDP per capita is 16,424 USD and its main revenues are from natural gas and oil. Today, there are 1,149 public schools in the country educating a student population of 603,797 (Ministry of Education, 2019). However, ECE in Oman is predominantly left to the private sector. Although the government has been criticized in this regard, it cites financial hardship and budgetary considerations as excuses for not establishing a public ECE system and recruiting teachers. It should be noted that Oman is a heavily oil-dependent country and current oil prices mean that many projects, including educational ones, are being put on hold.

Currently, 579,024 students are enrolled in 1,125 public schools, and this figure increases to 748,464 when the 636 private and 44 international schools are included (National Center for Statistics and Information, 2020). While education costs a total of 11% of total government expenditures (Times of Oman, 2018), several education variables, including the preschool enrolment rate baseline (29%; UNICEF, 2017), are not at desired levels. Significant attempts are being made to increase the enrolment rate. On the other hand, Omani parents are becoming more enthusiastic about being involved in their children's education (Tekin, 2014). This demand from families has been echoed in the field of educational practices and by schools attempting to engage families more in young children's education. However, the aspects of these family engagement processes in these schools are ambiguous.

Although parental involvement is not mentioned explicitly in major ECE steering documents in Oman many guidelines are available at various levels/sources to encourage parents' involvement and participation in schools, and these also provide advice and lay out best methods for helping children to succeed. In general, parental involvement in Oman is left to be regulated by schools. The country's official documents such as the Philosophy of Education and the Omani Child Law, and major official reports and documents such as the report prepared by the Ministry of Education jointly with the World Bank *Education in Oman, The Drive for Quality* (2013) or *Educational Journey in Oman* do not mention parental involvement. However, The Ministry of Education has designated a separate section on their website "Services to Parents/Guardians." This section, while in Arabic only, provides parents with tips and advice on how to develop their children's higher order thinking skills in addition to short, interesting stories targeting the development of peer relationships at schools and in the community.

The Omani Child Law addresses the child's right for education (Tekin, 2015). In Oman, the child's family or guardian is obligated to enroll the child in school for the basic education phase until grade 10. Parents are held officially responsible for failing to enroll their children in school, providing the means for their attendance, and preventing them from dropping out for the stated period (Article 36). Education is available for free up to grade 12.

Parent involvement in teacher training

Furthermore, parent involvement courses are provided in early childhood teacher education programs at higher education institutions in Oman. The Early Education Department at Sultan Qaboos University (SQU) sets a model in this regard. This program is recognized by the National Association for the Education of Young Children (NAEYC) and accredited by the Council for the Accreditation of Educator Preparation (CAEP). The whole study plan of the program has been developed according to the standards of NAEYC and CAEP; hence, it includes courses on family-school-community partnerships. In these courses, the teacher candidates are equipped with contemporary knowledge, skills, and dispositions concerning parent involvement at an international level. The courses are designed to integrate the aspects of how to work collaboratively with families from diverse backgrounds in early childhood education (ECE) as well as to recognize their differences and meet their needs.

However, there is no ECE Act or similar legislation in Oman that sets standards for becoming an ECE teacher. Therefore, most graduates are currently unemployed because private sector operators mostly recruit unqualified teaching staff to save money and make higher profits. Currently, no university degree is required to work as teaching staff in Oman, which means teachers have no formal early childhood teacher education in general or parent involvement credentials in particular.

Related literature

Research on parental involvement in Oman at the ECE stage has not received much attention. While the field needs more studies, some research has been conducted to examine parents' involvement at other educational levels. For instance, Al-Harrasi and Al-Mahrooqi (2014) investigated the nature of Omani parental involvement in their children's schooling without specifying the ages of the children; however, their survey addressed parental involvement at both the elementary and secondary school levels. The researchers found that parents did perceive the importance of parental involvement in promoting students' involvement but they viewed their involvement as home-based by helping their children complete homework and school projects. On a different level, Al-Barwani, Albeely, and Al-Suleimani (2012) conducted a study to examine the role of the family in Omani higher education institutions as perceived by parents and higher education-level students. The researchers found that parents viewed themselves as key in their children's education at higher education institutions; these views were supported by the students. Shifting to a different group of students, El Shourbagi (2017) studied the perceptions of teachers on parental involvement roles in the education of their children with disabilities in inclusive classrooms in Oman. The researcher concluded that the teachers believed that parental roles were important; however, parents did not activate their involvement, which stemmed from lack of awareness on the ways they could be involved.

Al-Mahrooqi, Denman, and Al-Maamari (2016) examined the benefits, challenges, and practices of Omani parents' involvement in their children's English language literacy. The researchers found that Omani parents believed in the benefits of their involvement in their children's academic, social, and psychological development related to their English language literacy. However, their actual involvement was limited. All the studies mentioned emphasized the importance of establishing a clear partnership between schools and parents to strengthen parental involvement and make the best use of their engagement in their children's education. Tekin (2011) stressed this point and emphasized the importance of developing a model of partnership between parents and ECE settings.

However, no research has been conducted to date in Oman to address the current practices and challenges of parent involvement in ECE. It is critical to start with understanding these issues from the perspectives of ECE administrators as they are the ones in charge of planning, managing, and coordinating parent involvement in schools. Thus, this study was done with ECE school administrators in Oman, and attempts were made to address two overarching research questions: 1) what are parent involvement practices in ECE in the Omani context? and 2) what are the challenges of parent involvement in their schools?

Method

Qualitative inquiry methods were used in this study since it is believed that qualitative methods such as interviewing participants are more appropriate for collecting in-depth information and rich data and to provide detailed participant insights into specific topics (Merriam & Tisdell, 2016). The purposeful sampling method was used to gather more concrete, solid, detailed data and information on the target group.

Participants

The participants of the study were the administrators of early childhood settings serving children aged three to six. The researchers contacted 50 ECE administrators currently working in the capital Muscat and invited them to participate in the study. The potential participants were informed about the aims and scope of the study. Participation was voluntary. Thirty-six (80%) ECE administrators agreed to be interviewed, while the rest did not respond.

Data collection

After securing the initial consent from the participants, interview sessions were scheduled with each of them at their convenience. The participants were informed about the scope, purpose, and confidentiality of the study. All information gathered in this study was kept in a password protected computer by the principal investigator. At the onset of the interviews, the participants were asked to provide basic information about themselves including their age, gender, educational background, and the years of their experience in teaching and administrative roles. Following this step, the participants were asked to address two major questions: 1) what parent involvement activities do they practice? and 2) what are the challenges of parent involvement in their schools? Although there was no time limit, the interview sessions lasted between 30 and 60 minutes. Following the interviews, the participant administrators were asked to clarify their responses and ensure they had been understood correctly. This triangulation procedure was employed as a verification method to support the validity issues as proposed by Creswell (2016). Arabic is the first language in the Omani context. Therefore, all interviews were conducted in

Arabic, then transcribed and translated into English by bilingual experts in the field of education. The researchers also employed back translation procedures to ensure the accuracy of the collected data.

Data analysis

Once the data collection steps were completed, the researchers used basic descriptive and qualitative study procedures to analyze the data. Henceforth, the responses from the participants were initially categorized per the research questions by using the thematic analysis method that enables an inquiry's findings to be reported in a more systemic and organized way. Furthermore, the researchers deployed the recursive examination of data through peer review as suggested for verification confirmability (Creswell, 2016). While reporting the study, representative participant answers were also quoted as suggested to convey the findings of the study in a clearer, more organized way and to be able to identify the statements mentioned in rank according to their frequency and to prioritize them.

Findings

Looking first at the characteristics of the participants, their average age was 42. The youngest administrator was 28 years old while the oldest was 62. Of the 36 participants, only two were males (5.6%) and the rest 34 were females (94.4%). Regarding their educational background, it was found that 11 (30.6%) were high school graduates, four (11.1%) had diploma degrees, and 21 (58.3%) held university and higher degrees. Only six (16.7%) of the participants reported having a bachelor's degree in ECE.

Parent involvement practices

One of the aims of this study was to understand the parent involvement practices in ECE in the Omani context. The participant reported practices were mapped according to six types of parent involvement model, which included: 1) parenting, 2) communicating, 3) volunteering, 4) learning at home, 5) decision-making, and 6) collaborating with the community proposed by Epstein et al. (2002). The following Table 16.1 shows the frequency of the participants who reported sample practices for each type of involvement.

As indicated in Table 16.1, the most commonly reported parent involvement practice was found to be "Communicating" by 25 (69.4%) participants. For example, Participant 21 said:

> We are constantly communicating with parents via diaries, newsletters, phone calls, and social media. In the past, we would do it with one-way methods but nowadays we practice multi-way communication thanks to technology. First, we have the so-called podcast program through which

TABLE 16.1 Frequency distribution of the participants

Frequency of Practiced Parent Involvement Types according to Epstein's Model (N= 36)

Type	Definition	Frequency	Percentage
Communicating	Communicate with families about school programs and student progress. Create two-way communication channels between school and home.	25	69.4%
Learning at home	Involve families with their children in academic learning at home, including homework, goal setting, and other curriculum-related activities.	20	55.5%
Volunteering	Improve recruitment, training, activities, and schedules to involve families as volunteers and as audiences at the school or in other locations.	16	44.4%
Parenting	Assist families with parenting skills, family support, understanding child and adolescent development, and setting home conditions to support learning at each age and grade level.	10	27.8%
Decision making	Include families as participants in school decisions, governance, and advocacy activities through school councils or improvement teams, committees, and parent organizations.	8	22.2%
Collaborating with the community	Coordinate resources and services for families, students, and the school with community groups, including businesses, agencies, cultural and civic organizations, and colleges or universities.	0	0%

parents are informed about whatever is implemented in the school such as events. The second way that we use is emailing in which we cover a report on what their children learned for the previous week and what they will learn for the next week. Also, we have something called the three-way-conference, where the students, parents, and teachers are present, and the children talk about the skills and information that they have learned; the teachers provide feedback and suggestions, and parents share their insights about their children's progress.

The majority of the administrators also mentioned the use of social media platforms such as WhatsApp, Instagram, and Twitter in their communication with the parents. The second most common involvement type was "Learning at home" reported by 20 (55.5%) of the participants. For instance, Participant 6 reported:

We have a writing program. In this program, the parents read any paragraph with the child and rewrite it in their home. Then the child talks about it in circle time within the classroom. Also, we encourage parents to read stories with their children and help them in their homework. They can support their education by providing a good environment in the house. So, in this case, we try to help the parents by offering them workshops, lectures, and informational booklets to support and encourage them to improve their learning at home skills.

Furthermore, 16 (44.4%) of the participants reported they practice the "Volunteering" type of involvement such as engaging in fundraising and charity events, invited speeches, facility improvement, organizing trips, and other activities and events, Moreover, ten (27.8%) of the administrators claimed that the "Parenting" type of activities mainly took place in the form of lectures and workshops to improve parents' skills to contribute to their children's learning. Eight participants also reported the practice of the "Decision-making" type of involvement and claimed involving parents mainly in the decision-making, the process of the teaching methods and strategies as well as assessment and evaluation of the students. On the other hand, none of the participants reported any sample practice that would fall into the "Collaborating with the community" type of involvement.

Interestingly, although gender issues in involvement were not among the investigation points of the present study and were not initially asked the interviewees, 12 administrators reported that they would involve only mothers and exclude fathers in the child's education. For example, Participant 19 said:

In my opinion, fathers throughout these ages are far from the education of children. The mother is the only one responsible for this mission. Therefore, we continue to communicate only with the mothers of students using the ways that I mentioned before.

Consistent with the earlier statement, Participant 34 asserted:

> We do our best to involve the mothers. As for fathers, their participation in the school is limited to providing funds and making the payments for school fees. We prefer mothers' involvement instead of them because all teachers and staff in the school are women. We do not have any plan to involve fathers.

Lastly, one of the participants stated that they did not practice any type of parent involvement in their school.

Challenges

The second research question about the challenges of parent involvement was analyzed on the basis of the participants' reports. The answers were aggregated into major common statements. Table 16.2 shows the list of challenges faced by the administrators in rank order according to their frequencies.

As indicated in Table 16.2, 15 (41.7%) participants reported that a low level of parental interest is a major challenge in their parent involvement experiences. For example, Participant 14 stated:

> Many families are not interested and do not see any value in participating in school activities or projects, and they do not believe their involvement would result in any meaningful change. There are parents who are not interested to taking up any role in their children's education, they just send the child to school every morning and do not follow the activities and have no interest in knowing what we do at school with their children.

TABLE 16.2 *Challenges of parental involvement*

Reported Challenges of Parent Involvement (N = 36) Definition	Frequency	Percentage
Low parental interest in getting involved	15	41.7%
Low parental interest in children's education overall	11	30.6%
Low level parental awareness for the importance of involvement	11	30.6%
Parents lack time and energy for involvement	10	27.8%
Belief in children's education is only the school's responsibility	9	25%
Communication problems with families from diverse backgrounds	6	16.7%
Parents lack knowledge and skills for involvement	5	13.89%

Moreover, 11 (30.6%) of the participant administrators claimed that parents in their school were not even interested in their children's overall education in this period. For instance, Participant 12 said:

> Most of the parents think that their children go to preschool to spend time so the mothers can rest when their children are at school. Some of them see preschool simply as a care center for their children and believe that early education does not have effective value that can change their children's whole lives. They do not take it as a serious part of educational life.

Furthermore, 11 (30.6%) of the participants reported a low level of parental awareness of involvement. For example, Participant 3 said:

> Parents are not aware of the effectiveness and positive content that the child can gain from their involvement in the activities. They are not even aware of what they can do or how they can contribute to their children's development through involvement. Therefore, they think it is a waste of time.

More to the point, ten (27.8%) of the participants reported that the parents do not have enough time or energy for involvement activities, and nine (25%) administrators stated that parents believe that children's education is only the school's responsibility. For instance, Participant 28 said:

> It is a cultural belief here that the school is solely responsible for educating children. Unfortunately, this has the greatest impact, and it is the biggest challenge that causes a low level of partnership between the parents and the school. This approach must change and everybody needs to understand that education of children does not stop at the school borders, it continues in their families and communities.

Lastly, six (16.7%) of the participants reported challenges in communicating with families from diverse educational, cultural, and linguistic backgrounds and five (13.89%) administrators claimed that parents do not have the required knowledge or skills to become involved. Other challenges reported by fewer than three participants are not presented in this study for data redundancy and representativeness purposes.

Discussion and conclusion

The current study sheds a light on this much understudied topic in the context of Oman. We found several significant pieces of evidence to provide a path for practitioners, policy-makers, parents, and researchers. Of course, the study was limited in its methods and geographical boundaries. Further studies should be conducted using quantitative methods and in areas outside the capital city to obtain a broader picture of the parent involvement phenomenon. While the present study was conducted only with school administrators, empirical studies must be conducted that recruit teachers, parents, and even policy-makers as participants so that the multidimensionality of different perspectives enriches the relevant information. However, the current study was significant as it revealed important information.

Regarding the first research question, it was revealed that the schools do not carry out all types of parent involvement activities to serve families and children, and it can be said plainly that the types of involvement practiced are not at the desired level and fail to provide sophisticated and diverse samples of practices. The involvement practices were mostly found to be universal types, for example, communicating, which is almost inevitable in the current educational system. However, it was seen that social media and other technological means such as electronic portals were used very frequently to communicate with parents. Learning at home and volunteering were other common practices that were found to exist in Omani early education settings based on the participants' reports. On the other hand, the other types of involvement were practiced by a small percentage of the participants. Interestingly, none of the participants reported any practice for collaborating with the community, which is very critical and beneficial in young children's education and development. The interview findings clearly showed that the current state of parent involvement practices in early education settings is far from being even standard. The findings implied that school administrators, who are the ultimate decision-makers and persons-in-charge along with teachers, are not knowledgeable enough about parent involvement practices in the first place. For example, several negative comments were made about fathers' involvement, which is very urgent in the early years of education (Tekin, 2012). The authors suggest that this is due to the lack of their educational background in educating young children as it was found that only a small percent of the administrators had degrees in the field.

An additional point of discussion is related to the second research question regarding the challenges of the parent involvement experienced by the participants. We found it interesting that the participant administrators' answers did not report any challenges from their point of view or even that of the teachers. This could be from a lack of enough involvement opportunities, for example. Instead, their responses simply revealed that they saw the parents as the source of all the challenges they are faced with in their efforts. This finding implies the existence of a misperception of the phenomenon. This finding is consistent with some previous studies that reported similar attitudes of school professionals blaming parents (e.g., Savacool, 2011). Nonetheless, many of them complained about the parents' low level of interest in getting involved and even in the overall education of their children. Low levels of awareness, a lack of responsibility, time, and energy, and required knowledge and skills for involvement among parents were the other challenges the participants listed. Communication problems with diverse families were also reported. The following is our list of proposed solutions to improve parent involvement in Omani early education settings:

- School administrators and teachers should be trained in effective parent involvement strategies to increase their knowledge, skills, and dispositions. Parent involvement courses should also be provided for in-service teachers and administrators. For example, practitioners should learn how to deal with diverse families.
- An awareness campaign to promote parent involvement should be started by policy-makers to emphasize the importance of parent involvement and collaboration in the education of young children. Informational printed material should be provided to all stakeholders, particularly parents. Seminars and workshops should be designed and delivered on the importance of early education and on how parents can contribute to their children's learning and development in this period through sample practices.
- Every ECE setting should be mandated to develop a structured parent involvement program and held accountable to following it under supervision.
- A parent involvement bureau should be established at the Ministry of Education to coordinate and serve as a resource for schools, parents, and communities.
- An Early Childhood Act similar to those in developed countries should be introduced to set the guidelines for required educational standards for both teachers and administrators.
- Alternative involvement opportunities and schedules for parents should be made available.
- More empirical research should be supported and conducted in the Omani context to gain in-depth, multidimensional, sophisticated information.
- Teachers should be equipped with research and collaboration skills that would enable them to actively investigate and learn about families from both mainstream and diverse backgrounds to transfer the knowledge and skills that families have accumulated and developed culturally throughout their history to their practice in the classroom. They should be able to utilize this valuable resource by accepting parents as founts of knowledge and make an educational change in the child's life as this type of approach would serve as a bridge between the home and school and make the young children's education continuous.

In conclusion, this study revealed that parent involvement practices were not at the desired level in the Omani context. Young children could not reap the utmost benefit from their education without the effective involvement of their families. All stakeholders could work cordially and benefit from the suggestions given earlier to initiate a comprehensive educational approach that values an important source – the families of young children.

References

Al-Barwani, T. A., Albeely, T. S., & Al-Suleimani, H. (2012). Parental involvement in higher education in Oman. *Jurnal Pendidikan Malaysia, 37*(1), 13–24.

Al-Harrasi, S., & Al-Mahrooqi, R. (2014). Investigating Omani parents' involvement in their children's schooling. *European Journal of Scientific Research, 117*, 272–286.

Al-Mahrooqi, R., Denman, C., & Al-Maamari, F. (2016). Omani parents' involvement in their children's English education. *SAGE Open, 6*(1), 1–12.

Bronfenbrenner, U. (1979). *The ecology of human development*. Cambridge, MA: Harvard University Press.

Creswell, J. (2016). *Educational research: Planning, conducting, and evaluating, quantitative and qualitative research* (6th ed.). New York: Pearson.

El Shourbagi, S. (2017). Parental involvement in inclusive classrooms for students with learning disabilities at Omani schools as perceives by teachers. *Journal of Psychology and Cognition, 2*(2), 133–137.

Epstein, J. L., Sanders, M. G., Simon, B. S., Salinas, K. C., Jansorn, N. R., & Van Voorhis, F. L. (2002). *School, family, and community partnerships: Your handbook for action* (2nd ed.). Thousand Oaks, CA: Corwin.

Merriam, S. B., & Tisdell, E. J. (2016). *Qualitative research: A guide to design and implementation* (4th ed.). San Francisco, CA: Jossey Bass.

Ministry of Education. (2013). *Education in Oman: The drive for quality*. Retrieved from https://documents1.worldbank.org/curated/en/246211468291645003/pdf/757190ESW0v10W0port0Summary-English.pdf

Ministry of Education. (2019). *Educational indicators*. Retrieved from http://home.moe.gov.om/arabic/index.php

Moll, L. C., Amanti, C., Neff, D., & Gonzalez, N. (1992). Funds of knowledge for teaching: Using a qualitative approach to connect homes and classrooms. *Theory into Practice, 31*(2), 132–141. doi:10.1080/00405849209543534

National Center for Statistics and Information. (2020). *Monthly statistical bulletin*. Muscat, Oman: Oman Government.

Savacool, J. L. (2011). *Barriers to parental involvement in the pre-kindergarten classroom*. Retrieved from http://eric.ed.gov/?id=ED519173

Tekin, A. K. (2011). Parent involvement revisited: Background, theories, and models. *International Journal of Applied Educational Sciences, 11*(1), 1–13.

Tekin, A. K. (2012). *Father involvement in early childhood education*. Paper presented at the International Conference on Educational Research, Bangkok, Thailand, 739–751. doi:10.13140/2.1.4349.8883

Tekin, A. K. (2014). Omani young children's language proficiencies: The outcomes of a bilingual education program. *Mediterranean Journal of Social Sciences, 5*(22), 784–791. doi:10.5901/mjss.2014.v5n23p784

Tekin, A. K. (2015). Improving child rights in the Gulf: Expectations from the brand-new child law of Oman. *Children and Youth Services Review, 50*, 12–19. doi:10.1016/j.childyouth.2015.01.008

Tekin, A. K. (2016). Parental perceptions of life context variables for involvement in their young children's education. *Education, 3–13, 44*(3), 353–366. doi:10.1080/03004279.2015.1059870

Tekin, A. K. (2019a). Parent involvement in the education of children with chronic diseases. In M. Gordon (Ed.), *Challenges surrounding the education of children with chronic diseases* (pp. 151–164). Hershey, PA: IGI Global. doi:10.4018/978-1-4666-9452-1.ch008

Tekin, A. K. (2019b). How to achieve early childhood education for all: Goal 4 of the United Nations sustainable development. *Journal of Sustainable Development Education and Research, 39*(1), 71–80. doi:10.17509/jsder.v3i1.17173

Times of Oman. (2018, July 23). *Number of school students in Oman growing steadily.* Retrieved from https://timesofoman.com/article/138639/Oman/Number-of-school-students-in-Oman-growing-steadily

UNICEF. (2017). *Annual report 2017: Oman.* Retrieved September 11, 2019, from www.unicef.org/about/annualreport/files/Oman_2017_COAR.pdf

Vygotsky, L. S. (1978). *Mind in society.* Cambridge, MA: Harvard University Press.

World Bank. (2019). *Annual report 2019: Oman.* Retrieved February 15, 2020, from http://pubdocs.worldbank.org/en/523771570664044067/EN-MPO-OCT19-Oman.pdf

17
PARENTAL INVOLVEMENT IN ECEC IN POLAND

Alicja Renata Sadownik and Ewa Lewandowska

Introduction

The democratic turn of 1989 and following years when a new act on education came into force witnessed the increased hope for a school which would be different and better than "a communist" one. In Poland, we expected a change for the better in all aspects of social life, including schooling. The feeling of going in the democratic direction was strengthened when local authorities started to take over schools. Not central authorities but local governments were to support schools and decide about who would become a head teacher, which was a significant difference if compared to the totalitarian system of the People's Republic of Poland. Local government, recognized due to democratic elections as the close one, gave hope for "ourness" of schools functioning under its influence and supervision (Mendel, 2012, p. 72).

The social and political transformation in 1989 also resulted in creating analogical conditions for the democratization of ECEC settings. The analogical expectation of an increased sense of the ECEC setting "being ours" with increased parental involvement as a sign of its realness also applied to the ECEC sector. Although not clearly articulated in the accessible literature, parental involvement was supposed to open up the ECEC setting to the local community represented by the parents. This was supposed to transform the ECECs into locally significant arenas for creating the best possible conditions for children's learning, development, and well-being. Partnerships among schools, homes, and local communities that manifest the joint "care for the children we share" (Epstein, 1995, p. 701) were encouraged (Mendel, 2007, 2012); however these were mostly related to school as the center of the community that brings together parents, teachers, and local government around the topic of children's well-being. Now, 30 years after the transformation, the knowledge on parental involvement in ECEC is still limited. In this chapter we

DOI: 10.4324/9780367823917-17

trace it by analyzing the steering documents for ECEC and ECEC teacher education and the literature presented to ECEC teacher education students.

The steering documents

The steering documents for ECE in Poland are: a) the School Education Act (1991, updated in 2017); and b) the Core Curriculum for Pre-school Education for Kindergartens and Pre-primary departments in Primary Schools (2017). The Core Curriculum for Pre-school Education for Kindergartens and Pre-primary Departments in Primary Schools focuses on provisional tasks, learning goals, and providing conditions for achieving them. Communicating with parents is mentioned as one of the kindergartens' tasks. "Teachers systematically inform parents about progress made in their child's development, encourage the implementation of the preschool's educational program at homes, and prepare school readiness assessments for children that will start school in a given year" (Polish Ministry of Education, 2017, p. 11, own translation). This places the parent in the role of an information receiver and an "implementor" of the preschool's educational program at home. No possibility of input to the kindergarten program based on parental knowledge and experience is mentioned. However, it is the parents' board that must approve the preschool's educational plan as is stated in the School Education Act.

In a further part of the Core Curriculum that focuses on child cognitive development states that a child who is ready for school is able to say what jobs and/or professions her/his parents and the people in her/his closest environment perform and explain what activities these jobs entail (Polish Ministry of Education, 2017, p. 10). This encourages information exchange between the parents and the preschool on the subject of parental jobs, and, as we mention later in the chapter, visits to parents' places of employment or parental visits to the preschool to speak about their jobs, professions, and occupations.

Lastly, parents are referred to in the project method that the preschools are supposed to implement. "The project can embrace one or more subjects. They permit collaboration between the preschool and the local community and also parental engagement" (Polish Ministry of Education, 2017, p. 16, own translation). This again opens up a way to exploit parental knowledge, skills, and social capital that can be valuable for the ECEC setting.

The School Education Act (1991, updated in 2017) is another steering document, but it is of a more legal character. It addresses several issues in relation to parents. For example, it explains that the word "caregivers" is also implied when the word "parents" is used. It sets forth procedures for when a child is not accepted into the preschool the parents applied for, or if the kindergarten that the child is attending is liquidated. This document also regulates the roles of parents when applying for a preschool place and for the municipality that provides the place. The School Education Act also regulates issues related to parental consent for any type of special educational assistance and possible diagnostic testing that are conducted in collaboration with psycho-pedagogical services.

What we find discriminatory in the steering documents is the assumption about who parents or caregivers are. In a rather homogenous society in terms of nationality (Polish) and religion (Catholic), silencing minorities in official documents is not a sign of progressing integration, but rather an unawareness of the marginalization of minority groups. In a relatively young democracy, with limited experience of diversity stemming from 40 years of isolation (1949–1989) behind the Iron Curtain, articulating and affirming diversity in policy documents is necessary if institutional discrimination is to be avoided and eliminated. Silencing diversity makes being a non-Polish, non-Catholic, and/or a non-heterosexual parent a private problem, the resolution of which depends on individual teacher's attitudes, which is not a topic that is addressed in teacher education. This again can empower expression of teachers' individual biases, or prevent such parents from collaborating honestly.

Individual and collective collaboration

As in other countries, parental collaboration happens at the individual and collective levels in Poland. At the individual level it focuses on the individual child's upbringing, learning, and development. School readiness is of no lesser importance. According to national standards, individual co-operation is expected to be trust-based and focused on the child's development and well-being.

Parental involvement at the collective level is realized through parents' boards, and is regulated by the School Education Act (1991, updated in 2017). A parents' board should have at least seven parents/caregivers who are elected anonymously during a parents' meeting. The parents' board regulates itself in terms of internal structure and how it works and meets. It can submit proposals and opinions referring to any possible issue or aspect connected to the institution to the head of the preschool and also to the municipality and/or supervisory institutions.

Within 30 days of the start of a new preschool year, the parents' board must issue their opinion of the education and prevention program. If there is disagreement, the teachers' board negotiates with the parents' board. The parents' board is also authorized to collect money for the preschool from both parents and other sources for use by the preschool. Any concept of, or requirement for children's uniforms has to be presented to and then discussed and accepted by the parents' board. The parents' board also gives its opinion and suggestions about the institution's hours of operation and about any proposals for digital monitoring and/or extraordinary monitoring procedures. As a collective, the parents influence the preschool institution to a great degree. This collective power can encourage various parental projects in the preschool that are mentioned in the Core Curriculum. Formally, various activities are possible, like voluntary work, thematic projects, free-time activities for children after opening time, or lifelong learning for the community. However, research on how such initiatives actually function is limited to schools and families in local communities (Mendel, 2007).

Preparing teachers for parental collaboration

Since many of the issues in the steering documents are open to professional interpretation, teachers' competences developed during higher education play a role. The National Standards for Teacher Education and Preparation for the Profession (Polish Ministry of Science and Higher Education, 2019) first mentions parents in the description of the goals of practical training in in-service kindergartens, one of which is the conscious building of relationships among children, parents or caregivers, and coworkers (page 30).

The other context in which the parents appear in the National Standards for Teacher Education is in reference to working with children. "The graduate can use effectively in her/his work with a child information pertaining to the child that is provided by specialists such as speech therapists, psychologists, pedagogues, and doctors and also the child's parents or caregivers" (Polish Ministry of Science and Higher Education, 2019, p. 32, own translation). This aspect of co-operation is developed so as to "build on trust-based relationships with all actors involved in a child's upbringing and education, including parents or caregivers, and to include them in activities that facilitate educational efficiency" (Polish Ministry of Science and Higher Education, 2019, p. 33, own translation). That includes also parental conferences as well as communication with parents through technological devices (p. 36).

Another ability expected of the graduate is to participate in teamwork with other teachers, specialists, parents, and other members of the local community. The National Standards for Teacher Education designates parents as an important source of information on the child and as important actors in the child's life with whom the preschool institution should be able to build a trust-based relationship to facilitate the child's learning and development in the best possible way. The co-operation competences with both parents and various specialists are emphasized especially with regard to children with special educational needs (Polish Ministry of Science and Higher Education, 2019, p. 55). With healthy children, cooperation with parents and other members of the local community remains most important, which, again, strengthens the possibility for various joint projects involving preschools, parents, and the local community.

What the steering documents do not regulate is knowledge of diversity in both parents and communities as an important issue in initial teacher education. This means that anti-discriminatory cooperation in education among diverse groups of families is dependent on the attitudes of academic staff at individual higher education institutions, which, again, potentially facilitates unawareness and the reproduction of biases among large groups of future teachers. In such biased settings, developing trust-based relationships between the parents and ECEC teachers is impossible.

Parental collaboration in practice

The practice of parental involvement in ECEC is definitely a topic that has not yet been adequately researched in Poland. In this part of the chapter we summarize what is accessible to us at the moment: 1) literature used in preschool teacher education at various Polish universities, 2) the results from our own small netnographic study, and 3) parental stories that we had access to when cooperating with the ECEC sector in Poland.

The literature analyzed for this article is included as a list (see Appendix 1). The analysis of the literature with a focus on how preschool teachers were instructed or inspired by the authors to deal with parents permitted us to reconstruct the following ways of dealing with parental involvement:

1. *Know-how* – is a category that includes handbooks on parental co-operation in which parents are often presented as a problem that teachers have to deal with effectively. This type of literature provides answers and strategies, but it does not invite reflection on the phenomenon;
2. *Interaction and communication* – is a category that includes publications that employ communication or therapeutic communication theories or concepts to describe and reflect on contact between the ECEC institution and children's parents and caregivers. The focus on psychological or psychoanalytical aspects, like personality type, temperament, extraverts or introverts, or one's own childhood, are what determine collaboration with the home, which characterizes this group of literature;
3. *Collaboration and co-operation* – is a group of publications that focus more on forms of organization and collaboration than on the individual features of the people involved. It underscores the importance of partnerships and encourages opening up at various levels (including with parents) that are important to the child's development;
4. *Critical and emancipatory* – is the most reflective category as it anchors ongoing collaboration in broader socio-economic and cultural contexts. Teachers are the reflective ones who in their interactions with parents have to consider their socio-economic background, sexual orientation, religion, cultural capital, needs, and aspects such as the space into which the parents are invited. Parental collaboration is described here in terms of asymmetric power relations, and there is a focus on how deep reflection and awareness are needs to enhance good collaboration with disadvantaged parents (of children who need and will benefit most from parental engagement with the preschool).

Among these categories, only point 4 approaches parents as a highly diverse group of individuals in an asymmetric power relationship with preschool institutions, which again are not aware of their own institutional discrimination. The institutional unawareness of preschools with regard to their own power in relation to parents and children, especially with those from minority groups, can lead to the decreased parental involvement reported in our netnography (Kozintes, 2015).

Our aim was to analyze archived discussions on various forums for ECEC teachers that turned up when we performed Google searches for expressions such as "involving parents in ECEC," "how do you involve parents in your ECEC."

Our search led to only one discussion on the forum *Bliżej przedszkola* (English: Closer to kindergarten). The discussion cluster that turned up in the Google search was entitled "parental involvement" and the first question posed by a kindergarten teacher was: "How do you engage 'your' parents in preschool life? Do they engage easily, or do you have to convince them for a long time? Maybe they initiate something or maybe they don't care at all?" (Blizej Przedszkola, 2010). The qualities of parental engagement that appeared in the teachers' discussion placed them at the intersection of volunteering and home-based involvement. They mentioned parents taking time off work to participate in events at the preschool during operational hours (related to Christmas, Grandmother and Grandfather's Day,[1] children's theatrical performances), baking cakes for these invents, or participating in an event such as a parental theatrical performance for the children. In the discussion analyzed, the teachers spoke about decreasing parental interest in these types of participation, and they discussed how harmful this could be for the child when no one comes. One voice in the discussion stated that there are various forms of involvement, and maybe the preschool should adjust to parents' needs, but this post received no responses.

This unanswered post is highly relevant to the stories that are being told to us by the field. These are voices of parents who cannot find their place in mainstream ECEC settings or cannot stand witnessing their child being pacified by unreflective, standardized education. Nevertheless, their voices are being heard in school research when they employ their own initiative and powers to establish quasi-schools for their children (Uryga & Wiatr, 2019). Unfortunately, ECEC initiatives have not yet been researched, but they do happen. The "forest preschools" (*Leśne Przedszkola*) that we describe here are the product of a joint parent and ECEC teacher movement that has developed a network of ECEC settings. Because of formal requirements, it is registered as an NGO running a non-public network of preschools that implement the Core Curriculum in outdoor, settings that are close to nature. Parents are involved in registering and formalizing the schools' legal status and ensuring it passes formal state monitoring inspections. The parents also sponsor purchasing equipment and participate in developing activities that respect the Core Curriculum and the needs of the children and families. The parents who we contacted us told us about their time-consuming, but worthy, involvement in the ECEC because it permits them to be honest about who they are in contact with both teachers and other parents. This is highlighted by rainbow or atheist families and other families as well as whose values and beliefs about what is good for children do not correspond to mainstream policy and pedagogy in which diversity is silenced.

Conclusion

We conclude that the silent assumption in the policy documents that parents are heterosexual Poles who follow Catholic traditions contradicts community projects and trust-based relationships with parents. Relationships that teachers should be able to lead according to the National Standards for Teacher Education and Preparation for the Profession (Polish Ministry of Science and Higher Education, 2019). Silencing diversity can facilitate unwitting discrimination in teacher education, during which biases can be reproduced in ECEC contact with parents and in interactions among parents. This raises questions regarding the sense of the ECEC setting "being ours" for which abolishing communism gave hope. Polish policy documents remain unaware and unreflective regarding who belongs and who is excluded from "our ECEC" settings. However, many non-public, parent-initiated ECEC alternatives indicate clearly that many who do not belong in mainstream ECEC settings, do not give up own agency, and create alternative, diversity friendly options.

Note

1 Grandmother's Day is celebrated on January 21 and Grandfather's Day on January 22. Kindergartens often celebrate these on one of the days by inviting grandparents to the preschool for a children's performance, cakes, and tea.

References

Blizej Przedszkola. (2019). *Spolecznosci blizej przedszkola* [*Association closer to kindergarten*]. Retrieved from https://blizejprzedszkola.pl/temat-58,248,jak-rodzice-uczestnicza-w-zyciu-przedszkola

Dziennik Ustaw. (2017). *Prawo oswiatowe* [*The school education act*]. Retrieved from http://prawo.sejm.gov.pl/isap.nsf/download.xsp/WDU20170000059/U/D20170059Lj.pdf

Epstein, J. L. (1995). School, family, and community partnerships: Caring for the children we share. *Phi Delta Kappan, 76*(9), 701–712.

Kozintes, R. (2015). *Netnograhy: Redifined*. London: Sage.

Mendel, M. (2007). *Rodzice i nauczyciele jako sprzymierzeńcy*. Gdańsk: Wydawnictwo Harmonia.

Mendel, M. (2012). Polish minischools: Microhistories of democracy and portraits of parental involvement. *International Journal About Parents in Education, 6*(1), 69–79.

The Polish Ministry of Education. (2017). *Podstawa programowa wychowania przedszkolnego i ksztalcenia ogolnego dla szkoly podstawowej* [*The core curriculum of pre-school education for kindergartens and general education in primary schools*]. Retrieved October 30, 2019, from www.ore.edu.pl/wp-content/uploads/2017/05/wychowanie-przedszkolne-i-edukacja-wczesnoszkolna.-pp-z-komentarzem.pdf

The Polish Ministry of Science and Higher Education, Załącznik 2 – standard kształcenia przygotowującego do wykonywania zawodu nauczyciela przedszkola i edukacji wczesnoszkolnej (klasy I – III szkoły podstawowej). *Educational standard for teacher profession in kindergarten and early years at school*. Retrieved October 30, 2019, from www.gov.pl/web/nauka/informacja-w-sprawie-standardow-ksztalcenia-przygotowujacego-do-wykonywania-zawodow

Uryga, D., & Wiatr, M. (2019). Quasi schools: New parental ventures on the fringes of the Polish educational system. In M. Mendel (Ed.), *Parent engagement as power: Selected writings* (pp. 73–87). Gdansk, Warszawa: Wydawnictwo UG.

Appendix 1

The list of literature used in the analysis of required reading in ECEC teacher education at 7 Polish universities.

1. Adamek, I. (1997). *Podstawy edukacji wczesnoszkolnej*. Kraków: Oficyna Wydawnicza Impuls.
2. Adamek, I. (2002). *Projektowanie i modelowanie edukacji zintegrowanej*. Kraków: Wydawnictwo Naukowe Akademii Pedagogicznej.
3. Adler, R. B., Rosenfeld, L., & Proctor, R. (2006). *Relacje interpersonalne: Proces porozumiewania się*. Poznań: Dom Wydawniczy REBIS.
4. Andrukowicz, W. (2000). *Teoria kształcenia integralnego*. Kraków: Oficyna Wydawnicza Impuls.
5. Andrzejewska, J. (2003). Współudział rodziców w planie rozwoju i działalności przedszkola. In A. Karpińska (Ed.), *Teoria i praktyka kształcenia w dialogu i perspektywie* (pp. 435–443). Białystok: Wydawnictwo Trans Humana Wydawnictwo Uniwersyteckie.
6. Andrzejewska, J. (2005). Wspieranie rozwoju dziecka przez współpracę nauczyciela z rodziną. In S. Guz & J. Andrzejewska (Eds.), *Wybrane problemy edukacji dzieci w przedszkolu i szkole* (pp. 113–124). Lublin: Wydawnictwo UMCS.
7. Argyle, M. (1991). *Psychologia stosunków międzyludzkich*. Warszawa: PWN.
8. Babiuch, M. (2002). *Jak współpracować z rodzicami trudnych uczniów*. Warszawa: WSiP.
9. Banasiak, M. (2013). *Współpraca rodziców ze szkołą w kontekście reformy edukacji w Polsce*. Toruń: Wydawnictwo Naukowe UMK.
10. Biedroń, M., & Prokosz, M. (Eds.). (2001). *Teoretyczne i praktyczne aspekty współczesnej pedagogiki opiekuńczej*. Toruń: Wydawnictwo Adam Marszałek.
11. Braun-Gałkowska, M. (1985). *Test Rysunku Rodziny*. Lublin: Wydawnictw KUL.

12 Braun-Gałkowska, M. (2007). *Poznawanie systemu rodzinnego*. Lublin: Wydawnictwo KUL.
13 Brągiel, J., & Badora, S. (Eds.). (2005). *Formy opieki, wychowania i wsparcia w zreformowanym systemie pomocy społecznej*. Opole: Wydawnictwo UP.
14 Breguła, I. (2015). Komunikacja z rodzicami w dobie technologii. *Życie Szkoły*, *8*, 23–24.
15 Bulera, M., & Żuchelkowska, K. (2006). *Edukacja przedszkolna z partnerskim udziałem rodziców*. Toruń: Wydawnictwo Edukacyjne Akapit.
16 Christopcher, C. J. (2003). *Nauczyciel-rodzic. Skuteczne porozumiewanie się*. Gdańsk: GWP.
17 Cudowska, A. (Ed.). (2011). *Kierunki rozwoju edukacji w zmieniającej się przestrzeni społecznej*. Białystok: Trans Humana Wydawnictwo Uniwersyteckie.
18 Deptuła, M. (Ed.). (2004). *Diagnostyka pedagogiczna i profilaktyka w szkole i środowisku lokalnym*. Bydgoszcz: Wydawnictwo Akademii Bydgoskiej im. Kazimierza Wielkiego.
19 Deutsch, M., & Coleman, P. (Eds.). (2005). *Rozwiązywanie konfliktów: Teoria i praktyka*. Kraków: Wydawnictwo Uniwersytetu Jagiellońskiego.
20 Dumont, H., & Istance, D (2013). *Istota uczenia się: Wykorzystanie wyników badań w praktyce*. Warszawa: Wydawnictwo Wolters Kluwer.
21 Ferenz, K. (2009). *Role współczesnego nauczyciela w zmieniającej się rzeczywistości społecznej*. Wrocław: Oficyna Wydawnicza ATUT.
22 Filipiak, E., & Smolińska-Rębas, H. (2002). *Od Celestyna Freineta do edukacji zintegrowanej*. Bydgoszcz: WSP.
23 Frąckowiak, M. (2011). *Gdy rodzic staje się roszczeniowy: Poradnik dla nauczycieli*. Poznań: Wydawnictwo EMPI2.
24 Frydrychowicz, A. (et al.) (2004). *Testy psychologiczne i pedagogiczne w poradnictwie. Przewodnik metodyczny*. Warszawa: Centrum Metodyczne Pomocy Psychologiczno-Pedagogicznej.
25 Gajewska, G. (2004). *Pedagogika opiekuńcza i jej metodyka. Wybrane zagadnienia teorii, metodyki i praktyki opiekuńczo-wychowawczej*. Zielona Góra: PEKW GAJA.
26 Goetz, M. (2016). Działania szkoły nakierowane na wspomaganie rodziców w wychowaniu dzieci. *Życie Szkoły*, *1*, 28–32.
27 Gondek, D. (2015). Szkoła dla uczniów i rodziców. *Psychologia w Szkole*, *2*, 106–112.
28 Gozdowska, E., & Uryga, D. (2014). *Rada szkoły: między ideą a społeczną praktyką*. Warszawa: Wydawnictwo APS.
29 Grzegorzewska, S. (2009). *Różnicowanie kształcenia w klasach początkowych*. Kraków: Oficyna Wydawnicza Impuls.
30 Janke, W. (Ed) (2005). *Pedagogiczna relacja rodzina – szkoła. Dylematy czasu przemian*. Bydgoszcz: Wydawnictwo Uczelnia WSP.
31 Jarosz, E., & Wysocka, E. (2007). *Diagnoza psychopedagogiczna: Podstawowe problemy i rozwiązania*. Warszawa: Wydawnictwo Akademickie Żak.

32 Jąder, M. (2009). *Efektywne i atrakcyjne metody pracy z dziećmi*. Kraków: Oficyna Wydawnicza Impuls.
33 Kaleta, W. (2015). Miejsce rodziców w szkole. *Dyrektor Szkoły, 8*, 15–18.
34 Kamińska, U. (2003). *Zarys metodyki pracy opiekuńczo – wychowawczej w rodzinnych i instytucjonalnych formach wychowania*. Katowice: Wydawnictwo Uniwersytetu Śląskiego.
35 Karbowniczek, J., Kwaśniewska, M., & Surma, B. (2011). *Podstawy pedagogiki przedszkolnej z metodyką*. Kraków: Wydawnictwo WAM.
36 Kawula, S. (Ed.). (2005). *Pedagogika społeczna: Dokonania – aktualność – perspektywy*. Toruń: Wydawnictwo Adam Marszałek.
37 Kawula, S., Brągiel, J., & Janke, A. (2002). *Pedagogika rodziny: Obszary i panorama problematyki*. Toruń: Wydawnictwo Adam Marszałek.
38 Kelm, A. (2000). *Węzłowe problemy pedagogiki opiekuńczej*. Warszawa: Wydawnictwo Akademickie Żak.
39 Klus-Stańska, D., & Szczepska-Pustkowska, M. (Eds.). (2009). *Pedagogika wczesnoszkolna, dyskursy, problemy, rozwiązania*. Warszawa: WSiP.
40 Koc, R. (2011). Promocja szkoły i jej współpraca ze środowiskiem lokalnym In S. Kowalik (Ed.), *Psychologia ucznia i nauczyciela: podręcznik akademicki* (pp. 303–333). Warszawa: PWN.
41 Kujawiński, J. (2010). *Ewolucja szkoły i jej współczesna wizja*. Poznań: Wydawnictwo Naukowe UAM.
42 Lulek, B. (2008). *Współpraca szkoły, rodziny i środowiska*. Rzeszów: Wydawnictwo Uniwersytetu Rzeszowskiego.
43 Łaniewska, G. (Ed.). (2001). *Współpraca szkoły z rodzicami*. Białystok: ODN.
44 Łobocki, M. (1985). *Współdziałanie nauczycieli i rodziców w procesie wychowania*. Warszawa: Nasza Księgarnia.
45 McKay, M., Davis, M., & Fanning, P. (2005). *Sztuka skutecznego porozumiewania się*. Gdańsk: GWP.
46 Mendel, M. (2001). *Rodzice i szkoła. Jak współuczestniczyć w edukacji dzieci?* Toruń: Wydawnictwo Adam Marszałek.
47 Mendel, M. (2000). *Człowiek, szkoła, wspólnota*. Toruń: Wydawnictwo Adam Marszałek.
48 Mendel, M. (2000). *Partnerstwo rodziny, szkoły i gminy*. Toruń: Wydawnictwo Adam Marszałek.
49 Mendel, M. (2004). Aktywna szkoła – bierni rodzice: anomia, mit czy przemieszczenie znaczeń. In A. W. Janke (Ed.), *Pedagogika rodziny na progu XXI wieku: Rozwój, przedmiot, obszary refleksji i badań* (pp. 297–310). Toruń: Akapit.
50 Mendel, M. (2007). *Rodzice i nauczyciele jako sprzymierzeńcy*. Gdańsk: Wydawnictwo Harmonia.
51 Mendyk, M. (2014). Współpraca z rodzicami z perspektywy nauczycieli edukacji wczesnoszkolnej – raport z badań. In J. M. Łukasik, I. Nowosad, & M. J. Szymański (Eds.), *Codzienność szkoły: Nauczyciel* (pp. 199–210). Kraków: Oficyna Wydawnicza Impuls.

52 Nyczaj-Drąg, N., & Głazewski, M. (Eds.). (2005). *Współprzestrzenie edukacji: szkoła, rodzina, społeczeństwo, kultura*. Kraków: Oficyna Wydawnicza Impuls.
53 Oleksa, K. (2016). Zebrania z rodzicami: Jak formalne spotkania przerodzić w owocną współpracę. *Głos Pedagogiczny, 79*, 59–63.
54 Pawlak, B. (2003). *Jak współpracować z rodzicami uczniów klas początkowych?* Kraków: Wydawnictwo Naukowe Akademii Pedagogicznej.
55 Piwowarski, R. (Ed.). (2003). *Dziecko – nauczyciel – rodzice. Konteksty edukacyjne*. Białystok – Warszawa: Wydawnictwo UB i IBE.
56 Popiela, B. (2015). Współpraca pomiędzy nauczycielami oraz współpraca z rodzicami – podstawa budowania społeczności szkolnej. *Polonistyka, 4*, 44–47.
57 Putkiewicz, E. (1990). *Proces komunikowania się na lekcji*. Warszawa: WSiP.
58 Reczek-Zymróz, Ł. (2009). *Współdziałanie pedagogiczne szkoły podstawowej ze środowiskiem lokalnym*. Kraków: Oficyna Wydawnicza Impuls.
59 Rogala, S. (1989). *Partnerstwo rodziców i nauczycieli*. Warszawa-Wrocław: PWN.
60 Rosiński, M. (1997). *Organizacja pracy opiekuńczo-wychowawczej w świetlicach*. Szczecin: Centrum Psychologiczno-Pedagogiczne.
61 Rydlewski, G., & Rydlewski, R. (2014). Rodzice w szkole – edukacyjni partnerzy. *Wychowanie Fizyczne i Zdrowotne, 6*, 40–42.
62 Sałasiński, M., & Badziukiewicz, B. (2003). *Vademecum pedagoga szkolnego*. Warszawa: WSiP.
63 Sawicka, A. (1991). *Współpraca przedszkola z rodzicami*. Warszawa: WSiP.
64 Segiet, W. (2013). *O związku edukacji z rodziną: Społeczne konteksty i jednostkowe biografie*. Poznań: Wydawnictwo Naukowe UAM.
65 Sitarczyk, M. (2001). Działalność informacyjno – edukacyjna przedszkola w kształtowaniu postaw wychowawczych rodziców. In S. Guz (Ed.), *Edukacja przedszkolna na przełomie tysiącleci* (pp. 103–114). Warszawa: Wyższa Szkoła Pedagogiczna Towarzystwa Wiedzy Powszechnej.
66 Sowisło, M. (2003). *Dla dobra dziecka: O warsztacie pracy nauczyciela wychowawcy*. Kraków: Wydawnictwo WAM.
67 Szlendak, T. (2019). *Socjologia rodziny*. Warszawa: PWN.
68 Sztejnberg, A. (1997). *Komunikacja między nauczycielem a uczniem w procesie edukacyjnym*. Opole: Uniwersytet Opolski.
69 Tłowińska-Królikowska, E. (2013). Współpraca szkoły ze środowiskiem lokalnym – nowe zadania szkoły? In G. Mazurkiewicz (Ed.), *Przywództwo i zmiana w edukacji: ewaluacja jako mechanizm doskonalenia* (pp. 141–153). Kraków: Wydawnictwo Uniwersytetu Jagiellońskiego.
70 Trempała, E. (2003). *Środowisko rodzinne dziecka a sytuacja szkolna ucznia*. Włocławek: Wyższa Szkoła Humanistyczno-Ekonomiczna.
71 Urbanek, B. (2015). Wspierajmy rodziców w wychowaniu. *Nowa Szkoła, 5*, 9–14.
72 Węglińska, M. (2002). *Jak się przygotować do zajęć zintegrowanych*. Kraków: Oficyna Wydawnicza Impuls".
73 Wierzchnicki, W. (2014). Relacje rodzina-szkoła: Dylematy czasu przemian. *Edukacja i Dialog, 11–12*, 62–65.

74 Więckowski, R. (1993). *Pedagogika wczesnoszkolna*. Warszawa: WSiP.
75 Winiarski, M. (2000). *Rodzina – szkoła – środowisko lokalne*. Warszawa: IBE.
76 Zieja, Z. (Ed.). (2003). *Poradnik metodyczny dla wychowawców*. Jelenia Góra: Wydawnictwo Kolegium Karkonoskiego.
77 Zyzik, E. (2009). Współpraca szkoły z rodzicami dzieci sześcioletnich oraz ze środowiskiem lokalnym. In J. Karczewska, M. Kwaśniewska (Eds.), *Dziecko sześcioletnie w szkole* (pp. 239–249). Kielce: Wydawnictwo Pedagogiczne ZNP.
78 Żłobicki, W. (2000). *Rodzice i nauczyciele w edukacji wczesnoszkolnej*. Kraków: Oficyna Wydawnicza Impuls".

18
COLLABORATING WITH PARENTS FOR SOUTH SÁMI LANGUAGE LEARNING

A study in an indigenous preschool in Norway

Heidi Harju-Luukkainen, Karianne Berg and Asbjørn Kolberg

Introduction

The indigenous Sámi languages of the Nordic countries and North-West Russia have, during the last decades, gained more official recognition across the Nordic countries, but many challenges remain (Keskitalo, Uusiautti, & Määttä, 2012). This has led to a situation, where the nine different Sámi languages, as well as different language and culture-related aspects of educational practices, have been studied more than before. Despite some positive developmental trends, there are still areas that need to be discussed and studied further. One of these areas is the parental collaboration during ECEC in an indigenous language setting.

One important part of teacher's work is the collaboration with parents. The learning of the children is happening in ecology with home, ECEC, community, through different media channels and other places where children have a possibility to learn and to be engaged (see Cho, Shin, & Krashen, 2004). The younger the child is, the stronger the family's influence in these environments is. However, not all parents are equally equipped to support their child and here professional expertise and specific competence from the teacher are needed (Uusimäki, Yngvesson, Garvis, & Harju-Luukkainen, 2019; Cho et al., 2004). However, there are great variances in how this collaborative work with parents is viewed in the Nordic countries' steering documents, which is the foundation for the work in ECEC setting (Uusimäki et al., 2019)

Further, there are also variances in how different Nordic countries' steering documents support children's language learning possibilities (Garvis, Harju-Luukkainen, & Flynn, 2018). The different approaches may reflect ideological differences toward languages and language learning (García, 2009). For instance, in Finland the steering documents make Sámi language immersion programs possible starting from early childhood education (Finnish National Agency for Education,

DOI: 10.4324/9780367823917-18

2016). This has led to Sámi language immersion in language nest programs in Finland (Äärelä, 2016). Similar supportive structures in the steering documents, cannot be found in the Norwegian context. Therefore, Albury (2016) argues that the Norwegian policy rhetoric has not been operationalized to benefit all Sámi languages or for instance to promote Norwegian familiarity with the Sámi languages.

From these premises, we have formulated a research question. How do teachers in ECEC work with parents in order to support children's language development in South Sámi language? This research paper was conducted as a part of a research project called "How to support language learners in South Sámi language? A study of teachers' competence in instructional strategies." The study was conducted in an ECE unit, in a municipality situated in Norway and it was funded by Regionale forskningsfond (RFF) of Norway. The data were collected with the help of structured interviews during fall 2019. The socioculturally oriented framework of this study is largely influenced by the latest empirical research connected to indigenous Sámi language context and parental collaboration.

Sámi education context in Norway

The Sámi population of the Arctic region, living across four countries, is constituted of people speaking nine different languages. The population is scattered and the indigenous language spoken poses specific educational challenges (Keskitalo et al., 2012; Albury, 2016). However, the Sámi population have attempted to maintain a unified culture by constituting a Sámi parliament and creating among others a national flag (Keskitalo et al., 2012). There are no official statistics on the number of speakers of the Sámi languages and therefore all of the numbers are estimates. The estimation for South Sámi speakers in Norway is around 300 (Ethnologue Languages of the World, 2020), which makes the language severely endangered by UNESCO (Cocq, 2012).

The South Sámi is the southernmost population, frequently described as a minority within the minority (Hermanstrand, Kolberg, Nilssen, & Sem, 2019). The traditional land of the South Sami covers large areas in Norway and Sweden and there are only a few public arenas where the language can be used on a daily basis. In Norway, the Sami Act of 1987 states that Norwegian and Sami are official languages and that they should be used on equal terms in the municipalities belonging to the Sami administrative area (Sami Act, 1987 (§ 1.5, Chapter 3); Regulations of the Sami Act, 2018; Education Act, 2020). The Norwegian Framework Plan for the Content and Task of Kindergartens (2017) highlight the special position of the minorities with an official status. According to the Norwegian Framework Plan for the Content and Task of Kindergartens (Kunnskapsdepartamentet, 2017) and Kindergarten Act (2005), "Sami kindergartens shall promote the children's Sami language skills, strengthen their Sami identity and promote Sami values". In these preschools Sami is the main language of instruction. However, there are no further description of what Sami culture is and what traditional learning and working methods are. Therefore all of the Sami preschools might interpret it differently, even if the Framework Plan for the Content and Task of Kindergartens (Kunnskapsdepartamentet, 2017) states here in particular that "Sami kindergarten children shall be supported in preserving and developing their language, their knowledge and their culture irrespective of where in Norway they live." (p. 25).

In practice, in the Norwegian context, this means various forms of distance education, especially for the South Sámi speaking children, due to the smallness and sparseness of the population. Further, there is a lack of qualified teachers speaking fluent South Sámi outside the South Sámi administrative area, that is a challenge for education providers. Other challenges are connected to adequate teaching material but also according to Keskitalo et al. (2012) to the need to develop an education paradigm that aligns with the needs of the Sámi community. There is (ibid. p. 59) a need to transform the Sámi community's own culture and tradition, its values, stories, expectations, norms, roles, ceremonies, and rituals into school knowledge, which would improve multiculturalism and the inclusion of Sámi culture in schools where Sámi curriculum would be utilized. The same would, without a doubt, be beneficial for the early childhood education context as well.

Parental collaboration

How parental collaboration is viewed in each country is dependent on the national context (Hujala, Turja, Gaspar, Veisson, & Waniganayake, 2009). The Norwegian ECE regarding parental collaboration is stipulated by two main documents: 1) by The Kindergarten Act (2005) and 2) by The Framework Plan for the Content and Task of Kindergartens (Kunnskapsdepartamentet, 2017). The Framework Plan for the Content and Task of Kindergartens (Kunnskapsdepartamentet, 2017) is a regulation under the Kindergarten Act and it provides a more detailed provision on the purpose and content of kindergartens. These documents highlight the importance of parental collaboration for children's well-being, learning, and overall development on a relatively general level. However, they highlight that parents and the preschools have to acknowledge that they have a shared responsibility for the child's well-being and development and further that the best interests of the child shall always be the primary consideration in all co-operation between the home and the kindergarten (Kunnskapsdepartamentet, 2017, p. 29).

Parents and teachers are differently equipped for the teacher–parent partnership where also cultural attributes play a key role. However, it is important to note that a good teacher–parent interaction is a positive determinant of child's later student performance (Xu & Gulosino, 2006; Bergroth & Palviainen, 2016). Teachers need expert skills in collaborating and engaging with the parents of the child (Chan & Ritchie, 2016; Mahmood, 2013), in a Sámi setting these expert skills are connected among other variables to culture and language. According to Alasuutari (2010), the challenge in this teacher–parent collaboration is to agree on the interpretation of partnership and participation for all partners (see also Cheatham & Santos, 2011). According to Xu and Gulosino (2006), teacher quality is one of the important factors affecting this teacher–parent partnership and therefore the teacher education should focus more on teacher behavioral attributes (see also Mahmood, 2013). Here, especially important in the Sámi setting would be for the teachers to get service training regarding the specific characteristics of the Sámi culture and language (see Äärelä, 2016). Further, Chan and Ritchie (2016) highlight a need to move from hegemonic safe zones of traditional teacher-dominated practices toward opening up spaces of dialogic, fluid engagement with families. This is important in an era of increasing super diversity and especially with families whose background differs from teacher's own.

Data and methods

This study was conducted in Norway in a South Sámi preschool. In total three teachers from this preschool were interviewed during fall 2019, with the help of semistructured interviews. These interviews were in length between 57 and 66 minutes. The textual data considering the question "how the teacher collaborated with parents in order to support child's language development in South Sámi" was analyzed with the help of content analysis. Content analysis examines patterns and structures from textual data. It selects out the key features that researchers want to pay attention to, develops categories and aggregates them into perceptual constructs in order to grasp the meaning (Gray & Densten, 1998). According to Weber (1990), content analysis may address language, content meaning, techniques of communication, specific events, or all of these simultaneously. Further, according to Leedy and Ormrod (2001, p. 155), content analysis examines the data in a systematic way for the purpose of identifying patterns, themes, or biases. The analysis started with coding the specific practices teachers used. These practices were then studied closer and thematically coded into two main categories. These two main categories were divided into subcategories. The thematic coding was reviewed and reorganized where needed by the research group members and finally names that best described the themes were defined.

Since this study was conducted in a South Sámi context and the researchers did not speak the language, all of the interviews were conducted in Norwegian. However, it is important to note that the teachers in the preschool considered themselves as bilinguals and fluent Norwegian speakers. The transcribed interviews were then translated to English. As regards ethical considerations, this study adheres to the international and national guidelines for research ethics, including those set by the The Norwegian National Committees for Research Ethics (2019), with special considerations to research with indigenous people. This research has provided its participants adequate information about the field of research, the purpose of the research, who will receive access to the information, the intended use of the results, and the consequences of the research project. This research also respected participants' autonomy, integrity, freedom, and right for co-determination. The data have been processed in such a way that personal matters and information were held confidential.

Findings

According to the results, preschool teachers work with parents in several ways, in order to support children's language learning. Teachers described the context for their parent–teacher collaboration from three larger frames of reference. These are important to understand when the results are interpreted. These three frames were: shared cultural understanding, shared goals, and shared responsibility. Shared cultural understanding refers to the South Sámi culture and how the teachers could use the natural South Sámi cultural settings in order to enhance children's language learning, without a need to explain themselves or a need for special permissions from the parents to work so. Shared goals refer to a mutual understanding between parents and teachers regarding the goals of the education. It refers to how they all work toward making children fluent South Sámi speakers. The shared responsibility refers to the mutual understanding, that this work is everyone's responsibility, in order to fulfill the goal in making the children fluent South Sámi speakers. Overall, the teachers described the relationship with the parents as a good one, with close ties, within the relatively small South Sámi community.

The methods teachers use in order to collaborate with parents regarding children's South Sámi language learning could be divided into two main categories. These were "Seeing preschool as an open arena regarding language learning' and 'Supporting parents in South Sámi language usage." These were then further divided into subcategories as following:

1 Seeing preschool as an open arena for language learning
Being available for questions regarding language
Parents are always welcome to join
2 Supporting parents in South Sámi language usage
Encourage the use of South Sámi
Provide parents with vocabulary

The first main category deals with practices connected to collaboration between teachers and parents, where the preschool is the acting arena for an open and supportive communication regarding language learning. The second one focuses on how teachers support the interaction between parents and their child(ren) at home.

Seeing preschool as an open arena for language learning

All teachers talked about how they worked to keep the threshold low for parents to contact them. Being a small preschool, with only a few children, teachers described how it was relatively easy for them to set aside time to talk with parents when they came to bring and to pick up their child(ren). Teachers expressed that they were available for questions that parents might have for instance regarding the South

Sámi language and thereby they were able to support them in various ways. One teacher described the situations as following:

> Being available when they [the parents] bring and pick up, it is important to be there, chat, messages. It is our experience that they come to us with their questions, many of them, what does that mean, my kid says this, what does that mean?

Another practice teachers described important was showing parents that they are welcome to come in and join the children and teachers if they have time for it, as following:

> If they have the time for it we let them come in for a cup of coffee . . . the parents tell us that they appreciate this opportunity, they can sit down and aren't rushed off.

One advantage with the parents coming into the classroom is that they get the opportunity to observe how teachers work with the children regarding language learning. One teacher described this as following:

> They [the parents] have told us that we just have to speak Sámi language to the children even if they are there, that way they learn at the same time as they can observer how much their children know.

Supporting parents in South Sámi language usage

Teachers talked about the fact that many of the parents were not fluent South Sámi speakers and how this might impact children's language learning. All of the teachers expressed a desire to offer language courses to parents so that they could learn South Sámi language parallel to their child.

> I hope we would be able to offer workshops for parents in order to give them the same language learning possibility as their children receive.

As described by teachers, language learning courses are not available on a regular basis in the municipality. Being aware of this, teachers described what they do to support parents in their South Sámi language learning. Teachers encourage parents to use South Sámi language as much as they know, as following:

> We tell parents to use South Sámi language they know and as much as possible, that's our philosophy.

A practical way to support parents and further children's South Sámi language learning is to provide parents with wordlists and to use communication supportive tools like communication supporting and language learning software (Mykid and Bravo). This was done in order to expand the parents' (and later children's) vocabulary. Teachers provided parents with wordlists covering words from themes that they had been working on in the preschool that week.

> We use Mykid [communication software], we post pictures and we write a little bit every every day, what we've done in Bravo [language learning programme], and we post wordlists.

The reason for this was to make parents better equipped to both understand potential new words that their child(ren) might use at home and to encourage the use of these words in conversations at home. This was done in order to strengthen the children's acquisition regarding new words. One of the teachers described the following, when asked about whether they talked to the parents about what they could do:

> Well, it is important that they follow up at home, because we write on Mykid what we have done . . . It is something for them to talk about when they come home.

Conclusions

According to Ethnologue Languages of the World (2020), the South Sámi population in Norway consisted of around 300 people with South Sámi as their primary or secondary language, all of them being multilingual. This makes South Sámi a severely endangered language and the research connected to its revitalization can be considered as extremely crucial. This in order to develop the understanding of the specific needs of this sparse population. The data for this study were collected with the help of semistructured interviews in a South Sámi preschool in Norway.

This study has several limitations since it is a case study conducted in only one preschool. It is important to note that the results of this study cannot be generalized to a wider population. Further, like in any qualitative research, there is a risk of researcher bias and the study cannot be replicated. Nevertheless, a case study enables a close examination of a specific context. According to the results, teachers described the context for their parent–teacher collaboration from three larger frames of reference. These frames were parallel to the Framework Plan for the Content and Task of Kindergartens (Kunnskapsdepartamentet, 2017) and curriculum and Kindergarten Act (2005), that highlights the promotion of children's Sami language skills, strengthen their Sami identity and promote Sami values. These three frames were: shared cultural understanding, shared goals, and shared responsibility.

According to Alasuutari (2010), the challenge in teacher-parent collaboration is to agree on the interpretation of partnership and participation for all partners. In a Sámi setting, the interpretations of Sámi culture and language appeared to be somewhat common and accepted. The methods teachers used in order to collaborate with parents regarding children's South Sámi language learning could be divided into two main categories. The main categories were "Seeing preschool as an open arena regarding language learning" and "Supporting parents in South Sámi language usage." In this preschool, teachers had managed to open a safe space which enables dialogue. This, according to Chan and Ritchie (2016) and Cheatham and Santos (2011), is of importance. The traditional 'teacher-dominated practices' were not existing in the descriptions of teachers and therefore an open dialogue was created.

This study indicates a clear lack of research on parental collaboration in the Norwegian context but also in the Norwegian indigenous settings. Parental collaboration is especially important as parents are their child's first educators and they have made the decision to enroll their child into a Sámi language preschool and further raise their children as speakers of the South Sámi language (see further research on heritage language support by Cho et al., 2004). We know from previous literature that with a good collaboration between the educational context and the parents, children's language development can be supported (Cho et al., 2004). Even though the teachers used several practices, more could be done. Teachers for instance indicated the need for South Sámi language classes for parents, something that is crucial for children's language learning, maintenance and further in the revitalization work. Also, other practices and new tools (regarding language acquisition) could be developed. The work that the teachers do is crucial for the South Sámi language maintenance and revitalization. Therefore, teachers need to receive the latest in service training in how to support children's language learning from parental as well as from other perspectives.

References

Äärelä, R. (2016). *Dat ii leat dušše dat giella ["Se ei ole vain se kieli"] Tapaustutkimus saamenkielisestä kielipesästä saamelaisessa varhaiskasvatuksessa*. Acta Universitatis Lapponiensis 335. Rovaniemi: Lapin yliopistokustannus.

Alasuutari, M. (2010). Striving at partnership: Parent–practitioner relationships in Finnish early educators' talk. *European Early Childhood Education Research Journal, 18*(2), 149–161. doi:10.1080/13502931003784545

Albury, N. (2016). Holding them at arm's length: A critical review of Norway's policy on Sámi language maintenance. *Journal of Home Language Research (JHLR), 1*, 1–16.

Bergroth, M., & Palviainen, Å. (2016). The early childhood education and care partnership for bilingualism in minority language schooling: Collaboration between bilingual families and pedagogical practitioners. *International Journal of Bilingual Education and Bilingualism, 19*(6), 649–667. doi:10.1080/13670050.2016.1184614

Chan, A., & Ritchie, J. (2016). Parents, participation, partnership: Problematising New Zealand early childhood education. *Contemporary Issues in Early Childhood, 17*(3), 289–303.

Cheatham, G., & Santos, R. (2011). Collaborating with families from diverse cultural and linguistic backgrounds. *Young Children, 66*(5), 76–82.

Cho, G., Shin, F., & Krashen, S. (2004). What do we know about heritage languages? What do we need to know about them? *Multicultural Education*, (2004), 23–26.

Cocq, C. (2012). The Sami languages and the UNESCO's atlas of endangered languages. In *Challenging traditions*. A Blog about Sami Folklore and Internet. Retrieved from https://challengingtraditions.wordpress.com/2012/08/30/the-sami-languages-and-the-unescos-atlas-of-endangered-languages/

Education Act. (2020). *Chapter 6, Sami education*. Ministry of Education and Research, Norway. Retrieved from https://lovdata.no/dokument/NLE/lov/1998-07-17-61#KAPITTEL_7

Ethnologue Languages of the World. (2020). Retrieved from www.ethnologue.com/language/sma

Finnish National Agency for Education. (2016). *National core curriculum for ECEC 2016*. Määräykset ja ohjeet 2016:17. Yliopistopaino: Finnish National Agency for Education. Retrieved from www.oph.fi/download/179349_varhaiskasvatussuunnitelman_perusteet_2016.pdf

García, O. (2009). *Bilingual education in the 21st century: A global perspective*. Malden, MA: Wiley-Blackwell.

Garvis, S., Harju-Luukkainen, H., & Flynn, T. (2018). A descriptive study of early childhood education steering documents in Finland, Sweden and Australia around language immersion programmes. *Asia Pacific Journal of Research in Early Childhood Education, 12*(3), 1–22.

Gray, J. H., & Densten, I. L. (1998). Integrating quantitative and qualitative analysis using latent and manifest variables. *Quality & Quantity, 32*, 419–431.

Hermanstrand, H., Kolberg, A., Nilssen, T. R., & Sem, L. (2019). Theoretical and methodological perspectives. In *The indigenous identity of the South Saami: Historical and political perspectives on a minority within a minority* (Chapter 1). Cham: Springer Open. Retrieved from https://link.springer.com/book/10.1007%2F978-3-030-05029-0

Hujala, E., Turja, L., Gaspar, M. F., Veisson, M., & Waniganayake, M. (2009). Perspectives of early childhood teachers on parent-teacher partnerships in five European countries. *European Early Childhood Education Research Journal, 17*(1), 57–76.

Keskitalo, P., Uusiautti, S., & Määttä, K. (2012). How to make the small indigenous cultures bloom? Special traits of Sámi education in Finland. *Current Issues in Comparative Education, 15*(1), 52–63.

Kunnskapsdepartamentet. (2017). *Framework plan for the content and task of kindergartens*. Retrieved from www.udir.no/globalassets/filer/barnehage/rammeplan/framework-plan-for-kindergartens2-2017.pdf

Leedy, P., & Ormrod, J. (2001). *Practical research: Planning and design* (7th ed.). Thousand Oaks, CA: SAGE Publications.

Mahmood, S. (2013). First-year preschool and kindergarten teachers: Challenges of working with parents. *School Community Journal, 23*(2), 55–85.

Norwegian Kindergarten Act No. 64. (2005). Retrieved from www.regjeringen.no/globalassets/upload/kd/vedlegg/barnehager/engelsk/act_no_64_of_june_2005_web.pdf

The Norwegian National Committees for Research Ethics. (2019). *General guidelines for research ethics*. Retrieved from https://www.etikkom.no/en/ethical-guidelines-for-research/general-guidelines-for-research-ethics/

Regulations of the Sami Act. (2018). *Forskrift om endring av forskrift om forvaltningsområdet for samisk språk (with the latest Sami administrative municipalities)*. Retrieved from https://lovdata.no/dokument/SF/forskrift/2018-04-20-598?q=samisk%20forvaltningsomr%C3%A5de

Sami Act. (1987). *Act of 12 June 1987 no. 56 concerning the sameting (the Sami parliament) and other Sami legal matters (The Sami Act)*. Retrieved from www.regjeringen.no/en/dokumenter/the-sami-act-/id449701/

Uusimäki, L., Yngvesson, T. E., Garvis S., & Harju-Luukkainen, H. (2019). Parental involvement in ECEC in Finland and in Sweden. In S. Garvis, H. Harju-Luukkainen, S. Sheridan, & P. Williams (Eds.), *Nordic families, children and early childhood education: Studies in childhood and youth* (pp. 81–99). Cham: Palgrave Macmillan.

Weber, R. (1990). *Basic content analysis* (2nd ed.). Thousand Oaks, CA: Sage.

Xu, Z., & Gulosino, C. (2006). How does teacher quality matter? The effect of teacher-parent partnership on early childhood performance in public and private schools. *Education Economics, 14*(3), 345–367.

19
PARENT PARTICIPATION IN PRESCHOOL EDUCATION IN SERBIA

Challenges and perspectives

Dragana Pavlović Breneselović, Lidija Miškeljin and Tijana Bogovac

Introduction

In the last two decades, there has been a tendency in most countries to ensure the greater participation of parents in decision-making in public education by introducing legislative measures. This trend comes as the result of efforts to increase (by the greater involvement of parents) the quality of the conditions in which children grow up and learn, and also as the result of the expressed social needs for democratizing and strengthening the doctrine of parents' rights. The rights of parents in education imply, on the one hand, the right to influence their children's education, and on the other hand, the need to strengthen the responsibilities of parents in the educational process. Through greater participation in decision-making, attempts have been made to give parents the role of participants and active citizens, thus reflecting a shift in understanding civil rights from the users' social rights to participatory rights with their obligations and responsibilities (Pavlović Breneselović, 2011). The chapter refers to issues regarding the participation of parents in preschool education and is focused on the review of the limitations of existing policy and practice. A systemic approach, as an alternative, has been elaborated to review this issue and to propose measures for improving on existing practice.

Policy documents and parental involvement in preschool education in Serbia

There is a general consensus on the need for family and kindergarten cooperation, both theoretically and in the field of education policy, among all relevant actors – experts and parents – and in public opinion (Pavlović Breneselović, 2014). The relationship between practitioners and families is widely seen as one of the indicators of the quality of preschool education, although the underlying meaning behind this concept differs frequently from context to context.

The need to open up preschool institutions to local communities and families, and to develop cooperation with families, is emphasized in legislative acts in Serbia. The Law on Education specifies the participation of parents on school boards (three representatives each – parents, school, and municipality representatives), and the establishment of parent councils at the school level with representatives of parents from all classes. This legislative solution is not entirely new since the law envisaged the participation of parents in these bodies decades ago (Pavlović Breneselović, 2011).

In the Law on the Foundation of the Education System (2019b) cooperation with parents or other legal representatives and the wider community is stated as one of the elements of the quality of education and upbringing in the Republic of Serbia. Cooperation with families and the involvement of parents or other legal representatives, local communities, and wider communities is listed as one of the general principles of the system of education (Strategy for education development in Serbia, 2012; Law on the Foundation of the Education System, 2019b). Parent involvement is one of the quality goals. Parent councils have an advisory role in various tasks concerning well-being and the education and financial plans of educational institutions. In recent years, local parent councils have been established legally. They consist of representatives from the parent councils of all institutions at municipality or city levels (Law on the Foundation of the Education System, 2019b).

The principles of preschool education such as democracy, transparency, and development support parent involvement within the Law on Preschool Education (Law on Preschool Education, 2019a). These principles provide an appreciation of the needs and rights of children and families, including the right to have one's opinion heard, the right to participate actively, the right to participate in decision-making processes, and the right to accountability. Preschool education should be based on building relationships with families, other parts of educational systems, and the local and broader communities and on developing various forms and programs in accordance with the needs of children and families and the opportunities afforded by local communities (Law on Preschool Education, 2019a).

Quality with regard to parent involvement is described in more detail in the Rulebook on Quality Standards in Institutions (Rulebook on Quality Standards in Institutions, 2018b). The Rulebook points that children and parents should participate in the design and enrichment of the physical environment, and this should reflect shared participation and learning. Moreover, program development takes into consideration the initiatives, proposals, ideas, and experiences of children and parents. Institutions should respect diversity and the rights and needs of children and families, and they should develop different programs and forms based on the needs identified. Different ways of involving families should be applied in institutions, and the supportive role of institutions is also emphasized.

The presentation of educational policy documents reveals a "manifest model of family participation" in which family participation is operationalized through organizational structures and areas of activity and forms of realizing relations with families (Pavlović Breneselović, 2014, p. 113). Legislation emphasizes the forms of cooperation with families, their diversity, and the reach and frequency of parental engagement. Partnership is defined in the field of communication, management, parents' participation in the program, and education for parenthood. The existing approach to the participation of parents in preschool education tends to increase the participation of parents through measures for regulating and introducing forms of participation and neglects the context of establishing relationships and the question of the quality of relationships, which includes questions of trust, respect, and sharing.

Research on parental involvement in preschool education in Serbia

The preceding shows that there is a legal and curriculum basis for parent participation in Serbia. However, there is no systematic or comprehensive research on the issue of parent participation in preschool education. Still, research shows that the legislative regulation of parental involvement does not ensure the actual involvement of parents (Kernan, 2012; Pavlović Breneselović, 2013b; Vranješević, 2012). It shows that real parent participation is a challenge even though it is proclaimed by law (Powell, 2010; Pavlović Breneselović, 2011, 2013b, 2014; Spasić & Mihajlović, 2014). In practice, the forms of parents' cooperation with educational institutions are often found to be inadequate, insufficient, and unsatisfying for both parents and preschool teachers (Spasić & Mihajlović, 2014). The latest situational analysis and recommendations on preschool education in Serbia (Baucal et al., 2016) showed that even though parents' participation in decision making is supported by legal regulations, their actual participation in the decision-making process is underdeveloped in practice and remains formal. Moreover, parent involvement is most often organized from the perspective of the needs and requirements of preschool and rarely from the perspective of the needs and interests of families (Baucal et al., 2016).

There is support for families available from preschools. The majority of preschools have established associates, i.e., pedagogues, psychologists, speech therapists, and social workers, who implement preventive, consultative, and advisory activities with parents (Baucal et al., 2016).

Baucal et al. (2016) argue that parent participation without well-developed quality relations through mutual trust, dialogue, and support can contribute to situations of mutual animosity in which parents are not sincerely welcome and teachers feel exposed to pressure from parents. Because of the uneven distribution of institutions and the lack of capacities to meet the needs of all families, children from more affluent families, whose parents possess higher educations and who reside in urban areas, are enrolled at higher percentages in kindergartens which brings in inequality as an issue of interest linked to the issue of parent participation. Research also indicates that children from vulnerable groups are under-represented in preschool institutions (Macura-Milovanovic, 2013, Krnjaja & Pavlović Breneselović, 2017). This also means their parents are underrepresented on parent councils. This deepens the issue of participation as one directly linked to the value of inclusion and democratic values that needs to be addressed further.

Parental involvement in preschool teacher education

The initial education for preschool teachers in Serbia is highly heterogeneous. There are different vocational and academic programs that last from three to four years (Bogovac & Miškeljin, 2019). Heterogeneous curricula and substantial differences in teaching methodology and training are also characteristics of preschool teachers' initial education in Serbia (Krnjaja & Pavlović Breneselović, 2013, Miskeljin, 2018, Bogovac & Miškeljin, 2019). The vision of a preschool teacher as a reflective practitioner with an emphasis on openness to families and the local community as well as diversified programs and forms of preschool education is underlined by many authors (Krnjaja & Pavlović Breneselović, 2013; Pavlović Breneselović, 2013a, 2014; Miskeljin, 2018; Baucal et al., 2016; Bogovac, 2019; Bogovac & Miškeljin, 2019).

With regard to content, initial teacher education is disciplinary and parent involvement is not highlighted as a specific area of interest. There are various areas of knowledge that students who are future preschool teachers need to possess. However, this approach to education where competences are perceived as isolated bodies of knowledge should be transformed. It is often highlighted that the initial education of preschool teachers should be built on the vision of teachers as creators and researchers with an emphasis on openness to local communities and to families (Baucal et al., 2016; Miskeljin, 2018). Providing opportunities for preschool teachers to engage in collaborative learning and critical reflection; cooperating with other institutions, experts, and children's families inside and outside of the system; networking with researchers and initial education institutions; and a coherent system of support are all needed (Bogovac & Miškeljin, 2019).

Parental participation in preschool education practice in Serbia

There has been a move toward more inclusive, democratic preschool education in recent years. Understanding parent participation is further expanded in the new Preschool Curriculum Framework entitled Years of Ascent (2018a). It emphasizes that the curriculum should be built on the basis of partnerships with families. These partnerships are perceived broadly from spatial-organizational indicators that range from indicating that families are invited and respected to family familiarity with the curriculum philosophy. There are various ways and modes of involving families that should be developed through dialogue with parents who assume different roles: as members of parent council, as volunteers, and as participants in activities with children. The curriculum framework emphasizes respect for the diversity of families and calls for various ways of involving them. Moreover, the framework stipulates building strategies to overcome any obstacles or difficulties for the inclusion of certain families (Preschool Curriculum Framework – Years of Ascent, 2018a).

Throughout piloting the new Preschool Curriculum Framework, there has been growth in the understanding of parent involvement in practice. The Preschool Curriculum Framework promotes programs that are created through joint participation in an environment that is inspiring and provocative for the child in which they can freely explore, play, think, cooperate with others, experiment, and meet the world around them. The data from the evaluation of piloting the new Preschool Curriculum Framework – Years of Ascent indicated that there was a high level of family involvement when it came to different ways of involvement, family engagement, and the frequency of their participation in developing curriculum. In the new program, parents most often participated by being involved in developing projects with children and educators, being informed in writing about events at kindergartens, providing technical assistance, and in activities with children in kindergartens.

Comparing family involvement in the program during the first and third quarters of the piloting the new Preschool Curriculum Framework – Years of Ascent, there was an almost twofold increase in parental involvement in project development, technical support, written information, and parent involvement in activities with children in the local community (Years of Ascent, Technical Report, 2018). Data from parent focus groups showed that partnerships with families were developed and that parents rated the quality of the program regarding benefits for children and families highly. Parents were well acquainted with the concept of the program, everyday life in kindergartens, changes in kindergarten spaces and the way they used spaces, as well as how they as parents could participate in the program. Parents emphasized the significant benefits for their children from participating in the program: satisfaction with being in kindergartens, developing close relationships, as well as developing new interests, commitment, and perseverance, and interests in research. Parents also emphasized their own benefits from the program when it came to strengthening parental competences (understanding their child and what is important to them, getting to know themselves as parents, and empowering them in their roles), their own well-being as parents (expressing their interests, skills, opportunities for new experiences, relaxation), and the impact on the quality of the time spent with children and the quality of family life.

> We do the same thing with flour at home and all these jars – we do it very often. It is a complete delight, since they get completely dirty and covered with flour. And then what they do, it is an exhibition and it stands, no one can touch it. And to us, when we do those projects at home, it really is relaxing, a fun time with them. Each of us has it with our children, but in

different ways, when they participate, when you ask them what they want, how to do something. To me as a parent it shows what kindergarten is and those who are part of it.

(Years of Ascent – Technical Report, 2018)

The process of piloting the new Preschool Curriculum Framework showed that, in practice, partnerships with families should be built first through meaningful joint activities with children, parents, and teachers that emphasize the quality of relationships and through mutual trust and respect.

How the family-preschool partnership should be developed

Understanding and developing partnerships is a question of perceiving and changing the position of the actors in social interactions through the roles they play. The legislative regulation of parental participation in preschool education and the Preschool Curriculum Framework are necessary pre-conditions, but they are certainly not enough to ensure the actual participation of parents.

Forms of parental involvement cannot occur as ready-made forms of partnership, but conversely, partnerships develop through the process of developing these forms. This process does not take place in a vacuum but is conditioned by a number of contextual variables that must also change (Weiss, Caspe, & Lopez, 2006; Weiss, Kreider, Lopez, & Chatman-Nelson, 2010; Lopez, Kreider, & Caspe, 2004). Existing models of cooperation with families focus on individual plans for the school-parent relationship. Instead, models of cooperation with families should focus on the empowerment of the social role of parents in education by strengthening the civilian role of parents as citizens (Hargreaves, Earl, Moore, & Manning, 2001; Vincent, 1996) and systemic and institutional changes that would improve educational conditions for both children and families (Weiss et al., 2006). Increasing the power of the parents' social role by strengthening the citizens' role through connecting, identifying common interests, lobbying for necessary changes, engaging in social actions, and genuine participation in management and decision-making creates the basis for equal participation of families in public education, and, thus, its higher quality.

In this section, we will attempt to develop a systemic approach to the issue of the family – preschool partnership. Such an approach implies a holistic, dynamic, contextual view of the relationship as a complex system of different, mutually conditioned, mutually connected, and mutually dependent social, program, personal, and organizational dimensions (Figure 19.1).

Partnership roles of parents and professionals can develop from the redefinition of concepts in all four dimensions mentioned earlier. In the social dimension, reconceptualizing the social role of professionals and parents should be done by deconstructing hierarchical relationships by changing the structure of power from *power over* others into *power with* others. The power of professionals is not based

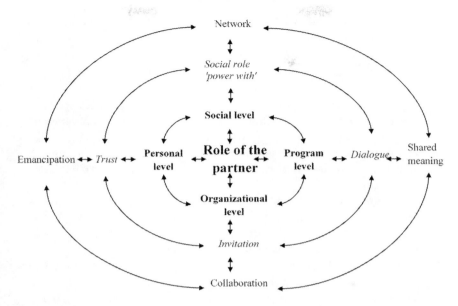

FIGURE 19.1 Systemic operationalization of partnerships through dimensions of roles (Pavlović Breneselović, 2011)

on a hierarchy of expert knowledge, but on the potential to create conditions for empowering others (by which *power for* and one's own feeling of self-respect are developed) and strengthening *power with* (Chambers, 2004). In the program, it means an exchange through *dialogues* where

> one will perceive his/her own beliefs about children, teaching and learning, not as neutral and independent, but as historically and culturally conditioned, and thus open to interpretation, criticism and reconstruction, one's own and of other people's, and encouraging parents to perceive their beliefs in the same way.
>
> *(Hughes & MacNaughton, 2007)*

At the organizational level, it refers to changes in the structure and culture of the institution that implements a program of family inclusion by which *invitation* (Hoover-Dempsey, 2005; Henderson & Mapp, 2002) and participation are promoted through the organization of space and time that enables participation; transparent procedures of participation; a culture of collaboration and continuous learning, etc. On a personal level, it means trust, and a readiness to expose oneself to others, that is developed through social interactions based on respect, attention, integrity, and the competencies of the other party (Bryk & Schneider cited in Mendoza, Katz, & Robertson, 2003). Mutually connected and supportive dimensions of dialogue (sharing power, trust, and participation) generate the essence of the partnership. The *network* is the structure of the relationship based on shared power (Capra, 1998) and social capital and the development of *shared meaning*, *collaboration*, and *emancipation* and the empowerment of one's own capacities for understanding children, their needs and capacities, and learning and changing social practices.

If we view the relationship of families and preschools as a complex system, the nature of this relationship is determined by characteristics of certain dimensions, and in order to change it, it is necessary to have a systemic approach to change. This approach implies a strategy based on the co-construction of the relationships between families and preschools through systemic changes in all the dimensions of these relationships.

Based on the systemic approach, we propose the following issues that need to be considered in order to develop genuine family – kindergarten partnerships:

1) **Autonomy and decentralization**. Changes in relationships between families and preschools are impossible without appropriate changes at the policy level. If the policy of the institution is agreed upon at the centralized level, and if, through a financial monopoly, a monopoly on decision-making is introduced (as well as if there is uniformity in the programs), then the participation of families in decision-making remains merely formal. Greater autonomy for preschools in organizational, financial, and program terms is a necessary precondition for partnerships with families.

2) **Learning community**. Developing partnerships with families is not an issue of multiplying forms of cooperation, but an issue of institutionalizing procedures and culture that allows for the equal and authentic participation of families through a process of exchange and respect. Raising awareness of one's own position and the diversity of perspectives, recognition of the needs and interests of children and parents, dialogue and elaborated mechanisms of involvement in preschool activities, decision-making procedures, and procedures for involvement in planning all have to be incorporated in a coherent program of preschool functioning. This is also an issue of meaningful exchange between parents and teachers on topics of education through appropriate organizational forms and not a separate area of activities implemented through various forms of involvement.

3) **Restructuring preschools**. The organizational structures of institutions have to be compatible with the partnership nature of relationships. Changes in the nature of relationships with families cannot be expected without appropriate relationships among preschool employees. Thus, the organizational structure of preschool employees must shift from linear and hierarchical towards team-functioning and the development of a learning community to create a common vision of partnerships with families. This, for example, raises issue of group sizes and existing standards for professional associates, as well as issues of the organization of time at work.

4) **Involvement of children**. Partnerships between families and preschools should not be limited to dyadic relationships between parents and teachers; it has to involve those for whom it is developed (i.e., the children). Children are not only mediators but they also have to be active participants and creators in these relationships. The strongest motivational factor for the involvement of parents is the feeling of being invited not only by preschools but also by their own children.
5) **Teacher as researcher and reflective practitioner**. Teachers play the key role in establishing partnerships. The issue of teachers' relationships with families cannot be the issue of any personal attitude, private philosophy of education, or regulatory program requirement, but it must be an integral part of teacher education as professionals whose role consists of the capacity to develop and reflect on their own practice as a continuous process of learning through collaboration, capacity building, and learning about children and families.
6) **Social capital and networking**. In this process, teachers have to be supported not only in the working environment but also in developing social capital within the stimulating network of connections and exchanges of different systems that participate in the education of children: preschools, families, universities, the civil sector, and relevant ministries. This requires restructuring some of these systems (e.g., universities and the government should become more open and flexible).
7) **Democratization**. The issue of relationships between families and preschools is that of the relationship between individuals and institutions as well as among institutions. Therefore, it is an inseparable part of the democratization of institutions and society as a whole. On the one hand, awareness should be raised about the right to choose, taking initiative, and exercising influence and personal responsibility. Nevertheless, awareness should be raised that public institutions and activities function for the public, not that the involvement of the public is an incidental concession, and that this contributes to the development of a preschool – family partnership. This is a long-term process, but each long-term process has to have initial steps; preschools could be the natural context through which society, by supporting the role of families as partners in the education of children, supports parents in their civic roles.

References

Baucal, A., Pavlović Breneselović, D., Miškeljin, L., Koruga, D., Stanić, K., & Avramović, M. (2016). *Early childhood education and care (ECEC) in the Republic of Serbia: Situational analysis and recommendations. Consulting report for World Bank*. Washington, DC: World Bank.

Bogovac, T. (2019). The issue of parent participation in preschool education in Serbia: Teachers' and families' perspectives. In S. Phillipson & S. Garvis (Eds.), *Early childhood education and care: Early childhood education in the 21st century* (Vol. II, p. 182). London: Routledge.

Bogovac, T., & Miškeljin, L. (2019). Early childhood workforces in Serbia as a policy issue. In S. Garvis & S. Phillipson (Eds.), *Policification of early childhood education and care: Early childhood education in the 21st century* (Vol. III, pp. 192–199). London: Routledge. vbk://9781351397858

Capra, F. (1998). *Mreža života: Novo znanstveno razumevanje živih sustava*. Zagreb: Liberata.

Chambers, R. (2004). *Ideas for development: Reflecting forwards*. Working Paper No. 238. Brighton: Institute of Development Studies.

Hargreaves, A., Earl, L., Moore, S., & Manning, S. (2001). *Learning to change: Teaching beyond subjects and standards*. San Francisco: Jossey-Bass.

Henderson, A., & Mapp, K. (2002). *A new wave of evidence: The impact of school, family and community connections*. Austin: SEDL.

Hoover-Dempsey, K. V. (2005). Why do parents become involved? Research findings and implications. *Elementary School Journal*, *106*(2), 105–130.

Hughes, P., & MacNaughton, G. (2007). Who is the expert? Reconceptualising parent-staff relations in early education. *Australian Journal of Early Education*, *24*(4).

Kernan, M. (2012). *Parental involvement in early learning – a review of research, policy and good practice*. Retrieved from https://icdi.nl/media/uploads/publications/parental-involvement-in-early-learning.pdf

Krnjaja, Ž., & Pavlović Breneselović, D. (2013). *Gde stanuje kvalitet – Politika uspostavljanja kvaliteta u predškolskom vaspitanju Knjiga 1* [*Where does the quality live: Policies of building early childhood education quality*] (Vol. I). Belgrade: Institute for Pedagogy and Andragogy, Faculty of Philosophy, University of Belgrade.

Krnjaja, Ž., & Pavlović Breneselović, D. (2017). The justness of preschool education in Serbia: Ensuring equal opportunities. *Journal of Contemporary Educational Studies/Sodobna Pedagogika*, *68*(3), 230–246.

Lopez, E. M., Kreider, H., & Caspe, M. (2004). Co-constructing family involvement. *Harvard Family Research Project: The Evaluation Exchange*, *10*(4). Retrieved from https://archive.globalfrp.org/evaluation/the-evaluation-exchange/issue-archive/evaluating-family-involvement-programs/co-constructing-family-involvement

Macura-Milovanovic, S. (2013). Pre-primary education of Roma children in Serbia: Barriers and possibilities. *CEPS Journal: Center for Educational Policy Studies Journal*, *3*(2), 9.

Mendoza, J., Katz, L., & Robertson, A. S. (2003). *Connecting with parents in the early years*. Urbana: University of Illinois, Early Childhood and Parenting Collaborative Campaign.

Miskeljin, L. (2018). Serbia ECEC workforce profile. In J. Peeters & L. Miskeljin (Eds.), *Towards a new initial training for ECEC teachers in Serbia*. Consulting Report for UNICEF Serbia (not published).

Official Gazette. (2012). *Strategy for education development in Serbia 2020*. Belgrade: Author.

Official Gazette. (2018a) *Osnove programa predškolskog vaspitanja i obrazovanja Godine uzleta* [*Preschool curriculum framework – years of ascent*]. Belgrade: Author.

Official Gazette. (2018b). *Rulebook on quality standards of work of institutions*. Belgrade: Author.

Official Gazette. (2019a). *Zakon o predškolskom vaspitanju i obrazovanju* (*Law on preschool education*]. Belgrade: Author.

Official Gazette. (2019b). *Zakon o osnovama Sistema obrazovanja i vaspitanja* [*Law on the foundations of the education system*]. Belgrade: Author.

Pavlović Breneselović, D. (2011). *Participation of parents in decision-making: From obligatory to genuine partnership*. ESP Working Paper No. 25. Retrieved from https://karl.soros.org/communities/esp-working-papers

Pavlović Breneselović, D. (2013a). Kompetencije ili kompetentnost: Različiti diskursi profesionalizma vaspitača. *Vaspitanje i obrazovanje*, *34*(2), 57–68.

Pavlović-Breneselović, D. (2013b). Partnership between family and school as a dimension of quality: Controversy of parents' participation in decision making in school. *Journal of Institute of Pedagogy and Andragogy*, *1*, 185–208.

Pavlović Breneselović, D. (2014). *Partnerstvo sa porodicom: Tri paradigme, dva modela, jedna ili više stvarnosti* [*Partnership with family: Three paradigms, two models, one or more realities*]. Paper presented at the Nacionalni naučni skup: Identitet profesije pedagog u savremenom obrazovanju.

Piloting the Draft Preschool Curriculum Framework – Years of Ascent. (2018). *Technical report*. Belgrade: Institute of Pedagogy and Andragogy, Faculty of Philosophy University of Belgrade (not published).

Powell, D. (1994). *Families and early childhood programs*. Washington, DC: NAEYC.

Spasić, B., & Mihajlović, M. (2014). *Parents have a say, too initiative*. Retrieved from www.cipcentar.org/en/PDF/Parents%20Have%20a%20Say,%20Too%20Initiative.pdf

Vincent, C. (1996). Parent empowerment? Collective action or inaction in education. *Oxford Review of Education*, *22*(4), 465–482.

Vranješević, J. (2012). Participation of parents in the educational-pedagogical process: Possibilities and limitations. *Inovacije u nastavi-časopis za savremenu nastavu*, *25*(3), 15–26.

Weiss, H., Caspe, M., & Lopez, M. E. (2006). *Family involvement in early childhood education*. Cambridge, MA: Harvard Family Research Project, No. 1.

Weiss, H. B., Kreider, H., Lopez, M. E., & Chatman-Nelson, C. (Eds.). (2010). *Preparing educators to engage families: Case studies using an ecological systems framework* (2nd ed.). Thousand Oaks, CA: Sage Publications, Inc.

20
TAMING THE TIGER

Exploring parental involvement in early childhood education in Singapore

Eugenia Koh-Chua, Sarah Somarajan, Lucas Ku-Wang and Sivanes Phillipson

Research has shown that parental involvement in young children's education has a direct impact on children's educational success (Anthony & Ogg, 2019; Epstein & Sanders, 2002; Huat See & Gorard, 2015; Jeynes, 2005). Parental involvement is a multi-faceted construct (Epstein & Sanders, 2002) that can manifest in three principal ways: home-based involvement where parents initiate home-based educational activities, school-based involvement where parents participate in activities organised by the school and home-school communication (Anthony & Ogg, 2019, Epstein, 1995). In addition to partnerships with families, Epstein (2010b) posits for schools to build relationships with the community as a holistic three-sphered influence for supporting children's learning needs.

In Singapore, the working terms for parental involvement across various educational settings are 'parent engagement' and 'school-home partnerships' (Manzon, Miller, Hong, & Khong, 2015). Parent engagement, in Singapore, is defined as

> the beliefs, attitudes, and activities of parents to support their children's learning from birth to adulthood, occurring across home, school, and community contexts, as a shared and co-constructed responsibility with the school and based on a trusting relationship between the school and parents.
> *(Manzon et al., 2015, p. 5)*

This notion took root in the late 1990s when the Ministry of Education established an advisory council – COMmunity and PArents in Support of Schools (COMPASS) to promote stronger home-school partnership (Khong & Ng, 2005; Ministry of Education, 2019a).

At the early childhood education setting, Singaporean parents are actively involved in their children's education through different ways such as reading at home, providing enrichment and tuition programmes as well as volunteering at school (Early Childhood Development Agency, 2014; Khong & Ng, 2005). It can be said that this is a marked shift as compared to the past when parents were primarily involved only for children's behavioural or academic issues in school (Khong & Ng, 2005). The increased parental involvement has been attributed to rising economic affluence and increasing academic competition in a high-staked educational landscape (Manzon et al., 2015).

Singapore's education landscape

Singapore has undergone several waves of educational reforms since the nation's independence in 1965. Replacing an old industrialisation model in the early nation-building days, Singapore schools presently embrace a new educational paradigm aimed at developing learners with problem-solving skills and critical and creative thinking, under the 1997 Teaching Schools, Learning Nation (TSLN) vision (Ministry of Education, 2018b). The TSLN vision is a holistic education reform targeted at all educational levels, from preschool to university, to ensure the country's labour force remains adequately competitive yet adaptive to changing global economic conditions (Koh, 2004).

In terms of early years education, the Ministry of Education implemented the Nurturing Early Learners (NEL) Framework in 2003. This nation-wide kindergarten curriculum framework aims to transform the traditional educational focus on rote learning and academic excellence towards a holistic educational approach (Khong & Ng, 2005). The framework focuses on six main areas, namely aesthetics and creative expression, discovery of the world, language and literacy, motor skills development, numeracy and social and emotional development (Ting, 2007). As such, the NEL Framework is a child-centric learning approach which recognises children as active learners and calls for more opportunities for play as they learn (Ling-Yin, 2006).

Whilst the NEL Framework has been implemented for more than a decade, Singaporean parents continue to struggle with the reconciliation of a play-based learning approach (Jones, 2019). In 2012, as high as 80% of Singaporean parents believed tuition is beneficial to children's education, especially for the average performing students (Private Tuition in Singapore: A Whitepaper Release, 2012). The same data showed that almost one in three Singaporeans think children should start tuition in preschool years and 46% of Singaporeans think tuition is necessary for children to stay competitive with their peers (Private Tuition in Singapore: A Whitepaper Release, 2012). Due to these firm beliefs and hothousing behaviours, Singaporean parents have been socially labelled as 'tiger parents' (Bach & Christensen, 2017) or '*kiasu*' parents' (Ng, 2017), with '*kiasu*' being a vernacular term for 'fear of losing out competitively'.

Tiger parenting is a social phenomenon strongly identified with Asian-heritage families (Juang, Qin, & Park, 2013). The term was first popularised by Chinese American Amy Chua's (2011) autobiographical account of her own child-rearing practices, in which she called herself a 'tiger mother' – a mother of Chinese ethnicity, highly focused on her children's academic success and achievements, often depriving them of free play and social dates. The book brought scholarly attention to parenting practices within Asian-heritage families, with studies exploring the influence of tiger parenting on children's educational outcomes and socio-emotional well-being (Choi, Kim, Kim, & Park, 2013; Doan et al., 2017; Kim, Wang, Orozco-Lapray, Shen, & Murtuza, 2013; Tam, Kwok, Ling, & Li, 2018). Despite these studies being conducted on different Asian-heritage cultures, the association between tiger parenting and the Chinese culture remains prominently established. With more than 74% of Singapore's population predominated by the Chinese race (Singapore Department of Statistics, 2018), it appears a strong likelihood the *kiasu* parent phenomenon stems from Singapore's deeply ingrained cultural appreciation for high academic achievements (Ng, 2017).

The dissonance Singaporean parents experience with the national play-based curriculum approach is further fuelled by the preparatory function performed by early childhood education in Singapore (Choy & Karuppiah, 2016; Mathews, Lim, & See, 2017). In a study conducted on Singaporean parents with preschool-aged children (Ebbeck & Gokhale, 2004), school readiness was found to be the most significant concern parents had. It has been suggested that such parental anxieties are largely attributed to concerns on the expected academic rigour within the primary school education system despite recent removal of examinations for early primary years (Costales & Anderson, 2018; Private Tuition in Singapore: A Whitepaper Release, 2012). In turn, these anxieties translated to increased parental involvement where Singaporean parents have been criticised for displaying overly competitive behaviour (Mokhtar, 2018).

Taming the tiger: parental involvement in ECE in Singapore

The Singapore government recognises that parents are vital stakeholders and important agents of change with regard to educational reforms (Retna & Ng, 2016; Yeong & Ng, 2009). It is posited that Singaporean policymakers view these 'unreformed passions of *kiasu* parents' (Christensen, 2015, p. 566) as the most significant barrier for education reform (Bach & Christensen, 2017). In the words of the Minister of Education, "for this shift to succeed, we will also need to bring the most important stakeholder – parents – on board" (Ministry of Education, 2018a). While the education reform was initially targeted at student development, the focus of the reform is now re-directed towards 'civilising parents' (Bach & Christensen, 2017, p. 138) to refrain from *kiasu* behaviour. It seems then the resulting conflict between parental expectations and the government's education reform directive remains lucid.

Nevertheless, parents continue to perceive the need to provide their children with extra enrichment programmes in addition to preschool education, whilst preschool teachers and leaders perceive life skills to be more critical for children's school readiness (Choy & Karuppiah, 2016; Ebbeck & Gokhale, 2004). On the other hand, to ensure parents fully embrace the paradigm shift towards holistic education, the Ministry of Education recognised the need to instil cultural change within the parent community (Ng, 2017). As part of the government's efforts to engage in 'positive and meaningful school-home partnerships' (Ministry of Education, 2019b), the Ministry of Education developed a set of partnership guidelines for parents (Koh, 2019). Nation-wide advertising campaigns including through the use of social media were launched to promote the importance of play-based learning in early years (Gov.sg, 2017). More recently, the government actively advocates for joyful learning through play (Ministry of Education, 2019a) and encourages parents to let children play more during school holidays (Ministry of Education, 2019b). While the reform policies were initially targeted at structural changes, following policy initiatives place greater emphasis on creating cultural shifts within the parent community (Ng, 2017).

Purpose of the study

This study explores and illustrates the role of parental involvement in early childhood education in Singapore. Specifically, the two guiding research questions are:

- How do stakeholders in Singapore's early childhood education settings – school leaders, educators and parents, define parental involvement in children's early years of education?
- How do Singaporean parents respond to play-based classroom practices in relation to recent policy initiatives to create a cultural shift amongst parents?

By analysing and triangulating the perspectives of the three stakeholders of K2 children in Singapore preschools, findings from this study provide narratives for future directions in early childhood education, particularly with enabling educators and parents to work collaboratively to support the education reform.

Method

This study adopted an exploratory qualitative methodology to gain insights into the perspectives of parents, preschool educators and leaders on parental mindsets towards the government's play-based initiatives. To perform this research objective, semi-structured one-on-one interview was chosen as the research approach. A total of six interviews were conducted face-to-face for stronger authenticity and on all three stakeholders for triangulation purposes. The interviews were conducted in private meeting rooms within the respective centre premises and lasted 30 minutes each.

Participants

A total of six participants – two school principals, two Kindergarten Two (K2)[1] teachers and two parents of K2 children from two local preschool centres, took part in the study. One of the preschool centres is an anchor operator,[2] and the other is a private preschool operator. Parental involvement levels have shown to possess a direct correlation to the socio-economic conditions, type of job and education background of parents (Goodall, 2017). Hence, the centres were chosen to represent sampling sets from diverse social-economic backgrounds.

The school principals and teachers selected for this study have worked in varied early years settings – both government-subsidised and private centres. The principals have more than 11 years of experience each, and the teachers have taught different early years levels for more than six years. The teachers' experience in working with K2 children and families are also mixed. One has taught three different K2 cohorts in the same centre, while the other followed the same class from pre-nursery up to K2 level.

Data collection instrument

Three sets of interview questions were prepared for each participant type (i.e. Principal, Teacher and Parent). Each participant set was interviewed using the same question set involving their perspectives on parental involvement in relation to the national play-based pedagogy framework. Example questions were such as '*How well does the NEL Framework align with the way you support and aspire for your child's learning*'? (for Parents), '*How supportive are the parents of K1 and K2 students towards play-based learning activities'?*" (for Principals and Teachers) and "*How do you think parents can better support play-based learning at home for their children and at school?* (for Principals and Teachers). The interviews were audio-recorded to ensure authenticity and validity of the verbatim transcriptions.

Data analysis

The six transcribed interviews were analysed in two steps: a manual thematic coding analysis followed by a Leximancer software analysis. Using the Leximancer analysis, the software's logarithmic analysis avoids researcher bias that could exist in a human inductive analysis method. However, the human analyst's subjectivity in the manual thematic coding includes semantic and socio-cultural background knowledge, which the Leximancer software does not possess (Smith & Humphreys, 2006). The semantic background is critical to this study as the participants are mostly Singaporeans who used Singlish, a colloquial variation of the standard English language. The grammatical structure of Singlish can deviate quite drastically from the standard English, as it borrows lexical components from the Malay language and Chinese dialects (Bokhorst-Heng, 2005). Hence, in using both analytical methods for this study, we hope to increase the validity of the data analysis, in view of the limitations in the sampling size.

In the manual thematic coding analysis, we manually scanned through the verbatim transcripts to identify recurring patterns and central organising concepts in the data that is meaningful to the research questions (Braun & Clarke, 2013). The themes were then validated with the Leximancer thematic summary. In the Leximancer analysis, underlying core themes and associations between themes were identified based on a logarithmic analysis built on word frequency and lexical co-occurrence (Smith & Humphreys, 2006). The themes are ranked by connectedness using the summed co-occurrence with all other themes.

Findings and discussion

There are two main findings from the analysis in this study. Both findings are related to how parents are involved in their children's education to ensure the desired outcomes for their children. The first finding explains the types of parental involvement, the challenges that such involvement raise, and the strategies schools adopt to encourage parental involvement. The second major finding is concerned with how parents' involvement addresses their perception of play as important to be part of their children's upbringing and education. In the following sections, we present and discuss these two main findings.

Parental involvement in Singapore ECE settings: types, challenges and strategies

The Leximancer results indicate two main concepts as themes in response to the research question of this study. Figure 20.1 shows that the concept, Child is the main theme with 628 verbatims hits and 2331 connectivity between key concepts in the study. The connectivity in the map supports the relationships found through the manual coding, where three types of parental involvement were identified. Concurring with literature (Anthony & Ogg, 2019; Epstein, 1995, 2010b), these involvements revolve around school-based involvement, home-based involvement and home-school communication. In addition, stakeholders articulated the importance of a tripartite type of involvement that consists of a partnership between parents, school and community, which reflects Epstein's (2010b) advocacy for home-school-community partnerships. Parents in this study were found to focus more on home-based involvement and home-school communication while educators hope for parents to be more actively engaged in school-based involvement.

Examples of school-based involvement reported in the study include parents-led in-class curriculum programmes (e.g. storytelling and inquiry-based experiments), parent-and-child participation in school-based charity activities, and parents attending children's performances in celebratory events. Home-based involvement firstly manifests as parents conducting home-coaching to help children be on par with required learning milestones and objectives. One parent shared that '*she* (her child) *is slightly behind in terms of numbers, so I do take more time at home to work with her*'. These home-coaching activities are welcomed by teachers interviewed in this study who emphasised the need for '*parents' help at home* [because] . . . *time* [within school hours] *is very tight*' to sufficiently cater to the learning needs of every single child. Enrichment programmes are also regarded as an effective type of home-based involvement, especially when parents lack time or subject knowledge needed to conduct home-coaching. One school principal remarked that *'parents don't grow up learning phonics, so it's a concept where they find it hard to support their child and learning, whereas putting into enrichment class would be more helpful for the child'*. The most popular educational programmes in both schools are Chinese enrichment and English reading classes. For home-school communication, both schools interviewed in this study make use of a plethora of communication platforms to update parents of their children's academic progress and daily well-being, with mobile phone applications being one of the most popular communication methods for parents.

In terms of home-school-community involvement, Epstein (2010a) proposed for relatives of the extended family, members of other families or the wider community to provide support for children's learning needs. In this study, grandparents and domestic helpers are reported to play active roles alongside parents in supporting children's learning at schools. Through working as parent volunteers, parents also contribute as community members who *'get to know not only your child in the class but* [also] *other children'*. These partnerships are critical for children's academic success as they help create conditions to support children's emotional well-being (Epstein, 2010b).

Overall, the definition of parental involvement by Singapore stakeholders interviewed in this study is found to be consistent with the definition adopted by policymakers (Manzon et al., 2015). According to Epstein (2010a), the early years of a child are critical in determining his/her future success. Parents who recognise this importance invest in equipping their children with skills and educational programmes and support their learning with guidance to better prepare them for school (Epstein, 2010a). Similarly, we found Singaporean parents to exhibit such beliefs, attitudes and behaviours through the three types of parental involvement.

Along with the types of involvement come challenges for parents to be involved in their child's education constructively. Referring to Figure 20.1, several key concepts stand out, and they are firstly the issue of time or lack of time for parents to be involved, parents' feelings that arise from trust in teachers and the relationship they have with their child's teachers. Parents' level of involvement is also dependent on which point of schooling their child is at.

In Singapore, it is common to find the caregiving role performed by domestic helpers and extended family members due to heavy work commitments and government policies that encourage mothers to work (Cheo & Quah, 2005; Ebbeck & Gokhale, 2004). As such, it is understandable parents listed time as their greatest challenge in parental involvement, as they perceive the school expectations as *'a little bit tedious'*, *'very tiring to be so involved'* and *'challenging'*.

Trust, being the other critical factor identified by educators in this study, is foundational for successful home-school partnerships, along with respect (Epstein, 1995). When parents and educators share a strong base of mutual trust and respect, conflicts and differences are easier to be resolved (Epstein, 1995). As reinforced by one of the teachers interviewed, once *'you win the trust of the parents, [they] will just come naturally to your school'*. However, in view of the time constraint faced by

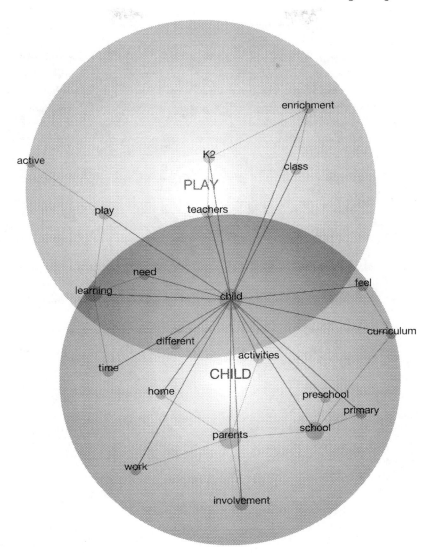

FIGURE 20.1 Leximancer concept map displaying the intersection of the key concepts within the main themes of Child and Play

many Singaporean parents, the work involved for teachers to establish a strong, trusting relationship with parents is paramount. Frequent communication of the child's daily well-being and in-class activities was articulated by one teacher to be highly effective in gaining the trust of parents, especially amongst the younger children. With preschools creatively using multiple communication platforms to engage with parents frequently, such active school-home engagement efforts may help compensate for the hectic schedules of Singaporean parents.

Considering the challenges that parents face in being involved, the findings also highlighted strategies that teachers and principals recognised as vital to encourage parental involvement. These include face-to-face communication, curriculum sharing sessions, gaining an understanding of the parents' background information, actively inviting parents to participate in school events and curriculum activities, as well as an open-door policy where parents are welcome in their children's classroom at any time to gain a better understanding of their children's learning in school. These forms of contact and efforts to better engage and communicate with parents are fundamental in ensuring stronger home-school collaboration and shared responsibilities in enacting national policies (Epstein & Sanders, 2002), such as the play-based pedagogical vision of the NEL Framework.

Singaporean parents' transition to play-based pedagogy: perceptions and concerns

The Leximancer results as displayed in Figure 20.2 highlights play as the second theme with 204 verbatim hits and 455 connectivity between key concepts in the study. The connectivity in the map supports the relationships found through the manual coding that showed how Singaporean parents embrace play as an important pedagogical trend in educating their children.

Parents of both schools were found to be generally supportive of play and recognised its importance for young children's development and well-being. However, parents of the anchor operator are mixed in terms of their level of understanding of the NEL Framework's vision, despite the government's communication initiatives. Many parents of the anchor operator grapple with the definition of play and are unsure how it leads to learning for their children. The principal of this centre shared the approaches undertaken by the school, such as curriculum sharing sessions and an open-door policy, to further educate parents on the benefits of play-based learning. In contrast, parents of the private operator are well-versed with play-based concepts, and the principal identified its play-based curriculum being one of the main reasons for parents' choice in the school.

Besides the shared view on the importance of play, parents of both schools were found to be deeply concerned with their children's academic abilities in ensuring a smooth transition to primary school. These parental anxieties exist regardless of parents being aware of policy initiatives to remove examinations for lower primary levels (Davie, 2018). Parents believe they '*cannot tone down*' on the preparation work for primary school transition as the academic rigour in the overall education system remains unchanged and '*the gap* [between preschool and primary school] *is so high*'. Educators share similar sentiments that "*there should be a continuum between preschool and primary school* [curriculum]". Despite firmly believing in children's need for play, one parent commented '*we got to tone* [play] *down*', especially for the higher preschool years. Both parents interviewed in this study also expressed concerns on the balance between play and academic emphasis but lamented '*it is a bit sad but there is no choice*'. Contrary to popular social beliefs that parents who send

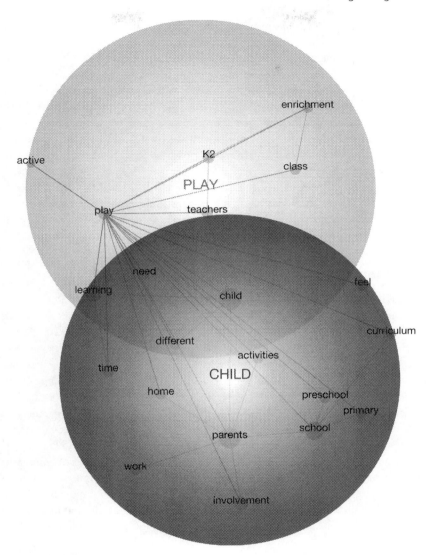

FIGURE 20.2 Leximancer concept map displaying the connectivity of the key concepts within the main theme of play in relation to Child outcomes

children for enrichment classes are 'tiger parents' or being *kiasu* with exceedingly high academic expectations, parents in this study hope these extra classes can help their children "*maintain* [their] *interest in education and to learning*" and to sustain the child's positive self-esteem at schools. They believe the additional coaching can aid children to "*stay afloat in the middle* [performance range]", as one parent expressed her aspirations that her child '*don't have to be the top . . . but not to be the bottom*'.

The interview results reflected that all the students in a K2 class in the private preschool attend enrichment classes outside of curriculum hours. Teachers believe the reason for parents choosing enrichment classes are due to concerns on school readiness for their children. This finding is consistent with other research on Singaporean parents' concerns relating to the role of preschool education (Choy & Karuppiah, 2016; Clarke & Sharpe, 2003). In fact, Ebbeck and Gokhale (2004) found all K2 children in the childcare centre of their study to attend tuition classes due to the same concerns. The tension between Singaporean parents' desire for a carefree childhood for their children and concerns for school readiness concur with other research on Singapore's educational context (Bach & Christensen, 2017; Early Childhood Development Agency, 2014; Ling-Yin, 2006; Phillipson, Koh, & Sujuddin, 2019). This deep-seated worry amongst Singaporean parents appears to be the ongoing greatest challenge for policymakers in garnering parental support and collaborative home practices for the national play-based learning vision.

Conclusion

This study contributes to literature on the role of parental involvement in Singapore's early childhood education settings in several areas. Three dominant types of parental involvement identified from stakeholders' perspectives, and the entrenched challenges for stronger parental involvement were examined and discussed. Strategies undertaken by school leaders and teachers to encourage stronger school-home partnerships were also explored. The main finding of this study is the dilemma that Singaporean parents face in terms of negotiating between their shared vision of play with policymakers and the academic rigour expected in reality. On a policy level, parents and educators support the vision for holistic education. However, in practice, parents and preschool educators struggle to reconcile with this vision as the academic rigour in primary school curriculum remains unchanged. As policymakers continue with endeavouring efforts to collaborate with parents to support the holistic education reform vision, it is imperative to conduct further investigations on parents' voice to understand their dissonance and dilemmas. Until then, the paradigm shift in Singaporean parents' mindset towards a holistic education emphasis may remain transitional.

Limitations and future directions

There are several limitations to this study worth noting. Further investigations can be conducted on a better-represented sample size, diverse family demographics and variables influencing parents' understanding of play-based pedagogical beliefs and practices. A larger number of preschools and range of preschool operator types can be included in these future studies. We also recommend further studies on parents' voice to gather better representation on the challenges and dilemmas Singaporean parents experience within the education reform in supporting the play-based learning vision. We believe further research in these areas would shed light on future directions for Singapore's education reform in supporting a smoother transition to play-based learning.

Notes

1 Kindergarten Two, or K2, refers to the final year of preschool education in Singapore.
2 Anchor operators are selected preschool operators who receive government funding support to offer quality preschool education at affordable school fees for the mass population, including children from lower income and disadvantaged backgrounds.

References

Anthony, C. J., & Ogg, J. (2019). Parent involvement, approaches to learning, and student achievement: Examining longitudinal mediation. *School Psychology, 34*(4), 376.
Bach, D., & Christensen, S. (2017). Battling the tiger mother: Pre-school reform and conflicting norms of parenthood in Singapore. *Children & Society, 31*(2), 134–143.
Bokhorst-Heng, W. D. (2005). *Debating singlish*. Berlin: Walter de Gruyter.
Braun, V., & Clarke, V. (2013). *Successful qualitative research: A practical guide for beginners*. London: Sage.
Cheo, R., & Quah, E. (2005). Mothers, maids and tutors: An empirical evaluation of their effect on children's academic grades in Singapore. *Education Economics, 13*(3), 269–285. doi:10.1080/09645290500073746
Choi, Y., Kim, Y. S., Kim, S. Y., & Park, I. J. (2013). Is Asian American parenting controlling and harsh? Empirical testing of relationships between Korean American and Western parenting measures. *Asian American Journal of Psychology, 4*(1), 19.
Choy, M. Y., & Karuppiah, N. (2016). Preparing kindergarten two children for primary one in Singapore: Perceptions and practices of parents, kindergarten teachers and primary schoolteachers. *Early Child Development and Care, 186*(3), 453–465.
Christensen, S. (2015). Healthy competition and unsound comparison: Reforming educational competition in Singapore. *Globalisation, Societies and Education, 13*(4), 553–573.
Chua, A. (2011). *Battle hymn of the tiger mother*. New York: Penguin Press.
Clarke, C., & Sharpe, P. (2003). Transition from preschool to primary school: An overview of the personal experiences of children and their parents in Singapore. *European Early Childhood Education Research Journal, 11*(sup1), 15–23. doi:10.1080/1350293X.2003.12016702
Costales, G. S., & Anderson, R. (2018). Preschool teachers' and parents' perspectives on primary school preparation in Singapore. *New Zealand International Research in Early Childhood Education, 21*(1), 87.
Davie, S. (2018, September 28). Schools to cut mid-year exams for several levels; primary 1 and 2 pupils will not be graded. *The Straits Times*. Retrieved from www.straitstimes.com/singapore/schools-to-cut-mid-year-exams-for-some-levels-primary-1-and-2-pupils-will-not-be-graded-or
Doan, S. N., Tardif, T., Miller, A., Olson, S., Kessler, D., Felt, B., & Wang, L. (2017). Consequences of "tiger" parenting: A cross-cultural study of maternal psychological control and children's cortisol stress response. *Developmental Science, 20*(3), e12404.
Early Childhood Development Agency. (2014). *Early childhood parenting landscape study 2014*. Retrieved from file:///C:/Users/ekoh/Downloads/Executive%20Summary_Parenting%20Study.pdf
Ebbeck, M., & Gokhale, N. (2004). Child-rearing practices in a selected sample of parents with children in childcare in Singapore. *Contemporary Issues in Early Childhood, 5*(2), 194–206.
Epstein, J. L. (1995). School/family/community partnerships. *Phi Delta Kappan, 76*(9), 701.
Epstein, J. L. (2010a). *School, family, and community partnerships: Preparing educators and improving schools* (2nd ed.). Boulder, CO: Westview Press.

Epstein, J. L. (2010b). School/family/community partnerships: Caring for the children we share. *Phi Delta Kappan*, *92*(3), 81–96. Retrieved from https://journals.sagepub.com/doi/abs/10.1177/003172171009200326

Epstein, J. L., & Sanders, M. G. (2002). *Family, school, and community partnerships* (pp. 407–437): Erlbaum Mahwah, NJ: Lawrence Erlbaum.

Goodall, J. (2017). *Narrowing the achievement gap: Parental engagement with children's learning*. London: Routledge.

Gov.sg. (2017). *Learning through play*. Retrieved from www.gov.sg

Huat See, B., & Gorard, S. (2015). The role of parents in young people's education – a critical review of the causal evidence. *Oxford Review of Education*, *41*(3), 346–366.

Jeynes, W. H. (2005). Parental involvement and student achievement: A meta-analysis. *Family Involvement Research Digest*, *9*, 241–273.

Jones, S. A. (2019). Home school relations in Singaporean primary schools: Teachers', parents' and children's views. *Oxford Review of Education*, *45*(1), 32–49. doi:10.1080/03054985.2018.1481377

Juang, L. P., Qin, D. B., & Park, I. J. (2013). Deconstructing the myth of the "tiger mother": An introduction to the special issue on tiger parenting, Asian-heritage families, and child/adolescent well-being. *Asian American Journal of Psychology*, *4*(1), 1.

Khong, L. Y. L., & Ng, P. T. (2005). School–parent partnerships in Singapore. *Educational Research for Policy and Practice*, *4*(1), 1–11.

Kim, S. Y., Wang, Y., Orozco-Lapray, D., Shen, Y., & Murtuza, M. (2013). Does "tiger parenting" exist? Parenting profiles of Chinese Americans and adolescent developmental outcomes. *Asian American Journal of Psychology*, *4*(1), 7.

Koh, A. (2004). Singapore education in "new times": Global/local imperatives. *Discourse: Studies in the Cultural Politics of Education*, *25*(3), 335–349.

Koh, F. (2019, February 16). Ministry of education introduces guidelines on how parents and schools can work together. *The Straits Times*. Retrieved from www.straitstimes.com/singapore/education/ministry-of-education-introduces-guidelines-on-how-parents-and-schools-can-work

Ling-Yin, L. A. (2006). Steering debate and initiating dialogue: A review of the Singapore preschool curriculum. *Contemporary Issues in Early Childhood*, *7*(3), 203–212.

Manzon, M., Miller, R., Hong, H., & Khong, L. (2015). *Parent engagement in education*. Singapore: National Institute of Education.

Mathews, M., Lim, L., & Teng, S. (2017). *Parents' perceptions of the Singapore primary school system*. Institute of Policy Studies Working Papers No. 27.

Ministry of Education. (2018a, September 28). *Speeches/interviews: Opening address by Mr Ong Ye Kung, minister for education, at the schools work plan seminar*. Retrieved from www.moe.gov.sg/news/speeches/opening-address-by-mr-ong-ye-kung-minister-for-education-at-the-schools-work-plan-seminar

Ministry of Education. (2018b, July 11). *Speeches/interviews: Parliamentary motion "education for our future" response by minister for education, Mr Ong Ye Kung*. Retrieved from www.moe.gov.sg/news/speeches/parliamentary-motion-education-for-our-future-response-by-minister-for-education-mr-ong-ye-kung

Ministry of Education. (2019a, March 18). *Compass*. Retrieved from www.moe.gov.sg/compass

Ministry of Education. (2019b). *Guidelines for school-home partnership: preparing students for the future*. Press release. Retrieved from www.moe.gov.sg/news/press-releases/guidelines-for-school-home-partnership-preparing-students-for-the-future

Mokhtar, F. (2018, September 28). Govt has no intention to ban tuition, but parents should take a step back and give children more space: Ong Ye Kung. *Today Online*. Retrieved from www.todayonline.com/singapore/govt-has-no-intention-ban-tuition-parents-should-take-step-back-and-give-children-more

Ng, P. T. (2017). *Learning from Singapore: The power of paradoxes*. London: Routledge.

Phillipson, S., Koh, E., & Sujuddin, S. (2019). Academic or else: Singapore parents' aspirations for their children's early education. *Teachers' and Families' Perspectives in Early Childhood Education and Care: Early Childhood Education in the 21st Century, 2*, 193.

Private Tuition in Singapore: A Whitepaper Release. (2012). Retrieved from www.blackbox.com.sg/wp/wp-content/uploads/2012/09/Blackbox-You-Know-Anot-Whitepaper-Private-Tuition.pdf

Retna, K. S., & Ng, P. T. (2016). Singapore principals' understanding and perceptions of the challenges of "teach less, less more" policy. *International Journal of Educational Reform, 25*(4), 426–442.

Singapore Department of Statistics. (2018). *Population trends 2018*. Retrieved from https://www.singstat.gov.sg/-/media/files/publications/population/population2018.pdf

Smith, A. E., & Humphreys, M. S. (2006). Evaluation of unsupervised semantic mapping of natural language with Leximancer concept mapping. *Behavior Research Methods, 38*(2), 262–279.

Tam, H. L., Kwok, S. Y., Ling, C. C., & Li, C. I. K. (2018). The moderating effects of positive psychological strengths on the relationship between tiger parenting and child anxiety. *Children and Youth Services Review, 94*, 207–215.

Ting, T. C. (2007). Policy developments in pre-school education in Singapore: A focus on the key reforms of kindergarten education. *International Journal of Child Care and Education Policy, 1*(1), 35.

Yeong, A. Y. E., & Ng, P. T. (2009). An examination of project work: A reflection on Singapore's education reform. In *Reforming learning* (pp. 109–128). Cham: Springer.

21
PARENTAL INVOLVEMENT IN EARLY CHILDHOOD EDUCATION IN CATALUNYA, SPAIN

Sílvia Blanch Gelabert, Ana María Forestello and Gabriel Lemkow-Tovias

Introduction

In the last 20 years Catalunya has experienced an increased interest towards parental involvement, thus leading to a change in the Early Childhood Education (ECE) settings, practices, programmes and the promotion of studies in this field. International and national research showed the importance of parental involvement in schools and other programmes to promote a healthy development and successful learning in children. For this reason, the ECE curriculum emphasises the importance of working in collaboration with parents, but there are still some challenges in order to achieve a significant partnership, such as improving teacher training programmes in Catalan universities and also changing some concepts about the teacher's role and relations with the families.

Local research has been recently developed around the families' institutional involvement. Most of these studies have been developed by the Spanish Government, Universities, Family associations, Foundations, and others. Some of their main results are presented below:

- **Most vulnerable families don't have access to nurseries (0–3 years).** Only 38.4% of children aged 0 to 2 years in Catalunya are schooled (Ferrer, Rivas, & Tobalina, 2019). In addition, research focused on Barcelona's population shows that the lower income districts have a significantly lower percentage of schooling, and only 7% of the foreign population have access to ECE services (Institut Infància, 2016). For this reason, it is necessary to widen the nurseries' offer for more children to be able to attend and to increase the families' support services through them (Blasco, 2016).
- **The socio educational playgroups for families with children younger than three favour a responsive upbringing.** Different research (Blanch,

2010; Ferrer, 2008) shows that family support programmes promote an upbringing improvement and more educational involvement in families.
- **Expectations, home environment, and family communication are key aspects for the educational success** (Blasco, 2018). The families' expectations towards their kids are related to the opportunities, interest and facilities given by the parents. The materials, such as books, a space to read or play, are key aspects for the children's learning. Also, school life is important, especially the parents' interest towards it. The family–school communication processes help children to connect both contexts and to boost their development. Parent involvement in the school facilitates conversations about the school at home, and this is one of the key elements for the children educational success.
- **Support groups between parents favour responsive upbringing** (Blanch & Badia, 2015). Evidence from national and international programmes show how families going to activities with other families, and with the accompaniment of professionals, reinforce the parenting capacities and promote the development of supporting networks.
- **Families demand acknowledgement for their role in schools** (Comas, 2018). Families are increasingly demanding a voice in the decision-making processes of education centres, at both pedagogical and organisational levels. However there is still some resistance in schools (Blanch, Gimeno, & Careta, 2016). This may be because it is still difficult to move from an educational model based on experts/clients to one based on real partnership based on distribution of roles.

The research shows that the collaboration between families and schools becomes essential for the children's academic performance at schools and summer programmes (Alegre, Todeschi, & Segura, 2018; Blanch, Duran, Valdebenito, & Flores, 2013; Park & Holloway, 2018). Moreover, parents are central for the children's upbringing and education processes within a communitarian development context (Bronfenbrenner, 1979). Therefore, it is essential to point out the importance of acknowledging parents and finding different ways to engage with them.

In this sense, this chapter will focus on different ways to support families through different programmes and successful parental engagement experiences at school.

Parental social perspective: policies to promote parental involvement

In this section, we will emphasise the key-steering documents that promoted this paradigm shift, favouring the parental role in ECE, in nurseries, preschool settings, and other kinds of services to support families with young children. Previous research shows that, from a cognitive, social, emotional and physical standpoint, families play a central role in the children's global development (Blasco, 2018). Due to this, the latest regulations provide support for a paradigm shift towards the strengthening of the social upbringing vision, where society is responsible for accompanying the parents in their children's education so that they can develop holistically and with educational success.

Since the Children's Rights Convention (UN, 1989, November 20), there has been a change in conceptualising the child as a person endowed with full rights. This convention was also endorsed by the Catalan Parliament in March 1991. In this document, some policies regarding Childhood were promoted, some of them taking into consideration the parents' upbringing role, the child's right of growing up with its family and its right to be protected in case of family negligence.

Departing from this different approach, at a national level different laws regarding parental responsibility were promoted and regulations were set up for the creation of new meetings and support for parental spaces with the professionals' accompaniment. An example is the Law of Family support 18/2003 that was partially deployed in Catalonia through ordinance 151/2009, regarding complementary services and help for families with special attention for single-parented and large families.

Another important regulation is the Council of Europe Committee of Ministers Recommendation (REC-19, 2006) which supports a social upbringing view where the child is the centre and the community should provide support to the parents so that they can provide positive and responsive parenting.

In relation to ECE, we could highlight the Catalan decree 101/2010 that regulates school and family partnership: an initial contact between parents and educators before the child's incorporation for the first time in the nursery, which takes the form of a day of open doors before summer holidays; in September, before the infant joins the nursery. An interview is set up with each family; daily contact during entry and exit at nursery are encouraged; regular meetings with the families of the same group of infants are also established. At least two annual written reports are guaranteed to families and one at the end of the ECE (3 year old) reflecting the assessment of the progress and difficulties observed, the evolutionary and personal aspects of the infant, and the complementary strategies or resources that may have been adopted, related to educational and learning processes.

Teacher training: parental involvement in the ECE teacher higher education degree programmes

The 0–6-years-old period in Spain is currently being carried out as an educational period, non-compulsory, and free for children from 3 years old, under the LOMCE (Organic Law for the improvement of educational quality) law. In order to enhance quality, the professionals who work in ECE need to hold specialised studies at university to work with children in nurseries, preschools, and other ECE services. In that sense, it is important to include in the teacher's initial training parental involvement contents.

Although there were previous studies and teacher training at university since 1845 in Barcelona, in 2009–2010, in the context of the ECTS European credits, a new 4-year ECE degree was created. Today, seven faculties offer the ECE Degree in Catalunya. As well as this, high schools offer ECE courses on National Vocational Qualifications to work as an assistant teacher in schools, especially in nurseries (0–3-years-old children).

At university level, in some of the ECE degree curriculum for the 0–3 and 3–6 periods there are references to the family's importance in the children's upbringing although still in a very general way and not always taking into consideration the different socioeconomic and cultural specificities of families (Lemkow-Tovias, 2018). So, a challenge for universities is to search for strategies to bring students and families together to learn from relevant situations. For example, in Universitat Autònoma de Barcelona there are courses that address this in a practical way for students and families. There are also essays in which students must interview a mother or a father; they record some moments of family games or encourage family participation during their school internship. Also families and teachers are invited by the university to give talks, among others.

However, parental involvement awareness in the ECE degrees is still pending due to its general treatment in the curriculum and it is often the professors' decision to give more or less importance to families.

In addition, the students' school internships allow them to approach families in an important way. However, BA students are not allowed to attend the parents' meetings or interviews, so it is difficult for future teachers and practitioners to learn how to engage with families without participating in real situations.

Families' services to support families with young children

In the previous section we showed how the international and national legislations have been long promoting policies from a social standpoint that support actions to enhance the parents' competences, to contribute to the positive responsive parenting in favour of a holistic development of children.

These policies are essential to develop support services for the families because Early Childhood is a key period for their development and health (Bueno, 2019). In this sense, different support programmes to the families have been created, with the aim of strengthening their ability to support the children's upbringing and education, as well as to promote a culture of parent's engagement with the community.

Below, some of the ECE services in Catalunya are presented, in which the parents' involvement becomes a central aspect through the following categories (Àngel, 2004):

Socio educational playgroups

Socio educational playgroups are groups conducted by professionals with different backgrounds, mostly from Psychology, Education or Pedagogy, to provide emotional, social, and educational support to the families' upbringing and education processes regarding their children. In this program they can find appropriate information and training, share experiences with other mothers or fathers and have some time for themselves. Examples of these are the Family Group and Playgroup programmes such as the *We already have a child* programme and the *Babygroup* programme designed for the first year of the child's life. The parents always come with their children and the professionals provide the families with adequate conditions for their educational involvement (De Febrer, 2003). Families can also enrol to programmes for children from three to six years to support the family health and logistics, especially for families with disabled children.

Children and family services at social risk

Services are addressed to families with social and structural complex situations, such as the Technical Service Meeting point, to help communication between children and parents. Also, the *Mothers in Prison Unit* facilitates the coexistence of children from 0 to 3 years with their mothers while they are in jail. Another example of service for families at social risk is the *Raval Infant House*, where vulnerable families are welcomed and accompanied in coordination with other communitarian agents from the third sector, to provide better global support to these families.

Leisure services

Playhouses for early childhood offer stimulating play proposals for children that are accompanied by an adult and supervised by qualified personnel, provide families guidance and promote nursery schools' groups to attend, in order to enhance playing with different resources. Such is the case of the municipal network of toy libraries in the city of Lleida.

Cultural services

Children's libraries (from 0 to 6 years old) with rooms specifically designed for children, such as Can Butjosa Library in Parets del Vallès, also play an important role for families. The aim is to promote interest in children, through family engagement, towards literature. Some of Barcelona's Art Museums (Picasso Museum and Fundació Miró) offer activities addressed for children (0–6 years) and their families and educators. Also, theatres such as LaSala Miguel Hernandez (Sabadell city) offer similar types of family activities.

Science and technology services

Some Science and Technology centres have specific areas for children and their families. Examples of these are the Science Nest in the Barcelona's Natural Science Museum and the Lab 0_6: Discovery, Research and Documentation Centre for Science Education in Early Childhood in Manresa, located in the Manresa's University.

Different strategies to promote parental engagement and collaboration at school

The research shows that the partnership between families and kindergartens is essential for children's success, but many of the programmes are often aimed at families that have a favourable cultural and environment with stimulating experiences. However, not all families can have such positive realities and thus schools must facilitate accompaniment strategies during schooling. For instance, some nurseries and preschools promote the creation of social networks between families in order to stimulate their confidence and encourage their mutual collaboration. In this sense, the design of learning environments will be central to create comfortable spaces, that could offer quality time for parents and also to boost positive relations between parents and their children.

Different families have different contexts, geographical, and cultural origins, as well as vulnerable and complex, permanent or temporary situations and this should be taken into account. Moreover, some families seldom participate due to specific issues, such as linguistic difficulties or cultural realities that become labelled by others.

In this respect, schools try to offer different family-school types of collaboration at a different level. Some successful examples of family-school initiatives are described in Table 21.1.

How can we redesign the parent-teacher conferences?

In this context, in which the families' support is basic, we will present a specific example: the initiative "Redesign the parents conference" (*Redissenyem la reunió amb famílies*) promoted by the Jaume Bofill Foundation to boost the parental involvement starting from the initial meeting (with the teacher at the beginning of the course) to act as a lever to favour the relations between families and teachers. This initiative is based upon the international initiative "How can we redesign parent-teacher night" from the Teachers Guild (IDEO & RSA).

To modify family meetings, a guide schools was published, based on the design thinking process. The process includes creative instruments that go beyond the usual ideas, through brainstorming processes, journey plot activities, and the creation of prototypes before action.

Thus, the process is organised through four relevant moments explained below:

1 **To explore**. Creation of a promoting group (ideally mixed between teachers, families and, if possible, also students). In this phase it is important to know the teachers' voice, but above all, the families' voice in order to have a better idea of what they think about the initial conference and their expectations. Activities are proposed to promote empathy, to listen to the families' and their expectations

TABLE 21.1 Successful examples of family-school initiatives

At home	• Programmes for the promotion of linguistic competences with parents
	• Programme for the promotion of mathematics with parents
	• Support with homework
Education system	• Representative institutions (school council)
In school	• Classroom/school direct participation
	• Family associations (AFA/AMPA/FAPAC etc.)/ Representative (School Council)
	• Mixed commissions (Parents & Teachers): gardening; school contents; events; infrastructures; lunch time; leisure; activities, etc.
	• Groups of parents (pedagogical coffee, positive upbringing. . .) meetings
	• Workshops chosen by teachers and parents
	• Social educators accompanying families within the school.
	• Volunteers to support activities
	• Parent Governors
	• Mothers acting as a link with members of minority groups
	• School promoters (e.g. for/with Roma Community)
Communication issues	• Diversity: documents, panels, apps, web, blog, social networks. . .
	• Course meetings
	• Interviews
	• Meeting opportunities: children's arrival and collection.
With the community	• Calls and Video Calls
	• Formal and informal networks (only families, families with teachers, and families & others)
	• Families or mixed conferences/workshops
	• Community programmes

2   **Cocreation.** Definition of the challenge, for example, by promoting more participatory conferences. Once defined, a brainstorming process is promoted and finally an idea is selected following three criteria chosen by the promoters, if these are realistic and sustainable.

3   **Prototyping and action.** The team prepares a creative prototype of the meeting, such as a video, a sculpture, or an illustration . . . and tests the prototype in order to validate the proposal with a small group of people (families, teachers. . .). Further changes can be done if required. After this, a new meeting is set.

4   **Assess.** Once each parent conference is finished, the community gathers to assess how the meeting went and which changes are proposed for the next ones.

Some facilitating aspects in these meetings are:

- **Calendar**. Having all the programmed meetings from year to year so that everyone has the meetings set up in their respective calendars (e.g. during the first Monday of October every year is reviewed).
- **Schedule**. To check which schedule fits better for the families, some schools or nurseries do them in the morning, others at noon, and most in the afternoon.
- **Meeting announcement**. To be creative with the meeting announcements, create surprising situations by involving the children through videos, invitations notes, voice recordings, etc.
- **Space.** The meeting can provide an opportunity to better understand the different spaces in the school, by suggesting walking itineraries and activities that can take place in different learning areas.
- **Teaching staff participation**. Presence of all the teaching staff involved in the children's activities, both specialist teachers and tutoring teachers and the management team, helps out in getting to know them and providing confidence to the families.
- **Activities**: Create some activities so that parents can meet and get to know each other, if the families have an opportunity to talk and meet each other, they can start establishing links and networking amongst themselves.
- **Information.** To help out in providing information through the use of different media. Everything that would make reference to the pedagogical aspects can help in providing closer experiences such as organising different spaces and materials so that they can walk and experiment as well as ask and understand better how their children work in school.
- **Students**. Think about how they can take part of the decision-making processes during the scheduling process or how they can express their worries, etc.
- **Leisure moment.** To include food or a breakfast snack helps during informal moments to talk, to know each other, etc. These are key ingredients for establishing a cooperative spirit with the school.
- **Assessment**. Listening to families, students and teachers helps in adjusting the next meetings programmed.

This process can be adapted to the individual meetings, a more accurate term than the "interviews" still being used in many nurseries and preschool settings.

Redesigning the family meetings allows progressing towards a more democratic school. To do so, spaces, time, and activities for the mutual encounter are conceived to create complicities and to promote the global development of children, even though teachers and parents may play different roles.

Challenges on parental involvement

After detailing some of the policies, research and services available for families, it is possible to observe the current positive context of involving and accompanying families in the schooling process. But why is it difficult to put this into practice?

In Catalonia many families with children are unable to cover their basic needs. For the FEDAIA, a platform that connects children, adolescents, and families at risk, it is required to implement and develop actions, programmes, services, and policies that could empower them and that could focus on the children's care. That is the challenge is to invest in the 0–3 education period in those most neglected environments through services such as Family Educational Playgroups and other annual programmes in the schools that are long-standing, better conditions could also be covered in formal education, leisure spaces, free time, culture and sport services, thus guaranteeing that the health and living issues are being appropriately taken care of.

There are many programmes to support parents in bringing up their young children, but they often depend upon different administrations, for example, some belong to the Education Department and others to the Social Services Department. This increases the difficulty in providing an appropriate coordination and an offer made for the families' needs. Sometimes these programmes don't even have enough family demand, maybe because they are not tailor-made to the parents' needs from this or that community. Moreover, the absence of dissemination and budget creates barriers for family participation, due to lack of information or to the uncertainty of not knowing how the activities will be developed.

On the other hand, to improve parent involvement it's important to start analysing our own beliefs, that is, those ideas regarding the "other", because it is one of the biggest barriers for including and approaching families in the school life. This belief promotes expectations that relate to one's own actions; therefore it's important (Blanch, 2010). Many teachers are afraid of the family participation, because they will be observed and thus, parents can become critical to their working habits or pedagogical strategies. In reality, there are no relevant problems in the schools being open to the families. The aim is that families become the centre and can be guided through the process to allow them to empower themselves towards a positive and responsive children upbringing process.

Another way to confront the fears towards the family meetings and to improve the confidence with them would be to promote experiences in the teachers' initial training and during their lifelong learning courses. For example, by facilitating meeting places such as Edhacks or Edcamps, where teachers, families, students, and other professionals/experts can take part and meet one another to suggest or develop solutions to the potential challenges encountered.

Schools have the main responsibility to encourage parent's engagement offering different channels of participation and co-creating to resolve the challenges they have agreed together.

References

Alegre, M. A., Todeschini, F., & Segura, A. (2018). *¿Puede un programa de verano mejorar las oportunidades educativas del alumnado? Evaluación de impacto del programa Èxit Educatiu.* Madrid: Fundación Ramón Areces.

Àngel, C. (2004). *Lliçó magistral-comiat. Visió panoràmica de l'atenció educativa a la petita infància dins un marc europeu.* Bellaterra: Universitat Autònoma de Barcelona, Departament de Psicologia Bàsica, Evolutiva I de l'Educació.
Blanch, S. (2010). *Expectatives parentals i pràctiques socioeducatives familiars. Influència mútua* (Tesi doctoral), Universitat Autònoma de Barcelona, Barcelona.
Blanch, S., & Badia, G. (2015). *A criar fills se n'aprén.* Barcelona: Fundació Jaume Bofill.
Blanch, S., Duran, D., Valdebenito, V., & Flores, M. (2013). The effects and characteristics of family involvement on a peer tutoring programme to improve the reading comprehension competence. *European Journal of Psychology Education, 28*(1), 101–119.
Blanch, S., Gimeno, X., & Careta, A. (2016). *Territoris d'intersecció entre els centres educatius i les famílies. Un estudi en l'etapa de l'educació infantil.* Bellaterra: ICE UAB.
Blasco, J. (2016). *De l'escola bressol a les polítiques per a la petita infància.* Barcelona: Fundació Jaume Bofill.
Blasco, J. (2018). *Els programes per fomentar la implicació parental en l'educació serveixen per millorar el rendiment escolar?* Barcelona: Fundació Jaume Bofill.
Bronfenbrenner, U. (1979). *The ecology of human development.* Cambridge, MA: Harvard University Press (Trad. Cast.: La ecología del desarrollo humano. Barcelona, Ediciones Paidós, 1987).
Bueno, D. (2019). Genetics and learning: How the genes influence educational attainment. *Frontiers in Psychology.* doi:10.3389/fpsyg.2019.01622
Comas, M. (2018). *La veu de les famílies en el sistema educatiu: Aposta pel bé comú o estratègia de clausura?* (Tesi doctoral), Universitat Autònoma de Barcelona, Barcelona.
De Febrer, V. (2003). Més enllà de l'escola bressol. *Revista de Girona, 216,* 76–81. Retrieved from www.raco.cat/index.php/RevistaGirona/article/view/94907/155176
Ferrer, A., Rivas, E., & Tobalina, G. (2019). *On tot comença. Educació infantil de 0 a 3 anys per igualar oportunitats. Annex Catalunya.* Save the Children. Retrieved from www.savethechildren.es/sites/default/files/imce/docs/donde_todo_empieza_cat.pdf
Ferrer, M. (2008). *Suport a les famílies en la primera infància. Estudi de cas d'un programa socioeducatiu* (Tesi doctoral), Universitat de les Illes Balears, Palma.
Institut Infància (2016). *El baròmetre de la infància i les famílies de Barcelona.* Retrieved from http://institutinfancia.cat/mediateca/barometre-infancia-families-barcelona/
Lemkow-Tovias, G. (2018). The Catalan case: Cultural diversity and pedagogical practices in ECE contexts. In *The intercultural needs of educators in early childhood services.* Italy: MECEC+ Project, European Commission.
Park, S., & Holloway, S. (2018). Parental involvement in adolescents' education: An examination of the interplay among school factors, parental role construction, and family income. *School Community Journal, 28*(1). Retrieved from https://www.adi.org/journal/2018ss/ParkHollowaySpring2018.pdf
Recomendación Rec 19. (2006). *Comité de Ministros a los Estados Miembros sobre políticas de apoyo a la parentalidad positiva.* Retrieved from www.mscbs.gob.es/ssi/familiasInfancia/parentalidadPos2012/docs/informeRecomendacion.pdf

22

PARENTAL INVOLVEMENT IN SWEDISH PRESCHOOLS

A reflection of current steering documents

Tina Yngvesson and Susanne Garvis

Introduction

In Sweden the preschool is part of the educational system and has since the 1970s become established as one of the primary pillars upon which Swedish family policy is built (Gunnarsson, Korpi, & Nordenstam, 1999; Hiilamo, 2004; Yngvesson & Garvis, 2019). The task of fostering children is thus considered a two-pronged task shared between the individual (family) and the state (preschool). By two-pronged is meant that Swedish ECE has two goals: 1) to ensure that both parents regardless of gender face equal opportunities for work and 2) assist and support in the development of children's overall healthy development (Swedish National Agency for Education, 2010). This heavy focus on engagement between home and preschool makes relevant a management between the two, where the engagement between family and preschool teachers (hereafter referred to as teachers) is seen as a collaborative- and strengths-based process through which the child and his or her family is assimilated into the Swedish educational system. This partnership requires that both family and preschool make a commitment to creating and sustaining an ongoing partnership that supports child well-being and an overall healthy development. In this chapter we will apply the Bronfenbrenner Ecological Systems Theory to address some aspects within this complex sphere of private (home) and public (preschool) relations and through mapping what the key steering documents say about parent engagement – comparing briefly the Lpfö 98 and the more recent 2018 revision, offer a discussion on how parent engagement in Sweden is put into practice, as well as how parent engagement in terms of children's learning and general well-being is in partnership with teachers. Furthermore, the chapter will tackle the question of how parental engagement is integrated into the Swedish ECE teacher education. Conclusively, the literature study will offer reflections in regard to possible paths to development in terms of how parent engagement and

DOI: 10.4324/9780367823917-22

home – preschool partnerships can be developed. Engaging with the ecological systems model, it shares a relational understanding of parental engagement within Sweden and opens up possibilities to explore the specific context of ECE.

Next the chapter shares findings from a document analysis seeking understanding around curriculum and teacher education from key Swedish documents. The chapter describes key phrases and statements before highlighting current gaps in the Swedish teacher education.

Parent engagement in Sweden

Encouragement of the Swedish approach to common fostering is strongly supported by the UN Convention on the Rights of the Child (1989) which states children's right to respect, to dignity, to make informed decisions and to self-determination. In the year 2018, in an effort to ensure the legal rights of children, the Swedish Parliament voted in favour of the government's proposal and the amendments came into force on the 1st of January 2020 (Riksdag, 2018). Thus, the provision of quality ECE as provided from government institutions means that early learning educators have a legal responsibility to ensure children's rights and that the child is given forum for, as well as encouraged and enabled to make their view known in all issues that affect them.

Since the Curriculum for Preschool was introduced in 1998, the ambition of what parent engagement in the preschool is was defined and entered into the curriculum with a heavy focus on which rights parents have in terms of information, participation and influence. Moreover, the curriculum dictated that the responsibility of establishing contact and relationships between the home and the preschool be placed on the preschool. However, the teacher education was not reformed to accommodate this change and the understanding of what parent engagement is was left vulnerable to interpretation (Flising, Fredrikson, & Lund, 1996). For the purpose of this study, this type of engagement refers to an interaction between the child's home and preschool; parent engagement in preschool is thus a collaboration concerning the well-being and development of the child, defining the interconnected relations between adults and children, as well as the negotiation of meaning and understanding therein (Yngvesson & Garvis, 2019).

Literature review

In his book, The Ecology of Human development, experiments by nature and design (1979), Urie Bronfenbrenner describes human development as a "lasting change in the way in which a person perceives and deals with his environment" (p. 3). Bronfenbrenner argues that "the ecological environment is conceived as a set of nested structures, each inside the next, like Russian dolls" (Bronfenbrenner, 1979, p. 3) and that "the innermost level is the immediate setting containing the developing person" (Bronfenbrenner, 1979, p. 3). The first and perhaps most important of Bronfenbrenner's definitions is the one summarizing the process upon which the theory is built

> the ecology of human development involves the scientific study of the progressive, mutual accommodation between an active growing human being and the changing properties of the immediate settings in which the developing person lives, as this process is affected by relations between these settings, and by the larger contexts in which the settings are embedded.
> *(Bronfenbrenner, 1979, p. 21)*

Thus, the goal of this literature review is to synthesise some of the existing research, thus illuminating the discrepancies between the research emphasis placed on a child perspective and the adult's perspective, in a home-preschool relationship sphere – and also to provide an overview of the research executed into the construct of children's – parents and teachers understanding of parent engagement in preschool as embedded in the curriculum and teacher education.

Nordic perspective

An increased interest surrounding the subject of parent engagement in preschool is a Swedish context that has emerged in recent years and scholars have made substantial progress in developing the knowledge base in the field of research concerning parent engagement in ECE (Hayakawa, Englund, Warner-Richter, & Reynolds, 2013; Levinthal de Oliveira Lima & Kuusisto, 2020; Swedish National Agency for Education, 2010; Tunberger & Sigle-Rushton, 2011; Yngvesson & Garvis, 2019). Recent years have witnessed an overall heavy emphasis on establishing strong teacher-parent relationships in the Swedish National Curriculum for Preschools, and parent engagement in preschool is seen as important for reasons such as promoting a healthy development of the child, as well as socialization and learning through play (Löfdahl & Hägglund, 2006; Rouse & O'Brien, 2017; Råde, 2020). However little or no investigation has been done into which level parent engagement is integrated into the Swedish ECE teacher education.

The above international context is in stark contrast to the ongoing current debate in Nordic countries, which in recent years has been particularly concerned with research primarily on partnerships between ECE areas, as well as attitudes and behaviours within these partnerships (Hakyemez-Paul, Pihlaja, & Silvennoinen, 2018; Hujala et al., 2009; Venninen & Purola, 2013) on the background of parents being encouraged to assume a more active role in their children's pedagogical day in preschool. As Swedish children are usually introduced to preschool between 15 and 18 months of age, teachers are in accordance with Lpfö 98, responsible for ensuring that each family has a good introduction to their child's start at preschool (Swedish National Agency for Education, 2016; OECD, 2017). When compared to other nations, parents in Sweden share the task of childcare with professional early years educators in preschool, which means that this relationship between home and preschool is of great significance for the child's healthy cognitive development and self-concept (Nisbett et al., 2012; Phillipson & Phillipson, 2017). Swedish children are thus subject to the supervision, care and education of both parents and teachers in two different settings, that of the home and that of the preschool, making engagement between the microsystems of preschool and home all the more significant. Whilst an increasingly large amount of international research is currently highlighting many changes in society and education policy in which the significance of parents' democratic rights to influence their children's education through preschool/school and home cooperation is emphasised (Björnsson, 2005; Lightfoot, 2004; Vincent & Tomlinsson, 1997; Wernersson, 2006), research in the Swedish context are limited in their representation of perspectives. According to the OECD, there is an increasing global interest concerning the area of parent engagement in ECE (OECD, 2017) existing research primarily represents the teacher's voice (Hakyemez-Paul et al., 2018; Hujala et al., 2009; Venninen & Purola, 2013), leaving it overrepresented in comparison to the parent's and child's voice.

An accepted view in Sweden is that parents and preschool teachers should maintain close communication in order to preserve the child's best interest, whilst also adhering to the steering documents. Hence, the domain between home and preschool in Sweden today is one that is widely discussed in the academic debate, and although many studies have shown that positive cooperation between the child's ECEC microenvironments has been of great benefit to the child's learning and development (Persson & Tallberg Broman, 2017; Markström & Simonsson, 2017; Murray, McFarland-Piazza, & Harrison, 2014; Vlasov & Hujala, 2017), very few of these include the child's perspective. According to Markström and Simonsson (2017), a dominating discourse in educational research regarding parent engagement in ECE is that the home and preschool should enter into cooperation and "act as close partners in the best interest of the child" (Markström & Simonsson, 2017). However, few researchers have taken their point of departure from the perspective of the teacher education curriculum and/or studied how the education prepares the teacher candidate for the psychological meeting between teacher and family and how to best promote a partnership between the two.

The Nordic tradition of inclusion has resulted in several research projects where parent engagement has been focal and by comparison, Finland for instance, initiated the International Parent-Professional Partnership (IPP) research study, which was conducted by Hujala et al. (2009). This initiative focused on the contemporary challenges of the parent-teacher partnerships in early childhood education from a cross-cultural perspective. The study explored the teacher-parent partnerships in ECEC services in five countries (Estonia, Finland, Lithuania, Norway and Portugal) and emphasis was placed on the teachers' views of parents' engagement in preschools. The results indicated that there exist discrepancies between teachers' approaches to parent-teacher partnerships between societies as well as within each country. The study also found that parents differed in their capacity to establish and maintain relationships with teachers. In another study conducted by

Hakyemez-Paul et al. (2018), with a sample of 287 educators (with both qualitative and quantitative data), it was identified that the Finnish preschool teachers generally possess a positive attitude towards parent engagement – and that participants found the difficulties of parent engagement to often times be caused by poor motivation on the parents behalf, as well as lack of time on both parents' and preschools part.

The aforementioned research conducted a) in a trans-national perspective and b) in a Finnish perspective indicates that it is beneficial for Sweden to undergo similar research – particularly since the role of the parent in the Swedish preschool curriculum embodies the idea that Swedish society has a comprehensive and holistic view of the child (Uusimäki et al., 2019) and existing research in this area typically places emphasis on the teacher's voice, leaving it over-represented in comparison to the children's and parents' voices. Furthermore, many studies have shown that positive cooperation between the child's ECEC microenvironments has been of great benefit to the child's learning and development (Persson & Tallberg Broman, 2017; Markström & Simonsson, 2017; Murray et al., 2014; Vlasov & Hujala, 2017) and a dominating discourse in educational research regarding parent engagement in ECEC is that the home and preschool should enter into corporation and act as close parties in the best interest of the child (Markström & Simonsson, 2017). In reality, however, how this is to be achieved is a matter of interpretation on both the home's and preschool's behalf.

The Bronfenbrenner Ecological Systems Theory

The overall consensus of this chapter is that children will, in a well-being, development and learning perspective, do better with parents who are actively engaged in their pedagogical development (Borgonovi & Montt, 2012; Desforges & Abouchaar, 2003; Emerson, Fear, Fox, & Sanders, 2012) Thus, designing pathways in order to develop the communication between home and preschool is considered a significant factor in children's developmental outcomes (Hayes, O'Toole, & Halpenny, 2017). Urie Bronfenbrenner (1979), who is best known for his ecological systems theory of child development, a theory which demands that a child's world is considered on a multitude of levels, promotes a theory which investigates a child's development within the context of the system of relationships that constitute a child's environment. The theory defines six layers of environment, each of which is considered imperative in understanding the wholeness of a child's development. When exploring the understandings that a child possesses, it is important to keep in mind the contextual and cultural differences present in his various environments or systems (see figure 2). The first and perhaps most important of Bronfenbrenner's definitions is that

> the ecology of human development involves the scientific study of the progressive, mutual accommodation between an active growing human being and the changing properties of the immediate settings in which the

developing person lives, as this process is *affected by relations between these settings, and by the larger contexts in which the settings are embedded.*

(Bronfenbrenner, 1979, p. 21)

Thus, children find themselves in various systems throughout their day (Bronfenbrenner, 1979) and are doubtlessly affected, in a well-being and healthy development perspective, by how the adults pertaining to the various systems communicate (Bronfenbrenner, 1979; Yngvesson, 2019; Yngvesson & Garvis, 2019). In an ecological system's perspective, the role of the home- and of the preschool is to primarily house the child's innermost intimate relationships within one or more microsystems, meaning that the teacher plays an overall significant role in a Swedish preschool child's life (Swedish National Agency for Education, 2016).

Method

A document analysis is described as a form of qualitative research that incorporates the coding of themes from public documents (Bowen, 2009; O'Leary, 2014). The researchers follow the eight-step process of planning for document analysis from O'Leary (2014) to develop a pattern of recognition within the document's data (Bowen, 2009). Bowen (2009, p. 33).describes this process as "evaluating documents in such a way that empirical knowledge is produced and understanding is developed". In this chapter, new understandings are developed around two research questions:

1 What does the curriculum say about parental engagement?
2 What do teacher education steering documents say about parental engagement?

The initial search was for documents that had words of 'parent' or 'parent engagement' in preschool steering documents. After the initial search, two documents were found – the Swedish Preschool Curriculum and preschool teacher education descriptions. The documents were then analysed to develop understanding and meaning in relation to the research questions.

The researchers developed and maintained a high level of objectivity and sensitivity in order for the findings to be credible and valid (Bowen, 2009). A key strength of this approach was that the documents could be reviewed multiple times and remains unchanged by the research process (Bowen, 2009). The researchers executed the evaluation of the relevant steering documents separately before coming together to discuss the main ideas that emerged and the findings from the document analysis were discussed in relation to Bronfenbrenner's ecological systems theory. The process of linking the document analysis with ecological systems theory also allowed the creation of future research questions and gaps in current knowledge and understanding.

Parent engagement in the curriculum

The Swedish national goals for ECEC are drawn up by the Swedish Parliament and the Swedish government. Preschool (children 1–6 years) and preschool class (children 6–7 years) are regulated by the (a) Swedish National Agency for Education and the Education Act 2010, which sets out the general objectives for the education system as a whole and (b) the Curriculum for Preschool 2018 (hereafter referred to as Lpfö 18) where all principles, goals and values for early childhood education and care are specified. The ambition of what parent engagement in the preschool is in Sweden was defined with the introduction of Lpfö 98, where in paragraph 2.4 it was stated that

> The guardian is responsible for their child's upbringing and development. The pre-school should supplement the home by creating the best possible preconditions for ensuring that each child's development is rich and varied. The preschool's work with children should thus take place in close and confidential co-operation with the home. Parents should have the opportunity within the framework of the national goals to be involved and influence activities in the preschool. A prerequisite for children and parents to have the opportunity of exercising influence is that the preschool is clear about its goals and what its work involves.
>
> *(Skolverket, 2010)*

The Lpfö 98 was, as the year implies, first introduced in 1998, then revised in 2010 and first translated to English in 2011. The Lpfö 98 has since been revised again and Lpfö 18 took effect on the first of July 2019. In the new revision, paragraph 2.4 states that "In order to create the best possible conditions for children to be able to achieve rich, versatile development, the preschool should cooperate in a close and trusting way with the home" (Skolverket, 2018), a significant shift in accountability from the previous 1998 version, where the opening phrase was that 'the guardian is responsible for their child's upbringing and development'. Today, the curriculum places no accountability on the home; other than that *the preschool should cooperate in a close and trusting way with the home*. As its overarching goal, the Lpfö 18 highlights not only the fundamental values and tasks of the preschool but also the importance of maintaining a close and confidential partnership with the home. Furthermore, the opening statement places the responsibility of establishing such relationship on the preschool. A prerequisite for this, however, is that children and parents are extended the opportunity of engagement and that the preschool is clear about its goals and what its work involves (Swedish National Agency for Education, 2018). This indicates that if a child is to receive a rich and varied life in preschool, the teachers as well as the parents must strive towards establishing lasting relationships where not only the child's well-being and development are central, but where the child is also included in the dialogues concerning the child's well-being and development

(Yngvesson, 2019; Yngvesson & Garvis, 2019). Since the introduction of Lpfö 98 in the year 1998, establishing relationships between home and preschool has been an area of responsibility assigned to the preschool and its staff. Thus, the guidelines dictate that in order to achieve such relationships, the teachers and work team are to divide the areas of responsibility as follows: Preschool teachers are responsible for

- respecting and satisfying children's needs, and enabling them to experience their own intrinsic value,

1 applying a democratic approach where children are actively involved,
2 actively including a gender equality perspective so that all children have equal opportunities for extended perspectives and choices, regardless of gender, and

- developing norms and approaches for the work and coexistence in the group of children.

The work team should

1 show respect for the individual and help in creating a democratic climate in the preschool, where children have the opportunity to feel a sense of belonging and to develop responsibility and solidarity,
2 cooperate in work on active measures to prevent discrimination and abusive treatment,
3 work consciously and actively on gender equality,
4 stimulate interaction between children and offer them help and support to resolve conflicts, work out misunderstandings, compromise and respect each other,
5 emphasise and approach the problems involved in ethical dilemmas and questions of life in everyday situations,
6 make children aware that people may have different values that determine their views and actions while at the same time reinforcing the fundamental values, and
7 collaborate with guardians, and discuss rules and approaches in the preschool with guardians, to promote the child's development to become a responsible person and member of society (Skolverket, 2018)

This suggests that a mutual engagement between the preschool and the home is central in the welfare state's task to provide Swedish children with the necessary prerequisites to maintain well-being and a healthy development within the sphere of ECEC. The emphasis on both *person* and *environment* is central in Swedish preschools, as they are duty-bound to follow the national curriculum and must therefore actively promote both understanding and communication between the parents and the teachers. The purpose of this understanding and communication is thus to build trust between the home and the preschool in order to ensure a safe environment in which children are respectfully and as individuals. Furthermore, the task of the preschool is to also help families by supporting them in their role of bringing up and helping their children to grow and develop, further promoting the theory that the systems of a child's world is interconnected (Bronfenbrenner, 1979; Swedish National Agency for Education, 2016). The task of the preschool is thus to cooperate in a close and trusting way with the home in order to ensure the healthy development of the child.

Parent engagement in teacher education, theory and praxis

According to the Swedish National Agency for Education and EACEA, 84% of all children aged 1–5 years, 97% of all children aged 4–5 years and 98% of all children aged six are currently enrolled in the preschool system (Swedish National Agency for Education, 2016) and although long-established, the domain between home and preschool in Sweden today is still one of constant negotiations between understanding various terminologies – personal background – and home culture as well as views on how to raise and educate children (Persson & Tallberg Broman, 2017).

This negotiation of parent engagement often results in a lack of clarity between the expectations and the reality of both parents and teachers, particularly perhaps in the increasing multicultural society that is emerging. While the Swedish preschool and preschool class teacher programme clearly states that *the candidate must demonstrate knowledge regarding the organisation of the educational system, relevant steering documents, curricula and various pedagogical and didactic perspectives.* Parental engagement' is limited only to the steering documents and the teacher's interpretation of these. There are currently no modules within the Swedish preschool teacher programme designed to target parent-to-teacher and teacher-to-parent-relations and the psychological meeting within these relations. Furthermore, the preschool teacher programme does not offer any formal training in cultural sensitivities that would better prepare the candidate for how to exercise the 'home and preschool' stipulations of the steering documents with non-Swedish families; how to better prepare the preschool and its staff for welcoming war- or otherwise traumatised refugee children and their parents; how to bridge the gap between the many cultures that found todays multicultural Sweden.

This, in spite of the huge influx of refugees between 2015–2018. According to Swedish Immigration Agency, in 2017 alone most asylum seekers came from war-conflicted countries such as Syria, Iraq and Eritrea and statistics show that of the around 35,500 asylum seekers that received a decision from the Swedish

Migration Agency in 2018, 11,000 (32 per cent) were granted asylum in Sweden, compared with 27,000 of 66,500 (41 per cent) in 2017 and 67,000 of 112,000 (60 percent) in 2016 (Swedish Migration Agency, 2018). Considering that in Swedish educational culture it is assumed that the majority of children will spend up to 8–10 hours a day in preschool where early learning educators are responsible for the children's pedagogical as well as social activities, it seems a gross oversight that the teacher education has not been reformed to a) accommodate the educational needs the teachers may have for managing the gap between home and school and b) for navigating the cultural sensitivities that may dominate many families and/or individual children during the assimilation process into Swedish preschool (and society).

Conclusion

This chapter outlined in broad strokes the current state of parent engagement in the Swedish preschool and against the background of steering documents investigated how this is reflected in the teacher education as well as how it is put into practice. A literature review and a document analysis were conducted. The focus of the chapter was thus to identify how the steering documents – preschool teacher curriculum – and praxis in regard to parent engagement (home-preschool partnerships) align and whether or not these strive harmoniously, or not, towards the overarching goal of creating and sustaining an ongoing partnership that supports child well-being and a healthy development.

The Bronfenbrenner Ecological Systems Theory dictates that conceptual models that are typical to a child's various systems are inevitably passed across from one system to the next by channels of communication such as parents (home) and preschool teachers (preschool) and also any kind of administration of activity that suggests to intermediate a child's processes of socialisation (Bronfenbrenner, 1979). However, in order to do this, teachers much receive the necessary training providing them with the pedagogical tools required to establish and maintain these monumental conversations between home and preschools – in order to ultimately encourage parents to participate in successful partnerships (Yngvesson & Garvis, 2019). Against this background, we promote the argument that it is crucial that preschool teacher competencies are developed and lifted in order to maintain the pride that the Swedish system places in its 'holistic approach to the child' (Skolverket, 2010). The absence of adequate preschool teacher education in Sweden in areas such as psychology and cultural sensitivity may be symptomatic of an overall void in understanding between what we see on a document and how we interpret that information into practice and moving forward, the primary goal of the Swedish preschool must be to revise and reform Swedish preschool teacher education to better accommodate the needs of 21st-century children and their families.

References

Björnsson, M. (2005). *Kön och skolframgång: Tolkningar och perspektiv* [*Gender and school success: Interpretations and perspectives*]. Stockholm: Swedish National Agency for School Improvement.

Borgonovi, F., & Montt, G. (2012). *Parental involvement in selected PISA countries and economies*. OECD Education Working Papers No. 73. Paris, France: OECD Publishing. doi:10.1787/5k990rk0jsjj-en

Bowen, G. A. (2009). Document analysis as a qualitative research method. *Qualitative Research Journal*, *9*(2), 27–40.

Bronfenbrenner, U. (1979). *The ecology of human development: Experiments by nature and design*. Cambridge, MA: Harvard University Press.

Desforges, C., & Abouchaar, A. (2003). *The impact of parental involvement, parental support and family achievement and adjustment: A literature review*. Research Report RR433. Nottingham: DfES.

Emerson, L., Fear, J., Fox, S., & Sanders, E. (2012). *Parental engagement in learning and schooling: Lessons from research*. Canberra, Australia: Australian Research Alliance for Children and Youth (ARACY) for the Family-School and Community Partnerships Bureau. Retrieved from www.aracy.org.au/publications-resources/area?command=recordandid=10

Flising, L., Fredrikson, G., & Lund, K. (1996). *Parent engagement: A book on creating, maintaining and developing successful parent-participation: A handbook*. Stockholm: Stockholm's Informationsförlag.

Gunnarsson, L., Korpi, B. M., & Nordenstam, U. (1999). *Early childhood education and care policy in Sweden: Background report prepared for the OECD. Thematic review of early childhood education and care policy*. Stockholm: Ministry of Education and Science.

Hakyemez-Paul, S., Pihlaja, P., & Silvennoinen, H. (2018). Parental involvement in Finnish daycare – what do early childhood educators say? *European Early Childhood Education Research Journal*, *26*(2), 258–273.

Hayakawa, M., Englund, M. M. Warner-Richter, M. N. & Reynolds, A. J. (2013). Early parent involvement and school achievement: A longitudinal path analysis. *National Head Start Association Dialog*, *16*(1), 193–197.

Hayes, N., O'Toole, L., & Halpenny, A. (2017). *Introducing Bronfenbrenner: A guide for students and practitioners in early years education*. London: Routledge.

Hiilamo, H. (2004). Changing family policy in Sweden and Finland during the 1990s. *Social Policy and Administration*, *38*(1), 21–40.

Hujala, E., Turja, L., Gaspar, M. F., Veisson, M., & Waniganayake, M. (2009). Perspectives of early childhood teachers on parent-teacher partnerships in five European countries. *European Early Childhood Education Research Journal*, *17*(1), 57–76.

Johansson, E., & Samuelsson Pramling, I. (2006). Play and learning-inseparable dimensions in preschool practice. *Early Child Development and Care*, *176*(1), 47–65.

Levinthal de Oliveira Lima, C., & Kuusisto, E. (2020). Parental engagement in children's learning: A holistic approach to teacher-parents' partnerships. In K. Tirri, & A. Toom (Eds.), *Pedagogy in basic and higher education*.

Lightfoot, D. (2004). Some parents just don't care: Decoding the meanings of parental involvement in urban schools. *Urban Education*, *39*(1), 91–107.

Löfdahl, A., & Hägglund, S. (2006). Power and participation: Social representations among children in pre-school. *Social Psychology of Education*, *9*(2), 179–194.

Lundqvist, Å., & Roman, C. (2008). Construction(s) of Swedish family policy, 1930–2000. *Journal of Family History*, *33*(2), 216–236.

Markström, A. M., & Simonsson, M. (2017). Introduction to preschool: Strategies for managing the gap between home and preschool. *Nordic Journal of Studies in Educational Policy*, *3*(2), 179–188.

Murray, E., McFarland-Piazza, L., & Harrison, L. J. (2014). Changing patterns of parent–teacher communication and parent involvement from preschool to school. *Early Child Development and Care*, *185*(7), 1031–1052.

Nisbett, R. E., Aronson, J., Blair, C., Dickens, W., Flynn, J., Halpern, D. F., & Turkheimer, E. (2012). Intelligence: New findings and theoretical developments. *American Psychologist*, *67*(2), 130–159.

O'Leary, Z. (2014). *The essential guide to doing your research project* (2nd ed.). Thousand Oaks, CA: Sage.

Organisation for Economic Cooperation and Development. (2017). *Family database, key characteristics of parental leave systems*. OECD – Social Policy Division – Directorate of Employment, Labour and Social Affairs. Retrieved from www.oecd.org/els/family/database.htm

Persson, S., & Tallberg Broman, I. (2017). Early childhood education and care as a historically located place – the significance for parental cooperation and the professional assignment. *Nordic Journal of Studies in Educational Policy*, *3*(2), 189–199.

Phillipson, S., & Phillipson, S. N. (2017). Generalizability in the mediation effects of parental expectations on children's cognitive ability and self-concept. *Journal of Child and Family Studies*, *26*(12), 3388–3400. doi:10.1007/s10826-017-0836-z

Råde, A. (2020). The involved, engaged or partnership parents in early childhood education and care, universal. *Journal of Educational Research*, *8*(7), 2833–2841.

Riksdagen. (2018). *UN Convention on the rights of the child to become law in Sweden*. Retrieved from www.riksdagen.se/en/news/2018/jun/18/un-convention-on-the-rights-of-the-child-to-become-law-in-sweden/

Rouse, E., & O'Brien, D. (2017). Mutuality and reciprocity in parent-teacher relationships: Understanding the nature of partnerships in early childhood education and care provision. *Australasian Journal of Early Childhood*, *42*(2), 45–52.

Swedish Migration Agency. (2017). *Asylum*. Retrieved from https://www.migrationsverket.se/Om-Migrationsverket/Statistik/Asyl.html

Swedish Migration Agency. (2018). *Granted residence permits overviews*. Retrieved from https://www.migrationsverket.se/Om-Migrationsverket/Statistik.html

Swedish National Agency for Education [Skolverket]. (2010). *Education act 2010:80*. Stockholm: Author.

Swedish National Agency for Education [Skolverket]. (2016). *Preschool curriculum* [*Läroplan för förskolan, Lpfö*]. 1998 and the amended Preschool Curriculum 2010. Stockholm: Skolverket.

Swedish National Agency for Education [Skolverket]. (2018). *Preschool curriculum* [*Läroplan för förskolan, Lpfö*]. 2018 and the amended Preschool Curriculum 2018. Stockholm: Skolverket.

United Nations. (1989). *Convention on the rights of the child*. Geneva: Author.

Tunberger, P., & Sigle-Rushton, W. (2011). Continuity and change in Swedish family policy reforms. *Journal of European Social Policy*, *21*(3), 225–237.

Uusimäki, L., Yngvesson, T. E., Garvis, S., & Harju-Luukkainen, H. (2019). Parental involvement in ECEC in Finland and Sweden. In S. Garvis, H. Harju-Luukkainen, S. Sheridan, & P. Williams (Eds.), *Nordic families, children and early childhood education* (pp. 81–99). Cham: Palgrave Macmillan.

Venninen, T., & Purola, K. (2013). Educators' views on parent participation on three different identified levels. *Journal of Early Childhood Education Research*, *2*(1), 48–62.

Vincent, C., & Tomlinson, S. (1997). Home-school relationships: The swarming of disciplinary mechanisms? *British Educational Research Journal, 23*(3), 361–377.

Vlasov, J., & Hujala, E. (2017). Parent-teacher cooperation in early childhood education – directors' views to changes in the USA, Russia, and Finland. *European Early Childhood Education Research Journal, 25*(5), 732–746.

Wernersson, I. (2006). *Gender perspective on education.* Stockholm: Swedish National Agency for Higher Education.

Yngvesson, T., & Garvis, S. (2019). Preschool and home partnerships in Sweden, what do the children say? *Early Child Development and Care.* doi:10.1080/03004430.2019.1673385

23
PARENTAL INVOLVEMENT IN EARLY CHILDHOOD EDUCATION DISCOURSE IN UGANDA

Godfrey Ejuu

Introduction

There is now greater recognition that parental involvement and quality support are critical in promoting holistic child education and general academic progress (Shahidullah, 2015). This recognition comes from the acknowledged fact that parents are their children's first teachers in their early years of life. In the case of Uganda, parents traditionally have been involved in the education of their children prior to the colonial period in 1896 (Ezati, McBrien, Stewart, Ssempala, & Ssenkusu, 2016). However, with the introduction of formal education, that emphasized knowing that was relatively new, schools took over both parenting and teacher roles as parents were considered "illiterate" to participate in school activities. This sidelining of parents continues in most school or learning environments up to this date. Some parents have, however, struggled to be involved in their children's learning process, sometimes with limited support.

The genesis of parental involvement in formal education of their children in Uganda started in 1963, immediately after Uganda had got her independence in 1962. The Uganda Education Act of 1963 that was passed gave government management control of all grant aided schools, while parents and religious institutions with teachers formed the Parents and Teachers' Association (PTA). Government took over general management of schools, while the PTA controlled the welfare of the school (Ssekamwa, 1996). Through the PTA, parents got involved in starting projects in schools, contributing to teacher welfare, general discipline in schools, and having a say on what charges were to be levied in the school.

While the earlier scenario is largely an affair of primary and secondary education, early childhood education centres are largely modelling the same approach, although in a slightly different way. First, up to this year 2020, we still do not have a government supported early childhood education centre for young children.

While parents in the primary or secondary schools are more eager to manage their schools, in the case of early childhood centres, parents are reluctant to take up the challenge. The general understanding of parental involvement is still not clear to many, as they want participation that is more common in primary or secondary schools.

Different people understand parental involvement in different ways. This understanding may influence how they get involved, which can be either direct involvement or participation. Fan and Chen (2001) see parental involvement as basic obligations of parents and the involvement of parents in daily routines of the school and at home, while parental participation is seen as influence of parents on organizational and policy level of the school (Suzuki, 2002).

In this situation where parents are not yet so clear on what parental involvement is, it becomes challenging to know which direction to lead parents to. This is coupled with the ever-changing parenting patterns among the 56 tribal groups in Uganda, where each tribe would like to pursue their own approach to parental involvement as a way of preserving or promoting their culture. What many people here see as a way of harmonizing parental involvement without compromising parental cultural values is through use of nationally coordinated parental involvement framework or strategy. This strategy and documents may be used to as key steering documents to guide parents. Some of documents currently being used to steer the country are discussed later.

What key steering documents say about parental involvement in Uganda

Different key documents have been developed in Uganda to promote parental involvement. The first key document is the Uganda Education (Pre-primary, primary and post-primary) Act (MoES, 2008). The Education Act in section 10 (2)(a) states that provision of pre-primary education in Uganda shall be the responsibility of parents. This act dictates that parents must be involved in their children's schools as part of management. Section 28(1), of the Education Act of (2018) states that all institutions declared as schools must have a board of governors or management committees. The same Act in section 5(2)(f) requires parents to participate in providing community support to the school (MoES, 2008).

Another key document is the guidelines for Early Childhood Development centres. This document, under section 6.5 (a–i), states that parents are to be involved in provisions of basic child survival requirement; preparing children to attend school; providing a safety, guidance, and support for learning centres where their children are enrolled; and participating in community activities that are aimed at promoting the children's learning (MoES, 2010).

A new document that was passed in 2018 is the parenting policy. This policy has a number of clauses that enjoin parents to be involved in the education of their children. The parenting policy in section 2.3.1 considers parenting as a cardinal responsibility that cannot be substituted for any other. However, whereas parenting is shared, section 2.3.2 notes that each stakeholder or parent plays unique but complementary roles to raise an emotionally balanced child. This is done in the context of community to recognize that it takes a village to raise a child (Ministry of Gender, Labour and Social Development (MoGLSD), 2018). Other sections in the same policy, for example, section 3.0 of the parenting policy state that parents, guardians, and caregivers shall ensure that children of all ages learn and imitate positive values, norms, and practices for child growth and development (MoGLSD, 2018). Similarly, the same policy in sections 3.1–3.14 guides that every parent, guardian and caregiver shall ensure that they express love; spend quality time with children; effectively communicate; build children's self-esteem and confidence; instil cultural and religious values; live by example; provide for children's needs; respond to children's sexuality; raise hardworking and ethical citizens; inculcate value of wealth creation and saving; discipline children; raise children with special needs; monitor and keep in close touch with the child; and promote the right to play (MoGLSD, 2018).

In total, the National Integrated Early Childhood Development policy in section 1.3.4 states that in Uganda, the family will be the first line of response in early childhood development service delivery. Thus, programs ought to actively engage and empower families and communities to participate in the care and development of their children. Section 2.2.5(b) proposes promoting parenting and child support programs (MoGLSD, 2016).

What is clear about the policy documents mentioned earlier is that government recognizes the critical role played by parental involvement in education of children in the early years. The documents also go ahead to give guidelines and responsibilities to different stakeholders to play their roles in promoting parental involvement. However, all these steering documents fall short of declaring sanctions on institutions or parents who deliberately refuse to do their part.

What research has been done on parental involvement in ECEC in Uganda

Parental involvement in ECEC, still being a new area in Uganda, is yet to attract much literature. A study by Boothby, Mugumya, Ritterbusch, Wanican, Bangirana, Pizatella, Busi and Meyer (2017) to identify community perceptions of protective and harmful parenting practices in three districts in Uganda. The findings suggested that parenting practices can be grouped into seven basic themes that include: investing in children's future, protection, care, enterprising, relationship with neighbours, intimate partner, and child rearing (Boothby et al., 2017).

How the above practices lead to better involvement is another issue. A study by Berg and Noort (2011), aimed at finding out how schools in Uganda involved parents in the education of their children, found there was a lack of cooperation between parents and schools. It also found out that few schools created opportunities for parents to volunteer in school (Berg & Noort, 2011).

In another study, Ezati et al. (2016) explored the relationship between historical effects and parental responses to education in northern Uganda. The study concluded that a complexity of factors including poverty, dislocation, fear, alcohol consumption, and misunderstanding of policy contributed to reduced parental involvement (Ezati et al., 2016).

A study conducted to promote men's involvement in a parenting program to reduce child maltreatment and gender-based violence in Uganda found that men experienced social pressure to conform to conventional masculinity, suggesting the need to instil intervention values at community level (Siu et al., 2017).

Another study conducted by Twaweza in partnership with Ipsos Synovate focused on involvement of young parents in their children's education. Findings revealed that parents exhibited difference in the way they were involved in their children's education. Forty-three percent of parents never checked their children's homework, while 48% of the parents never bothered to talk to their children's teachers about a child's progress (Twaweza, 2013).

The common pattern we see from all these studies is the limited nature of parental involvement in their children's education. The attitude is still negative and no adequate mechanism is yet in place to enforce better parental involvement. More sensitization and action may be needed starting from curriculum changes in the teacher training institutions.

How parental involvement is "treated" in early childhood teacher education in Uganda

The current move toward active parental involvement teacher education is largely seen as a foreign phenomenon rather than a naturally grown concept. Most parents believe that teacher training institutions are an area where they have no contribution. The training institutions on the other hand recognize the critical role played by parents when they are involved in children's school activities. The training institutions therefore try as much as possible to create opportunities to guide teacher trainees to harness parental support and work with them to promote children's learning. This concept has led to three key strategies that are being used to promote parental involvement in schools in teacher education.

The first strategy is one of teacher practicum to simulate parental engagement in different school activities. It is becoming more fashionable for schools or learning centres to have a parents', class visitation, academic, sports, music, speech, or exhibition days. In these days, parents are obliged to come to the school to support their children in given activities on offer. Since parents' participation is more of a requirement by the school, teachers or caregivers are obliged to involve parents in different activities in those days. In the training, teachers are guided on how to manage those school days in such a way that allows better parental involvement.

The second strategy is the introduction of short courses called "parenting programs" to support parents to respond to opportunities school provide for them to be involved in school activities. Usually these are short, less-structured programs mainly supported by local and foreign agencies, and implemented in communities. The facilitators are mainly teacher trainees, but are sometimes done by community workers, child protection staff, or project officers in charge of such interventions. The themes tackled range from child care practices, providing opportunities for child stimulation, child abuse and neglect, child health and nutrition. This training content is what teacher trainees are also taken through in the colleges as parental and community engagement courses.

The third strategy is of curriculum review to introduce course units called "parental and community engagement" in early childhood teacher education. These courses started being introduced in early childhood teacher education courses in 1990s with the coming of certificate teacher programs. Later in 2012, they were formally consolidated in the Ministry of Education and Sports approved Early Childhood Development Caregiver Training Framework (MoES, 2012). The units include different strategies that teachers are to use to involve parents and communities in the education of their children, what kind of support they should give their children, and how they should work with parents. A home visit component was also introduced for trainees to interact with parents about their children. Later, the trainees would compile a "child study" report that details their experiences with a given child and parents, and what kind of support they are proposing to improve the education of the given child.

The parental involvement courses are found in four different programs. The first program is called the Community Child Care Program. This is a parenting program that is meant to provide child care skills to caregivers and parents who have an interest in learning about children. There is no specific academic requirement, save for one's interest. The second program is the Child Care program that admits persons who have completed lower secondary education, but did not pass. So, when a given community initiates an early childhood centre, they are among the target to be seconded by communities to work in child care centres. The third program is the Certificate in Education, designed to prepare early childhood teachers to work in kindergartens. This program admits only those persons who completed and passed the lower secondary examinations. After training, these persons can be posted as teachers in early childhood education centres. The fourth program is the diploma in education course. It is a course that admits those persons who have completed the certificate course and are ready to upgrade to the diploma level. Usually upon graduation, they are given opportunity to teach the certificate group of teachers and also facilitate parenting sessions in communities.

All these four programs have elements of parenting education or involvement. What should be noted about this curriculum strategy is that while the courses are essentially parental engagement courses, they are not actually meant for parents. Instead, the courses are designed in such a way that they are exclusively for teachers. The courses provide information about how teachers should interact with parents. They do not cater for how the parents should engage with the teachers, thus, leaving a gap for effective collaborative involvement as only one side is empowered.

How parental engagement is practiced in some Ugandan schools

Parental involvement in children's education has not been as explicit as it is in the West. This has been due to the belief that school and home are two distinct institutions. In this belief, parents belonged to homes, while teachers belonged to school. It was also believed that parents were not knowledgeable to give advice on what is to be done in school, even when it involved issues to do with their children. Parents picked this cue so well such that many of them have always stayed away from school activities as they don't see themselves being of any benefit there.

In the same way, most teachers believe that school is for teachers. They are the ones who are more competent to have a say in what goes on in a school. Thus, teachers find it difficult to involve parents in any school activity. Teachers in most cases are only comfortable to have parents at school to either pay school dues, drop, or pick their children. A parent who stays around will be considered going beyond expected boundaries.

The concept of school in early childhood education in the Ugandan context may be rather confusing. Early childhood education and care services in Uganda are provided in pre-primary, sometimes also called pre-school centres. In this context, school is a formalized system, while early childhood education is informal and sometimes family or community child care activities. For the purpose of this article, we shall understand the word school to mean early childhood education centres, where children of the ages 0–3 or 3–6 years are supported for early learning stimulation within families, communities, or institutionalized centres.

In the earlier settings, parenting involvement is seen as critical in ensuring that children are adequately prepared and made ready for school. Since these early childhood care and education services are largely provided by private individuals or communities and families, the main work of government is to provide guidance and oversight function to allow parents to be involved in different child care and education support to their children within the acceptable standards within ECCE settings.

In the context of ECCE, there are many community-based ECCE centres all over the country. Up to this year 2020, there are still no government ECCE centres in Uganda. The centres are initiated by communities, with government providing oversight function. The oversight function is in different areas that include caregiver quality, parental engagement and education, facility standards, basic requirements, and minimum standards (M0ES, 2007). However, quality standards in most centres largely depend on the status of the community it serves. Low socio-economic status communities have largely low quality centres in the perspective of the government officials. In offering oversight function, government of Uganda has produced the following guidelines to promote parenting education and involvement. Under Ministry of Gender Labour and Social Development, we have National Integrated Early Childhood Development Policy (2016), Uganda National Parenting Guidelines (2018), and Uganda National Parenting guidelines (2018). Under Ministry of

Health, we have the 26 key family care practices. Under Ministry of Education and Sports' Directorate of Education Standards (DES) we have the Early Learning and Development Standards (2015).

With all the earlier guidelines in place, there seemed to be too many of them that potentially showed conflicting information. We note that NGOs, especially those with international collaborators or funders also introduced foreign based parenting practices that were seen to be conflicting with local cultural beliefs about parenting. In view of the above, the government through the National Curriculum Development Centre (NCDC) initiated a parenting framework. The goal of the framework is to provide parental education that helps to strengthen families by providing relevant, effective education, and encouraging an optimal environment for the growth and development parents and children (NCDC, 2020). The key areas in the framework include Parent development, children's early learning and stimulation, approaches to learning, cultural development, community engagement and involvement, family development, and life skills and values (NCDC, 2020). This framework is meant to harmonize the key messages that are supposed to be given to parents while maintaining community best practices. The key principles of this parenting framework include: Parents have the mandate of nurturing their children; families shall be empowered to provide holistic development of healthy and productive children; communities shall be empowered to support families to provide holistic needs for children; and the rights of children must be safe guarded in all community cultural practices (NCDC, 2020).

Parenting education is a largely private sector led in Uganda. It is an area that has been taken up by Non-Governmental Organisations (NGOs). Some of the NGOs with parenting education programs include Children at Risk Network (CRANE) Services; Healthy Child; Brac Uganda, Plan Uganda, Learning Through Play (LTP); Literacy and Adult Basic Education (LABE); World Vision; Parenting Uganda; Child Fund; Save the Children; Catholic Relief Services (CRS); Geneva Global; and Stromme Foundation among others.

There are four basic approaches being used to in parental engagement in ECCE in Uganda. The first approach is where local or international non-governmental organisations (NGOs) start ECCE centres and later pass them on to parents and communities to take over, run, and maintain them. One such organization is BRAC Uganda that is initiating children's play labs. The NGO identifies communities that deserve to get the play labs, start the labs, and train seconded parents from the communities to support children's learning in play way mode (BRAC, 2019). BRAC uses parenting manuals that caregivers and other parent educators use to improve parents' knowledge on their roles to support child well-being both at home and at school (BRAC, 2019). The areas of focus in the parenting education include child development and its importance, child brain structure and development, effects of parents' negative and positive thinking on children; promoting cognitive development through play; mothers' self-care practices; role of father in supporting children; parents behaviour toward children; and child safety at home and school readiness (BRAC, 2018). Parents are brought together to attend the sessions, facilitated by play leaders (Teachers) employed by BRAC to support the communities (BRAC, 2019). When time comes for BRAC to leave, the centres are handed over to parents to manage them. Some centres have managed to flourish, but many have collapsed after BRAC left.

The second approach is through parent education with the aim of parents using the knowledge to get involved in taking care of their children at home and school appropriately to promote school readiness. This approach is spearheaded by NGOs like PLAN Uganda. This organization uses a Community Led Action for Children (CLAC) strategy that aims at increasing parent's skills, knowledge, and capacity to fulfil and meet the care and development of children (PLAN Uganda, 2016). Usually, they have parenting groups of between 30 and 35 members who meet regularly to discuss issues related to child welfare. These groups are usually of specific gender, although sometimes they can have all of them in one meeting when need arises (PLAN Uganda, 2016). Parenting sessions are facilitated by volunteers trained and mentored by PLAN staff. In addition to the training sessions, they also have home visits, material, technical, and financial support to families depending on their need (PLAN Uganda, 2016). The challenge with this strategy is that most parents only come because the funds given to the groups by the NGO are an income generating activity. Greater participation is also seen among mothers, and not fathers who make the decisions in most homes. Also, tracking parental involvement in homes can be a challenge.

The third approach is by engaging parents to be involved in initiating, managing, and sustaining ECCE centres within their community spaces. This approach is spearheaded by NGOs like LABE have taken another approach towards parental involvement. In their approach, parents are mobilized to initiate an early childhood education centre in a home of one of the parents. The same parents then volunteer as teachers for the children in that home or be members of savings scheme. Others come as helps to support with preparation of hot snacks, play with children, or repair play equipment made by parents from local materials (LABE, 2019). The parents also form the management committee to hire other trained caregivers to work with them from time to time. The parents discuss with the caregivers their remuneration that can be either cash or labour in caregivers' gardens (LABE, 2019).

The fourth approach is one by individual parents who take it upon themselves to listen to what is being said or done elsewhere so that they can come and do it with their children. These activities could involve direct participation with children in planting greeneries, adopting pets, starting home projects, attending school meetings, or supervising a child when doing school work at home. Other parents are using mobile phone apps based on simple, practical advice from their teachers and counsellors focusing on three features that include: Something to talk about; activities to share; and guidance to encourage children (GEMS Education, 2019) to promote better parental involvement in the learning of the child. This involvement, however, is largely to promote school goals, very academic and is only common among the middle-class parents who are able to appreciate such engagements.

What may be clear about all these engagements with parents is that most of them are involved in what they call retooling, empowerment, knowledge sharing, or parental awareness depending on who is doing what with parents. This approach is largely a hand-to-mouth effort that makes parents to be passive recipients of information about their children, but rarely involved in doing things for their children. Government is providing guidance, which is information, while NGOs are providing training, which is another information. Parents have not yet started being involved in ECCE.

How parental engagement and collaboration can be developed in Uganda

The Government of Uganda has put in place a number of policies and guidelines to show that it is committed toward promoting a more active parental engagement in school. However, the policies alone are not achieving the desired effects. What comes clearly now is that a multi-faceted strategy may be needed to evoke results. We could start with the following suggestions.

Parent education on the roles they are expected to play in the school or while with their children. A number of parents believe that they have limited roles to play at school, as what goes on there is for teachers. These parents believe that once they have paid school dues and provided all requirements as expected of them by respective schools, then they are done for the school term.

Parents like children also need guidance in form of activities or projects to accomplish together with their children either at home or at school. Schools that have been able to use such approach have made parents to be more involved in school activities as parents become part of the children's learning process.

Constant communication with parents to get ideas from them on how they want their children to be educated is key in attracting them to schools (Bridge, 2019). This constant communication has been key in helping Bridge schools in Uganda maintain a certain loyal proportion of parents to their schools despite challenges they faced in the initial stages of establishment where government had to close some schools.

While some schools have used bylaws to condition parents to be involved in some school activities, it is not sustainable. This is because some parents feel use of bylaws make the process a force instead of a free participation. The result of this is parents complying by being there but don't offer to participate freely.

Conclusion and implications

The parental involvement in ECCE in Uganda is still at the infancy state with most actors still not sure of what to do. Government gives guidance, but since it does not have ECCE centres, the officials have no experience to share with parents. In the same vein, most parents either are inexperienced or come from a cultural background that does not understand the basis for parental involvement as being guided by government. The NGOs bring in much-needed financial and technical support; however, most of this initiative is misunderstood by some parents as income generating activities as opposed to a means of helping them support their children to be ready for school.

The implications for this situation include: Government needs to provide the parental involvement guidelines and mentors to work with parents to implement them. Absence of this just make parents go back to what they have done before since they may not have understood what is expected of them even after training sessions.

Agencies that are supporting parents to pick up parental involvement practices need to use parents' cultural knowledge on parent involvement and explore that to support them. Use of parenting best practices from the west will not be sustainable. This is because, some of the parents may not be convinced about the practices.

Government officials who are working with parents need to model the parenting involvement they are preaching. Use of mentors or trainers who have no children themselves will only lead to apathy of the guidelines.

References

Boothbya, N., Mugumyab, F., Ritterbuschc, A. E., Wanican, J., Bangiranae, C. A., Pizatellaf, A. D., Busig, S., & Meyer, S. (2017). Ugandan households: A Study of parenting practices in three districts. *Child Abuse & Neglect, 67* (2017) 157–173. http://dx.doi.org/10.1016/j.chiabu.2017.02.010

Berg, R. D., & Noort, L. (2011). *Parental involvement in primary education in Uganda: How primary schools in Bukedea, Kumi and Mbale district involve parents in the education of their children.* Utrecht: Utrecht University.

BRAC. (2018). *Parenting manual.* Kampala: Author.

BRAC. (2019). *Early childhood development parenting manual* (Vol. 2). Kampala: Author.

Bridge. (2019). *Ugandan parents cite education quality as their motivation for school choice.* Retrieved from www.bridgeinternationalacademies.com/uganda-bridge-parents-2019/

Ezati, B. A., McBrien, J. L., Stewart, J., Ssempala, C., & Ssenkusu, P. (2016). Parents, pay attention! Factors related to parental involvement with education in Northern Uganda. *Australasian Review of African Studies, 37*(2), 9–32. doi:10.22160/22035184/ARAS-2016-37-2/9-32

Fan, X., & Chen, M. (2001). Parental involvement and students' academic achievement: A meta-analysis. *Educational Psychology Review, 13*, 1–19.

Directorate of Education Standards (DES) (2015). *Early Learning and development standards.* Kampala: DES.

GEMS Education. (2019). *Parental engagement.* Retrieved from www.gemseducation.co.ug/parents/parental-engagement

LABE. (2019). *Mid-term review of the scaling up children's school readiness and retention (SURE) project.* Kampala: LABE.

Ministry of Gender, Labour and Social Development (MoGLSD) (2016). *The national integrated early childhood development policy action plan of Uganda (2016–2021).* Kampala: MoGLSD. Retrieved from http://health.go.ug/sites/default/files/FINAL_National_Integrated_ECD_ACTION_PLAN_Approved.pdf

MoGLSD (2016). *The national integrated early childhood development policy*. Kampala: Uganda. MoGLSD. file:///C:/Users/USER/Downloads/FINAL_NIECD_POLICY_FINAL_BOOK_approved_by_Acting_PS__Mpagi.pdf

Ministry of Gender, Labour and Social Development. (2018). *The Uganda national parenting policy*. Kampala: MgLSD.

Ministry of Gender, Labour and Social Development. (2018). *The Uganda national parenting guidelines*. Kampala: MoGLSD. chrome-extension://efaidnbmnnnibpcajpcglclefindmkaj/viewer.html?pdfurl=https%3A%2F%2Fmglsd.go.ug%2Fwp-content%2Fuploads%2F2021%2F05%2FThe-Uganda-National-Parenting-Guideline.pdf&clen=1725573&chunk=true

MoES. (2008). *Education (Pre-primary, primary and post-primary) act, 2008*. Kampala: Author. Retrieved from https://ulii.org/ug/legislation/act/2015/13

MoES. (2012). *The early childhood development caregiver training framework*. Kampala: Author.

MoES. (2007). *The early childhood development policy*. Kampala: MoES.

MoES (2010). *Guidelines for early childhood development centres*. Kampala: MoES.

National Curriculum Development Centre. (2020). *Parenting education framework*. Kampala: Author.

PLAN Uganda. (2016). *Lesson learned: Implementing ECCD/CLAC approach by plan international Uganda*. Kampala: Plan International.

Shahidullah, S. (2015). *The impact of parents' education on parenting and pedagogy on child's development and learning*. ARNEC Connection: Working together for Early Childhood, 9. Retrieved from www.academia.edu/33124323/Community_of_practice_in_Early_Childhood_Development_Experience_of_ChildFund_India?email_work_card=title

Siu, G. E., Wight, D., Seeley, J., Namutebi, C., Sekiwunga, R., Zalwango, F., & Kasule, S. (2017). Men's involvement in a parenting programme to reduce child maltreatment and gender-based violence: Formative evaluation in Uganda. *The European Journal of Development Research, 29*(5), 1017–1037. doi:10.1057/s41287-017-0103-6

Ssekamwa, J. C. (1996). *History and development of education in Uganda*. Kampala: Fountain Publishers. Retrieved from www.nzdl.org/gsdlmod?e=d-00000-00off-0unescoen-00-0-0-10-0-0-0direct-10-4-0-1l-11-en-50-20-about-00-0-1-00-0-4-0-0-11-10-0utfZz-8-00&a=d&cl=CL2.3.1&d=HASH5a996944f627034add15bf.16

Suzuki, I. (2002). Parental Participation and Accountability in Primary Schools in Uganda. *Compare 32*(2):243-259. DOI: 10.1080/03057920220143200

Twaweza. (2013). *Are parents involved in education?* Twaweza Monitoring Series. Retrieved from www.twaweza.org/uploads/files/Education-14112014ty.pdf

24
UNITED KINGDOM – FOUR NATIONS IN ONE COUNTRY

Diversity in policy, research, and practice

Catherine Carroll-Meehan

Introduction

This chapter outlines the context in which parent partnerships in Early Childhood Education and Care (ECEC) exist in the United Kingdom. Relevant recent policy, research, and practice highlight the complexities that exist in a country made up of four nations. In order to illustrate the differences and similarities of the four countries of the United Kingdom, it is critical to present contextual information about the United Kingdom regarding what the nature is of parent partnerships in each nation.

The quote from Save the Children (2013) "Parents and families are a critically important part of a child's learning and development" highlights the central role that families play in the lives of children. Families as partners in learning is a frequently used phrase among adults working with children and families in ECEC in the United Kingdom. The relationship between teachers and families can be problematic as each holds differing sets of values about education and knowledge and the power imbalances in these relationships. The intention to create effective partnerships is strong but the reality in practice is not always easy because of barriers to partnership that exist for both families and teachers and practitioners working with young children.

Tett (2001) suggests that "genuine partnerships" between educators and families are possible if "power, responsibility and ownership in ways which show a high degree of mutuality" are embedded in the fabric of the relationship (p. 194). The majority of educator and family relationships are based physically and professionally in the educators' place of work, language, and social and organisational structures, which can lead to families feeling like junior partners in this relationship (Tett, 2001, p. 195).

The chapter focuses on the context of the United Kingdom by outlining the policy approach in the four nations, and it presents an overview of parent partnership research and training and continuous professional development available for professionals working with families.

Context of the United Kingdom

As mentioned in the introduction, the United Kingdom is a country consisting of four nations: England, Northern Ireland, Scotland, and Wales. Historical, political, economic, and social factors all led to the creation of the United Kingdom. The four nations were part of the larger British Empire of the ruling monarch. Over time, the British Empire declined, and now many Commonwealth countries retain the ruling monarch as head of state, but many have sought independence. Within the United Kingdom, we have witnessed tensions that have led to an increased devolution of powers by England to the three nations (Scotland, Wales, and Northern Ireland). This has been a political mechanism to maintain the "Union" by the government in Westminster (London, England). The current reigning monarch, Queen Elizabeth II, is a strong supporter of the Union. Current political challenges related to Brexit, potentially threaten the continued union of the four nations. Rather than the United Kingdom, the United Kingdom might become the "Untied Kingdom."

The devolved governments in each nation have the responsibility for all education and care, including for early childhood. There is no single overarching set of policies or strategies for the United Kingdom. Each nation has their policy and strategies for children and their education. Following ten years of austerity policies of the United Kingdom government that resulted in the loss of funding for many services that targeted children and families, there has been a significant increase in the role of non-governmental organisations (NGOs) and charities in filling the gap left by the discontinuation of government services. Cutbacks to education, health, and social care budgets have meant that work to support families has left families unable to access services to support their role in raising children.

In setting out the case for the United Kingdom, it is important to set the scene with regard to the complexity of diverse socio-political and economic circumstances. In spite of all the efforts previously in education to reduce the impact of inequality through education, such as accelerated literacy and numeracy skills for children and their families (e.g., children's centres, Sure Start), the gap is widening. One of the greatest challenges in the United Kingdom is the level of social, educational, and health inequality.

Declining birth rates and positive migration rates influence public perceptions about the causes of inequality. The populist media fuels racism, and right wing nationalist radicalism blames migrants for poverty and unemployment. Figure 24.1 shows the percentage of children living in poverty in each of the four nations. Scotland has been consistently lower than all four countries, while Wales is consistently higher. Formerly, the lowest rate of 21% in Scotland in 2010–2011 has seen a steady increase under the Conservative government's austerity policies. Shamefully, on average about 30% of United Kingdom children live in poverty. Children in

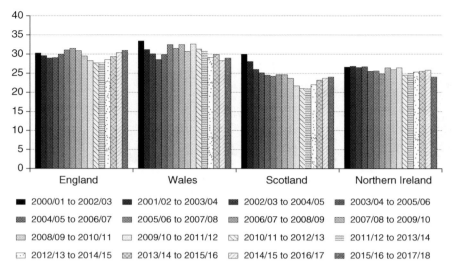

FIGURE 24.1 Child poverty rates in England, Wales, Scotland, and Northern Ireland: Households Below Average Income. (UK Gov, 2019)

families with more than one child are more likely to be living in poverty. Children from working households also live in poverty as a consequence of low minimum wages and casual working. An increased number of families rely on foodbanks to feed themselves, and parents report going hungry so their children can eat.

The next section of this chapter outlines the policies and strategies adopted in each nation with examples provided.

Policy related to family involvement in the United Kingdom

The prevailing common feature of policy in the United Kingdom related to family involvement recognises the prime role and importance of families in the lives of children and their education. Defining what family involvement looks like in policy and practice is evidence of the variation among countries. Families are involved with ECEC settings or schools, and they support learning in the home. The majority of family education initiatives are related to ensuring that families are able to support a rich learning environment at home from birth until the end of compulsory schooling.

Policy and legislation differ in each of the four nations. The United Kingdom signed the United Nations Convention on the Rights of the Child in 1989. Each country then ratified the convention into law in the following ways.

Gordon Brown (then the Chancellor of the Exchequer) introduced the Sure Start policy in 1998 for all four countries. There were localised arrangements in each of the four countries. The Children Centre model that evolved in England under the Blair government linked health, social care, and education services into one service for families. The coalition and Conservative governments from 2010 oversaw reductions in funding. This resulted in many children's centres closing around England with some local authorities maintaining Sure Start hubs with ring-fenced budgets. Sure Start services for families of children from birth to three still exist in Northern Ireland and Wales (Flying Start). Sure Start in Scotland is a one-off maternity payment of £500.

England

In England, the legislative and policy view of families and their involvement in the education system is set forth in the Education Act in 1996, which was revised in 2004. The Act focuses on the roles of schools and teachers and parents are portrayed as customers or users of the education system. Prior to the Conservative government, in 2008 the former Department for Children, Schools, and Families (DCSF) published a report focusing on the impact of families in children's education. The key findings of this report include some prevailing narratives that underpin current policy and practice in England more than ten years later. Namely, early family involvement in children's learning is one of the most significant factors in improving children's educational achievements and life chances. The nature of this involvement differs among families; for fathers, it is the quality and nature of the involvement that matters, whereas for mothers, it is time and their own educational achievements and qualifications that have the greatest impact on children's success in education. The report also highlighted the importance of family learning, in particular, with regard to the development of children's reading, writing, and numeracy. Other significant factors were family attitudes, aspirations for children, and belief in children, which were also identified as determinants of children's success in education (DSCF, 2008).

In 2011, the United Kingdom government commissioned a review to explore best practices for family engagement (Goodall et al., 2011). The review focused on the education system of five- to 19-year-olds and neglected family engagement in ECEC services. This report provided guidance with four recommendations for the education sector for best practice for working with families.

Recently, a further review by the Education Endowment Fund sought to explore the ways that teachers and settings could enhance relationships with families in an effort to support learning and improve life chances (Education Endowment Fund, 2018).

Scotland

In Scotland, the government commissioned a review of the impact of Scottish Schools (Parental Involvement) Act 2006. Scotland is unique in the four countries as it is the only one in the United Kingdom to legislate family involvement in education. The review was done in 2016, ten years after the legislation was enacted. The review found that the increase in family involvement in Scottish education has a positive impact on children and their learning. Further work is still required to build on the changes made and to continue to embed best practice consistently in Scotland for all children and families (Education Scotland, 2019).

Guidance from the Scottish Schools (Parental Involvement) Act 2006 states that "Parental involvement is about supporting pupils and their learning. It is about families and teachers working together in partnership to help children become more confident learners" (p. 9 review).

The Act sets forth provisions in the following prioritised areas, and local education authorities must develop and implement the following schemes:

1   Learning at home,
2   Home/School partnerships,
3   Family representation (Scottish Government, 2006).

The Scottish Act identifies six types of family involvement. The underpinning philosophy is that family involvement leads to family engagement. The involvement is classed as:

1   Family support programmes, home visits, and family education;
4   Communicating with families about school, progress, and effective communication;
5   Volunteering recruitment, training, and work for families in schools and settings to support children's education;
6   Learning at home and supporting families to work with children at home to do homework and other curriculum related activities;
7   Decision-making by providing opportunities for families to be part of governance and advocacy for children's educational settings;
8   Collaboration and advocacy in the local community to source resources and services for children and families (Scottish Government, 2006).

The National Parenting Strategy (2012) Scotland reinforces the critical importance of families in children's educational success and recognises the asset that families are in education (Scottish Government, 2012).

Northern Ireland

In Northern Ireland, Sure Start provides a targeted service for children from the most disadvantaged backgrounds (Northern Ireland Government, 2018). The "Getting Ready to Learn" programme aims to increase levels of family participation and involvement in collaboration with ECEC providers. The Northern Ireland government has a dedicated website and toolkits for settings and practitioners to highlight the importance of early intervention and the impact on children's learning and development. The website contains "bite-sized" information related to the key themes of the programme, which include:

1. Enhancing family understanding and appreciation of the role of play in learning and what this means in the curriculum,
9. Raising awareness of health and well-being, in particular the critical importance of physical activity,
10. Giving families critical information about their child's development through awareness of the ages and stages they may be witnessing at home,
11. Promoting reading at home and encouraging good bedtime routines to provide structure for children (Getting Ready to Learn, 2017).

Wales

The devolved government in Wales has responsibility for education. Like other governments in the United Kingdom, the Welsh Assembly has responded to the particular challenges of their local population. Poverty rate in Wales is higher than that in any other part of the United Kingdom, with one in three children living in households at or below 60% of the median income and 14% living in severe poverty. Unemployment rates in Wales are also higher than those in any other part of the United Kingdom (Poverty and Social Exclusion, 2017).

The Welsh Government, like the other countries in the United Kingdom, has responded to OECD reports about improving education and children's outcomes. For example, the Building a Brighter Future: Early Years and Childcare Plan (2013) for Wales outlines the government's commitment and vision for young children. It builds on other strategies and brings together in one place a comprehensive plan for those who work with children (birth to seven years) and their families. This includes a range of multidisciplinary teams such as health, social care, and education professionals.

The Flying Start initiative (Welsh Government, 2019), which is similar to the now defunct English Sure Start policy, provides targeted support for children from birth to three and their families. Targeted services support children's development and early intervention services are provided as required. The Welsh Government website states that the following is provided for families:

1. Part-time childcare for two to three year olds,
12. Enhanced Health Visiting service,
13. Access to parenting programmes,
14. Support for children in learning to talk and communicate (Welsh Government, 2019).

Working with families is a theme in Welsh government documents related to education and care for children from birth to seven years. One example is the Good Practice in Parental Involvement in Primary Schools paper produced for Estyn

(Welsh Inspectorate for Education and Training in Wales) from 2009. This document reports that parental involvement mostly involves mothers and that parental and family involvement typically declines as children get older because of their own limited aspirations, poor basic skills creating a barrier to accessing school, their own negative experiences of education, a lack of confidence and competence with homework tasks, and cultural/language differences (Estyn, 2018, pp. 12–13).

Research related to family involvement in ECEC in the United Kingdom

Research undertaken in the United Kingdom about family involvement is widespread. A systematic review of the literature since 2015 related to family involvement or engagement in ECEC identified the following themes (see Table 24.1).

Some examples of research are outlined later. The Organisation for Economic Cooperation and Development (OECD) undertakes large-scale systematic studies

TABLE 24.1 Themes emerging in research about family involvement from systemic literature review in the UK (2015–2020)

Families and reading	Encouraging family/carer involvement	Family involvement and voice in services, e.g. health, SEN, justice, social care
Father involvement and children's behaviours and academic achievement	Families' perceptions about involvement in education	Factors affecting family involvement
Families and children's academic achievement	Family-Teacher communications	Fathers and ECEC involvement
Family education	Family-child relationships as predictors of children's social competence	Attachment
Family involvement in primary schools	Home environment and influence on education, e.g., unpredictable environments	Interventions with families and impact on reducing inequality
Emerging technologies, families, children, home and school-family literacy practices	Maternal time and children's outcomes	Family factors associated with childhood anxiety, depression and well being
Households, employment, gender and children's outcomes	Involving families in children's learning	Therapeutic work with families and children
Identification of 'good' parenting practices	Early intervention	Family 'over aspiration'
Family 'under aspiration'	Families impact on children's development e.g. language, cognition, social/emotional	Poverty, child abuse, neglect and inequality

of countries. Two recent OECD studies focused on Scotland and Wales school improvement. The Welsh report outlined the importance of family involvement and found that most primary schools employed a broad range of strategies to engage families in children's learning. This finding was mirrored in ECEC settings (OECD, 2014). Similarly, the report on Scotland recognised the long tradition of family involvement in education. Notably, families were viewed as being critical in developing children's skills, health, social, and emotional well-being (OECD, 2015).

The findings of the Effective Provision of Pre-School Education (EPPE) research from 2004 have shaped ECEC policy and practice in England and internationally (Sylva, Melhuish, Sammons, Siraj-Blatchford, & Taggart, 2004). This research found that the quality of home learning was more important that many other factors outranking family education, job, and income (Sylva et al., 2004, p. 9). With regard to relationships between early childhood settings and home, the research recommended that ECEC settings should engage families in children's learning by sharing educational aims with them (Sylva et al., 2004, p. 15). The research highlighted that the most effective ECEC settings enabled families to support children at home through shared goal setting.

In England, the report "The Impact of Parental Involvement on Children's Education" (2008) produced by the Department of Schools, Children, and Families found that family socio-economic status affected three domains. These domains included cognitive attainment, cooperation/conformity, and confidence. These domains had an impact on children's performance in education, and the relationship between home and school was paramount to children's success. Living in single parent families, young families, poorer families, or less qualified families further reduced the life chances of the children. These risks and poor outcomes can, however, be reduced by high home learning environment scores. Higher home learning environments might include routines and structures at home, such as regular bed times and regularity for children. Children should also have opportunities to socialise with peers outside of the home. The report concluded that what "families do is more important than who families are" (p. 29).

Teacher and practitioner training and families in the United Kingdom

Across the four countries, there are a range of post-secondary schooling qualifications for working with young children and their families. For the purpose of this chapter, the approach used in England is highlighted. There are slight differences in each country; however, England's journey provides an example of how changes in political priorities change the shape of training.

The Early Years Initial Teacher Training (EYITT) pathway in England is one example of how one of the four nations trains teachers. Since September 2013, EYITT, which awards the Early Years Teacher Status (EYTS), replaced the Early

Years Professional Status. The aim of EYTS is to raise the status of the qualification to that of teachers working in other phases who, at the end of their training, earned Qualified Teacher Status (QTS). The EYTS standards mirror QTS but focus on those staff with specialist knowledge for children from birth to five years who deliver the Early Years Foundation Stage (EYFS) curriculum. By the end of the training, Early Years Teachers must:

1   Set high expectations that inspire, motivate, and challenge all children;
2   Promote good progress and outcomes by children;
3   Demonstrate good knowledge of early learning and EYFS;
4   Plan education and care while taking into account of the needs of all children;
5   Adapt education and care to respond to the strengths and needs of all children;
6   Make accurate and productive use of assessment;
7   Safeguard and promote the welfare of children, and provide a safe learning environment;
8   Fulfil wider professional responsibilities (Department for Education, 2019).

The preamble to the text states that EYTs will "forge positive professional relationships and work with parents and/or carers in the best interests of babies and children." Specific references to parents are made in six places in the Teacher Standards (Early Years). For example, EYTs must:

1   2.7 Understand the important influence of parents and/or carers, working in partnership with them to support the child's wellbeing, learning, and development;
2   4.3 Promote a love of learning and stimulate children's intellectual curiosity in partnership with parents and/or carers;
3   6.3 Give regular feedback to children and parents and/or carers to help children progress towards their goals.

Future aspirations and developments for family involvement and engagement in the United Kingdom

Reducing barriers to family involvement is the goal of early childhood education in the United Kingdom. The literature on tackling educational inequalities strongly states that home and school partnership is critical. There are barriers both for teachers and schools and for parents and families. Extrinsic barriers for teachers can include educational system policy and perceptions about family expectations of teachers and work place culture. Intrinsic barriers can include confidence and competence, feelings about themselves, and control, values, and beliefs. Future training and education of teachers and those working with young children and their families must include greater awareness of the barriers family/parents feel in an effort to reduce power imbalances (Meehan & Meehan, 2017).

Concluding comments

Whilst there are policy differences and priorities in each of the four nations, the reality that unites the four nations is that early childhood educators work in a highly regulated context (Education Workforce Council [Wales], 2019). For example, inspections about the quality of provision by Ofsted (England) (OFSTED, 2019), Education and Training Inspectorate Northern Ireland ([ETINI], 2019), Her Majesty's Inspectorate of Education (Education Scotland, 2019), and Estyn (2019, Wales) mean that teachers work in a pressurised context to ensure compliance, and this can undermine teacher creativity, confidence, and responsiveness. The mythical aspiration of seeking to achieve "best practice" sees educators in the United Kingdom on an infinite treadmill meeting regulation, accountability, and quality imposed on their day-to-day practice by legislation, regulation, and funders.

Additionally, Miller (2008) suggests that

> the diverse roles and responsibilities of early years practitioners, the variety of settings they work in, and the lack of a professional registration body and formal pay structures make it difficult to agree what constitutes an early years teacher in England.
>
> (p. 266)

This is also a common feature of all four nations. The changes in England that provide for the new qualification of Early Years Teacher Status attempt to recognize the need for qualified teachers working with children from birth to five years. Although the teacher training requirements are comparable with other teacher training routes, there is still a great divide for early years teachers in terms of pay and conditions when compared with teachers with the same qualifications working in schools (Carroll-Meehan, Bolshaw, & Hadfield, 2017).

This perpetuates the complex professional and working conditions in the early childhood sector and remains a challenge for effective partnerships with parents and families.

Harris and Goodall (2007) remind us that working with parents and families is "multifaceted in nature because parental involvement subsumes a wide variety of parental behavioural patterns and parenting practices" (p. 23). Some examples of parental involvement include parental aspirations for their children's academic achievement, parental communication with their children about school, parental participation in school activities, parental communication with teachers about their child, and parental rules at home that are considered to be related to education.

In conclusion, this chapter outlines the United Kingdom context and conditions for policy, research, and practice in the four countries.

References

Carroll-Meehan, C., Bolshaw, P., & Hadfield, E. (2017). New leaders in early years: Making a difference for children in England. *Early Child Development and Care*, *189*(3), 416–429. doi:10.1080/03004430.2017.1324436

Department for Education. (2019). *Teachers' standards (early years)*. Retrieved from https://assets.publishing.service.gov.uk/government/uploads/system/uploads/attachment_data/file/211646/Early_Years_Teachers__Standards.pdf

Department of Schools, Children and Families. (2008). *The impact of parental involvement on children's education*. Retrieved from https://webarchive.nationalarchives.gov.uk/20120504214534/www.education.gov.uk/publications/eOrderingDownload/DCSF-Familyal_Involvement.pdf

Education and Training Inspectorate Northern Ireland (ETINI). (2019). *ETINI website*. Retrieved December 31, 2019, from www.etini.gov.uk/

Education Endowment Fund. (2018). *Working with parents to support children's learning: Guidance report*. Retrieved from https://educationendowmentfoundation.org.uk/public/files/Publications/FamilyalEngagement/EEF_Familyal_Engagement_Guidance_Report.pdf

Education Scotland. (2019). *Early learning and childcare*. Retrieved from https://education.gov.scot/education-scotland/scottish-education-system/early-learning-and-childcare-elc/

Education Workforce Council (Wales). (2019). *Education workforce council website*. Retrieved from www.ewc.wales/site/index.php/en/14-english/about.html

Estyn. (2018). *Involving parents' communication between schools and parents of school-aged children*. Retrieved from https://www.estyn.gov.wales/thematic-report/involving-parents-communication-between-schools-and-parents-school-aged-children

Estyn. (2019). *Estyn website*. Retrieved from www.estyn.gov.wales/language

Getting Ready to Learn. (2017). *Getting ready to learn*. Retrieved from www.gettingreadytolearn.co.uk

Goodall, J., Vorhaus, J., Carpentieri, J. D., Brooks, G., Akerman, R., & Harris, A. (2011). *Review of best practice in parental engagement: Practitioners summary*. Retrieved from https://assets.publishing.service.gov.uk/government/uploads/system/uploads/attachment_data/file/182507/DFE-RR156_-_Practitioner_Summary.pdf

Harris, A., & Goodall, J. (2007). *Engaging families in raising achievement: Do families know they matter?* Research Report. DCSF-RW004. Warwick: University of Warwick, DCSF.

Her Majesty's Inspectorate of Education (Education Scotland). (2019). *HMI education website*. Retrieved from https://education.gov.scot/education-scotland/what-we-do/inspection-and-review/

Meehan, C., & Meehan, P. (2017). Trainee teachers' perceptions about parent partnerships: Are parents partners? *Early Child Development and Care*. Retrieved from www.tandfonline.com/doi/full/10.1080/03004430.2017.1286334

Miller, L. (2008). Developing professionalism within a regulatory framework in England: Challenges and possibilities. *European Early Childhood Education Research Journal*, *16*(2), 255–268. doi:10.1080/13502930802141667

Northern Ireland Government. (2018). *Sure start*. Retrieved from www.education-ni.gov.uk/articles/sure-start

Office for Standards in Education, Children's Services and Skills (Ofsted). (2019). *Ofsted website*. Retrieved from www.gov.uk/government/collections/education-inspection-framework

Organisation for Economic Cooperation and Development (OECD). (2014). *Improving schools in Wales: An OECD perspective*. Retrieved from www.oecd.org/education/Improving-schools-in-Wales.pdf

Organisation for Economic Cooperation and Development (OECD). (2015). *Improving schools in Scotland: An OECD perspective*. Retrieved from www.oecd.org/education/school/Improving-Schools-in-Scotland-An-OECD-Perspective.pdf

Poverty and Social Exclusion. (2017). *Wales child poverty report*. Retrieved from www.poverty.ac.uk/report-wales-child-poverty/wales-has-worst-child-poverty-uk

Save the Children. (2013). *Too young to fail*. Retrieved from www.savethechildren.org.uk/content/dam/global/reports/education-and-child-protection/too-young-to-fail.pdf

Scottish Government. (2006). *Parental involvement act. Legislation*. Retrieved from www.legislation.gov.uk/asp/2006/8/crossheading/involvement-ambitions-objectives-and-performance

Scottish Government. (2012). *National parenting strategy*. Retrieved from www.gov.scot/publications/national-parenting-strategy-making-positive-difference-children-young-people-through/

Sylva, K., Melhuish, E., Sammons, P., Siraj-Blatchford, I., & Taggart, B. (2004). *Effective Pre-School Education*. Final Report. London: Institute of Education, DfES.

Tett, L. (2001). Parents as problems or parents as people? Parental involvement programmes, schools and adult educators. *International Journal of Lifelong Education, 20*(3), 188–198.

UK Gov. (2019). *Households below average income (HBAI) statistics*. Retrieved from https://www.gov.uk/government/collections/households-below-average-income-hbai--2

Welsh Government. (2013). *Building a brighter future: Early years and childcare plan progress report*. Retrieved from www.childreninwales.org.uk/policy-document/building-brighter-future-early-years-childcare-plan-progress-report-2013-14-140714-w/

Welsh Government. (2019). *Flying start initiative website*. Retrieved from https://gov.wales/get-help-flying-start

25
FAMILY ENGAGEMENT IN EARLY CHILDHOOD

Policy and practice in the United States

Carola Oliva-Olson, Mari Estrada, Soodie Ansari, Annie White and Jaime Matera

> Children grow and learn in the contexts of family, school, and community that often influence one another dynamically and interactively.
> (California Department of Education [CDE], 2009, p. 3)

Introduction

School readiness and future academic success are the driving goals behind the designation of federal and state funding to meet the needs of the increasingly diverse early childhood population of the United States. Furthermore, with evidence from research that systematic inclusion of families in their child's early education results in children's improved performance in school and better likelihood to graduate from high school (Yoshikawa et al., 2013; Barnett, 2011), efforts to build on research in teaching theory and pedagogical practice have resulted in the engagement of families as a national priority for early care and education programs (U.S. Department of Education & U.S. Department of Health and Human Services, 2016). As the United States continues to become a superdiverse nation – with linguistically and culturally diverse families bringing their own child-rearing, cultural, and educational practices and values into their children's education – family engagement in early childhood education (ECE) has become increasingly and critically important. Likewise, the superdiversity construct must be addressed in the development and delivery of quality early childhood programs and their respective family engagement efforts.

Defining superdiversity

The concept of superdiversity responds to the growing differences in ethnicity, country of origin, and other multiple variables, including different immigration statuses, gender and age, language, religion, place of settlement, and transnationalism

DOI: 10.4324/9780367823917-25

(Vertovec, 2007). The United States is superdiverse: children of immigrants comprise over 25% of all children under the age of 8, and their parents are of low income (45%) and have limited English proficiency (47%) (Park & McHugh, 2014). Superdiverse families can experience a variety of stressors, including low income, low employment, low levels of education, and limited access to health care and healthy nutrition. Such stressors can result in children starting kindergarten behind and staying behind.

Superdiverse families

Early childhood policy in the United States builds on the research that high-quality early learning brings children social, emotional, academic, and cognitive benefits. Public programs attempt to bolster skill formation and provide information to parents of all incomes, ethnicities, and cultures. Both the affluent family as well as the family with limited access to resources benefit from "strong family environments through their attachment, warmth, and investment in time and caring" (Elango, Garcia, Heckman, & Hojman, 2016). However, there is no dispute that high-quality early childhood experiences are particularly advantageous to children from low-income communities and those who are learning English as their second language. Well-designed support for children who are dual language learners (DLLs) can unlock the cognitive advantages of bilingual speakers (National Academies of Sciences, Engineering, & Medicine [NASEM], 2017) as well as improved capacity to retain cultural ties and identity as DLLs develop their proficiency in a home language as well as English.

Nevertheless, the data demonstrate that an academic achievement gap has persisted between white and Latino students, specifically, and that DLLs have been overrepresented in grade repetition and special education. At the state level, however, American voters have begun to reverse English-only policy in response to DLLs who represent one-third of children and historically have scored low in assessments. Family engagement, in particular, is an essential strategy that supports DLLs (Institute of Medicine and National Research Council, 2015) by employing tools that help address the curricular, assessment, and social – emotional needs of DLLs.

Although a growing diversity can require modifications to educational systems, supporting diversity is critical in early childhood development and an investment in the future of a nation. As the world becomes ever more connected, a diverse society provides social, cultural, and economic advantages. Markers of diversity such as language, for example, provide children access to cultural knowledge largely transmitted orally by family members, a sense of social and cultural belonging in a country that may not be their place of origin, and the "leg up" that being linguistically diverse can benefit them as they move toward higher education and eventually enter the workforce. Addressing diversity is critical because it benefits the individual and society in general and incorporating families as active participants in their children's education will positively impact their learning and social – emotional growth.

Research on family engagement in the United States

Current definitions of family engagement reflect the expansion in U.S. research and practice from a focus on "parent involvement" to a perspective that embraces much wider concepts of family. Historically, "parent involvement" has been understood as parents supporting their child's development by participating in classroom activities, usually with the encouragement and direction of the child's teacher(s) (Caspe & Lopez, 2006). Findings show the value of such engagement as a partnership that shifts from a focus on "fixing the families" to a strengths-based emphasis that responds not just to families but also to the communities being served.

The broader research focus on family engagement in children's early education shows many positive findings for learning, including a beneficial impact on children's readiness to enter the public school system (Sheridan, Moen, & Knoche, 2017); contributions to positive learning outcomes (Galindo & Sheldon, 2012; Mehaffie & Fraser, 2007; Mendez, 2010; Mistry, Benner, Biesanz, Clark, & Howes, 2010; Powell, Son, File, & San Juan, 2010; Serpell & Mashburn, 2012; Sheridan, Knoche, Edwards, Bovaird, & Kupzyk, 2010; Sheridan et al., 2017); and later academic achievement (Henrich & Gadaire, 2008; Ladd, Herald, & Kochel, 2006; Weiss, Caspe, & Lopez, 2006). The significance of such effects has led to wide consideration in the United States for family engagement as an important indicator for children's overall academic success (Fantuzzo, McWayne, & Perry, 2004; Ginsburg-Block, Manz, & McWayne, 2010).

Researchers looking in general at parental involvement have found many additional positive effects: young children benefit when parents participate in their education, which results in supportive, strong relationships with teachers (Mendez, 2010); a school's commitment to partner with and involve parents, and parents' high educational expectations, are associated with gains in reading and math achievement in the early school years (Galindo & Sheldon, 2012); and parents' involvement with their child can positively affect language acquisition, self-regulation, and creativity (Ayoub, Vallotton, & Mastergeorge, 2011).

In contrast, but reinforcing such findings, low parental involvement in school and at home can negatively influence children's social skills (Bulotsky-Shearer, Wen, Faria, Hahs-Vaughn, & Korfmacher, 2012). And the benefits are not limited to children: parents who see themselves as making an impact on their child's education during the preschool years develop a sense of self-efficacy as evidenced by their greater effort to participate and engage throughout their child's education; parents who do not feel included have been found to lack a sense of self-efficacy (Pelletier & Brent, 2002). Furthermore, numerous studies have examined the lifetime impacts of early education and have consistently shown that these children are more likely to graduate from high school and stay out of jail, and less likely to become dependent on the social welfare system. These results produce exceptional economic returns for American society. An often cited statistic claims that for every $1 invested during the early years, the early childhood program produces a

$7–9 return by reducing public expenditures on criminal justice, welfare, and other remedial services (Deming, 2009).

A broader scope for research also produces encouraging evidence. Family-centered practices and services that support strong relationships with children and parents result in better family health and well-being as well as positive child outcomes (Dunst, Trivette, & Hamby, 2007; Glisson & Schoenwald, 2005; Portilla, Ballard, Adler, Boyce, & Obradović, 2014; Roorda, Spilt, & Koomen, 2017). Benefits such as improved health, well-being, and child outcomes have contributed to the paradigm shift away from the belief by U.S. educators that to fully support their child's education, parents need to be physically present and working in the classroom on tasks set by the teacher. Today, educators have a perspective that is more inclusive of the families' social and cultural backgrounds, and many teachers now listen to parents' thoughts, dreams, beliefs, and values (Ferlazzo, 2011). Further, program managers and educators seek opportunities to support parent and child relationships, reinforce beneficial child-rearing practices, and provide a variety of occasions for family members to become involved in children's learning activities at school and home (Baker, Wise, Kelley, & Skiba, 2016).

Research has shown the positive value of program practices such as creating a welcoming environment, gathering family information, considering the home as a rich learning environment, including parents in program decision-making and shared governance, and creating the role of parent liaison to connect school and home (Halgunseth, 2009). Family language and culture questionnaires are common effective family engagement program practices, particularly upon initial child enrollment (Oliva-Olson, Espinosa, Hayslip, & Magruder, 2020), and strong communication between teachers and families provides opportunities to develop a collective voice within the school environment (Durand, 2011; White, 2016, 2019). Finally, a welcoming setting encourages families to engage, for example, a room for parents to mix and mingle and for staff to greet family members at the door (Hoover-Dempsey et al., 2005; Constantino, 2008). Many U.S. educators are working diligently in these ways to collaborate with families using authentic dialogue that contributes to children's growth and learning.

One example of family engagement and research-based practice in the United States is Parent and Child Together (PACT) classes focused on facilitating parent and child bonding and development of positive relationships. These face-to-face sessions aim to enhance parents' understanding of child development and connect them to community services. The research-based approach focuses on building knowledge, confidence, and support to promote building a strong foundation for school and life. The PACT program can be seen in action via First 5 Ventura, in Southern California, which developed a set of best practices and implementation standards intended to standardize the approach, while individualizing for the local community's strengths and needs. During a PACT class, parents and children play and learn together while teachers model, coach, and affirm positive parenting skills and strategies. Developmentally appropriate activities for children to learn and explore alongside their peers help strengthen family relationships and enhance parent knowledge of their children's development.

Policies on family engagement in early childhood programs

Early childhood care and education

> includes a wide range of part-day, full-school-day, and full-work-day programs, under educational, social welfare, and commercial auspices, funded and delivered in a variety of ways in both the public and the private sectors.
> *(Kamerman & Gatenio-Gabel, 2007, p. 23)*

Although enrollment in early childhood programs, including kindergarten for 5-year-olds, is not mandated in the United States, the U.S. Department of Health and Human Services (USDHHS), not the U.S. Department of Education (USDOE), provides funding through the Office of Head Start for comprehensive early care and education to pregnant mothers and children from birth to age 5 experiencing poverty in the United States (USDHHS, 2019a). In 2016, the Office of Head Start began to mandate efforts targeting family engagement, which has led to an increased depth at the institutional level and to the production of guidelines and models of practice that are valuable and accessible to all U.S. early childhood programs. Serving more than a million children nationally, Head Start leads the way in early childhood programming, setting a high standard for states and local initiatives.

Head Start, from its inception in 1965, has been run on the premise that children cannot be served in isolation from their familial and social setting and background (USDHHS, 2019b),[1] and has provided a window into research-based engagement practices. The introduction of Head Start, with its aim to eliminate poverty, was shortly followed by the Elementary and Secondary Education Act of 1965, which mandated the incorporation of parental involvement as a way to increase equity in education in the United States.[2] The refinement and renewal of both legislative acts have since continued and reflect the evolution of the concept of parental involvement into family engagement as research and practice have defined its parameters. Beyond Head Start, family engagement has become a widespread mark of program quality (NASEM, 2017).

Head Start, drawing from a national review of research by the National Academies of Science, Engineering, and Medicine (2017) and investigations across the United States, provides the most comprehensive policy mandates for parent, family, and community engagement. The required standards define family engagement as:

> . . . an interactive process through which program staff and families, family members, and their children build positive and goal-oriented relationships. It is a shared responsibility of families and professionals that requires mutual

respect for the roles and strengths each has to offer. Family engagement means doing with – not doing to or for – families.

(USDHHS, 2018, p. 2)

Furthermore, according to the Office of Head Start, family engagement "focuses on culturally and linguistically responsive relationship-building with key family members in a child's life" and "honors and supports the parent-child relationships that are central to a child's healthy development, school readiness, and well-being." The definition goes well beyond "parental involvement," including as family members "pregnant women and expectant families, mothers, fathers, grandparents, and other adult caregivers" (Early Childhood Learning and Knowledge Center, 2019).

Political importance attached to parental involvement and family engagement has been signaled in the joint 2016 Policy Statement of the USDHHS and USDOE on "Family Engagement from the Early Years to the Early Grades" (USDOE & USDHHS, 2016). The statement is presented as a "Guidance Document" to assist state and local agencies to meet their educational requirements. It defines family engagement as "the systematic inclusion of families in activities and programs that promote children's development, learning, and wellness, including in the planning, development, and evaluation of such activities, programs, and systems." The USDHHS also provides a "Family Engagement Inventory" made up of definitions for specific disciplines, including ECE as defined earlier, in which families are "essential partners" (USDHHS, 2017).

The future of family engagement: highlights from California's quality rating and improvement system

Although family engagement has been critical in supporting childcare programs to achieve quality improvement across settings (e.g., childcare centers, family childcare homes), many efforts to work with families have been implicit. In the United States all 50 states and their territories are involved in either a quality rating and improvement system (QRIS) or other large-scale quality improvement initiative (USDHHS, 2019c). From 2010 to 2014 Race to the Top – Early Learning Challenge federal awards supported the formation of state QRISs from 17 regional consortia, with post-award First 5 California taking the lead by provisioning funding for continued infrastructure building of the state's own QRIS, Quality Counts California, and training and technical assistance for implementation at the local level. State and local agencies collaborate on the design, implementation, and delivery of Quality Counts California, which was launched in 2012 (USDHHS, 2019c).

In California, local counties receive funds to support services to parents, caregivers, and children ages birth to 5 from a 50-cent tax on tobacco products. This funding was secured to support all 58 counties with the passing of Proposition 10 in 1998 and led to the establishment of First 5 California.[3] Furthermore, over the last 20 years First 5 California has made a range of investments in initiatives and programs comprising family engagement. As of 2019, First 5 California is investing in six focus areas,[4] which include "Positive Parenting" and "Early Learning and Care." In turn, the 58 local county commissions invest in both state focus areas and additional initiatives based on local needs for education, health services, and childcare (First 5 California, 2019a). A focus on families is both implicitly and explicitly addressed across local initiatives, with state media campaigns promoting families as "children's first and most important teachers."

Quality Counts California is made possible via one of the most substantial First 5 California investments, IMPACT (Improve and Maximize Programs so All Children Thrive), which is an initiative authorized for a 5-year period, focused on the infrastructure and delivery of the QRIS, and delivered in partnership with California's Department of Education. Although Quality Counts California does not include an explicit requirement to address family engagement or partnerships, its seven elements of quality[5] contain implicit inferences to working with families. In element #2, Developmental and Health Screenings, childcare programs (and family childcare homes) work with families to help them understand what developmental observations include, what tool will be used, what the results will demonstrate, and how that information will inform learning experiences. In element #3, Minimum Qualifications for Lead Teacher (and family childcare homes), providers must have completed 12 education units of Early Childhood Education/Child Development, of which in California's Child Development Permit Matrix requires the core course of Child, Family, and Community.[6] As part of this course, typically delivered at the community college level, students learn "strategies that empower families and encourage family involvement in children's development" (CDE, 2015, p. 1).

In addition to funding support for programs, a substantial investment has been made in training and technical assistance for childcare programs and the early care workforce. In support of family engagement, First 5 California has invested in an interactive family engagement course for childcare program staff and the greater community that works and interacts with children and families. The course will be made available through California's online professional development training system, California Early Childhood Online (CECO). Reflective of the California approach to make self-selected professional development and resources as accessible as possible, training on CECO is provided at zero cost and in multiple languages. Because childcare providers who are part of Quality Counts California must demonstrate 20 hours of professional development annually, this family engagement training is one option to obtain those credentials.

First 5 county commissions, and other statewide agencies, have collaborated with the Center for the Study of Social Policy to implement California's Strengthening Families' network (nationally, 30 states are engaged in this work). These California partnerships began in 2010 to provide training and technical assistance and to formalize efforts to provide statewide approaches that "increase family strengths, enhance child development and reduce the likelihood of child abuse and neglect" (Center for the Study of Social Policy, 2017, p. 1), that are grounded in five protective factors,[7] and that focus on how providers interact with families to support them in building protective factors. California has incorporated online training on the protective factors into CECO, and training and resources support agencies and organizations to make changes to daily practice at the program and staff level. Local First 5 commissions have made significant investments in the Strengthening Families' approach, which has led to many QRIS programs completing training on the five protective factors.

California will continue to invest in quality early learning and care with a renewed 3-year investment of IMPACT 2020 and five new focus areas,[8] including an explicit focus on "Engage Parents and Families" (First 5 California, 2019b). The explicit focus area will ensure that childcare programs and early educators receive support to address family engagement approaches that fit their program model and capacity. The First 5 California Strategic Plan for 2019–2024 lists "family engagement" as a public education and outreach "priority or project" and as a part of "IMPACT 2.0."

Local snapshot of family engagement efforts: San Mateo County, California

San Mateo County (population of 718,451; U.S. Census, 2010), one of the nine counties bordering the San Francisco Bay, is home to superdiverse families with close to half (46.3%) of all people in the county speaking a language other than English at home. In response, the San Mateo County Office of Education provides a wide selection of educational programs that are culturally and linguistically responsive to the needs of the local communities they serve.

San Mateo County's family engagement efforts focus on shifting the understanding and practice of family engagement from one of parent education or "random acts of parent involvement" to authentic collaboration and partnership among families, educators, and the school system.

In 2014, the San Mateo County Office of Education received funding from the Kellogg Foundation, one of the largest philanthropic foundations in the United States, to infuse innovative research-based family engagement principles and strategies into its dual language learning professional development model, which is led by the Early Childhood Language Development Institute (ECLDI). ECLDI's multi-tiered professional development model for early childhood professionals (teaching staff and administrators) provides training, technical assistance, and coaching support to design and implement classroom practices and program policies that are culturally and linguistically responsive to the superdiverse children and families in the county, ultimately bridging the gap and transforming the educational system to one that is more equitable for all learners.

Furthermore, ECLDI has developed a parallel series of interactive workshops for families of DLL children with content that is aligned with the educator professional development modules. The ECLDI strategies are anchored in research that validates families' role in providing the cultural and linguistic foundation on which DLLs develop and learn. As such, a unique element of the ECLDI professional development model is its focus on family engagement as a fundamental strategy to develop leadership skills among families in the context of effective family – school partnerships and promote culturally responsive early learning experiences and practices that lay the foundation for children's academic and life success.

With additional funding from First 5 San Mateo, ECLDI bolstered its family engagement strategies over the recent years by launching Friday CAFEs (Community and Family Engagement), a monthly professional learning community designed to support capacity building and networking for family engagement practitioners that promotes a shift to a more collaborative approach to family engagement. The Conversation Catalysts at the CAFEs are charged with sparking innovative thinking by engaging the practitioners in discussions that challenge the status quo with a call to action (e.g., staying resilient as a community in the face of adversities such as a housing crisis). One practitioner eloquently articulated how she shifted her approach to family engagement after attending the CAFEs: "I want to switch from what I can *do* for families to what I can *be* with families."

Moreover, First 5 San Mateo also funds ECLDI's Early Learning Family Engagement Communities of Practice, which support teachers and family engagement practitioners with concrete family engagement strategies, including support with effective implementation of Parent Cafés – which, in contrast to the Friday CAFEs mentioned previously, aim to cultivate peer support opportunities for families and are rooted in California's Strengthening Families' protective factors – and other site-based family engagement offerings with the goal of enhancing family – school partnerships.

Conclusion

Family engagement is a critical component of effective ECE programs, and including families on children's educational journey is fundamental, particularly in places where the language of instruction and cultural norms are different from that of the home. As the United States becomes increasingly diverse, it has become imperative for educators and policymakers to integrate, *not* replace, cultural norms and home language into educational practices and policies. In addition, collaborating with parents to create and promote a home environment where learning at an early age is not only supported but also valued and validated increases the likelihood that children will succeed in school and in life.

Nationwide investments such as Head Start help facilitate best practice with their mandate of parental involvement as a way to increase equity in education. Given that each state, territory, and local community set their own standards for quality early childhood programs, the work of quality childcare continues in parallel and duplicated efforts. More work needs to be done for a systematic approach that will serve the growing diversity of children and families in the United States.

The San Mateo County approach described in this chapter offers a multi-tiered professional development model for early childhood professionals and demonstrates targeted training that emphasizes culturally and linguistically responsive practices for children and their families. These local efforts reflect the importance and effectiveness of enhanced family – school partnerships, taking the United States one step closer to closing the educational gap that exists between learners of different cultural and linguistic backgrounds. However, at a national level this continues to be a work in progress, one which requires a focus on actively engaging families, appropriate and sustained funding for ECE programs, and culturally appropriate teacher training.

Notes

1 "The Advisory Committee on Services to Families with Infants and Toddlers consolidated knowledge from the research literature and from practice into nine principles to guide Early Head Start programs: (1) high quality; (2) prevention and promotion; (3) positive relationships and continuity; (4) parent involvement; (5) inclusion; (6) culture; (7) comprehensiveness, flexibility, responsiveness, and intensity; (8) transition; and (9) collaboration. These principles, along with the revised Head Start Program Performance Standards, set the stage for quality as they guide programs to implement specific practices (for example, low child-teacher ratios in relation to high quality)" (Love et al., 2002, p. 15).
2 Head Start was formed partly in response to President Lyndon B. Johnson's "War on Poverty" (introduced in 1964) and was initially administered through the Office of Economic Opportunity. The 1968 Head Start Report included the descriptor "compensatory education" to refer to the program (Retrieved from https://eclkc.ohs.acf.hhs.gov/about-us/article/head-start-timeline).
3 "First 5 California was established in 1998 when voters passed Proposition 10, which taxes tobacco products to fund services for children ages 0 to 5 and their families. First 5 California programs and resources are designed to educate and support teachers, parents, and caregivers in the critical role they play during a child's first 5 years – to help California kids receive the best possible start in life and thrive" (First 5 California, n.d., *About us*. Retrieved from www.ccfc.ca.gov/about/about.html).
4 The six focus areas are Positive Parenting, Early Learning and Care, Effective Interactions and Teaching, Tobacco Cessation, Public Outreach, and Advocacy and Policy.
5 The seven elements of quality are 1. Child Observation, 2. Developmental and Health Screenings, 3. Minimum Qualifications for Lead Teacher/Family Child Care Home, 4. Effective Teacher-Child Interactions: CLASS Assessments, 5. Ratios and Group Size, 6. Program Environment Rating Scale, and 7. Director Qualifications.
6 See the course outline for Child, Family, and Community. Retrieved from www.child-development.org/cs/cdtc/print/htdocs/services_cap_8courses.htm.
7 The five protective factors are parental resilience, social connections, knowledge of parenting and child development, concrete support in times of need, and social and emotional competence of children.
8 The IMPACT 2020 focus areas are 1. Strengthen Adult-Child Interactions, 2. Engage Parents and Families, 3. Expand Access to Quality Childcare for Our Most Vulnerable Children and Providers, 4. Support Workforce and Ensure Data-Driven Continuous Quality Improvement, 5. Implement Sustainable Systems at Scale.

References

Ayoub, C., Vallotton, C. D., & Mastergeorge, A. M. (2011). Developmental pathways to integrated social skills: The roles of parenting and early intervention. *Child Development*, *82*(2), 583–600.

Baker, T. L., Wise, J., Kelley, G., & Skiba, R. J. (2016). Identifying barriers: Creating solutions to improve family engagement. *School Community Journal, 26*(2), 161–184.
Barnett, W. S. (2011). Effectiveness of early educational intervention. *Science, 333*, 975–978.
Barnett, W. S. (2011). Effectiveness of early educational intervention. *Science, 333*(6045), 975–978.
Bulotsky-Shearer, R. J., Wen, X., Faria, A. M., Hahs-Vaughn, D. L., & Korfmacher, J. (2012). National profiles of classroom quality and family involvement: A multilevel examination of proximal influences on Head Start children's school readiness. *Early Childhood Research Quarterly, 27*(4), 627–639.
California Department of Education. (2009). *Preschool English learners: Principles and practices to promote language, literacy, and learning* (2nd ed.) Sacramento: CDE. Retrieved from https://www.cde.ca.gov/sp/cd/re/documents/psenglearnersed2.pdf
California Department of Education. (2015). *California community colleges early childhood/ child development curriculum alignment project*. Retrieved from https://cccece.net/advocacy/curriculum-curriculum-alignment-project-and-curriculum-innovation/
Caspe, M., & Lopez, M. E. (2006). *Lessons from family-strengthening interventions: Learning from evidence-based practice*. Cambridge, MA: Harvard Family Research Project.
Center for the Study of Social Policy. (2017). *Strengthening families California: State profile*. Washington, DC: Author. Retrieved from https://cssp.org/wp-content/uploads/2018/08/California-2017.pdf
Constantino, S. M. (2008). *101 ways to create real family engagement*. Galax, VA: ENGAGE! Press.
Deming, D. (2009). Early childhood intervention and life-cycle skill development: Evidence from head start. *American Economic Journal: Applied Economics, 1*(3), 111–134.
Dunst, C. J., Trivette, C. M., & Hamby, D. W. (2007). Meta-analysis of family-centered help-giving practices research. *Mental Retardation & Developmental Disabilities Research Reviews, 13*(4), 370–378.
Durand, T. M. (2011). Latino parental involvement in kindergarten: Findings from the early childhood longitudinal study. *Hispanic Journal of Behavioral Sciences, 33*(4), 469–489.
Early Childhood Learning and Knowledge Center. (2019). *Family engagement*. Retrieved from https://eclkc.ohs.acf.hhs.gov/family-engagement
Elango, S., Garcia, J. L., Heckman, J. J., & Hojman, A. (2016). Early childhood education. In R. A. Moffit (Ed.), *Economics of means-tested transfer programs in the United States* (Vol. 2, pp. 235–297). Retrieved from www.nber.org/chapters/c13489.pdf
Elementary and Secondary Education Act of 1965. Retrieved from https://legcounsel.house.gov/Comps/Elementary%20And%20Secondary%20Education%20Act%20Of%201965.pdf
Fantuzzo, J., McWayne, C., & Perry, M. (2004). Multiple dimensions of family involvement and their relations to behavioral and learning competencies for urban, low-income children. *The School Psychology Review, 33*(4), 467–480.
Ferlazzo, L. (2011). Involvement or engagement? *Schools, Families, Communities, 68*(8), 10–14.
First 5 California. (2019a). *First 5 California – strategic plan 2019–2024*. Sacramento, CA: Author. Retrieved from www.ccfc.ca.gov/pdf/about/budget_perf/F5CA_Strategic-Plan_2019-24.pdf
First 5 California. (2019b). *First 5 California state commission approves $103 million for IMPACT 2020 to improve the quality of early learning and care*. Press Release. Retrieved from www.ccfc.ca.gov/pdf/about/news_events/pr/pr_2019-07-26_First_5_IMPACT.pdf
Galindo, C., & Sheldon, S. B. (2012). School and home connections and children's kindergarten achievement gains: The mediating role of family involvement. *Early Childhood Research Quarterly, 27*(1), 90–103.

Ginsburg-Block, M., Manz, P., & McWayne, C. M. (2010). Partnering to foster achievement in reading and mathematics. In S. Christenson & A. Reschly (Eds.), *Handbook of school-family partnerships* (pp. 176–203). Oxford: Routledge, Taylor.

Glisson, C., & Schoenwald, S. (2005). The ARC organizational and community intervention strategy for implementing evidence-based children's mental health treatments. *Mental Health Services Research*, 7(4), 243–259.

Halgunseth, L. (2009). Family engagement, diverse families, and early childhood education programs: An integrated review of the literature. *Young Children*, 64(5), 56.

Henrich, C. C., & Gadaire, D. M. (2008). Head start and parent involvement. *Infants & Young Children*, 21(1), 56–69.

Hoover-Dempsey, K. V., Walker, J. M., Sandler, H. M., Whetsel, D., Green, C. L., Wilkins, A. S., & Closson, K. (2005). Why do parents become involved? Research findings and implications. *The Elementary School Journal*, 106(2), 105–130.

Institute of Medicine and National Research Council. (2015). *Transforming the workforce for children birth through age 8: A unifying foundation*. Washington, DC: The National Academies Press. doi:10.17226/19401

Kamerman, S. B., & Gatenio-Gabel, S. (2007). Early childhood education and care in the United States: An overview of the current policy picture. *International Journal of Child Care and Education Policy*, 1, 23–34. doi:10.1007/2288-6729-1-1-23

Ladd, G. W., Herald, S. L., & Kochel, K. P. (2006). School readiness: Are there social prerequisites? *Early Education and Development*, 17(1), 115–150.

Love, J. M., Kisker, E. E., Ross, C. M., Schochet, P. Z., Brooks-Gunn, J., Paulsell, D., . . . Brady-Smith, C. (2002). *Making a difference in the lives of infants and toddlers and their families: The impacts of early head start* (Vol. I, Final Technical Report, Early Head Start Research and Evaluation Project). Washington, DC: Child Outcomes Research and Evaluation Office of Planning, Research and Evaluation Administration for Children and Families U.S. Department of Health and Human Services. Retrieved from www.acf.hhs.gov/sites/default/files/opre/impacts_vol1.pdf

Mehaffie, K. E., & Fraser, J. (2007). School readiness; definitions, best practices, assessments, and cost. In C. J. Groark, K. E. Mehaffie, R. B. McCall, & M. T. Greenberg (Eds.), *Evidence-based practices and programs for early childhood care and education*. Thousand Oaks, CA: Corwin Press.

Mendez, J. L. (2010). How can parents get involved in preschool? Barriers and engagement in education by ethnic minority parents of children attending head start. *Cultural Diversity and Ethnic Minority Psychology*, 16(1), 26.

Mistry, R. S., Benner, A. D., Biesanz, J. C., Clark, S. L., & Howes, C. (2010). Family and social risk, and parental investments during the early childhood years as predictors of low-income children's school readiness outcomes. *Early Childhood Research Quarterly*, 25(4), 432–449.

National Academies of Sciences, Engineering, and Medicine. (2017). *Promoting the educational success of children and youth learning English: Promising futures*. Washington, DC: The National Academies Press. doi:10.17226/24677

Oliva-Olson, C., Espinosa, L. M., Hayslip, W., & Magruder, E. S. (2020). Many languages, one classroom: Supporting children in superdiverse setting. In S. Friedman & A. Mwenelupembe (Eds.), *Each & every child: Teaching preschool with an equity lens* (pp. 91–97). Washington, DC: National Association for the Education of Young Children.

Park, M., & McHugh, M. (2014). *Immigrant parents and early childhood programs: Addressing barriers of literacy, culture, and systems knowledge*. Washington, DC: National Center on Immigrant Integration Policy, Migration Policy Institute.

Pelletier, J., & Brent, J. M. (2002). Parent participation in children's school readiness: The effects of parental self-efficacy, cultural diversity and teacher strategies. *International Journal of Early Childhood, 34*(1), 45–60.

Portilla, X. A., Ballard, P. J., Adler, N. E., Boyce, W. T., & Obradović, J. (2014). An integrative view of school functioning: Transactions between self-regulation, school engagement, and teacher-child relationship quality. *Child Development, 85*(5), 15–31.

Powell, D. R., Son, S. H., File, N., & San Juan, R. R. (2010). Parent – school relationships and children's academic and social outcomes in public school pre-kindergarten. *Journal of School Psychology, 48*(4), 269–292.

Roorda, D. L., Spilt, J. L., & Koomen, H. M. (2017). Teacher-child interactions and kindergartners' task behaviors: Observations based on interpersonal theory. *Journal of Applied Developmental Psychology, 53*(1), 74–85.

Serpell, Z. N., & Mashburn, A. J. (2012). Family – school connectedness and children's early social development. *Social Development, 21*(1), 21–46.

Sheridan, S. M., Knoche, L. L., Edwards, C. P., Bovaird, J. A., & Kupzyk, K. A. (2010). Parent engagement and school readiness: Effects of the getting ready intervention on preschool children's social emotional competencies. *Early Education & Development, 21*(1), 125–156.

Sheridan, S. M., Moen, A. L., & Knoche, L. L. (2017). Family-school partnerships in early childhood. In E. Votruba-Drzal & E. Dearing (Eds.), *The Wiley handbook of early childhood development programs, practices, and policies* (pp. 287–309). Malden, MA: John Wiley & Sons, Inc.

U.S. Census. (2010). *Quick facts California*. Retrieved from www.census.gov/quickfacts/CA

U.S. Department of Education & U.S. Department of Health and Human Services. (2016). *Policy statement on family engagement: From the early years to the early grades*. Retrieved from https://www2.ed.gov/about/inits/ed/earlylearning/families.html

U.S. Department of Health and Human Services. (2017). *Definitions of family engagement*. Family Engagement Inventory. Retrieved from www.childwelfare.gov/fei/

U.S. Department of Health and Human Services. (2019a). *Title of page*. Retrieved from www.acf.hhs.gov/ohs

U.S. Department of Health and Human Services. (2019b). *History of head start*. Office of Head Start. Retrieved from www.acf.hhs.gov/ohs/about/history-of-head-start

U.S. Department of Health and Human Services. (2019c). *State information*. QRIS Resource Guide. Retrieved from https://ecquality.acf.hhs.gov/states

U.S. Department of Health and Human Services, Administration for Children and Families, Office of Head Start, & National Center on Parent, Family, and Community Engagement. (2018). *Head Start parent, family, and community engagement framework*. Retrieved from https://eclkc.ohs.acf.hhs.gov/sites/default/files/pdf/pfce-framework.pdf

Vertovec, S. (2007). Super-diversity and its implications. *Ethnic and Racial Studies, 30*(6), 1024–1054.

Weiss, H., Caspe, M., & Lopez, M. E. (2006). Family involvement in early childhood education. *Family Involvement Makes a Difference, 1*, 1–8.

White, A. (2016). Creating new pathways for dialogue: Collaboration of diverse voices. *NHSA Dialog, 19*(3), 60–88.

White, A. (2019). Engaging families through observation and reflection: A collaborative approach to making learning visible. *Journal of Children and Poverty, 25*(1), 45–56.

Yoshikawa, H., Weiland, C., Brooks-Gunn, J., Burchinal, M., Espinosa, L., Gormley, W., Ludwig, J. O., Magnuson, K. A., Phillips, D. A., & Zaslow, M. J. (2013). *Investing in our future: The evidence base on preschool education*. New York: Foundation for Child Development and Ann Arbor, MI: Society for Research in Child Development. Retrieved from http://fcd-us.org/sites/default/files/Evidence%20Base%20on%20Preschool%20Education%20FINAL.pdf

26
INTERNATIONAL TRENDS IN PARENT INVOLVEMENT OF *SAYINGS, DOINGS,* AND *RELATINGS*

Alicja Renata Sadownik, Sivanes Phillipson, Heidi Harju-Luukkainen and Susanne Garvis

Introduction

Here we are after learning about parental involvement in ECEC in 24 countries, reflecting on the main thread of messages that we could take away as lessons of how parents involve and ensure their children are educated and cared for. As the chapters of this book demonstrate, parental involvement is an area of social practice, the performance of which is framed by policy documents and institutional contexts, as well as the knowledge and meaning-making processes of the social actors involved. Such complexity of parental involvement poses challenges for the theoretical approaches attempting to embrace it. The well-established model for parental involvement developed by Epstein (1995) is used widely in this book. By enabling both home-based and school-based involvement, as well as community-related partnerships, Epstein's model (1995) allows a meaningful description of the parental involvement situation in each country. However, the conclusions and future recommendations made by the authors in the majority of the chapters go beyond this model and other country-specific models, and boldly suggests links between institutional practices and teacher competence, as well as culturally, economically and socially anchored relationships between professionals and caregivers. This supposition is not far from what we have found in our previous works involving practice and policy in ECEC (Phillipson & Garvis, 2020).

We take our departure from the authors' method of conclusion and propose a theoretical approach that embraces the synergies of the polices, theoretical approaches, competence and individual meaning-making established by the chapters' authors. We therefore propose to describe parental involvement as a professional and social practice using the theory of practice architectures. The theory of practice architectures is a practice theory developed by Mahon, Kemmis, Franciso, and Lloyd (2017) that aims to respond to the challenging and complex realm of social/professional practices. This approach defines social practice as follows:

> Socially established cooperative human activity involving utterances and forms of understandings (*sayings*), modes of action (*doings*), and ways in which people relate to one another and the world (*relatings*) that hang together in characteristic ways. . . . How they hand together gives particular kinds of practices their distinctiveness.
>
> *(Mahon et al., 2017, p. 8)*

This statement means that every *social practice* constitutes various combinations of its semantic space achieved in the medium of language (*sayings*), its action in physical space-time conducted in the medium of activity and work (*doings*), as well as its social space (*relatings*) performed through and with power and solidarity relationships (Mahon et al., 2017).

Describing parental involvement in ECE within the context of each country requires reference to the *sayings*. In this book, the *sayings* include both meanings generated at the policy level, steering documents and theoretical approaches used to articulate and reflect on the phenomenon, as well as individual understandings represented by the professionals and caregivers. *Sayings* thereby articulate the meaning for the actions of parental involvement. Moreover, they relate various actors to one another and allocate power based on their positions.

The actual activity – *doings*, i.e. the worked-on and performed parental involvement in ECE institutions, may confirm, resist or overcome the *sayings*. It is this aspect of parental involvement that various theoretical models address and provide a matrix for evaluation purposes. The *doings* may then be home- or preschool-based or focused within the local community (Epstein, 1995). The activities are performed within a particular tradition of practices (*doings*), which may be centred around the preschool or the social pedagogy tradition (Bennet, 2005) of parental involvement. *Doings* are therefore related to various kinds of *sayings* deriving from a country's cultures, history and values associated with well-balanced parenting, a wholesome childhood, and participation in educational and care institutions. Moreover, *doings* constitute a physical and symbolic space for various *relatings* among the social actors such as families, parents, teachers and children. Though, it must be noted that the different groups of social actors may represent different *sayings*, different perspectives, values, and meanings. *Relatings* are therefore the aspect of social/professional practice that mediate *sayings* and *doings* and may be used to explain and highlight the main trends of policies and practices in ECE across the 24 countries. Moreover, *relatings* allow understandings relationships between *loyalty* and *power relations* that exist within particular ECE paradigms. The power and loyalty relations are possible to detect in some actors' loyalty to some *sayings* because of other actors' power of them, or loyalty to some ways of *doing* even when wishing to change the practice (at the level of *sayings*). At any rate, it is a dimension that usually enters into the picture when reflecting on unsuccessful implementations of particular models/programmes/strategies of parental involvement.

To support this theoretical analysis across the 24 chapters, we utilised Leximancer 4.5v software to explore the main threads of concepts framed to *Parent Involvement Sayings, Doings and Relatings*. Leximancer replicates the manual coding procedures used in content analysis to identify the underlying core themes and associations between themes (Smith & Humphreys, 2006). Content analysis takes place by determining the occurrences of words and similar meaning words that are then broken down to manageable categories of concepts and core themes (Leximancer, 2018). As Leximancer is an automated system, it generates a logarithmic analysis that is free of bias during the coding process, thereby removing issues such as coder reliability and subjectivity. Leximancer produces a thematic summary that includes a connectivity score to indicate the relative importance of the themes, with the most important theme at 100%, which would be the first theme originating at the top. The subsequent grouping of themes enables the mapping of any relationships between the concepts. Conclusively, Leximancer provides a visual concept map of the thematic grouping in the form of spheres, which includes their associations with each other (Smith & Humphreys, 2006).

Figure 26.1 presents the Leximancer visual concept map for this book's main themes that support the theory of practice architecture as the basis for parental involvement across 24 countries. The three main themes were clustered *as Parent Involvement Sayings*, *Parent Involvement Doings* and *Parent Involvement Relatings*. The biggest theme is Parent Involvement Sayings with 1150 hits of verbatims across the country contributions. The second theme is Parent Involvement Doings with 916 verbatim hits whilst the third and smallest theme is Parent Involvement Relatings with 82 verbatim hits. The next sections will detail the concepts found in each of the themes, followed by an analysis of the overlapping factors on how these themes work together in some countries presented in this book.

Parent involvement of sayings

As seen in the Leximancer map, the main theme Parent Involvement Sayings have nodes of concepts surrounding their role as parents of children and working to meet the needs of their children. These nodes point to a) policies and theories that define the role and significance of parents and their involvement in ECE services; as well as b) who is assumed as parents/caregivers by the official documents and reports. References to parents and families are the dominant paradigm for many policies in the 24 countries. For example, the UK and Australian contexts refer to parents as families, hence suggesting a more diverse inclusion of who parents are and what their role can be. In the UK context, families are said to be involved in supporting "a rich learning environment at home from birth till the end of compulsory schooling". Parents in Uganda are put forward as families who are first educators and carers of their children. The author advocated that parents and families should be empowered through the formal programs to participate in the care and

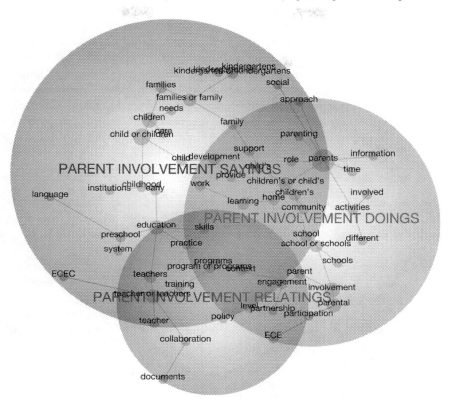

FIGURE 26.1 Leximancer concept map showing themes of parental involvement – Parent Involvement Sayings, Parent Involvement Doings and Parent Involvement Relatings

development of their children. In the same vein, Belarus' ECE context considers the role of parents including those being involved in articulating ways preschools teachers. Interestingly, the Polish context highlights the practice of marginalising sexual, cultural and religious minorities in the official steering documents through silent assumptions about parents as white, Polish and heterosexual.

The *sayings* centres on the essence and role of parenting in ECE related contexts. Whether the parenting is done by parents, grandparents, aunty or uncle or any member of a family, the action for sayings from the chapters is associated with parenting that leads to children's holistic development and growth or absence of such development and growth. Where there is an absence of parent involvement of sayings in the development and growth, the educators and teachers (or pedagogues, as mentioned in many of the European chapters) play a larger role. The Hungarian authors point out that such an approach signals a deficit view of parental role in their children's early education, and therefore a partnership model where both teachers and parents feel that they have a position in the sayings for children is much to desire. The authors from the US conclude that parent role is important in ensuring beneficial experience especially for children of disadvantage background.

Though most of the 24 countries in this book acknowledge that their governments do recognise the value of parental involvement; however, in some countries parents are not always given a clear and official status of their role in the policy documents. This phenomenon indicates that the sayings of parental involvement are not apparent within the socio-political systems of those countries. If parents are not given an official recognition in the policy documents as collaborative partners, parental involvement in early childhood settings becomes optional. Their involvement will pretty much depend on pedagogical traditions in learning institutions, teacher competence and parents' own personal attitudes in relation to be involved. Different countries' traditions for institutional participation and individuals' (parents and teachers) social or interactive skills may therefore play a decisive role in the quality of parental involvement.

Some chapters in the book (e.g., Chapter 4 on Belarus and Chapter 19 on Serbia) point out that low interest and participation of parents in ECE are derived from traditional and historical societal views and attitudes. If in such countries, the parental involvement is not safeguarded by liberal policies that encourage the sayings of parental involvement, the parental involvement itself can be paralysed by a lack of policy-based conditions for parental agency and dispositions towards active participation in their children's early learning and development. Parental involvement of sayings in these countries, however, is noted to be present in the form of single institutions-based educational and programs that link families and teachers from the ECE settings. Such changes are noted in Chapter 5 that focuses on Croatian changing paradigms about childhood, which is leaning towards understanding and respecting children's needs through the lense of supporting families and the parental involvement structure. Similar sentiments are found by the Hungarian authors that talked about how support for parents are closely aligned to the families' needs and perspectives. The same can be said for the Australian situation – where there is a clear inclination to support parents to provide for their children's needs with government providing broad policy statements through the early years framework and funding for universal access for children care.

The sayings of parental involvement are dominant in the dimensions of collective and mutual engagement for the child's best interest in many of the Scandinavian countries, where strong traditions for joint, social actions, together with the role of the feminist movement in establishing ECE services, has kept parental participation as an "inherent" way of sayings. The Swedish chapter authors stated that

> "a mutual engagement between the preschool and the home is central in the welfare state's task to provide Swedish children with the necessary prerequisites to maintain well-being and a healthy development within the sphere of ECE. The emphasis on both person and environment is central in Swedish preschools, as they are duty-bound to follow the national curriculum and

must therefore actively promote both understanding and communication between the parents and the teachers.

It is apparent then that the Swedish government takes pride in providing opportunities for parents' voice/perspectives to take priority in ensuring a true parental involvement happens in collaboration with teachers for the betterment of children. The true parental involvement happens when parents are able to effectively collaborate with teachers and the wider community in implementing actions or more precisely *doings* for their children.

Parent involvement of doings

Referring to Figure 26.1 again, we can see that the doings of parental involvement have nodes of concepts of actions linking parents with teachers, and schools and the wider community. The dimension of *doings* as in the theory of practice architecture highlights the practical side of parental involvement – as to who do parents work and engage with to support their children's development. The 24 countries' chapter authors have diverse explanation and discussion around the doings that parents are involved in to their own preferences and also in relation to teachers and their level of skills and training as well as community participations.

The unarticulated diversity of parents and forms of involvement seem to lead to a marginalisation of weaker and more vulnerable groups of parents. This marginalisation may occur at the level of *doings*, as asymmetric relationships between the professionals and caregivers (as mentioned in Belarus, Serbia, Croatia, UK, the Czech Republic, Hungary, Jordan, Oman and Singapore), where the latter are experts with consider power to 'colonise' the daily life and activities of children and families from disadvantaged backgrounds. However, this does not appear as a concern in the context of Azerbaijan, where parental involvement at the official document level is precisely about the "pedagogical-psychological enlightenment of parents", regardless of the resources and status they represent. Workshops and parent training programmes are the forms for involvement used, followed by various possibilities to participate in decision-making processes. One may wonder about the social class reference of the knowledge presented during the workshops and courses, but it does not appear as a concern in the chapter. It seems that, in terms of Azerbaijan, the lower involvement of fathers and grandfathers, as well as parents of boys, is of greater concern.

On another angle, a focus on school readiness and lifelong learning is also expected to unite caregivers from various socio-economic backgrounds and professionals in the UK. Here, however, the theoretical *sayings* presented by, for example, Tett (2001) points out that cooperation on the preschool premises with use of the educators' professional language leads many families to feel like 'junior partners' in the relationship, with less to do and involved with. Such concerns are facilitated even more in the chapter about the Czech Republic, the author of which directly asks about the premises on which social inclusion takes place in preschools. "Do we talk about equalising opportunities to fulfil the individual potential or rather normalising and assimilating children and their parents into predefined paths?" In the context of the Czech Republic, different methods of collaboration (that can be recognized as forms of doing) are offered to different parent groups by different ECEC settings that are affordable for them. While the middle-class parents, silently recognised as 'good', are given the opportunity to co-create educational environments, the parents from Roma background or lower socioeconomic backgrounds experience little facilitation in their collaboration with preschools. This discrepancy in opportunities for parents' involvement points to how different general official *sayings* on reducing inequalities and strengthening school readiness in collaboration with parents may be implemented at the level of *doings*. The chapter on Hungary points out the risk of school readiness as a phenomenon that is easily prioritised in preschool-family collaboration and that it is the professionals' responsibility to keep other relevant options of involvement and activities open. The chapters on Oman and Jordan therefore argue in favour of anchoring different forms of involvement, providing specific examples at the policy document level.

Parent involvement of relatings

When we look at Figure 26.1 with a focus on relatings of parental involvement, we notice nodes of concepts networking between programs, education, system and institution, to name a few. The dimension of *relatings* as in the theory of practice architecture highlights the factors such as partnership, collaboration and training that connects parental involvement that is being advocated at both policy level and institutional level with parental involvement that is operational. In other words, parent involvement of relatings can include those elements that educate and inform institutions and the wider community of the usefulness and benefit of parental involvement.

The chapter on the Norwegian South Sami Indigenous parents is a good example of parent involvement of relatings through language and collaboration as a form of doing. This chapter shows how the ECE service and Indigenous parents in Norway may be related to a joint cultural understanding, joint responsibility and the joint practice of supporting Sami language development among the children. Considering the value of language preservation, any asymmetrical power-knowledge relationships between ECE and families seem to be mutually accepted. The ECE staff and families support each other's knowledge and resources in order to facilitate language development among the children, and it happens that the ECE services provide the families with the necessary Sami vocabulary, which the generation of parents may not remember. This is particularly interesting, as this practice would be considered unacceptable if performed, for example, in relation to migrant and/or parents from disadvantaged backgrounds, who are not fluent uses of the majority language. This issue again calls into question the importance of a wide array of practices and activities, opening up for diverse and meaningful ways of parents getting involved with the service.

Early childhood professionals with less than desirable professional competence (or unqualified professionals) and the ability to reflect on their own practice of parental collaboration can sometimes *relate* to parents in negative ways. The chapters on Croatia, the Czech Republic, Poland, Germany and Oman report on ECE staff's *relatings* to parents as problems. Parents are viewed as more of a hindrance to the progress that early childhood professionals seem to want to move. The 'problem of parents', however, may relate to other values they present, resources at their disposal, a lack of time to participate in various ECE events or a lack of awareness of the importance of their involvement for the child's development (Phillips, Phillipson, & Tyler-Merrick, 2021).

The lack of parental involvement is therefore perceived by the professionals as due to a lack of time or awareness of the importance of personal involvement. However, this may be linked to a lack of inclusions of wider definitions in the available forms of involvement. Parents also may not see any point in participating in the defined activities while unable to have a say in an issue they consider important. The chapter on Belarus, for example, describes the phenomenon of parental committees with fictional influence, the participation in which is viewed as unimportant by both the professionals and caregivers. The chapter on Poland confronts the lack of parental involvement in the events arranged by preschools, with the relatively large parental movement resulting in the creation of 'Forest Preschools'. Creating ECEC based on specific educational and value-related principles requires daily involvement and considerable extra work, but it is meaningful and opens up for the free articulation of individual opinions and dialogue.

Parental involvement of sayings, doing and relatings – how do they intersect internationally?

The overlap between *sayings*, *doings* and *relatings* of parental involvement is evident in the Figure 26.1 through the context of how parental involvement manifests in children's development and education. Of note is that parents from the 24 countries comprise highly heterogeneous and diverse group of people with being parents of children being the only common factor. The super diversity among parents comes directly into play in the chapter on the US by presenting *sayings* that recognise the diversity of cultures and resources, and associating them with the same goal of child-rearing, school readiness and future academic success. Focusing the *sayings* around common goal changes the *relatings* from doing *for* parents into doing *with* parents. However, the goals of the partnership are defined from the academic perspective (school readiness, academic performance), which again expects and supports particular (often white middle-class) parenting styles and methods of involvement. The brief description of particular programmes of *doing* shows that parents are introduced to the supportive parenting styles through joint activities for parents and children, while diversity is encouraged at the language level.

Regardless of the approaches presented in the steering and policy documents or theoretical approaches, all of the book chapters point out various shortcomings in the realisation of those *sayings*. One of the obstacles pointed out as an important link to *doings* is the extended dimension of *sayings*, which is the professionals' understanding and anchored in professional knowledge and competences to act. It is the professional knowledge that seems to be the platform where the interpretation of the steering document and daily ECE life takes place. The chapters on the UK, Germany, Poland, the Czech Republic, Croatia, Hungary, Norway, Finland, Jordan, and Oman point out the importance of the professional competence of ECE staff in facilitating parental involvement. This professional competence refers to reading and understanding the general framework of the steering document on one hand, and continuous reflection on own practice of interacting with parents, on the other. The steering documents cannot function as a 'to-do' list or detailed instruction for institutional life. They draw the general semiotic landscape of meanings and values and recognise the role of potential social actors in the process of their realisation. The processes themselves can only be facilitated through professional reflection, linking the steering documents to the daily life of ECE and thereby dealing with ethical concerns involved in the collaboration with parents. Many chapters, however, present parental involvement as an underprioritised issue in preschool teacher education. In this book, we argue in favour of prioritising this aspect in preschool teacher education around the world, as well as hiring professionals and not unqualified cheap labour in ECEC services.

The Polish ECE parental movement 'Forest Preschools' (*Lesne Przedszkola*) is an example of parental power as citizens. The emergence of such movements in young democracies that have developed in Europe in the post-Soviet era reflects stronger civic society and growing civic disposition associated with initiative, responsibility and participation. The chapters on Serbia, Poland, Hungary, Belarus and the Czech Republic mention the socio-political transformation as greatly influencing parental rights and possibilities for involvement in their own children's education. Based on long traditions of the *sayings and doings* of parental subordination, they are suddenly supposed to be active parents who are involved with an ECE institution on behalf of their own and other people's children. This is mentioned as still difficult to achieve in the entire population of parents, regardless of theoretical approaches that promote partnership between preschool and community. This is why making ECE and professionals responsible for the quality of parental involvement, as is the case in Norway as well as Croatia, seems to be a solution in the right direction. It is the task of ECE to get parents involved, but it is important to create meaningful (for various groups of parents) arenas for such participation.

An interesting combination of *sayings, doings and relating* is presented in the chapter on Singapore, where both professionals and parents come together in their disbelief of the official *sayings* that promote play-based ECE and promote parental involvement that is less 'tiger-like', less competitive, less focused on academic performance and school readiness. Nevertheless, both parents and professionals are aware of the *doings* of the primary school (which at the level of sayings has omitted examinations, while maintaining academic rigour) continue school preparation within both ECE settings and extracurricular activities.

Conclusion

This chapter has presented a Leximancer concept mapping of parental involvement in 24 countries through the theory of practice architectures (Mahon et al., 2017). This ECE practices and parental involvement were examined in relation to the semiotic aspect of *sayings*, the real aspect of *doings,* and the socio-political aspect of *relatings*. Hence, with this examination we draw some conclusions for each of the parent involvement of sayings, doings and relatings of the ECE practices in the 24 countries in this book.

Sayings: We argue in favour of this practice as a starting point for more precise and inclusive definitions of parental involvement taking into account parents, their diversity and variety of their engagement. We stress that parent involvement of sayings do come in various forms of involvement and these involvements need to be properly defined and recognised by policy documents that pushes for better teacher education and early childhood education professionalism. We assert such a move facilitates professional knowledge and competence to enable and empower early childhood teachers to deal with the considerable contextual and ethical dilemmas in collaborating with parents.

Doings: On the level of *doing*, parental involvement seems to be full of ethical dilemmas, dealings that will have short- and long-term consequences on the lives of children and parents in the educational system. Instructing and 'colonising' parents into the 'right' way of being a parent at home and a parent in the ECE context poses to be problematic, including pacifying identity and diversity of the parents involved. Many parents tend to take a step back from being involved with their children's formal care and schooling because they are not recognised for who they are or because they do not consider the institutional activities to be meaningful. On the other hand, when families experience support from teachers or the community they tend to feel more comfortable in being involved. This is why professional competence is crucial at the level of doing, as it allows the negotiation of major concepts like 'social inclusion' or 'equalising educational opportunities for the children of disadvantaged families' with the need for respecting the identity and well-being of the actual parents and children. Hence to address these needs at the level of doings, it is imperative that more qualified early childhood trained professionals are positioned in the ECEC sector. This will be a wise investment for not only improving teacher competency but also enabling the teachers to work better with parents for children's well-being and development. Teacher education is a particularly important aspect of the social practice of parental involvement, as it is a social domain that joins professional *sayings* and *doings*, and through campus-based teaching and placements in ECE settings facilitates the development and competence to act of pre-service teachers (Aasen & Sadownik, 2019) in the area of parental collaboration by providing students with theoretical concepts to reflect on their own actions in practical settings (Aasen & Sadownik, 2019).

Relatings: As mentioned earlier, *relatings* may refer to the relationship between the social actors involved, between actors and sayings, as well as between past and present traditions of practice. As a conclusion, we would like to point out the fact that *relatings* both facilitate and inhibit potential in the realisation of good policies or good theories/models for parental involvement. This is why a high level of awareness and reflection on this dimension is necessary, which again points towards teacher education and continuous professional development as arenas for reflecting on various dimensions of own professional practice using conceptual toolkits that enable the unmasking of pre-assumptions and biases.

Without doubt, what is important for parents to be involved in the ECE is for them to be recognised not only as parents but also as stakeholders of early education. The practice of parental involvement takes not only the acknowledgement of governments and policy makers but also the prescription of better teacher education and professionalism that leads to community of practice (Phillips et al., 2021). The notion of community of practice is one of statements of act, doings of acts and collaboration of acts between all parties involved in children's early care and education. The building of a community of practice – where parental involvement is central to building children's future – regardless of country and cultural contexts, will take a concerted effort of resources, affirmation of acts and partnerships across boundaries of diverse perception, biases and prejudices.

References

Aasen, W., & Sadownik, A. R. (2019). Does the new kindergarten teacher education program in Norway provide good conditions for professional kindergarten teachers? *Universal Journal of Educational Research*, *3A*, 1–7. doi:10.13189/ujer.2019.071301

Bennett, J. (2005). Curriculum issues in national policy-making. *European Early Childhood Education Research Journal*, *13*(2), 5–23. doi:10.1080/13502930585209641

Epstein, J. (1995). School/family/community partnerships: Caring for the children we share. *Phi Delta Kappan*, *76*(9), 701–712.

Leximancer. (2018). *Leximancer user guide (version 4.5)*. Brisbane: Leximancer Pty Ltd.

Mahon, K., Kemmis, S., Francisco, S., & Lloyd, A. (2017). Introduction: Practice theory and the theory of practice architectures. In K. Mahon, S. Francisco, & S. Kemmis (Eds.), *Exploring education and professional practice: Through the lens of practice architectures* (pp. 1–30). Singapore: Springer.

Phillips, J., Phillipson, S., & Tyler-Merrick, G. (2021). *Growing children's social and emotional skills: Using the together programme* (1st ed.). London: Routledge.

Phillipson, S., & Garvis, S. (2020). Policy and childhood: Making sense of systems. In S. Garvis & S. Phillipson (Eds.), *Policification of early childhood education and care: Early childhood education in the 21st century* (Vol. III, pp. 274–285). London: Routledge.

Smith, A. E., & Humphreys, M. S. (2006). Evaluation of unsupervised semantic mapping of natural language with Leximancer concept mapping. *Behavior Research Methods*, *38*(2), 262–279. doi:10.3758/BF03192778

Tett, L. (2001). Parents as problems or parents as people? Parental involvement programmes, schools and adult educators. *International Journal of Lifelong Education*, *20*(3), 188–198.

INDEX

Äärelä, R. 212, 214
Aasen, W. 52, 315
Abayad Research and Marketing Consultancy 163
Abdel Jabbar, S. 167
Aber, J. L. 112
Abouchaar, A. 126, 260
Abu-Rudwan, E. 165
Abu Taleb, T. 165
acclimatization, in educational partnership 101
ACEA 76–77
Ackah-Jnr, F. R. 109, 112, 114, 115, 116, 117, 118
Active Involvement model 144, 145
Act on Early Childhood Education and Care 90
Act on ECEC 96
Act on Preschool Education 51, 53
Act on Social Care for Preschool Children 51
Adler, N. E. 295
Administration Guide for the 2017–2018 School Year 123, 125, 127, 128
age, parental involvement influenced by: in Australia 13; in Azerbaijan 24, 25, 30, 31, 32, 34, 35, 36; in Belarus 42; in Czech Republic 65; in Denmark 75; in Finland 90; in Germany 105; in Ghana 109; in Hong Kong 122; in Hungary 136, 138, 145–146; in Iceland 152, 158; in Jordan 162; in Oman 189, 190, 191; in Sweden 258; in United States 292–293, 296, 300
aided preprimary institutions 123
Alasuutari, M. 91, 92, 93, 94, 213, 217
Al-Barwani, T. A. 188
Albeely, T. S. 188
Albury, N. 212
Alegre, M. A. 247
Alexander, E. 138
AlFlasi, M. 167
Al-Harrasi, S. 188
Al-Hassan, O. 164
Al-Hassan, S. 166
Al Jabery, M. 167
Alkraisha, M. 166
Al-Maadadi, F. 167
Al-Maamari, F. 188
Al-Mahrooqi, R. 188
Al-Shboul, M. 167
Al-Suleimani, H. 188
Al-Thani, T. 167
Amanti, C. 186
Ampiah, J. G. 112, 113, 114
Andenæs, A. 74
Anders, Y. 103
Anderson, R. 234
Àngel, C. 249
ANOVA: Factorial 32, 34, 35; focused 34–35
Ansong, D. 112
Antal, B. 138

Anthony, C. J. 232, 237
Appiah, J. 112, 115, 117
Asante, J. 112
ASIPDE 28
attend, in Leximancer concept maps 16, 17
Australia 9–22; analysis in research 13; demographic information of participants in research 12–13; discussion and inclusion 20–22; explanation of educator's role and role of others in parental involvement 18–20; explanation of parental involvement in ECEC 13–15; explanation of parental role and role of others in parental involvement 15–18; introduction 9–10; method of research 11–13; overview 3; parental involvement in 10–11; parent involvement sayings, doings and relatings in 308, 310; results of research 13–20; visual representation of parental involvement 22
Australian Government Department of Education, Employment and Workplace Relations 10
autonomy 228
Ayoub, C. 294
AzEdu Education Portal 28
Azerbaijan 24–37; data analysis and results of study 31–35; demographic characteristics of participants in study 30–37; discussion and conclusion 36–37; ECE systems in, structure and organization of 24–25; Factorial ANOVA used in study 32, 34, 35; focused ANOVA used in study 34–35; instrument used in study 30–31; introduction 24; investigation of family engagement in ECE among Azerbaijani parents 30–35; Likert scale used in study 30, 32, 33; overview 3–4; parental engagement in teaching practice 27–30; parental involvement in ECE teacher education curricula 26–27; parent involvement sayings, doings and relatings in 311; participants and data collection in study in study 31; reliability analysis of scale used in study 31; role of parents in education, key steering documents about 25–26
Azerbaijan Muellimi Newspaper 28, 30

Babygroup programme 250
Bach, D. 233, 234, 242
bachelor's degree *see* teacher education
bachelor university study program (ISCED 5) 67

Bacigalupa, C. 40
back translation procedures 31, 190
Baden-Württemberg 101
Badia, G. 247
Badics, T. 141
Baker, M. 30
Baker, T. L. 295
Bakken, Y. 180
Bakonyi, A. 144
Bakonyi, P. 138
Baku State Pedagogical University 27
Ballard, P. J. 295
Bangiranae, C. A. 271
Barnett, W. S. 292
Basic Education Act 90
Baucal, A. 223, 224
Bavarian education and upbringing plan 101
Bečvařová, Z. 65
Behrman, J. R. 112
Belarus 40–47; conceptualisation of parental involvement 41–42; conclusion 46–47; educational policies related to parental involvement 42–44; introduction 40–41; language groups in 43; overview 4; parental involvement in practice 45–46; parent involvement sayings, doings and relatings in 309, 311, 313
beliefs, parental involvement influenced by: in Australia 16, 18, 21; in Catalunya, Spain 254; in Germany 104; in Ghana 109; in Jordan 167; in Poland 204; in Serbia 227; in Singapore 232, 233, 238, 240–241, 242; in Uganda 275; in United Kingdom 288; in United States 288
Benner, A. D. 294
Bennett, J. 307
Berg, R. D. 271
Bergroth, M. 213
Berlin educational program 101
Berliner, P. 78
Betawi, I. 167
Better Parenting Programme (BPP) 163–164, 166, 167
Bezrukova, V. S. 41
Bidwell, K. 115
Biesanz, J. C. 294
bilingualism 43, 190, 214, 293
Björk, L. G. 52
Björnsson, M. 259
Blanch, S. 246–247, 254
Blasco, J. 246, 247
Bleach, J. 51

Blizej Przedszkola 204
Bognar, B. 54
Bognár, M. 145, 146
Bogovac, T. 224
Bokhorst-Heng, W. D. 236
Bolshaw, P. 289
Bond, M. 10, 20
book, in Leximancer concept maps 16, 17
Boothbya, N. 271
Borgonovi, F. 260
Bosch, C. 10
Bourdieu, P. 2
Bovaird, J. A. 294
Bowen, G. A. 261
Boyce, W. T. 295
BRAC Uganda 275–276
Brandi, U. 78
Braun, V. 236
Bredekamp, S. 109
Brent, J. M. 294
Bridge 277
Brix, D. 77, 78–79
Bromell, L. 40
Bronfenbrenner, U. 185, 247, 257–258, 260–261, 264
Bronfenbrenner Ecological Systems Theory 185, 256, 260–261, 265
Brown, G. 282–283
Brown, J. 164
Browne-Ferrigno, T. 52
Bryk, A. 227
Bu, H. 10
Bueno, D. 249
Building a Brighter Future: Early Years and Childcare Plan 285
Bulotsky-Shearer, R. J. 294
Busig, S. 271
Business Optimization Consultants (BOC) 163

CAFEs (Community and Family Engagements) 300
Cakharevich, A. A. 40, 41
California: family engagement efforts in San Mateo County 299–300; quality rating and improvement system (QRIS) 297–299
California Department of Education (CDE) 292, 298
California Early Childhood Online (CECO) 298–299
Campbell-Barr, V. 139
Can Butjosa Library 250
capacity building 117

Cape Coast and University of Education, Winneba 114
Čapek, R. 68
Capra, F. 228
care, in Leximancer concept maps 14–16, 18–19
caregivers: in Ghana 110; in international trends 306–308, 311, 313; in Jordan 163–166; in Norway 176–177, 179–180; in Poland 200–203; in Uganda 271–276; in United States 297
Careta, A. 247
Carroll-Meehan, C. 289
Carson, N. 180
Caspe, M. 226, 294
Catalan decree 101/2010 248
Catalan Parliament 248
Catalonia, Spain 246–254; challenges on parental involvement 253–254; children and family services at social risk 250; cultural services 250; families' services to support families with young children 249; family-school initiatives 252; introduction 246–247; leisure services 250; overview 7; parental engagement and collaboration at school, strategies to promote 251–253; parental involvement in ECE teacher higher education degree programmes 248–249; parent-teacher conferences, redesigning 251–253; policies to promote parental involvement 247–248; science and technology services 250; socio educational playgroups 249–250; study results 246–247
Catholic Relief Services (CRS) 275
Ceglowski, D. 40
celebrations 43, 64, 67–70
Census and Statistics Department 124
Center for the Study of Social Policy 298
Centre for Harmony and Enhancement of Ethnic Minority Residents (CHEER) 132
Certificate in Education 273
Chambers, R. 227
Chan, A. 92, 94, 96, 213, 214
Chatman-Nelson, C. 226
Cheatham, G. 213, 218
Chechet, V. V. 40–41
Chen, M. 126, 129
Chenhall, R. 11, 20
Cheo, R. 238
Cheung, C. S. S. 122
Child, Family, and Community course 298

Child and Family Welfare Policy 111
childcare centres *see* day-care centres
Child Care Services Ordinance 122, 123
child/children, in Leximancer concept maps 13–16, 18–20
Child Development Permit Matrix 298
Child Fund 275
Children at Risk Network (CRANE) Services 275
Children Centre model 283
Children's Act 560 110
Children's Museum of Jordan 165
Children's Rights Convention 248
"Child Safety on Internet" project 28
Child Safety Programme 165
Cho, G. 211, 218
Choi, Y. 234
Chowa, G. A. 112, 113, 114, 115, 116
Choy, M. Y. 234, 242
Christenson, S. L. 52, 74, 77, 138, 233, 234
Christian values 175
Chua, A. 233–234
Čiháček, V. 67
Clark, S. L. 294
Clarke, B. L. 51, 54
Clarke, C. 242
Clarke, V. 236
Cloos, P. 99, 100
Cocq, C. 212
Code on Education (CE) 42–44
collaborating with parents: in Azerbaijan 26; in Belarus 43; in Catalunya, Spain 246; in Denmark 78; in Finland 92, 96; in Germany 99–106; in Iceland 153; international trends in 312, 314; in Norway 174–175; in Poland 202–204, 211; for South Sámi language learning 6, 211–218
collaborating with teachers 77, 83, 111, 115, 311
collaborating with the community domain, in Epstein's model: in Azerbaijan 28; in Denmark 83, 85; in Ghana 118; in Jordan 167, 169; in Oman 190, 191, 192, 195
College of Education, UCC 114
Comas, M. 247
Committee on Home–School Co-operation 126
Common Framework for Early Education 100
communicating domain, in Epstein's model: in Australia 17; in Azerbaijan 27–28; in Belarus 41, 47; in Denmark 79; in Ghana 116–118; in Jordan 167, 168; in Oman 190–191, 194, 195; in Poland 200; in United Kingdom 284
COMmunity and PArents in Support of Schools (COMPASS) 232
Community Child Care Program 273
community engagement 273, 300
Community Led Action for Children (CLAC) 276
compass system 15, 19
competency: *to be competent* and *to have competences,* distinction between 53; parent 131, 225, 249; teacher 52–53, 202, 212, 265, 306, 310, 315
Competent Parent program 25
Complex Preventative, Montessori Programme 137
Conference of Ministers of Culture and Youth 100
Connors, L. J. 79
Constantino, S. M. 295
Constitution of Government of Ghana 110
Constitution of the Republic of Belarus 42
cooperation, defining 51, 55
Correction and Development Training and Rehabilitation Centre (DC) 43
Corter, C. 40
Costales, G. S. 234
Cottle, M. 138
Coughlin, C. 167
Council for the Accreditation of Educator Preparation (CAEP) 187
Council of Europe Committee of Ministers Recommendation (REC-19) 248
Cox, D. 74
CREATE 113, 117
Creswell, J. 189, 190
critical policy analysis (CPA) 124
Croatia 50–59; challenges to parental involvement 53–54; codes and frequencies of data in research 56; conclusion 59; discussion of research findings 57–59; interviews in research 54–55; introduction 50; method of research 54–55; overview 4; parent involvement sayings, doings and relatings in 310, 311, 313, 314; participants in research 54; policy framework for parental involvement 50–51; research on parental involvement, previous 51–52; research on parental involvement in ECE 54–59; results of research

55–57; teachers' education for parental involvement 52–53
Croatian Universities, study programs of 53
Cronbach's alpha value 31
Crozier, G. 50
culture, parental involvement influenced by 1, 2, 3; in Australia 9–22; in Azerbaijan 28–29; in Belarus 46; in Catalonia, Spain 249, 250, 251, 254; in Croatia 52, 54; in Denmark 74, 76, 77, 78, 81, 83; in Finland 90, 92, 93, 97; in Germany 100, 105; in Ghana 109–110, 111, 112, 116–117; in Hungary 136, 137, 141, 144, 147, 148; international trends in 306, 307, 309, 312, 313, 316; in Jordan 169; in Norway 175, 176, 177, 179, 180, 182, 183; in Oman 185, 191, 194, 196; in Poland 203; in Serbia 227, 228; in Singapore 234, 235, 236; in South Sámi language learning 211–218; in Sweden 259, 260, 264–265; in Uganda 270, 271, 275, 277–278; in United Kingdom 286, 288; in United States 292, 293, 295, 297, 299–301
curriculum 1; in Australia 9, 10, 18; in Azerbaijan 26–27; in Belarus 42, 44, 45; in Catalunya, Spain 246, 249; in Croatia 51–52, 56, 57, 58; in Czech Republic 64–65; in Denmark 75–77, 79–86; in Finland 90–91, 93–97; in Germany 99–102, 106; in Ghana 111, 113–114, 116, 119; in Hong Kong 123–132; in Hungary 136, 139, 144, 145; in Iceland 151–155, 159–160; in international trends 310–311; in Jordan 168, 171; in Norway 175; in Oman 191; in Poland 200, 201, 204; in Serbia 223, 224–226; in Singapore 233, 234, 237, 240, 242; in South Sámi language learning 213, 217; in Sweden 3, 257–265; in Uganda 272–273, 275; in United Kingdom 284–285, 288
Czech Republic 63–72; final thoughts 71–72; introduction 63; overview 4; parental engagement in practice 68–69; parental involvement in key steering documents 65–67; parental involvement in teacher education 67–68; parent involvement sayings, doings and relatings in 311–312, 313, 314; private high-price facility 70; private low-price facility 70; private medium-price facility (forest pre-school) 70; public high-demand facility 69; public low-demand facility

69–70; public medium-demand facility 69; research on parental involvement in ECE 67–70; transformation and system context of ECE 64–65

daily exchange of knowledge 78
Dampson, G. 115, 116, 118
Daniel, G. 10, 74, 138
Danish model 76
Danish Parliament (Folketing) 76, 81
Danish Statistics 74
Danmarks Evalueringsinstitut 155
danning 177–178, 183
Davie, S. 240
Davis-Kean, P. E. 54
day, in Leximancer concept maps 16, 17
Day Care Act 75, 76, 85
day-care centres: in Czech Republic 68–69; in Denmark 75, 77, 78–81, 83, 85; in Finland 97; in Germany 101; in Ghana 109; in Hong Kong 130; in Iceland 152; in Jordan 163
De Bruïne, E. J. 52
decentralization 228
decision-making domain, in Epstein's model: in Azerbaijan 27, 28, 32, 33, 36; in Belarus 44; in Catalunya, Spain 247, 253; in Denmark 79, 82–83, 85; in Germany 100, 103; in Ghana 118; in Hong Kong 127, 130; in Hungary 138–139; in Iceland 155; international trends in 311; in Jordan 167, 169; in Oman 190, 192; in Serbia 221, 222, 223, 226, 228; in United Kingdom 284; in United States 295
De Febrer, V. 250
Deliné, F. K. 137
Deming, D. 295
democracy 5, 76, 151, 152, 154–155, 159, 201, 222
democratization 229
Dencik, L. 77
Denman, C. 188
Denmark 74–86; discussion on research findings 85–86; ECEC, key steering document for 75–77; Epstein's model of parental involvement in 83–85; goals from the national curriculum in which parental cooperation is mentioned 83, 84; introduction 74–75; limitations and areas for future research 86; method of research 79; overview 4, 75; parental involvement in ECE teachers' education curricula 83–85; parents' role in ECEC,

key steering documents on 80–81; research about parental involvement in practice 77–86; results of research 80–81; theoretical approach to research 79–80; universities' knowledge and proficiency goals, examples of 83, 84
Densten, I. L. 79, 214
Department for Children, Schools, and Families (DCSF) 283
Department for Education 288
Department of Basic Education (DBE) 114
Department of Schools, Children, and Families 287
Department of Social and Child Welfare Services 146
Department of Teacher Education of the University of Zadar 53
Desforges, C. 126, 260
Difficult Conversation Project 180
digital communication 78
Directorate of Education Standards (DES) 275
Disability Act 111
disadvantaged backgrounds: in Azerbaijan 311; defined 145; equalising educational opportunities for 315; in Hungary 145–146; in Northern Ireland 284; in Norway 312; in United States 310
Diversification of pre-school education in the Czech Republic 68
diversity, parental involvement influenced by: in Belarus 44–45; in Catalunya, Spain 252; in Czech Republic 69; in Denmark 79; in Finland 94; international trends in 311, 313, 315; in Norway 175, 182–183, 214; in Poland 201, 202, 204, 205; in Serbia 222–223, 225, 228; in United Kingdom 280–289; in United States 292–293, 300
Doan, S. N. 234
doings, parent involvement of 309, 311–315
Donkor, A. K. 112, 113, 114, 116
Downer, J. T. 132
Drugli, M. B. 181, 182
dual language learners (DLLs) 293, 299
Duan, W. 10
Dunst, C. J. 295
Duran, D. 247
Durand, T. M. 295
Dvořáčková, J. 66
Dýrfjörð, S. 151

EACEA 75, 76, 264
Earl, L. 226
Early Childhood Care and Development (ECCD) Policy 110, 115, 117
Early Childhood Development (ECD): centres 114, 270; settings/contexts 12; strategy 164; teachers 114, 118
Early Childhood Development Agency 233, 242
Early Childhood Development Caregiver Training Framework 273
early childhood education (ECE): definitions of parental involvement in, in Belarus 41–42; home-school-community involvement, in Singapore 238; investigation of, among Azerbaijani parents 30–35; investigation of family engagement in, in Azerbaijan 30–35; parental engagement in practice, in Ghana 115–117; parental involvement, in Singapore 237–240; parental involvement in teacher education curricula, in Azerbaijan 26–27; parental involvement in teachers' education curricula, in Denmark 83; research based on parental involvement, in Ghana 111–113; research on parental involvement in Croatia 54–59; research on parental involvement in Czech Republic 67–70; school-based involvement, in Singapore 237–238; steering documents for, in Poland 200–201; structure and organization of, in Azerbaijan 24–25; teacher higher education degree programmes in Catalonia, Spain 248–249; teachers' education curricula, in Denmark 83; transformation and system context of, in Czech Republic 64–65; treatments or attentions to parental involvement, in Ghana 113–115
early childhood education and care (ECEC) and parental involvement: in Australia 3, 9–22; in Azerbaijan 3–4, 24–37; in Belarus 4, 40–47; in Catalonia, Spain 7, 246–254; in Croatia 4, 50–59; in Czech Republic 4, 63–72; in Denmark 4, 74–86; in Finland 4–5, 90–97; in Germany 5, 99–106; in Ghana 5, 109–119; in Hong Kong 5, 122–133; in Hungary 5, 136–148; in Iceland 5, 151–160; international trends in 8, 306–316; in Jordan 5–6, 162–171; in Norway 6, 174–183, 211–218; in Oman 6, 185–196; overview 3–8; in Poland

6, 199–210; in Serbia 6–7, 221–229; in Singapore 7, 232–243; in South Sámi language learning 6, 211–218; in Sweden 7, 256–265; traditions in 2–3; trends in 306–315; in Uganda 7, 269–278; in United Kingdom 7–8, 280–289; in United States of America 8, 292–301
Early Childhood Language Development Institute (ECLDI) 299–300
Early Childhood Learning and Knowledge Center 297
Early Childhood Teacher Education Programme (ECTEP) 169–171
Early Education Department at Sultan Qaboos University (SQU) 187
Early Learning and Development Standards 275
Early Learning Family Engagement Communities of Practice 300
Early Years Foundation Stage (EYFS) curriculum 288
Early Years Initial Teacher Training (EYITT) 287–288
Early Years Learning Framework (EYLF) 9–10, 18
Early Years Teacher Status (EYTS) 287–288
Ebbeck, M. 234, 238, 242
ECCD Policy 109, 110, 115, 116, 117
Eccless, J. S. 54
Ecology of Human Development (Bronfenbrenner) 257–258
economic status *see* socioeconomic status, parental involvement influenced by
ECTS European credits 248
Edmondson, J. 124, 125
educare model 90
education, in Leximancer concept maps 14–16
Education Act 212, 262; Uganda 269, 270
Education Act 778 110–111
Educational Act 65
educational background, parental involvement influenced by: in Azerbaijan 30, 32, 34, 35, 37; in Belarus 46; in Czech Republic 68; in Ghana 119; in Oman 188, 189, 190, 195; in Singapore 233
educational institutions (EIs) 25–26, 28, 50, 51, 137, 140, 141, 177, 222, 223
Educational Journey in Oman 187
educational levels, parental involvement influenced by: in Azerbaijan 30, 32, 34,
35, 37; in Belarus 46; in Czech Republic 68; in Ghana 119; in Oman 188; in Singapore 188
educational partnerships 101
Educational programme of preschool education (MOE) 42
Educational standards for preschool education (MOE) 42
education and encouragement 117
Education and Manpower Bureau 122; *see also* Education Bureau
Education and Training Inspectorate Northern Ireland (ETINI) 289
Education Bill 111
Education Bureau 122, 125, 126, 127, 128, 129, 130, 132
Education Bureau and Social Welfare Department 123, 125, 126, 129
Education Endowment Fund 283
Education in Oman, The Drive for Quality 187
Education Ordinance 122, 123
Education Reform for the Knowledge Economy (ERfKE) 164, 167–168
Education Scotland 284, 289
Education Strategic Plan (ESP): Ghana 111; Jordan 165
Education Workforce Council 289
Edwards, C. P. 294
Effective Provision of Pre-School Education (EPPE) 287
Effective School project 28–29
Einarsdóttir, J. 151
Ejrnæs, M. 79
Elango, S. 293
Elementary and Secondary Education Act 296
Elias, J. 54
Elizabeth II, Queen 281
El-Kogali, S. 163
El Shourbagi, S. 188
emailing 192
emancipation 228
Emerson, L. 10, 260
Emilia, Reggio 155
Emmerová, K. 67
employment of staff: in Croatia 53; in Denmark 80, 83; in Oman 188
employment status, parental involvement influenced by: in Azerbaijan 30, 32, 34, 35; in Hong Kong 130; in Oman 186; in United Kingdom 281, 285, 286; in United States 293
empowerment 5, 152, 154–155, 159, 226, 228, 277

"Engage Parents and Families" 299
England 181–283, 287–289; *see also* United Kingdom
Englund, M. M. 258
Epstein, J. L. 1, 2, 27, 51, 52, 57, 77, 79, 80, 81, 116, 117, 118, 119, 169, 190, 199, 232, 237, 238, 240, 306, 307
Epstein's model of parental involvement 2, 4; *see also individual domains*; collaborating with the community domain 83, 85, 167, 169, 190; communicating domain 27, 81–82, 85, 167, 168, 190, 191; decision-making domain 27, 82–83, 85, 167, 169, 190; in Denmark 79–86; in Ghana 116, 118, 119; in international trends in parental involvement 306; in Jordan 163, 167–169; learning at home domain 82, 85, 167, 168, 190, 191; in Oman 190–193; parenting domain 81, 85, 167–168, 190; in Singapore 237, 238; types of family involvement 27; volunteering domain 27, 82, 85, 167, 168
Eraut, M. 53
"Erziehungs- und Bildungspartnerschaft" (educational partnership) 99
Espinosa, L. M. 295
ESS (European social survey) 3
Estonia 93, 259
Estyn 285–286, 289
ethnicity, parental involvement influenced by: in Denmark 78, 85; in Hong Kong 124, 131, 132; in Hungary 146; in Norway 179; in Singapore 234; in United States 292–293
Ethnologue Languages of the World 212, 217
Eurasia 24
European Commission (EU) 63, 66, 75
European Parents' Association (EPA) 96
Eurostat 75, 76
Eurydice 75, 76
EVA 78, 155, 159
exchange with parents, in educational partnership 101
Exemplary Charter of General School, MoE 26
Exemplary Charter of Preschool Educational Institutions 26
extracurricular activities 130, 166, 314
Ezati, B. A. 269, 272

face-to-face interactions 15, 17, 19, 116, 117, 235, 240, 295
Factorial ANOVA 32, 34, 35

family, in Leximancer concept maps 18–19
Family Educational Playgroups 254
family engagement: CAFEs 300; efforts, in San Mateo County, California 299–300; future of, in United States of America 297–299; investigation of, among Azerbaijani parents in Azerbaijan 30–35; investigation of in ECE, among Azerbaijani parents 30–35; policies in early childhood programs, in United States of America 296–297; research on, in United States of America 294–296
"Family Engagement from the Early Years to the Early Grades" (USDOE/USDHHS) 297
"Family Engagement Inventory" 297
Family Engagement Scale (FES) 30–31, 32
Family Pedagogy 53
family-school partnership 10, 52, 79, 115
Family-School Partnerships Framework 115
Family Support and Child Welfare Centres 146
Fan, X. 126, 129, 270
Fantuzzo, J. 294
Faria, A. M. 294
Fayez, M. 165
Fear, J. 10, 260
FEDAIA 254
Ferlazzo, L. 295
Ferrer, A. 246
Ferrer, M. 246–247
File, N. 294
Finland 90–97; cooperation with parents as a subject in Finnish teacher training programmes 93–94; future developmental objects 96–97; introduction 90–91; overview 4–5; parent involvement sayings, doings and relatings in 314; partnership in practice 94–96; research connected to parental participation 91–93
Finnish Education Evaluation Centre (FEEC) 90, 91, 97
Finnish National Agency for Education (FNAE) 90–91, 94, 96, 211–212
Finnish National Board of Education (FNBE) 90, 94
Finnish National Curriculum Guidelines for Early Childhood Education and Care 91
First 5 California 297–298
First 5 California Strategic Plan for 2019–2024 299
First 5 San Mateo 300

first step model 44
Fitzpatrick, A. 57
Fleischmann, F. 30
Flising, L. 257
Flores, M. 247
Flying Start 283, 285
Flynn, T. 211
focused ANOVA 34–35
Földesi, K. 140
Folketing 76, 81
Förbundet Hem och Skola i Finland r.f. 96
Forest preschools *(Leśne Przedszkola)* 204, 313, 314
"Forms of Collaboration between Kindergarten and Family" (course) 27
fostering children 256–257
Fox, S. 10, 260
Framework Education Programme for Preschool Education (FEP) 65–68, 71
Framework Plan for Kindergartens: Content and Tasks 174, 175, 177, 181, 212–213, 217
Francisco, S. 306–307
Fraser, J. 294
Fredrikson, G. 257
Free Quality Kindergarten Education Scheme 123
Friederich, T. 99, 102, 103, 104, 106
Friis-Hansen, M. 78
Fritzell Hanhan, S. 58
Fröhlich-Gildhoff, K. 99, 100, 102, 103, 104, 105
Fuller, K. 30
Fundació Miró 250

Gadaire, D. M. 294
Galindo, C. 294
Ganja State Pedagogical University 27
Ganley, D. D. 52
Garcaí, O. 211
Garcia, J. L. 293
Garvis, S. 41, 76, 91, 211, 256, 258, 306
Gaspar, M. F. 51, 93, 213
Gatenio-Gabel, S. 296
Gehlbach, H. 30
Geinger, F. 151
GEMS Education 276
gender, parental involvement influenced by: in Azerbaijan 30, 32, 34, 35, 113; in Denmark 78, 85; in Ghana 113, 116; in Jordan 163; in Norway 182; in Oman 189, 192; in Sweden 256, 263; in Uganda 272, 276; in United Kingdom 286; in United States 292

General Certificate of Secondary Education Examination 162
General Education Law 25–26
Geneva Global 275
Georgeson, J. 139
Gerard, M. 58
Gercke, N. 57
Germany 99–106; educational partnership in preschools, idea of 99–100; future perspectives and development tendencies of parental involvement 105–106; implementation of educational partnership in ECEC settings 102–104; overview 5; parental collaboration in ECEC teacher education 102; parental collaboration in steering documents 100–101; parent involvement sayings, doings and relatings in 313, 314; research on parental involvement in 104–105; responsibilities in ECEC in 100
"Getting Ready to Learn" programme 284–285
Ghana 109–119; capacity building for parental involvement 117; conclusion 119; developing parental engagement and collaboration in 117–118; education and encouragement for parental involvement 117; Epstein's model of parental involvement in 116, 118, 119; introduction 109; multifaceted two-way communication for parental involvement 117; overview 5; parental engagement for children's learning and general well-being and its partnership with teachers, schools and community in 118–119; parental engagement in practice in ECE 115–117; parental involvement in, steering documents on 109–111; parent engagement policy for parental involvement 117–118; research base on parental involvement in ECE in 111–113; treatments or attentions to parental involvement in ECE teacher education 113–115
Ghana Education Strategic Plan (ESP) 111
Ghana Inclusive Education Policy (GIEP) 111
Ghana's Sustainable Development Goal 2 111
Ghanney, R. A. 113, 114, 116, 117–118
Gimeno, X. 247
Ginsburg-Block, M. 294
Glaser, V. 181
Glisson, C. 295

goals: in Belarus 43–44; in Czech Republic 64; in Denmark 81–86; in Finland 93, 96–97; in Ghana 112; in Hong Kong 123, 126; in Iceland 157–158; in international trends 313; in Norway 175; in Oman 186; in Poland 200, 202; policymakers' 125; in Serbia 222; in South Sámi language learning 215, 217; in Sweden 256, 262; in Uganda 276–277; in United Kingdom 288; in United States 292
GOBAN 180
Goff, W. 12
Gokhale, N. 234, 242
Gonzalez, N. 186
Goodall, J. 51, 138, 236, 283, 289
Good Practice in Parental Involvement in Primary Schools paper 285–286
Gorard, S. 232
Government of Ghana (GOG) 110, 111
Gov.sg 235
Grady, S. 30
Gragert, N. 103
Grammatikopoulos, V. 74
Granata, A. 53–54
Gray, J. H. 79, 214
Greater Accra Region 112
Gregoriadis, A. 74
Grundmeyer, T. 138
Grůzová, L. 68
Guan, Y. 10
Guba, E. G. 54
"Guidance Document" 297
Gulf Cooperation Council (GCC) 186
Gulosino, C. 213–214
Gunnarsson, L. 256
Gurr, D. 11, 20

Haas, A. D. 30
Haavin, H. 74
Habermas, J. 5, 152, 155, 159
Hachfeld, A. 103, 105
Hadfield, E. 289
Hägglund, S. 258
Hahs-Vaughn, D. L. 294
Hakyemez-Paul, S. 92, 97, 258, 259, 260
Halgunseth, L. 295
Halpenny, A. 260
Hamby, D. W. 295
Handbook for Principals of Preschool Educational Institutions (MoE) 27
Hannula, H. 93
Hansèn, S. E. 44, 45
Hanssen, N. B. 41, 42, 43, 44, 45

Harðardóttir 155, 159
Hargreaves, A. 226
Harju-Luukkainen, H. 41, 91, 211
Harms, H. 104
Harris, A. 289
Harrison, L. J. 40, 41, 259
Hayakawa, M. 258
Hayes, N. 260
Hayslip, W. 295
Head Start 296–297
Healthy Child 275
Healthy School-Healthy Nation project 28, 29–30
Heckman, J. J. 293
Hedegaard, M. 124
Henderson, A. 227
Henrich, C. C. 294
Herald, S. L. 294
Her Majesty's Inspectorate of Education 289
Hermanstrand, H. 212
Hevey, D. 139
Higgins, T. 57
higher education: in Australia 11; in Azerbaijan 27, 30, 32, 35, 36; in Catalonia, Spain 248–249; in Croatia 53; in Czech Republic 67–68; in Denmark 75, 83; in Ghana 114; in Jordan 162, 169; in Oman 187, 188, 190; in Poland 202; in Serbia 223–224; in United States of America 292–294
high school specialisation (ISCED 3A) 67
Hiilamo, H. 256
Hill, N. E. 40, 41
Hindin, A. 52
Ho, E. S. C. 122, 125, 127, 128, 129, 131
Højholt, C. 78
Hojman, A. 293
Holloway, S. 247
Holm, A. 78
Holmes, C. 11
home-based involvement 2, 3, 122, 124, 125, 128, 204, 232, 237, 306
home–school communication 129, 232, 237, 238
home-school-community involvement, in Singapore 238
home-school partnerships 2, 131–132, 167, 232, 238
Hong, H. 232
Hong Kong 5, 122–133; conclusion and implications 131–133; definition and goals of parental involvement stated in policy and embedded values 126–127;

findings and discussion 126–131; guiding questions for data analysis 125; home- and kindergarten-based parental involvement 127; home-based parental involvement 128; introduction and background 122–123; kindergarten-based parental involvement 129–130; overview 5, 124; qualitative content analysis 124–125; underprivileged being left behind, benefits with 130–131
Hong Kong Council of Social Service 124, 131
Hoover-Dempsey, K. V. 227, 295
Horká, H. 68
Hornby, G. 50, 51, 57, 74, 78
Horvat, E. M. 63
"How can we redesign parent-teacher night" (Teachers Guild) 251
Howes, C. 294
"How to support language learners in South Sámi language? A study of teachers' competence in instructional strategies" 212
Hoyuelos, A. 154–155
Hreiðarsdóttir, A. M. 151
Huat See, B. 232
Hughes, P. 227
Hujala, E. 51, 93, 213, 258, 259
Human Resource Development (HRD) Strategy, 2016–2025 165
Humphreys, M. S. 13, 236, 308
Hung, C. L. 30
Hungary 136–148; conclusions and ways forward 147–148; families from disadvantaged backgrounds, working with 145–146; introduction 136; legislative and theoretical frame for parental involvement in 137–139; models of working with families 141–145; overview 5; paradigmatic shift between practice during socialist regime and today 140–141; parent involvement sayings, doings and relatings in 309–310, 311, 312, 314; pre-service training for working with families 147

Iannone, R. L. 77
Iceland 151–160; *see also* Iceland preschool project; context of 152; discussion 158–160; empowerment and democracy 154–155; introduction 151–152; overview 5; policies on parental involvement in preschools 152–154

Icelandic Association of Local Authorities 152
Iceland preschool project 155–158; beginning of 156–157; parent meetings 157; story of 156; teachers' discussion afterward 157–158
Igo, S. 51
Ihmeideh, F. 165–166, 167
IMPACT (Improve and Maximize Programs so All Children Thrive) 298, 299
"Impact of Parental Involvement on Children's Education" 287
important, in Leximancer concept maps 14–16, 18–19
Imre, N. 138
income *see* socioeconomic status, parental involvement influenced by
indigenous preschool in Norway, study in 211–218; conclusions 217–218; data and methods of research 214; findings from research 215–217; introduction 211–212; overview 6; parental collaboration 213–214; preschool as open arena for language learning 215–216; Sámi education context in 212–213; supporting parents in South Sámi language usage 216–217
individual family talk 78
induction and acclimatisation to day care 78
information, in Leximancer concept maps 14, 18–19
Institute of Medicine and National Research Council 293
Institut Infancia 246
International Parent-Professional Partnership (IPP) 93, 259
international trends in parental involvement 306–316; *see also* themes of parental involvement
interview analysis, Morris's stages of 55
investigation of family engagement among Azerbaijani parents, in Azerbaijan 30–35
involved/involvement, in Leximancer concept maps 15–17, 19–20
involvement of children 229
Ipsos Synovate 272
Issaka, C. A. 112

Janssen, J. 1, 151
Jarkovská, L. 66
Jaskóné Gácsi, M. 139
Jaume Bofill Foundation 251
Jeara, Y. 165

Jennings, K. 10
Jensen, B. 76, 77, 78
Jensen, E. 151
Jensen, H. 151
Jensen, N. R. 77, 78–79
Jeynes, W. H. 232
Jírová, M. 64
Johnston, C. 50
Jones, S. A. 233
Jónsdóttir, A. H. 151
Jordan 162–171; developing parental involvement and collaboration in 170–171; Epstein's model of parental involvement in 167–169; introduction 162–163; overview 5–6; parental involvement in early childhood teacher education 169–170; parental involvement in the Jordanian educational context 163–165; parent involvement sayings, doings and relatings in 311, 312, 314; research context 165–167
Jordan River Foundation 165
Juang, L. P. 233
Jugendministerkonferenz/ Kultusministerkonferenz (JMK) 100
Juhl, P. 75

Kaga, K. 164
Kallioniemi, A. 93
Kamerman, S. B. 296
Kampichler, M. 66
Kangas, J. 90
Karczewicz, Á 144
Karila, K. 74
Karner, B. 99, 100
Karuppiah, N. 234
Kasüschke, D. 99
Katz, L. 227
Katzev, A. R. 30
Kelley, G. 295
Kellogg Foundation 299
Kemmis, S. 306–307
Keřková, A. 64
Kernan, M. 223
Keskitalo, P. 211, 212, 213
Keyes, C. R. 51, 57
"Keys to Good Education, Upbringing and Care" 104
Khasawneh, S. 165
Khawaldeh, M. 165
Khong, L. Y. L. 232, 233
kiasu parents 233–234
Kim, S. Y. 234
Kim, Y. S. 234

kindergarten: in Azerbaijan 24–25, 27; in Belarus 43; in Catalonia, Spain 251; in Croatia 51, 55, 56; in Czech Republic 65; in Ghana 109, 112, 118; in Hong Kong 122–133; in Hungary 136–148; in Jordan 162–171; in Norway 174–183, 212–213, 217; in Poland 200, 202, 204; in Serbia 221, 223–224, 225–226, 228; in Singapore 233, 235–236, 242; in South Sámi language learning 212–213, 217; in Uganda 273; in United States of America 293, 296
Kindergarten 1 (KG1) 162, 163
Kindergarten 2 (KG2) 162, 163
Kindergarten Acts 51, 174–178, 181, 212, 213, 217
Kindergarten and Child Care Centre Fee Remission Scheme 123
kindergarten-based involvement 124, 125, 128–130
Kindergarten Education Curriculum Guide 123, 125–132
Kindergarten Knowledge Centre for Systemic Research on Diversity and Sustainable Futures 182
Kindergarten Two (K2) 235
Knoche, L. L. 294
Kochel, K. P. 294
Kocyigit, S. 40, 41
Koh, A. 233
Koh, E. 242
Koh, F. 235
Kolberg, A. 212
Koomen, H. M. 295
Korfmacher, J. 294
Korintus, M. 141
Korosteleva, T. M. 40
Korpi, B. M. 256
Koťátková, S. 65, 68
Kousholt, D. 78
Kovács, E. 148
Kozintes, R. 203
Kraft, C. 163
Kraft-Sayre, M. 57
Krashen, S. 211, 218
Kraus, G. 99
Kreider, H. 226
Krnjaja, Ž. 224
Kuchařová, V. 64
Kuger, S. 103
Kukhoreva, N. N. 41, 44
Kunnskapsdepartamentet 212, 213, 217
Kupzyk, K. A. 294
Kušević, B. 52

Kuusisto, E. 258
Kwok, S. Y. 234
Kwong, W. 131

Lab 0_6: Discovery, Research and Documentation Centre for Science Education in Early Childhood 250
Ladd, G. W. 294
Lafaele, R. 74, 78
Lam, C. C. 128
Lammi-Taskula, J. 92
language; *see also* South Sámi language learning: barriers 101, 130–132; Belarusian-language groups 43; bilingualism 43, 190, 214, 293; Cantonese 128, 129, 130, 132; Chinese 236; dual language learners 293, 299; illiteracy 131, 132, 269; Malay 236; Mandarin 128, 130; Singlish 236
Lankaran State University 27
Lansford, J. 166
Lareau, A. 63
Larsen, M. R. 78
LaSala Miguel Hernandez 250
Lastikka, A. L. 94, 97
Lau, E. Y. H. 124, 129, 130, 131, 132
Law of Family support 18/2003 248
Law on Child's Rights 42
Law on Preschool Education 222
Law on the Foundation of the Education System 222
Lazzari, A. 146
Lea, T. 11
learning, in Leximancer concept maps 13, 14, 19
learning at home domain, in Epstein's model: in Australia 10; in Azerbaijan 28; in Denmark 82; in Ghana 116, 118; in Hong Kong 129; in Jordan 167, 168; in Oman 190, 191, 192, 195; in Singapore 236; in United Kingdom 282, 284
learning community 228
Learning Potential App 11
Learning Through Play (LTP) 275
Leedy, P. 94, 214
Legankova, O. V. 40, 41, 45
legislation: in Azerbaijan 25; in Belarus 42; in Catalunya, Spain 249; in Croatia 51; in Denmark 75, 80, 85; in Hong Kong 123; in Hungary 136, 137–139, 146, 147, 148; in Oman 188; in Serbia 221, 222, 223, 226; in United Kingdom 282, 283, 284, 289; in United States 296
Lemkow-Tovias, G. 249

Levinthal de Oliveira Lima, C. 258
Leximancer software 13, 236–237, 240, 308; concept maps 14, 16, 19, 239, 241, 308, 309, 315; key concepts 13–15
Li, C. I. K. 234
Li, H. 130, 132
libraries 250
Lightfoot, D. 259
Lim, L. 234
Lincoln, Y. S. 54
Ling, C. C. 234
Ling-Yin, L. A. 233, 242
Literacy and Adult Basic Education (LABE) 275, 276
Lithuania 43, 93, 259
Ljubetić, M. 51
Lloyd, A. 306–307
Löfdahl, A. 258
Lokharde, M. 105
LOMCE (Organic Law for the improvement of educational quality) law 248
Lopez, M. E. 226, 294
Love, J. M. 294
Lpfö 18 (Curriculum for Preschool) 262
Lpfö 98 (Curriculum for Preschool) 256, 258, 262–263
Lund, K. 257
Lutheran State Church 174

Määttä, K. 211
MacNaughton, G. 227
Macura-Milovanovic, S. 224
Magruder, E. S. 295
Mahfouz, S. 165
Mahmood, S. 92, 93, 94, 96, 213, 214
Mahon, K. 306–307
Mahon et al., 2017 315
Malaguzzi, L. 154–155
Maleš, D. 51, 52
Malin, N. 77
Mamonka, V. V. 40–41, 45
Manning, S. 226
Manz, P. 294
Manzon, M. 232, 233, 238
Mapp, K. 227
Markström, A. M. 151, 259, 260
Marschall, A. 79
Masa, R. D. 113
Mashburn, A. J. 294
Mastergeorge, A. M. 294
master's degree *see* teacher education
Mastroleo, R. D. 54
Mátay, K. 141

Mathews, M. 234
McAllister Swap, S. 58
McBrien, J. L. 269
McCoy, D. C. 112, 115, 116, 117, 118
McDonald, M. 10
McFarland-Piazza, L. 40, 41, 259
McHugh, M. 293
McQuiggan, M. 30
McWayne, C. M. 294
Meehan, C. 288
Meehan, P. 288
Megra, M. 30
Mehaffie, K. E. 294
Mejri, O. 53–54
Melhuish, E. 74, 287
Mendel, M. 199
Mendez, J. L. 132, 294
Mendoza, J. 227
Merriam, S. B. 189
Meyer, S. 271
Mihajlović, M. 223
Millei, Z. 140, 141
Miller, L. 289
Miller, R. 232
Miller, S. 144
Milligan, K. 30
Ministerium fur Kultus, Jugend und Sport Baden-Wurttemberg (KM BW) 101
Ministry for Social Affairs 75
Ministry of Children and Education 76
Ministry of Children and Social Affairs 75, 76, 77, 80, 81
Ministry of Education 152, 153, 154, 187; of Azerbaijan 24, 25, 26, 27; of Belarus 42–43, 44, 45; of Ghana 111, 115; of Jordan 75, 162, 164–165, 167, 168, 170–171; of Singapore 232, 233, 234, 235
Ministry of Education, Science, and Culture 153, 154
Ministry of Education, Youth and Sports 65
Ministry of Education and Culture 90, 159
Ministry of Education and Sports (MoES) 273, 274; Directorate of Education Standards (DES) 275
Ministry of Gender, Labour and Social Development (MoGLSD) 271, 274
Ministry of Health 274–275
Ministry of Higher Education and Science 75, 83
Ministry of Higher Education and Scientific Research (MoHESR) 169
Ministry of Human Resources 136, 137, 138, 145, 148

Ministry of Social and Health Affairs 92
Miretzky, D. 58
Miškeljin, G. 224
Mistry, R. S. 294
Mitrosh, O. I. 41, 44
models; *see also* Epstein's model of parental involvement: Children Centre 283; educare, in Finland 90; Nordic/Danish 76; of parent involvement, in Hungary 141–145
MOE-GIEP 115
Moen, A. L. 294
Mokhtar, F. 234
Moll, L. C. 186
Molnár, B. 137, 141, 145, 146
Monrad, M. 79
Montgomery, C. 51, 138
Montt, G. 260
Moore, S. 226
Morgan, N. S. 51, 57
Morris, A. 55
Morris, V. G. 132
Morrow, G. 77
Mothers in Prison Unit 250
MŠMT 65, 66, 67
Mueller, M. 52
Mugumyab, F. 271
Muijs, D. 31
multifaceted two-way communication 117
Murray, E. 40, 41, 259, 260
Murray, J. 138, 139
Murtuza, M. 234

Naidoo, L. 21
Nakata, M. 20, 21
Nathans, L. 167
National Academies of Sciences, Engineering, and Medicine (NASEM) 293, 296–297
National Association for the Education of Young Children (NAEYC) 31, 187
National Center for Statistics and Information 186, 187
National Committee for Human Resource Development 165
National Core Curriculum for Early Childhood Education and Care (FNAE) 90, 91, 96
National Core Programme for Kindergarten Education 137–138, 146, 148
National Council for Curriculum and Assessment (NaCCA) 111
National Curriculum Development Centre (NCDC) 275

Index **331**

National Guidelines for Kindergarten Teacher Education 179
National Inspectorate Board (NIB) 111
National Integrated Early Childhood Development policy 271, 274
National Nursery Teachers' Training Centre (NNTTC) 113
National Parenting Strategy 284
National Partnership Agreement on Low Socio-Economic Status School Communities and the Parent Engagement Project 11
National Pre-Tertiary Education Curriculum Framework (NPTECF) 111
National Public Education Act 137
National Quality Framework (NQF) 9
National Quality Standard (NQS) 9
National report on the state of early childhood education and childcare for pre-school children in the Czech Republic (MŠMT) 67
National Standards for Teacher Education and Preparation for the Profession 202, 205
National Statistical Committee of the Republic of Belarus (Belstat) 43
National Team for Early Childhood Development 164
National Vocational Qualifications 249
Natural Science Museum 250
NCFA 164
necessarily, in Leximancer concept maps 16–17
Neff, D. 186
Nentwig-Gesemann, I. 101, 104
networking 228
Ng, M. L. 129, 130, 131, 132
Ng, P. T. 232, 233, 234, 235
Ng, S. W. 122, 124, 130, 131
Nicolai, K. 101
Niemi, H. 93
Nikonova, L. E. 40–41, 45
Nilssen, T. R. 212
Nisbett, R. E. 259
No Child Left Behind 115
Noftle, J. T. 52
NOKO 96
non-Chinese-speaking (NCS) parents 129–130, 132
Non-Governmental Organisations (NGOs) 113, 116, 119, 275, 276, 277, 278, 281
Noort, L. 271
Nordahl, T. 182
Nordenstam, U. 256

Nordic countries 6, 211, 258; *see also* South Sámi language learning
Nordic/Danish model 76
Northern Ireland 281–285, 289; *see also* United Kingdom
Northern Ireland Government 284
North-West Russia 6, 211; *see also* South Sámi language learning
Norway 174–183; *see also* indigenous preschool in Norway, study in; collective and individual involvement 178–179; improvements, needed 182–183; introduction 174; national evaluation involving parental perspective 180–182; overview 6; parent involvement sayings, doings and relatings in 314; preparing teachers for parental collaboration 179–180; research on teacher education 180; Sámi education in 212–213; *understanding* and *collaboration,* principles of 174–178
Norwegian Directorate for Education and Training 181
Norwegian Kindergarten Teacher Education 179
Norwegian Ministry of Education and Research (NMER) 175–177, 179–180
Norwegian National Committees for Research Ethics 214
Nurturing Early Learners (NEL) Framework 233, 236, 240
Nurturing and Educating Parents model 143, 144–145
Nyarko, K. 112

Obeng, C. S. 112, 115, 117, 118
Oberhuemer, P. 100, 147
Obradović, J. 295
O'Brien, D. 258
O'Byrne, M. 10
Ødegaard, E. E. 76, 177, 181–182
offers for parents, in educational partnership 101
Office of Head Start 296–297
OFSTED 289
Ogg, J. 232
Ohm, M. 180
Ojala, M. 90
O'Leary, Z. 261
Olender, R. A. 54
Oliemat, E. 166
Oliva-Olson, C. 295
Oman 185–196; context of 186–188; data analysis in research 190; data collection

in research 189–190; discussion and conclusion 194–196; Epstein's model of parental involvement in 190–193; findings from research 190–194; introduction and background 185–186; literature related to research 188–189; methods of research 189–190; overview 6; parent involvement challenges 193–194; parent involvement in teacher training 187–188; parent involvement practices 190–193; parent involvement sayings, doings and relatings in 311, 312, 313, 314; participants in research 189
Omani Child Law 187
Ombudsman Office 28
Onnismaa, E. L. 92
Onsøien, R. 181
Operation Manual for Pre-primary Institutions 123, 125, 127, 129
Opravilová, E. 67, 68
Organisation for Economic Co-operation and Development (OECD) 9, 63, 67, 80, 81, 147, 151, 153, 154, 160, 258, 259, 285, 286–287
Ormrod, J. 94, 214
Orozco-Lapray, D. 234
Osei-Akoto, I. 112
O'Toole, L. 260

Pálfi, S. 137, 141, 144
Palviainen, Å 213
Pang, I. W. 129
parental collaboration: Catalonia, Spain 251–253; Germany 100–101, 102; Ghana 117–118; indigenous preschool in Norway 213–214; Jordan 170–171; Norway 174–180; Poland 201–204; in South Sámi language learning 213–214; Uganda 277
parental engagement: in Australia 10, 11; in Azerbaijan 27–30; in Catalonia, Spain 247, 251–253; in Croatia 52; in Czech Republic 68–69; in Denmark 85; in Ghana 115–119; in Jordan 163, 165, 170, 171; in Poland 200, 203–204; in Serbia 223; in Sweden 256–257, 261, 264; in Uganda 272–277
parental involvement *see* early childhood education and care (ECEC) and parental involvement
Parental Involvement Initiative (PII) 164–165
parental involvement programmes (PIPs) 170
parental leave 42, 152

parental partnerships 2, 92, 94, 147
Parent and Child Together (PACT) 295–296
parent committee 43
parent engagement policy 117–118
parenting domain, in Epstein's model: in Australia 10, 16, 18, 20, 21; in Azerbaijan 27–29; in Catalonia, Spain 247, 248, 249; in Croatia 51–52; in Czech Republic 66–67; in Denmark 78, 79, 81, 83, 85; in Germany 101, 103–104; in Ghana 112, 117–118; in Hong Kong 128; in Hungary 138, 143, 144–145; international trends in 307, 309, 313; in Jordan 163–168, 169; in Oman 190, 191, 192; in Singapore (tiger parenting) 233–234; in Uganda 269–278; in United Kingdom 284, 285, 286, 289; in United States 295–296, 298
"Parenting Issues in a National Family Environment" (course) 27
parenting programmes 163, 165, 167–168, 272–273, 285
Parenting Uganda 275
Parent Involvement Doings 309, 311–315
Parent Involvement Programme 165
Parent Involvement Relatings 309, 312–316
Parent Involvement Sayings 308–311, 312–316
parents: in Leximancer concept maps 13–14, 16–19; roles of 51–52, 169; training programs for 32, 33, 36, 311
Parents and Spectators model 141, 142
Parents as Organisers model 141, 142, 144
Parents as Volunteer Labourers model 143, 144
parent-teacher association (PTA): in Azerbaijan 25; in Czech Republic 269; in Gahana 113, 115, 116, 117, 118, 119; in Uganda 269
Park, I. J. 233, 234
Park, M. 293
Park, S. 247
partnership, in Leximancer concept maps 16–17
Passiatore, Y. 77
Patrikakou, E. N. 52
Pavlović Breneselović, D. 221, 222, 223, 224, 227
Pedagogical Council 26
pedagogical integration 41
Pedagogical Universities 27
pedagogues, defined 137

"Pedagogy of Early Childhood Education" 102
Peeters, J. 146
Pelletier, J. 294
Performance Indicators: Kindergartens 123, 127
Perry, M. 294
Persson, S. 41, 259, 260, 264
Peters, S. 78
Petrović-Sočo, B. 51
Peucker, C. 103
Phillips, J. 313, 316
Phillipson, S. N. 124, 242, 259, 306, 313
Philosophy of Education 187
Pianta, R. C. 57
Piattoeva, N. 141
Picasso Museum 250
pick-up and drop-off situations 78, 85, 106
Pietsch, S. 99
Pihlaja, P. 92, 97, 258
Pirchio, S. 77
Pizatellaf, A. D. 271
PLAN Uganda 275, 276
Play-Movement-Communication Programme 137
Plowden Report 50–51
Pluto, L. 103
podcast program 190, 192
Podráczky, J. 138
Pol, M. 67
Poland 199–210; conclusion 204–205; individual and collective collaboration 201; introduction 199–200; literature used in analysis of required reading in ECEC teacher education 206–210; overview 6; parental collaboration in practice 202–204; parent involvement sayings, doings and relatings in 309, 313, 314; preparing teachers for parental collaboration 202; steering documents for ECE 200–201
Policy Statement of the USDHHS and USDOE 297
Polish Ministry of Education 200
Polish Ministry of Science and Higher Education 202, 205
politics: in Belarus 42, 46, 47; in Croatia 54; in Czech Republic 65; in Denmark 78; in Finland 93; in Ghana 109–110; in Hungary 136, 139, 140–141, 145, 147; in Iceland 153; in international trends 310, 314, 315; in Norway 175; in Poland 199; in United Kingdom 281, 287; in United States 297

Pomerantz, E. M. 122
Portilla, X. A. 295
Portugal 93, 259
poverty, parental involvement influenced by: in Ghana 113, 116; in Hungary 145; in Uganda 272; in United Kingdom 281–282, 285–287; in United States 296
Poverty and Social Exclusion 285
Powell, D. R. 223, 294
Power, K. 21
Pozdeeva, T. V. 40, 41
practice architectures, theory of 306–316; Parent Involvement Doings 309, 311–315; Parent Involvement Relatings 309, 312–316; Parent Involvement Sayings 308–311, 313–315
pre-primary education: in Finland 90; in Hong Kong 130; in Jordan 163; in Uganda 270
pre-school centres 274
Preschool Curriculum Framework – Years of Ascent 224–226
preschool education: in Azerbaijan 24–28; in Belarus 42–47; in Catalonia, Spain 247, 251, 253; in Croatia 51, 53; in Czech Republic 63–72; in Denmark 74–86; in Finland 90, 96; in Germany 99–106; in Iceland 151–160; international trends in 307, 309–314; in Jordan 162–163; in Norway 211–218; in Oman 187, 194; in Poland 200–204; in Serbia 221–229; in Singapore 233–236, 239–242; in South Sámi language learning 211–218; in Sweden 256–265; traditions in 2–3; in Uganda 274; in United Kingdom 287; in United States of America 294
Preschool Education Law 25–26
Preschool Pedagogy for Higher Education 27
Preschools Act 153
Pre-Tertiary Education Bill 111
Prichard, P. 10
primary education: in Australia 12–13; in Azerbaijan 24–25, 28–29, 31; in Finland 95; in Germany 103; in Ghana 110–111; in Hong Kong 127; in Hungary 137; in Iceland 153, 156, 160; international trends in 314; in Poland 200; in Singapore 234, 240–242; traditions in 3; in Uganda 269–270; in United Kingdom 285–287
Prior, J. 58
Private Tuition in Singapore: A Whitepaper Release 233, 234

Program Orientation of Early Childhood Education 51
Proposition 10 297
Pryor, J. 112, 113, 114
Purola, K. 92–93, 97, 258

Qatari ECE 167
Qin, D. B. 233
Quah, E. 238
Qualified Teacher Status (QTS) 288
Quality Counts California 297–298
Quality Education Fund 126
quality rating and improvement system (QRIS) 297–299
Queen Rania Foundation 164, 165
Quintanar, A. 52

Rabušicová, M. 64, 65, 67, 68
Race to the Top – Early Learning Challenge 297
Råde, A. 258
Rákó, E. 137, 146
Rania Al-Abdullah, Majesty Queen 164
Rao, N. 124, 132
Rapley, T. J. 55
Raval Infant House 250
"Redesign the parents conference" initiative 251
Regionale forskningsfond (RFF) 212
Regulations of the Sami Act 212
relatings, parent involvement of 309, 312–316
relationships, in Leximancer concept maps 16–17
religion: in Norway 175–176, 179; in Poland 201, 203, 204–205, 309; in Uganda 269, 271; in United States 292
Reschly, A. L. 138
Research Office Legislative Council Secretariat 123
restructuring preschools 228
Retna, K. S. 234
Reunamo, J. 97
Revelle, C. 167
Reykjavík city preschools 153
Reynolds, A. J. 258
Richter, S. 104
Riksdagen 257
Rimm-Kaufman, S. 57
Rinaldi, C. 155
Rintakorpi, K. 97
Ritchie, J. 92, 94, 96, 213, 214
Ritterbuschc, A. E. 271
Rivas, E. 246
Rizzi, F. 53–54

Robertson, A. S. 227
Roets, G. 151
Roffey, S. 138
Roggemann, K. 165
"Role of Families in a Child Care and Development" course 27
"Role of Family in Teaching Elementary Math Concepts" course 27
Røn Larsen, M. R. 76, 77, 78
Rönnau, M. 99
Ronnau-Böse, M. 99
Roorda, D. L. 295
Roth, X. 99
Rouse, E. 258
Rulebook on Quality Standards in Institutions 222
Ruskovaara, E. 93
Russia 24; *see also* South Sámi language learning
Ryberg, L. 151
Rydl, K. 64

Sabah, S. 165
SABER Country Report 26
Sadownik, A. R. 52, 180, 181–182, 315
Sámi Act 212
Sámi languages of Nordic countries and North-West Russia *see* South Sámi language learning
Sammons, P. 74, 287
Sand, S. 182
Sandberg, A. 51, 57, 77
Sanders, E. 10, 260
Sanders, M. G. 52, 79, 232
San Juan, R. R. 294
Santos, R. 213, 218
Satuvuori, T. 93
Savacool, J. L. 195
Save the Children 275, 280
Saxonberg, S. 64
sayings, parent involvement of 308–311, 313–315
Schmidt, L. S. K. 77
Schneider, B. 227
Schoenwald, S. 295
school, in Leximancer concept maps 15–16
School Act 1848 174
school-based involvement 129, 130, 232, 237, 306
school-based involvement, in Singapore 237–238
School Education Act 200, 201
School Management Committees (SMCs) 113, 117, 119, 127

Schreier, M. 79
Schreyer, I. 100
Schwarz, S. 99, 101
Science Nest 250
Scotland 281–284, 287, 289; *see also* United Kingdom
Scottish Government 284
Scottish Schools (Parental Involvement) Act 283–284
Seckinger, M. 103
secondary education: in Azerbaijan 25; in Belarus 45; in Denmark 75; in Ghana 112, 114; in Hong Kong 127; in Hungary 137, 143; in Jordan 162; in Oman 188; in Uganda 269–270, 273; in United Kingdom 287; in United States of America 296
Šeďová, K. 67
Segura, A. 247
Seikkula-Leino, J. 93
Sem, L. 212
Senatsverwaltung fur Bildung, Jugend und Wissenschaft
Senior, K. 11
Serbia 221–229; development of family-preschool partnership 226–229; introduction 221; overview 6–7; parental involvement in preschool teacher education 224; parental participation in preschool education practice in 224–226; parent involvement sayings, doings and relatings in 311; policy documents and parental involvement in preschool education in 221–223; research on parental involvement in preschool education in 223–224
Serpell, Z. N. 294
Services for Children and Young People (*Sozialgesetzbuch, SGB VIII – Kinder- und Jungendhilfe*) 100
Shahidullah, S. 269
share, in Leximancer concept maps 14, 18, 19
shared goals 77, 81, 215, 217
Sharpe, P. 242
Shaw, S. 50
Shehadah, S. 166
Sheldon, S. B. 294
Shen, Y. 234
Sheridan, S. M. 51, 52, 57, 294
Shin, F. 211, 218
Shukri, M. 165
Sigle-Rushton, W. 258
Siippainen, A. 92

Silova, I. 141
Silvennoinen, H. 92, 97, 258
Simonsson, M. 259
Singapore 232–243; conclusion 242; data analysis in study 236–237; data collection instrument in study 236; educational reforms 233–234; Epstein's model of parental involvement in 237, 238; findings and discussion from study 237–242; home-school-community involvement in ECE settings 238; introduction 232–233; limitations and future directions 242; method of study 235–237; overview 7, 234–235; parental involvement in ECE settings 237–240; parent involvement sayings, doings and relatings in 311; parents' transition to play-based pedagogy 240–242; participants in study 235–236; purpose of study 235; school-based involvement in ECE settings 237–238
Singapore Department of Statistics 234
Singlish 236
Siraj-Blatchford, I. 74, 287
Širanović, A. 52
Siu, G. E. 272
Skiba, R. J. 295
Skoglund, R. I. 175
Skolverket 262, 263, 265
Smart Parent Net 128
Smeds, K. 97
Šmelová, E. 64
Smidt, W. 103
Smith, A. E. 13, 236, 237, 308
social arrangements 78
social capital 228
social class *see* society, parental involvement influenced by; socioeconomic status, parental involvement influenced by
Social Code Book Eight (SGB VIII) 99, 100
social media 56, 190, 192, 195, 235
Social Service Act 75, 80
Social Welfare Department 122
society, parental involvement influenced by: in Azerbaijan 24; in Belarus 42; in Catalunya, Spain 247–248; in Croatia 50, 52; in Denmark 75–76; in Finland 93, 96; in Germany 99; in Hong Kong 124, 132; in Hungary 140–141, 147; in Iceland 154; in international trends 310, 314; in Jordan 162, 168; in Norway 175–176, 179, 180; in Oman 186; in Poland 201; in Serbia 229; in Sweden

259–260, 263, 264–265; in United States 293, 294
socioeconomic status, parental involvement influenced by: in Australia 12; in Belarus 42; in Catalonia, Spain 246, 249; in Croatia 54; in Czech Republic 63, 66–67, 71, 72, 312; in Denmark 78, 85; in Germany 100; in Ghana 112, 113, 116, 119; in Hong Kong 123, 130; in Hungary 136, 144–146; in Iceland 152; international trends in 306; in Oman 185; in Poland 203; in Singapore 233, 236; in Uganda 272, 274, 276, 278; in United Kingdom 281–282, 285–287, 311; in United States of America 293, 294, 296
Sociology of the Family or *Family Care and Education* 68
Somerville, M. 21
Sommer, D. 76
Son, S. H. 294
Sønsthagen, A. G. 181
South Sámi language learning 6, 211–218; conclusions 217–218; data and methods of research 214; findings from research 215–217; introduction 211–212; overview 6; parental collaboration 213–214; parent involvement sayings, doings and relatings in 312; preschool as open arena for language learning 215–216; Sámi education context in 212–213; supporting parents in South Sámi language usage 216–217
Spain *see* Catalonia, Spain
Spasić, B. 223
special education: in Azerbaijan 27; in Belarus 43; in Denmark 77; in Ghana 111, 114, 118; in Poland 200–201, 202; in United States of America 293
specialised secondary education (SSE) 45
special needs, children with 43, 77, 111, 118, 271; *see also* special education
Spilt, J. L. 295
SPSS 23.0 (Statistical Package for the Social Sciences) 31, 34
SPSS 23.0 (Statistical Package for the Social Sciences) for Windows 31, 34
Ssekamwa, J. C. 269
Ssempala, C. 269
Ssenkusu, P. 269
Stacey, M. 11
STAKES 91, 96
Stanek, A. 78
Starke dagtilbud – alle skal med I fallesskabet (2016 ECEC agreement) 76

State Institute of Education 27
State Statistical Committee (SSC) 25
State Strategy on Development of Education 25
Statistics Denmark 75
Statistics Iceland 152
steering documents for, in Poland 200–201
Steiner Rasmussen, O. 78
step-by-step educational model 44
Step-by-Step kindergarten programme 137
Stewart, J. 269
Stóka, G. 139
Strategy 2020 66
Strategy 2030+ 66, 69
Strategy for education development in Serbia 222
Strategy for Education Policy of the Czech Republic until 2020 66
Strengthening Families' network 298–299
Stromme Foundation 275
Strong ECEC settings – everyone must form part of the community (2016 ECEC agreement) 76
structure and organization of systems, in Azerbaijan 24–25
Sujuddin, S. 242
Sultan Qaboos University (SQU) 187–188
Suomen Vanhempainliitto 96
support, in Leximancer concept maps 14–15
sure, in Leximancer concept maps 18–19
Sure Start 281, 282–283, 284, 285
Sustainable Development Goals (SDGs) 111, 186
Suzuki, I. 270
Svinth, L. 75
Svobodová, K. 64
Sweden 256–265; conclusion 265; ecological systems theory, Bronfenbrenner's 260–261; introduction 256–257; literature review 257–260; method of research 261; Nordic perspective 258–260; overview 7; parent engagement in 257; parent engagement in curriculum 262–264; parent engagement in teacher education, theory, and praxis 264–265; parent involvement sayings, doings and relatings in 310–311
Swedish Migration Agency 264–265
Swedish National Agency for Education 256, 258, 261, 262, 264
Swedish Parliament 262
Sykes, G. 145

Sylva, K. 74, 287
Syslová, Z. 68
Szabadi, I. 138
Széll, K. 146
Szerepi, S. 137
Szilágyiné Szemkeő, J. 139

Taeschner, T. 77
Taggart, B. 74, 287
TALIS Starting Strong report 153, 160
Tallberg Broman, I. 41, 259, 264
Tam, H. L. 234
Tao, S. S. 124
Tartori, V. 30
Tawjihi 162
Taylor, S. I. 132
teacher as researcher and reflective practitioner 229
teacher education; *see also* early childhood education (ECE): in Azerbaijan 26–30, 37; in Belarus 45–46; in Catalunya, Spain 246, 248–249; in Croatia 53, 54; in Czech Republic 67–68, 72; in Denmark 75, 79, 80, 83, 85–86; in Finland 90–97; in Germany 102, 106; in Ghana 112, 113–115, 119; in Hong Kong 123, 131–133; in Hungary 147; in Iceland 152; international trends in 314–316; in Jordan 163, 169–171; in Norway 179–180, 183; in Oman 187–188, 190; in Poland 199–210; in Serbia 224–226, 229; in South Sámi language learning 213–214; in Sweden 256–265; in Uganda 272–273; in United Kingdom 287–288, 289
teacher–parent partnership 52, 213–214, 259
Teachers Guild 251
Teaching Schools, Learning Nation (TSLN) 233
Technical Service Meeting point 250
Tekin, A. K. 30, 163, 166, 186, 187, 188, 195
Teng, S. 234
Teszenyi, E. 137, 139
Tett, L. 280, 311
Textor, M. R. 99, 106
themes of parental involvement: overlap between 309, 313–314; parent involvement of doings 309, 311–312; parent involvement of relatings 309, 312–313; parent involvement of sayings 308–311
Thiersch, R. 99–100, 104

three-way conference 192
Tietze, W. 105
tiger mother 233–234
tiger parenting 7, 233–234
time, in Leximancer concept maps 16–17, 19–20
Times of Oman 187
Ting, T. C. 233
Tisdell, E. J. 189
Tobalina, G. 246
Todeschini, F. 247
Tomlinson, S. 259
Toom, A. 93
Török, B. 138–139, 147
traditions in parental involvement 2–3
transformation and system context of, in Czech Republic 64–65
transparency of the pedagogical work 101
Tritrini, C. 77
Trivette, C. M. 295
Trnková, K. 67
trust 238–239
Tschöpe-Scheffler, S. 104
Tucker, J. 113
Tunberger, P. 258
Turja, L. 51, 93, 213
Twaweza 272
Tyler-Merrick, G. 313
Tyson, D. F. 40, 41

UDIR 174, 175, 177, 178–179, 180, 181
Uganda 269–278; conclusions and implications 277–278; introduction 269–270; overview 7; parental and community engagement 273; parental engagement and collaboration developed in 277; parental engagement practiced in schools 274–277; parental involvement in, steering documents about 270–271; parental involvement in early childhood teacher education in 272–273; parent involvement sayings, doings and relatings in 308–309; research on parental involvement in ECEC in 271–272
Uganda Education Act 270
Uganda National Parenting Guidelines 274
UNESCO 24, 109, 163, 212
UNICEF 112, 113, 116, 117, 118, 163–164, 167, 187
United Kingdom (UK) 280–289; child poverty rates in 281–282; concluding comments 289; context of 281–282; future aspirations and developments for family involvement and engagement in

288; introduction 280–281; overview 7–8; parent involvement sayings, doings and relatings in 308, 311, 314; policy related to family involvement in 282–286; research related to family involvement in ECEC in 286–287; teacher and practitioner training and families in 287–288
United Nations (UN): Convention on the Rights of the Child (UNCRC) 42, 154, 159, 248, 257, 282; Population Division 24; Sustainable Development Goals (SDG) 111, 186
United States (US) 292–301; California's quality rating and improvement system in 297–299; conclusion 300–301; family engagement efforts in San Mateo County, California 299–300; future of family engagement in 297–299; introduction 292; overview 8; parent involvement sayings, doings and relatings in 310, 313; policies on family engagement in early childhood programs 296–297; research on family engagement in 294–296; superdiverse families in 293; superdiversity in 292–293
U.S. Agency for International Development (USAID) 164
U.S. Department of Education (USDOE) 292, 296, 297
U.S. Department of Health and Human Services (USDHHS) 292, 296–297
"Unity of Families and Preschool Institutions" (course) 27
Universitat Autònoma de Barcelona 249
University of Cape Coast (UCC) 114
University of Juraj Dobrila in Pula 53
Uryga, D. 204
Uusiautti, S. 211
Uusimäki, L. 41, 91, 92, 93, 94, 96, 211, 260

Valdebenito, V. 247
Vallotton, C. D. 294
values, parental involvement influenced by: in Azerbaijan 26; in Belarus 42; in Croatia 52; in Czech Republic 71; in Denmark 76, 77–78, 81; in Ghana 109; in Hong Kong 125, 126, 128; in Hungary 139, 145; in Iceland 154, 159; in international trends 307, 313, 314; in Norway 175–178; in Oman 196; in Poland 204; in Serbia 224; in South Sámi language learning 212–213, 217; in Sweden 262–263; in Uganda 270–272, 275; in United Kingdom 280, 288; in United States 292, 295
Vandenbroeck, M. 1, 63, 146, 151
Van Houtte, M. 63
Van Laere, K. 63
Varga Nagy, A. 137, 138, 139, 141, 145, 146
Veisson, M. 51, 93, 213
Velde Lønning, K. 180, 181
Venninen, T. 90, 92–93, 258, 259
Vertovec, S. 293
Viernickel, S. 99, 101, 102, 103, 104, 105
Villányi, G. 141
Vincent, C. 63, 226, 259
Visković, I. 51, 52
Višnjić Jevtić, A. 51, 52, 55
Vlasov, J. 93, 259, 260
vocational school training (ISCED 5A) 67
voluntarily and/or involuntarily left out parents 130–131, 132
voluntary work 78
volunteering domain, in Epstein's model: in Azerbaijan 27–28; in Denmark 79, 85; in Ghana 116; in Hong Kong 124, 129, 131; in Hungary 143, 144; in Jordan 167, 168; in Oman 190, 191, 192, 195; in Poland 204; in Singapore 232–233; in United Kingdom 284
Vranješević, J. 223
Vuorinen, T. 51, 57, 77
Vygotsky, L. S. 185

Waanders, C. 132
Wahle, M. 102
Wales 281–283, 285–287, 289; *see also* United Kingdom
Wang, Y. 234
Wanican, J. 271
Waniganayake, M. 51, 93, 213
Warner-Richter, M. N. 258
Warren, S. R. 52
Watine, L. 115
We already have a child programme 250
Weber, R. 214
Wegner, A. 11
Weiss, H. 294
Weiß, H. 104
Weiss, H. B. 226
Welsh Assembly 285
Welsh Government 285
Welsh Inspectorate for Education and Training in Wales 285–286
Wen, X. 294
Wernersson, I. 259

Western University of Applied Sciences 180, 182
White, A. 295
White, E. J. 177
Wiatr, M. 204
Wildemuth, B. M. 124
Williams, C. 94
Williams, P. 57
Winder, C. 40
Winters, W. 167
Winther-Lindqvist, D. A. 75, 76
Wise, J. 295
Wolf, B. 99
Wolf, S. 112, 115, 116, 117, 118
Wong, N. Y. 128
Woodrow, C. 21
Woods, K. E. 51
work, in Leximancer concept maps 14
World Bank 164, 186, 187
World Data on Education (WDE) 42, 45
World Vision 275
Wreekat, K. Y. 165
Wu, B. 12
Wunsche, M. 99

Xu, Z. 213–214

Yagublu, V. 28, 29
Yankey, J. 138
Yaro, K. 112, 114, 115, 116
year, in Leximancer concept maps 18–19
Years of Ascent, Technical Report 225–226
Yeong, A. Y. E. 234
Yngvesson, T. 41, 256, 257, 261, 263, 265
Yngvesson, T. E. 91, 211, 258
Yoshikawa, H. 292
You, H. M. 124
Young, 1999 124
Young, M. D. 124
Yuen, W. K. G. 124

Zachopoulou, E. 74
Zaza, H. 167
Zedan, R. F. 30
Zenker, L. 101
Zhang, Y. 124
Zhuk, A. A. 40, 41
Zsubrits, A. 138

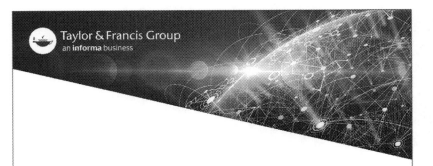

Taylor & Francis eBooks

www.taylorfrancis.com

A single destination for eBooks from Taylor & Francis with increased functionality and an improved user experience to meet the needs of our customers.

90,000+ eBooks of award-winning academic content in Humanities, Social Science, Science, Technology, Engineering, and Medical written by a global network of editors and authors.

TAYLOR & FRANCIS EBOOKS OFFERS:

- A streamlined experience for our library customers
- A single point of discovery for all of our eBook content
- Improved search and discovery of content at both book and chapter level

REQUEST A FREE TRIAL
support@taylorfrancis.com

Printed in the United States
by Baker & Taylor Publisher Services